D0812729

PARALLEL COMPUTATION AND COMPUTERS FOR ARTIFICIAL INTELLIGENCE

THE KLUWER INTERNATIONAL SERIES
IN ENGINEERING AND COMPUTER SCIENCE

PARALLEL PROCESSING
AND FIFTH GENERATION COMPUTING

Consulting Editor

Doug DeGroot

PARALLEL COMPUTATION AND COMPUTERS FOR ARTIFICIAL INTELLIGENCE

edited by

JANUSZ S. KOWALIK
Boeing Computer Services, Bellevue, Washington
and
University of Washington, Seattle, Washington

KLUWER ACADEMIC PUBLISHERS
Boston/Dordrecht/Lancaster

Distributors for North America:
Kluwer Academic Publishers
101 Philip Drive
Assinippi Park
Norwell, Massachusetts 02061, USA

Distributors for the UK and Ireland:
Kluwer Academic Publishers
MTP Press Limited
Falcon House, Queen Square
Lancaster LAI IRN, UNITED KINGDOM

Distributors for all other countries:
Kluwer Academic Publishers Group
Distribution Centre
Post Office Box 22
3300 AH Dordrecht, THE NETHERLANDS

Library of Congress Cataloging-in-Publication Data
Parallel computation and computers for aritificial
    intelligence.
    (The Kluwer international series in engineering and
computer science; SECS   . Parallel processing and
fifth generation computing)
    Bibliography: p.
    1. Parallel processing (Electronic computers)
2. Artificial intelligence.   I. Kowalik, Janusz S.
II. Series.
QA76.5.P3147   1987   006.3   87-3749

Printed in the United States of America

Typeset by Macmillan India Ltd, Bangalore 25.

CONTENTS

88-4643

PREFACE

It has been widely recognized that artificial intelligence computations offer large potential for distributed and parallel processing. Unfortunately, not much is known about designing parallel AI algorithms and efficient, easy-to-use parallel computer architectures for AI applications. The field of parallel computation and computers for AI is in its infancy, but some significant ideas have appeared and initial practical experience has become available.

The purpose of this book has been to collect in one volume contributions from several leading researchers and pioneers of AI that represent a sample of these ideas and experiences. This sample does not include all schools of thought nor contributions from all leading researchers, but it covers a relatively wide variety of views and topics and in this sense can be helpful in assessing the state of the art. We hope that the book will serve, at least, as a pointer to more specialized literature and that it will stimulate interest in the area of parallel AI processing.

It has been a great pleasure and a privilege to cooperate with all contributors to this volume. They have my warmest thanks and gratitude. Mrs. Birgitta Knapp has assisted me in the editorial task and demonstrated a great deal of skill and patience.

Janusz S. Kowalik

INTRODUCTION

Artificial intelligence (AI) computer programs can be very time-consuming. Researchers in the field and users of AI software hope that it will be possible to find and exploit high degrees of parallelism in large AI programs in order to reduce their processing time. We have reason to believe that this hope is justified.

Parallel computation may prove useful in shortening the processing time in AI applications that require substantial but not excessive speed-ups. What we mean is that parallel processing alone could not and will not overcome the exponential complexity that characterizes very hard AI problems. Also, we should keep in mind that some AI problems involve large amounts of numerical processing. In such applications both the numerical and the symbolic components of the hybrid software systems have to be computed in parallel modes to achieve significant speedups.

Many AI computer programs are pattern-directed. In pattern-directed computer programs, distinct computational modules, representing chunks of knowledge, are activated by successful pattern matches that occur in data bases. In contrast to conventional computer programs, the pattern-directed modules do not call each other explicitly but cooperate indirectly via commonly accessible data bases.

This structure of knowledge-based computer programs has the following major consequences:

1. The programs are very flexible; the system components are loosely connected and each module, such as an if-then rule, can be added or dropped without necessarily destroying the rest of the system.

2. Multiple modules can be processed in parallel, since the conditions that trigger their execution may be satisfied by more than one module.

The reader interested in pattern-directed programming is referred to Bratko [1], who presents a lucid discussion of the topic. For our purposes, it suffices to observe that AI computer program organization often lends itself naturally to parallel computation.

Some specialized AI systems such as blackboard architectures, also offer a very natural possibility for large-grain parallelism. Nii [2] enumerated and described three methods for using multiple processors in the blackboard systems:

1. Partitioning the solution space on the blackboard into separate, loosely coupled regions.
2. Using multiprocessors to place the blackboard data in a shared memory and distributing the knowledge sources on different processors.
3. Partitioning the problem into independent subproblems and solving each subproblem on a separate processor.

Still another source of parallelism can be found in AI programming languages such as Prolog and Lisp. Prolog clauses can be regarded as pattern-directed modules, which we have just discussed. Parallel Lisp's on the other hand, allow parallel execution by using special constructs and extensions to sequential dialects of this language.

We hope that by now our reader suspects that parallel processing may indeed play an increasingly important role in AI research and applications and is willing to take a closer look at some chapters of the book.

The first part of the book, entitled Parallel Computation, opens with Scott Fahlman's chapter on "Parallel Processing in Artificial Intelligence." He divides parallel approaches to AI into three broad categories:

1. General programming approaches, such as current dialects of Lisp offering small gránularity parallelism, or blackboards, which utilize larger modules of computation.
2. Specialized programming languages, such as Prolog or OPS5.
3. The active memory approach, which attempts to apply massive parallelism to the problems of locating relevant information in large knowledge bases, doing simple inferences, and identifying stored descriptions that match given inputs.

The last approach is the most radical departure from the current knowledge based methodologies. It replaces clever, hand-crafted programming by a massively parallel brute force method. It also offers some hope for fundamental advances in AI and may help us to understand how the human brain functions.

The general programming approach is represented in the book by the next three chapters. Chapter 2, by Robert Halstead, describes Multilisp, which is a version of the Lisp-like language Scheme, developed at MIT and extended to specify parallel execution using the *future* construct. In Multilisp a function may return a promissory note instead of an actual value and then attempt to find a processor for performing the actual computation. The *future* construct creates parallelism by manipulating partly computed data.

Multilisp has been implemented on Concert, a 28-processor shared-memory machine, and Butterfly (see Chapter 8). The performance of Concert Multilisp on two parallel test programs, tree insertion and Quicksort, is presented and discussed. One of the author's conclusions is that constructs such as *future* are only part of what is needed to exploit fully different levels of parallelism. In particular, we should have constructs that would allow various parts of a program to execute concurrently, that is a means to do parallel programming at large. Other needs include aids for the development and structuring of large programs plus debugging tools to help in finding both corrections and performance bugs. Moreover, any practical language must have an ability to construct modular programs. This is true for sequential programs, and the requirements for parallel programs will not be less important.

The following chapter, "Execution of Common Lisp Programs in a Parallel Environment," by Patrick McGehearty and Edward Krall, reports results of simulated parallel runs of several Lisp application kernels. They included numerical algorithms, a simple theorem prover, and the inference kernel of the EMYCIN expert system. The *future* construct from Multilisp has been used as a primary way of specifying parallel execution. The modifications to the selected Lisp kernels have been done mechanically. The simulated runs have shown speedups ranging from 1 to 500. The authors conclude that the *future* construct is of no value to a few programs, of great value to a few programs, and of moderate value to most programs. A parallel implementation of the inference kernel of the EMYCIN expert system has resulted in a negligible speedup. The system performs frequent operations on a blackboard which prevents parallel operations without use of synchronization. Consequently, the *future* construct has been of no value for this application.

Chapter 4 by Richard Gabriel and John McCarthy presents a variant of Lisp that features elegant style and extensions allowing two kinds of parallelism: (1) The parallelism derived from the parallel evaluation of arguments; and (2) the unstructured parallelism of process invocation, in which a number of processes are created and messages are passed among them, resulting in concurrent processing.

The parallel language called Qlisp is compact and provides only a few powerful primitives. The language design has been motivated by the following goals:

1. A shared memory architecture is assumed, since Lisp manipulates pointers.
2. There must be a means to limit the degree of multiprocessing at run-time, because any real parallel machine will have a fixed number of processors, and there will be a cost of creating and maintaining computational processes.

3. Qlisp should provide only minimal extensions to Lisp.
4. Conventional Lisp constructs should assume new meaning for parallel execution, and entirely new constructs should be avoided.
5. The Qlisp constructs should preserve meaning and work in a uniprocessor environment.

To speed up maximally large AI programs, it will be necessary to exploit different levels of parallelism from coarse-grain down to fine-grain parallelism. Qlisp should be very helpful in accomplishing in part this objective for programs written in Lisp.

The specialized programming language approach to parallel processing in AI is represented in this collection by Chapters 5 and 6. Chapter 5 is written by Doug DeGroot and entitled "Restricted AND-Parallel Execution of Logic Programs." Parallel execution of logic programming languages is a very active area of research for two reasons: (1) Logic programming exhibits high potential for concurrency; and (2) the Japanese Fifth Generation projects have been emphasizing this approach to computer programming since their inception.

In logic programming there are generally several alternative clauses that can be used to prove a given predicate or goal. Each clause in turn has several subgoals requiring the proof. Because any one clause may be used to prove the predicate, attempting this proof in parallel is called OR-parallelism. On the other hand, once a particular clause is selected for a proof attempt, all subgoals within this clause must be solved for the clause to succeed. Therefore, executing this subgoals in parallel is called AND-parallelism.

OR-parallelism appears to be easier to implement than AND-parallelism, because to prove a given predicate, separate, independent processes may be activated in parallel, one process for each clause that defines the predicate. Moreover, not all activated processes need to communicate with each other, and backtracking is unnecessary. However, there are two disadvantages of this approach: (1) If little nondeterminism exists (the number of clauses that can be attempted per goal), then OR-parallelism will be insignificant; and (2) OR-parallel models attempt to find all solutions to a problem, although only one may be required.

AND-parallelism models, instead of attempting to find all proofs of all solutions, attempt to produce the first answer as quickly as possible before trying to find another. Consequently, the amount of parallelism exhibited by AND-parallelism is independent of the amount of nondeterminism in the program. But there is one difficulty in this approach. AND-parallelism involves the parallel execution of goals that are usually highly interdependent, and a significant amount of communication between processes is required, which raises the cost of the potential parallelism. To keep this cost down, the amount of potential parallelism may need to be reduced. One method that restricts the potential AND-parallelism is presented by Doug DeGroot. In this approach, the parallelism is restricted so that tasks that cooperate to produce a single answer do not execute in parallel until no danger of creating binding conflicts exists. Several other restricted AND-parallelism models have been proposed, and their true merits can only be established empirically.

Chapter 6, "Parlog: Parallel Programming in Logic" by Keith Clark and Steve Gregory, is an introduction to a version of Prolog that incorporates both AND-parallelism and OR-parallelism. Parlog has some features in common with concurrent Prolog designed by Shapiro and Guarded Horn Clauses by Ueda, but there are also significant differences.

In Parlog, the attempt to find a solution to each condition of a parallel conjunction becomes a separate concurrent process. The shared variables of the conditions (the calls) are the communication channels between the processes. Because of mode declarations, which restrict the unification between a call and an invoked clause to "input matching" on certain arguments, usually only one process will be able to bind each shared variable. This process is called the *producer* process for the variable. Any other (consumer) process needing the value of the shared variable suspends until the variable is bound by the producer of the variable. Suspension waiting for a value of shared variable is the means of process synchronization in Parlog.

Parlog was initially implemented on the parallel machine ALICE. Currently work has begun on a new compiler from Parlog to ALICE Compiler Target Language in association with the Alvey "Flagship" project.

The last chapter in Part I written by Lubomir Bic, presents a model of computations, which integrates synergistically three fundamental concepts: semantic nets, logic programming, and data-driven computation.

"Semantic nets" are a well-known scheme of knowledge representation, used widely in various AI applications. Some of the appealing features of semantic nets are their intrinsic simplicity, their expressive power to represent related objects, and an organization that is exceptionally well suited for information storage and retrieval. There are also two potential problems with implementing an AI system based on semantic nets. The first difficulty is related to efficiency. If operations involving the traversal of many edges in the net are performed sequentially by a single processor, the processing time grows linearly with the size of the net. Bic describes an approach based on data-driven computation, which allows a large number of asynchronous processing elements to cooperate in parallel in solving a given problem. The second weakness of semantic nets is related to operations performed on semantic nets. Most systems define only the information represented by nets, but not the knowledge about how to interpret and use this information. Hence, there is a need to design a formalism capable of describing not only semantic nets but also operations that can be applied to extract information from or to modify the nets. For this purpose, a restricted form of logic programming has been selected. This allows operations to be expressed on a semantic net in a declarative fashion. This can be done without the necessity of specifying explicitly where parallelism is to occur. The execution of a program written using this restricted form of logic programming can be carried out in highly parallel manner by implementing the underlying semantic net as a dataflow graph, in which nodes can communicate with one another asynchronously by exchanging messages. Each node is an independent unit of computation, whose execution is triggered by the arrival of a message, i.e., in a data-driven fashion. The need for centralized control and centralized memory is eliminated.

The main contribution of this work is the idea that the semantic net is not just a passive representation of data, but a dataflow graph whose nodes are capable of receiving, processing and emitting messages.

The second part of this book is entitled Parallel Computers and contains six chapters describing selected AI machines. Comprehensive surveys of special-purpose computer architectures for AI, including multiprocessors and multicomputers, can be found in the Appendix and in the January 1987 special issue of the *IEEE Computer* journal.

The first chapter in this part by Donald Allen and N. S. Sridharan, describes the Bolt Beranek and Newman Advanced Computers's Butterfly, which consists of from one to 256 processor nodes connected through a proprietary high-performance switch network. Each processor node consists of an MC68020 microprocessor and a MC68881 floating point coprocessor, with one to four megabytes of memory. The memory of the processor nodes collectively forms the shared memory of the machine, which is accessible to all processors through the Butterfly switch network. The switch is a key element of the Buttefly multiprocessor. It uses packet-switched networking techniques to implement processor-to-memory communication. The cost of the switch is proportional to $N \log_4 N$, where N is the number of processor nodes. The switching nodes use packet address bits to route the packet through the switch network from source to destination along the appropriate path. The path is not dedicated and it is possible for messages to collide. When this happens, one message is allowed through and the others are retransmitted after a short, random delay. This technique and other ways to provide alternate paths help to prevent massive performance degradations due to the effect called "hot spots," which can occur in highly parallel shared-memory multiprocessors.

The Butterfly machine is programmed primarily in high-level languages: C, Fortran, and Lisp. For symbolic and AI applications, a Common Lisp programming environment has been developed for the Butterfly system. This environment includes Butterfly Common Lisp, user interface, and program development facilities implemented on a front-end Lisp machine, the Symbolics 3600. Butterfly Lisp uses the *future* construct, described in Chapter 2. In addition, an Expert System Tool Kit aids in development of expert systems, shells, and prototypes on the Butterfly parallel processor. Implemented in Common Lisp, it supports object-oriented programming (emulates the Xerox CommonLoops), annotated slots, and rule-system programming.

The Butterfly multiprocessor system combines hardware and software facilities for symbolic and numerical processing and may be useful in applications such as robotics, signal processing, machine vision, and expert systems coupling symbolic and numerical compututotion. The producer has started design of a successor machine, the Monarch, which is expected to feature an 8,000-processor configuration.

Chapter 9, entitled "On the Range of Applicability of an Artificial Intelligence Machine," by David Shaw, presents an overview of a prototypical multiprocessor, NON-VON, and summarizes performance projection, derived through detailed analysis and simulation, in the areas of rule-based inferencing, computer vision, and knowledge-base management.

The central goal on the NON-VON project is the investigation of massively parallel computer architectures capable of providing significant performance - and cost/performance improvements by comparison with conventional von Neumann machines in a wide range of AI and other symbolic computing applications. Central to the NON-VON machines is a massively parallel active memory composed of a large number of simple, area-efficient small processing elements (SPE's), which are implemented using custom very large scale integration (VLSI) circuits. In the current version of the machine, the SPE's are configured as a complete binary tree whose leaves are also interconnected to form a two-dimensional orthogonal mesh. Each nonleaf node of the active memory (except root) is connected to three neighbors, the parent and two children. Each leaf is connected to its parent and to its four mesh-adjacent SPE's. In the current simplest implementation, the entire active memory operates under control of a single large processing element (LPE) where the NON-VON programs are stored. Consequently this version of NON-VON is a single instruction stream, multiple data stream (SIMD) machine. The general NON-VON design provides for multiple large processing elements, each capable of broadcasting a different sequence of instructions to control the corresponding active memory subtree. The incorporation of multiple LPE's enables the NON-VON computer to function as a multiple instruction stream, multiple data stream (MIMD) or a multiple SIMD processor.

One of the most important advantages of the NON-VON machine is the highly efficient hardware support it provides for set of associative processing primitives useful in many AI applications. This fine-grain machine allows processing elements to be associated with individual data elements and provides the capabilities of a powerful content-addressable memory. The associative processing capabilities of NON-VON are employed in a number of applications whose performance is analyzed and reported in the chapter. These applications include production system, computer vision, and knowledge-base management.

Shaw concludes the chapter by stating that NON-VON's strong performance on any given AI problem is of less interest that the wide range of AI problems that would appear to be efficiently executable within a single architecture. The NON-VON architecture might serve as a step toward future general-purpose AI multiprocessor machines.

In Chapter 10, Leonard Hamey, Jon Webb, and I-Chen Wu deal with "Low-Level Vision on Warp and the Apply Programming Model." Low-Level vision algorithms include edge detection, smoothing, convolutions, contrast enhancement, color transformations, and thresholding. Related operations are often very time consuming because they have to be applied thousands of times to an image. Fortunately, low-level vision processing can be easily parallelized because calculations at every point in the image are often independent from point to point. Many parallel computers achieve good efficiency in these algorithms through the use of data parallelism. One of them is Warp, a programmable, one-dimensional array with identical processing cells. The authors have developed a specialized programming language, called Apply, which simplifies the task of writing the algorithm for this class of problems. Apply is limited to certain computations in the low-level vision domain. On the other hand, it appears possible to implement Apply on different computers. At this time, only Warp and Unix systems can run Apply programs.

In Chapter 11, "AHR: A Parallel Computer for Pure Lisp," Adolfo Guzman describes the design and operation of AHR, a multimicroprocessor that executes pure Lisp in parallel. Each microprocessor can execute any Lisp primitive operation, each has its own private memory, and all share access to three common memories: the grill that contains Lisp executable codes; the passive memory for data; and the variables memory, where bindings of variables tolvalues reside. The programmer using AHR does not control parallelism explicitly and does not need to be aware that the program is executed in parallel. The experimental multimicroprocessor AHR was constructed and performed as expected.

Another multiprocessor for symbolic computation is presented in Chapter 12 by Alan Davis. The machine, called FAIM-1, permits an unbounded number of processing elements called Hectogons to be interconnected by a communication topology. Hectogons communicate by passing messages, and nonlocal messages can be sent by using intermediate Hectogons. Each Hectogon is a medium-grain processing element containing a number of concurrent coprocessor subsystems. Processing elements are interconnected and form a processing surface. Any number of surfaces can be viewed as the homogeneously replicated processing element of the FAIM-1 architecture, or as a medium-grain, highly concurrent, heterogeneous, shared-memory multiprocessor. Externally Hectogons can be tiled together to form a distributed message-passing multiprocessing architecture. Internally each Hectogon is a shared-memory multiprocessor containing multiple specialized coprocessor subsystems that cooperate to handle the assigned tasks. This architecture allows software concurrency to be exploited in a variety of ways. A prototype of FAIM-1 is presently under construction.

The last chapter provides an overview of AI application-oriented parallel computer projects in Japan. Computers described by the author, Ryutarou Ohbuchi, are grouped into three categories, related to the primary language they support: logic languages, functional languages, and others. The overview includes the machines built by ICOT, Tokyo University, and Electrotechnical Laboratory.

In the Appendix, Benjamin Wah and Guo-Jie Li offer "A Survey on Special Purpose Computer Architectures for AI." The survey summarizes the state of the art in AI computer architectures and lists over 400 references.

REFERENCES

1. L., Bratko, *PROLOG Programming for Artifical Intelligence*, Menlo Park, CA; Addison-Wesley 1986.
2. H. P. Nii, "Blackboard Systems, and Blackboard Application Systems from a Knowledge Engineering Perspective," *AI Magazine*, Aug. 1986.

CONTRIBUTORS

Donald C. Allen, BBN Advanced Computers, Inc., Cambridge, MA
Donald Allen is a senior scientist at BBN where he supervises the development of a Common Lisp programming environment for the Butterfly multiprocessor system. He has been with BBN since 1972 and has been involved in numerous projects, including the design and implementation of a data collection, display and interpretation system for an oil-field services company; research in packet radio networks; and the development of design aids for custom VLSI circuits. He was also a member of the technical staff at Interactive Data Corp, a member of the technical staff at MIT Lincoln Laboratory, and a member of the technical staff in the Computer Research Department at the Cornell Aeronautical Laboratory. Donald Allen holds a B.S. degree in physics and an M.S. degree in mathematics from Stevens Institute of Technology.

Lubomir Bic, Department of Information and Computer Science, University of California, Irvine
Lubomir Bic received an M.S. degree in computer science from the Technical University of Darmstadt, West Germany, in 1976 and a Ph.D. in computer science from the University of California, Irvine, in 1979. After working one year for the Siemens Corp. in Munich West Germany, he joined the computer science faculty at the University of California, Irvine, where he is currently employed as associate professor. Lubomir Bic's research interests lie in the area of parallel computing. He is the principal investigator of a project aimed at developing

non–von Neumann models of computation for data base and knowledge-base application. These models abandon the principles of control-driven sequential processing and thus are suitable for implementation on highly parallel computer architectures. Lubomir Bic's research group is currently investigating the potential performance of a data-driven knowledge-base system and its applicability in NASA's Space Station Program. This research is sponsored by McDonnell Douglas Astronautics.

Keith Clark, Imperial College, London University, London, England

Keith Clark is a reader in computational logic in the Department of Computing at Imperial College. He heads the Parlog Research Group and is the president of the Association of Logic Programming. He has been active in the area of logic programming since 1975, contributing influential papers in the areas of language design, theoretical issues, and applications. He has wide experience in industrial consulting and is a founding director of Logic Programming Associates Ltd, the first company to market Prolog systems for microcomputers.

Alan L. Davis, Schlumberger Palo Alto Research, Palo Alto, CA

Dr. Davis received a B.S. degree in Electrical Engineering from MIT in 1969. He received a Ph.D. in computer science from the University of Utah in 1972. He then spent a year as an assistant professor of computer science at the University of Waterloo before joining the research staff at Burrough's Interactive Research Center (IRC) in La Jolla, CA. At the Burrough's IRC, he directed a project that produced the first operational dataflow prototype machine in 1976. He joined the computer science faculty at the University of Utah in 1977, where he continued his research interests in parallel dataflow computing and built another custom machine. In 1982, he joined the Fairchild Artificial Intelligence Laboratory (which later became part of Schlumberger Palo Alto Research) where he is directing the FAIM project.

Doug DeGroot, Consultant,

Doug DeGroot received a B.S. in mathematics and a Ph.D. in computer science, both from the University of Texas at Austin. While there, he was a member of the Texas Reconfigurable Array Computer (TRAC) project, with special responsibility for operating system design and machine performance simulations. Upon graduating in 1981, he joined IBM's T. J. Watson Research Center where he worked on the design of an internally parallel numeric and vector processor based on the IBM 801 processor architecture. Following this, he was made manager of IBM's Parallel Symbolic Processors Group, a new group formed to perform research in the area of parallel logic programming Lisp machines. In July of 1985 he became Vice President of Research and Development at Quintus Computer Systems. Presently, he is engaged in parallel processing research at Texas Instruments Computer Science Center in Dallas. Dr. DeGroot is currently the chairman of ACM's SIGARCH. He served as technical chairman of the IEEE 1985 International Conference on Parallel Processing and general chairman of the IEEE 1985 Symposium on Logic Programming. He is co-technical chairman of the ACM 1988 International Symposium on Computer Architecture. D. DeGroot is on the editorial boards of *IEEE Expert, New Generation Computing,* and *Future Generation Computing Systems.*

Scott E. Fahlman, Carnegie-Mellon University, Pittsburgh, PA
Scott E. Fahlman is a senior research computer scientist in the Computer Science Department of Carnegie-Mellon University. His primary research interest is the development of massively parallel "connectionist:" computing architectures for such artificial intelligence problems as recognition, knowledge representation, and simple kinds of search and inference. Dr. Fahlman has also been very active in the development of software tools for artifical intelligence research. He has been a major participant in the definition and standardization of the Common Lisp language. The public-domain Common Lisp implementation developed Dr. Fahlman's direction has been used by many major manufactueres as the starting point for their own Common Lisp implementation efforts. Dr. Fahlman received his Ph.D. degree form M.I.T. in 1977, where he also received his B.S. and M.S. His doctoral dissertation described the NETL architecture, a massively parallel marker–passing machine for representing large amounts of real world knowledge. Dr. Falhman has been at Carnegie-Mellon University since 1978. He is a founder of Lucid, Inc. and Expert Technologies, Inc. and is a consultant for Siemens Central Research Laboratories in Munich.

Richard P. Gabriel, Lucid, Inc.,
Richard P. Gabriel, President and Chief Technical Officer of Lucid, Inc., is the originator of Common Lisp. He was the manager of the S-1 Lisp Project and a senior research associate at Stanford University. He holds a B.A. in mathematics from Northeastern University, a M.S. in mathematics from the University of Illinois, and a Ph.D. in computer Science from Stanford University. He did extensive work on MacLisp at both Illinois and Stanford. He has published in the areas of artifical intelligence, Lisp systems, Lisp performance, and multipro-cessing Lisp. He has extensive experience with optimizing Lisp compilers.

Steve Gregory, Imperial College, London University, London, England
Steve Gregory is an advanced research fellow in the Department of Computing at Imperial College, London University. He is a founder member of the Parlog Research Group. His principal research interests are the design and implement-ation of parallel logic programming languages. Gregory received a B.Sc. (Eng.) in 1980 and a Ph.D. in 1985, both from London University.

Adolfo Guzman, Microelectronics and Computer Technology Corp. (MCC), Austin, TX
Adolfo Guzman obtained his Ph.D. from the Electrical Engineering Department at M.I.T. at the Artifical Intelligence Laboratory. He was a professor of computer science at the National University of Mexico and the National Polytechnic

Institute, also in Mexico. He was formerly an assistant professor at MIT. He has been director of the National Computing Center of the National Polytechnic Institute and the IBM Scientific Center for Latin America; head of the Department of Computer Science (IIMAS), National University of Mexico; and head and founder of the Computer Science Section at Cinvestav-National Polytechnic Institute. His professional interests, besides parallel processing, include vision, image processing, and pattern recognition. He currently develops novel architectures for symbolic processing at the Parallel Processing Program of MCC.

Leonard G. C. Hamey, Computer Science Department, Carnegie-Mellon University, Pittsburgh, PA
Leonard Hamey was born in Sydney, Australia, in 1958. He received the B.Sc. degree in 1982 from Macquarie University, Sydney, Australia, majoring in stastics, and the M.S. degree in computer science from Carnegie-Mellon University in 1985. Mr. Hamey has been a research assistant in the Computer Science Department at Carnegie-Mellon since 1982. His primary area of research is in computer vision, especially the analysis of visual textures. He has developed a number of tools for vision research including the prototype Apply compiler and the generalized image library, a powerful tool for manipulating image data.

Robert H. Halstead, Jr., Massachusetts Institute of Technology (MIT), Cambridge, MA
Robert H. Halstead, Jr., is an associate professor in the Department of Electrical Engineering and Computer Science at MIT. His research interests include languages, algorithms, and architectures for generalpurpose parallel processing, with an emphasis on symbolic computing. The Concert multiprocessor testbed was constructed at MIT under his supervision, and is now being used as a vehicle for the development of Multilisp and for other parallel computing research. He has taught in the areas of programming languages, computer architecture, compilers, and operating systems. Dr. Halstead received the B.S., M.S., and Ph.D. degrees from MIT, graduating with the Ph.D. in 1979. He is on the editorial board of the *International Journal of Parallel Processing* and is a member of the ACM and the IEEE.

Janusz S. Kowalik, Boeing Computer Services, Bellevue, WA
Janusz Kowalik is a manager in the Boeing Computer Services and an affiliate professor of computer science at the University of Washington in Seattle. Before, his current appointment he served as a scientist, a manager, and a professor in industry and at universities in Norway, Australia, Canada, and the United States. He received a Ph.D. in mathematics from the Polish Academy of Sciences in Warsaw. He has published books and papers in various areas of computer science including parallel computation. His research interest include computer architectures, supercomputing, and applications of artificial intelligence.

Edward J. Krall, Microelectronics and Computer Technology Corp. (MIC), Austin, TX

Edward Krall is an employee of NCR Corporation on assignment to MCC. He is a member of the Parallel Processing Program, one of the four advanced computer architecture programs at MCC. He received a Ph.D. in computer science from the University of Texas at Austin in 1971. From 1971 to 1975 he taught at the University of Dayton. In 1975 Dr. Krall joined the Corporate Research and Development Division of NCR Corporation in Dayton. There he specialized in system implementation languages. In 1982 he was assigned to the "Alpha-Omega" Task Force, which created the research charter for the ACA Program in MCC. He joined MCC in 1984, specializing in research of parallel Lisp architectures.

Guo J. Li, Academy of Science, Bijing, China

Guo J. Li graduated from Peking University, Bijing, China in 1968. He received a M.S. in computer science and electrical engineering from the University of Science and Technology, China Academy of Science, in 1985. Between 1985 and 1987 he was a postdoctoral research fellow at the University of Illinois. He is currently an associate researcher at the Academy of Science, Bijing, China. Research interests include parallel processing computer architecture and artificial intelligence.

John McCarthy, Stanford University, Stanford, CA

John McCarthy, is professor of computer science at Stanford University. He has been interested in artificial intelligence since 1949 and coined the term in 1955. His main artificial intelligence research area has been the formalization of common sense knowledge. He invented the Lisp programming language in 1958, developed the concept of time-sharing in the late 1950s and early 1960s, and has worked on proving that computer programs meet their specifications since the early 1960s. His most recent theoretical development is the circumscription method of nonmonotonic reasoning since 1978. McCarthy received the A. M. Turing Award of the Association for Computing Machinery in 1971 and served as president of the American Association for Artificial Intelligence in 1983–1984.

Patrick R. McGehearty, Microelectronics and Computer Technology Corp. (MCC), Austin, TX

Patrick McGehearty is an employee of MCC. He is a member of the Parallel Processing Program, one of the four advanced computer architecture programs at MCC. He received a Ph.D. in computer science from Carnegie-Mellon University in 1980. From 1980 to 1982 Dr. McGehearty worked for Mostek Corporation in the area of performance evaluation of computer architectures. In 1983, he joined Geotronics Corporation in Austin as Software Development Manager. He joined MCC at the start of 1984, specializing in parallel emulation environments.

Ryutarou Ohbuchi, Tokyo Research Laboratory, IBM Japan Ltd., Tokyo
Ryutarou Ohbuchi received a bachelor's engineering from the Sophia University, Tokyo, Japan, in 1981. He received a master engineering from the University of Electro-Commumications, Tokyo, in 1983. While he was in graduate school, he worked on the dataflow parallel processor architecture under Dr. Amamiya at Nippon Telephone and Telegraph Basic Research laboratory as his thesis work. He joined Tokyo Research laboratory, (Japan Science Institute, at the time) IBM Japan Ltd., in 1983, where he worked on graphics processor architecture for display and printer. Since August 1986, he has been at Computer Science Department, University of North Carolina at Chapel Hill, as a graduate student under IBM Japan's Foreign Study Program. His major interest is in parallel processor architecture.

David E. Shaw, Morgan Stanley & Co., New York, NY, Standford, CA
After receiving an M.S. in computer science from Stanford University in 1974, David Shaw served for three years as president an chief excetive officer of Stanford Systems Corporation, a Palo Alto-based computer systems firm, before returning to Stanford to pursue his doctorate. After receiving his Ph.D. in 1980, Dr. Shaw joined the faculty at Columbia University, where he was an associate professor of computer Science and director of the NON-VON Supercomputer Project, whose principal focus is the development of massively parallel computers for artificial intelligence and other symbolic applications. In 1986, he joined the investment banking firm of Morgan Stanley & Co. as Vice President in Charge of Automated Trading Technology. Dr. Shaw is the autor of 58 technical publications in the areas of parallel computer architectures and artifical intelligence.

N. S. Sridharan, FMC Corporation, Santa Clara, California
N. S. Sridharan is currently director of the artificial intelligence center at FMC Corporation in Santa Clara, CA. He was most recently a division scientist at BBN Laboratories in Cambirdge, MA, where his research interests included parallel programming languages, parallel algorithms for artificial intelligence, knowledge acquisition, knowledge representation, and plan formation and recognition. Dr. Sridharan joined BBN in 1984 from Rutgers University where he was an associate professor. He was also a director of software systems at LIAC Corporation in Plainview, NY. Dr. Sridharan holds a Ph.D. and an M.S. in computer science and artificiąl intelligence from the State University of New York at Stony Brook. He received a B.Tech. in electrical engineering from the Indian Institute of Technology.

Benjamin W. Wah, University of Illinois, Urbana-Champaign
Benjamin Wah is an associate professor in the Department of Electrical and Computer Engineering and in the Coordinated Science laboratory of the University of Illinois at Urbana-Champaign. He was on the faculty of the School of Electrical Engineering at Purdue University between 1979 and 1985. His

current research interests include parallel computer architectures, artificial intelligence, distributed data bases, computer networks, and theory of algorithms. He has authored *Data Management in Distributed Systems* and has coedited a *Tutorial on Computers for AI Applications*. He received a Ph.D. in computer science from the University of California at Berkeley in 1979.

Jon A. Webb, Computer Science Department, Carrnegie Mellon University, Pittsburgh, PA
Jon a. Webb is a research Computer Scientist in Carnegie-Mellon University's Computer Science Department. His research interests include the development of powerful tools to aid vision researchers and the use of those tools, particularly in the area of visual motion. With H. T. Kung and other CMU researchers, he is working on development of the Warp machine, a high-speed systolic processor intended for use in computer vision. He is developing Warp both as a tool for laboratory computer image processing, and for use with visual control of robot vehicles. Dr. Webb received his Ph.D. from the University of Texas at Austin in 1980, his M.S. degree from The Ohio State University, and his B.A. degree from the University of South Florida. In his doctral dissertation he studied problems in the interpretation of visual motion and proposed a new method of dealing with the interpretation of moving light displays.

I-Chen Wu, Computer Science Department, Carnegie-Mellon University, Pittsburgh, PA
I-Chen Wu was born in Taipei, Taiwan in 1960. He received the B.E. degree in elctrical engineering and the M.S. degree in computer science from National Taiwan University, Taipei, in 1982 and 1984, respectively. He is currently working towards the Ph.D. degree in computer science at Carnegie-Mellon University. Since 1986, he has been a research assistant in the Computer Science Department at Carnegie-Mellon. He has published papers on VLSI computation and systolic design. His research interests include VLSI computation, analysis of algorithms, computational complexity, systolic architecture, and software engineering.

I. PARALLEL COMPUTATION

1. PARALLEL PROCESSING IN ARTIFICIAL INTELLIGENCE

SCOTT E. FAHLMAN

1. INTRODUCTION

Intelligence, whether in a machine or in a living creature, is a mixture of many abilities. Our current artificial intelligence (AI) technology does a good job of emulating some aspects of human intelligence, generally those things that, when they are done by people, seem to be serial and conscious. AI is very far from being able to match other human abilities, generally those things that seem to happen "in a flash" and without any feeling of sustained mental effort. We are left with an unbalanced technology that is powerful enough to be of real commercial value, but that is very far from exhibiting intelligence in any broad, human-like sense of the word. It is ironic that AI's successes have come in emulating the specialized performance of human experts, and yet we cannot begin to approach the common sense of a five-year-old child or the sensory abilities and physical coordination of a rat.

In the earliest days of AI research, many machine arthitectures were considered, but then the successes began to flow from work on serial machines. Work on parallel approaches to AI fell into disfavor. Could it be that our pattern of success and failure in AI is a reflection of the machines we have been using? We seem to have succeeded in capturing the serial, symbol-processing part of intelligence on our serial symbol-processing machines; everything else has escaped us. Perhaps it is time to cast our net more widely and consider some radically different machine architectures in an attempt to get at these more elusive aspects of intelligence.

To what extent are the shortcomings of AI a result of the limited processing power available on our current serial computers? Are there areas where having more processing power would make a significant difference in what we can accomplish? If so, could some form of parallel processing provide that additional power? Could the application of really massive amounts of parallelism lead to some qualitative improvements in the abilities of our AI systems or some fundamental changes in the way our programs are structured? A number of researchers have begun to explore these possibilities.

In this chapter we will look at the various areas of AI in which parallel approaches are being explored, with special emphasis on those areas in which the application of parallelism might make a fundamental difference and not just make existing programs run faster. The goal is not to mention *every* such application, but merely to give the reader some idea of the variety of approaches being tried and what the prospects are for future advances.

AI programs are different in structure from the numerical programs that have received the most attention from the parallel processing community, and they present a different set of problems to anyone trying to apply parallel processing to them. Most of numerical programs do a lot of processing on a small amount of data; they typically spend most of their time in a few easily identifiable inner loops.

Because of their emphasis on symbolic, knowledge-based processing, AI programs typically must sift through vast amounts of stored information or vast numbers of possible solutions, but very little work is done in processing each item—usually just a comparison or two. The grand tradition within AI, as the field has developed on serial machines, is to reduce the search space through the use of *heuristics*: problem-specific hints about which parts of the search are most likely to succeed in various kinds of situations. Heuristic search programs contain a lot of decision points and a lot of branches, with each branch handling some special case or combination of cases, and with complicated interactions among the branches. As we will see, this kind of code is difficult to speed up dramatically on a parallel machine. The alternative is to be less clever and to perform exhaustive searches, counting on massive parallelism to provide enough power to get the job done this way.

We can divide the parallel approaches to AI into three broad categories, though the boundaries between them are often fuzzy:

The **general programming** approach attempts to detect and exploit any opportunities for concurrent execution that may exist in free-form AI programs written in some general-purpose language such as Lisp. In some of these systems, the programmer is expected to indicate where parallel processing is to occur; in others, the programmer pays no attention to issues of parallelism, and it is the system that must decide where parallelism is appropriate. In either case, the programmer is free to structure his program however he chooses, so it is possible to use search-guiding heuristics of arbitrary complexity.

The **specialized programming language** approach requires the programmer to write his code in some language that, while it may be fully general and Turing-equivalent, imposes some constraints on the programmer's style, either by favoring the heavy use of some central mechanism or by forbidding the use of certain kinds of side effects. In this category are the production system languages, the logic programming languages, and the functional programming languages. A restricted language of this sort may offer more opportunities for parallel processing than one finds in unrestricted, free-form programming.

The **active memory** approach attempts to apply massive amounts of parallelism to a group of closely related problems that occupy a central position in most AI systems: locating relevant information in a large knowledge base, doing simple inferences using such knowledge, and finding stored descriptions that match a set of inputs. The suggestion here is that perhaps we should worry more about applying parallelism to particular computationally demanding problems that are central to AI and less about finding opportunities for parallelism in arbitrary chunks of application-specific heuristic code.

In addition to these categories, a lot of research is going on in the application of parallel processing to other computationally demanding tasks in AI: low-level image processing for computer vision, low-level acoustic processing for speech understanding, and the control of multi-jointed robot manipulators. All of these tasks offer significant opportunities for parallel processing. However, these are specialized subfields with their own extensive literature, and I will not attempt to review that work here.

2. GENERAL PROGRAMMING APPROACHES

Many of today's AI programs are basically just a large mass of amorphous Lisp code. Other AI programs have an identifiable control structure, but little time is spent any one piece of code; for every type of input that the program has to deal with, there is a chunk of code to handle that case. A critical question is just how much concurrency of execution is possible in such a system.

There have been many proposals over the years for concurrent dialects of Lisp. It is clear that in many cases the arguments to a function or the branches of an AND or OR construct can be executed in parallel, but this generally buys us very little. Much of the program must still be executed in serial order, and much time is spent waiting for the slowest branch to complete its work. Where parallel execution does occur it is often only two-way or three-way—hardly enough to pay for the overhead of detecting these cases and sending them off to another processor.

Dataflow processing of amorphous Lisp code suffers from a similar limitation: much of the time, there is just not much opportunity for more than a few strands of processing to be going on at once. Because of side effects in the code, there are many synchronization constraints, and much time is wasted waiting for the slowest of the parallel branches to finish its work.

A number of researchers have explored general-purpose programming systems that attempt to minimize synchronization waits through the use of "eager beaver evaluation," in which results are computed in anticipation that they may be wanted later, and "futures," in which a token representing a data object can be passed around by one process while a separate process is working to fill in the contents of the object. The work of Halstead [1] is an example of a parallel Lisp system based upon such ideas. A function may return a promissory note instead of an actual value, and then attempt to find the resources needed to do the actual computation. The recipient of the promissory note can go on about its other business, and only has to stop when it actually needs to look at the contents of the returned data structure. By then, perhaps, the value will be ready. In principle, the recipient of a list could be looking at the head of it while the provider of the list is still busy computing its tail. Languages of this sort are the subject of active research, but they have not yet been accepted as a practical tool. It is still an open question whether this technique will lead to a significant increase in concurrency when applied to real problems and when the bookkeeping overhead is taken into account.

A different approach to parallel AI is exemplified by the Hearsay system [2]. In Hearsay, there is no attempt to discover and exploit opportunities for low-level concurrency in the code; instead, the problem is broken up into a number of large modules by the programmer. Each of these modules is an "expert" on some aspect of the problem, and each module is assigned to a separate processor. Communication among the modules is kept to a minimum; the small amount of necessary information is done by a shared data structure called the "blackboard." Any of the processors can write on the blackboard, and all of them can see it.

In the original Hearsay system, the domain was speech understanding. One module was the "expert" on phonological constraints, one on words in the lexicon, one on syntactic constraints, one on general knowledge about the subject being discussed, and so on. The Hearsay control structure has recently been abstracted and applied to other kinds of problems [3]. In addition, Hearsay-like arrangements are beginning to emerge by another route, as separately developed expert systems are tied together by local networks into larger composite systems.

The problems with the Hearsay approach are obvious: one must find a way to carve a problem up into a number of more-or-less independent chunks, with relatively little low-level communication among these chunks. It is not always easy to find such a partitioning. If there is too much message traffic among too many modules, the blackboard communication scheme becomes a bottleneck and must be replaced by yet another expert system whose job is to handle the message traffic and overall coordination. The most difficult problem, however, is that with many different subsystems working together, it is very hard to balance the load. Typically, the speed of the system is limited by the speed of one overloaded processor, while the rest have much less to do.

There is a price to be paid for the generality exhibited by all of these "general programming" systems. Each individual processor has to be able to execute code segments of arbitrary complexity and to communicate in complex ways with the other processors, so these are necessarily multiple instruction stream, multiple data stream (MIMD) systems. Since a processor in an MIMD machine requires its own program memory and enough logic to execute an arbitrary instruction stream, an MIMD machine will typically have fewer processors than a single instruction stream, multiple data stream (SIMD) machine of equivalent hardware cost. At present, MIMD systems being built in the United States range in size from a few Cray-class processors to a thousand single-chip microprocessors. Much larger SIMD machines are being designed, with up to a million processing elements. In addition, the general purpose processors usually cannot handle a particular subtask as quickly as more specialized hardware specifically tailored to the problem.

All of these systems, if well designed, offer the possibility for moderate amounts of speed up. This can be valuable in specific applications, either to get a certain job done faster or to do a more thorough job of problem-solving in a fixed amount of time. If the overall system can run twice as fast due to the judicious application of parallelism, the system could use that added speed to consider twice as many items of knowledge for possible relevance or to examine twice as many possible solutions to the problem. However, as valuable as this added speed might be in some practical applications, it seems very unlikely that these modest speed improvements will add up to a qualitative change in what AI can and cannot accomplish.

3. SPECIALIZED PROGRAMMING LANGUAGES

As noted above, the main problem in applying parallel processing to free-form heuristic programs is that the opportunities for concurrent execution are very limited. One way to attack this problem is to require the programmer to write his code in some restricted style or language that is more amenable to parallel processing. For example, the language might ban the use of certain kinds of side effects, as the functional programming languages do. Such a language may offer more opportunities for concurrent execution because there are many fewer synchronization points at which all of the concurrent program branches must wait for the slowest to finish. On the other hand, this approach imposes costs of a different kind. Because the functional modules in such programs are unable to communicate via side effects on shared data structures, everything that a function might need to see must be passed to it explicitly as an argument or must be bundled up into a closure. If not managed very carefully, the overhead resulting from all of this copying and passing of data can easily overshadow any performance gains due to increased parallelism. So far, functional programming has been of more theoretical than practical interest, but it is a very active area of research that might lead to practical AI applications in the future. For an overview of research in this area, see [4].

Prolog and other logic programming languages encourage the programmer to use a central piece of machinery—a resolution-based inference engine for simple

Horn clauses—in place of the great variety of heuristic search-limiting techniques that one finds in the more traditional style of AI programming. (The use of amorphous code and more complex search strategies is possible in most dialects of Prolog, but the idea is to avoid this whenever possible, sticking instead to the built-in search mechanisms.) By confining itself to a simple, uniform search strategy, Prolog gives up the performance advantages that search-limiting heuristics, hand crafted for a particular problem domain, could provide. On the other hand, since Prolog spends most of its time matching a large number of patterns against a data base of simple assertions, there is great potential for parallel processing. Several papers in this collection describe parallel implementation strategies for Prolog and related logic-programming languages. This is a very active area of research, due in part to the decision of the Japanese Fifth Generation Project to emphasize this approach.

Production system languages such as OPS5 [5] also spend most of their time matching patterns (the left-hand sides of their rules) against items in a data base (the working memory). Whenever such a match is found, the right-hand side of the rule is run; this is a piece of arbitrary code that, among other things, can modify the contents of the working memory.

The processing requirements of a production system's left-hand-side matcher are similar in principle to those of a Prolog matcher, and most of the same opportunities for parallel processing exist. However, most existing production system languages were designed with serial processors in mind, and they contain some elements that complicate the situation. For example, in OPS5 it is possible to require that two left-hand-side variables be bound to values in such a way that the values obey some complicated constraint. A simpler production system language might be a better choice for parallel processing, even if it is somewhat less convenient for the programmer.

On a serial machine, the OPS5 language is executed using some form of the RETE algorithm [6]. This algorithm takes advantage of the fact that the working memory changes slowly, so that much can be preserved from one match to the next, and that many of the left-hand sides share common sub-expressions. The tree-structured DADO machine [7] has been suggested as an appropriate parallel architecture for executing an OPS-like language. However, an analysis of a number of existing OPS5 programs by Forgy and colleagues suggests that the amount of possible concurrency in executing the RETE algorithm is only in the range of five to ten [8]. It is possible that these programs could be rewritten to increase the potential for concurrency; it is also possible that some algorithm other than RETE would be preferable for parallel processing. Again, this is an area of active research and discussion; within a few years we should know more about the potential for parallel processing in this area.

In general, then, these specialized languages may give up a great deal of the flexibility of the more general languages, but in exchange they offer much greater opportunities for concurrent processing. Similarly, they make it very easy to code certain kinds of problems, but the restrictive style gets in the way for many other problems. It remains to be seen whether the advantages will outweigh the disadvantages for real AI applications.

4. ACTIVE MEMORY APPROACHES

4.1. Opportunities for Parallel Processing

In the preceding sections, we looked at the problem of applying parallel processing to arbitrary AI programs, whether or not the programs are written in some special style to facilitate this task. An alternative is to identify certain time-consuming operations that most AI programs have in common, and to develop parallel subsystems to perform these selected tasks at very high speed, much as a floating-point accelerator takes over a particular set of arithmetic tasks from a general-purpose central processing unit (CPU). By confining our attention to a single problem, we can often make use of an SIMD architecture with a very large number of simple, specialized processing elements and with paths carefully tailored for the task.

The closely related problems of searching for particular items in a large knowledge base, performing simple deductions using the stored knowledge, and searching for the stored description that best matches some perceived set of features are good candidates for this sort of special-purpose parallelism. These tasks play a central role in most AI applications, they are often extremely time-consuming on a serial machine, and it is straightforward to break these tasks down into a large number of independent subtasks. A number of research groups are now investigating the use of massive parallelism to create an "active memory" system for AI.

Our serial AI technology does not do a good job of effectively using large bodies of diverse knowledge. This is a critical problem. Common sense, after all, is built mostly out of knowledge—millions of facts about the way our world works. By the time a human child is five, he knows a great deal about his environment: the kinds of objects in it, their parts, properties, and functions, a lot of informal physics, rules of behavior, the grammar and vocabulary of his native language, and so on. Anyone lacking this knowledge would be unable to function intelligently in our world, regardless of his powers of inference.

Contrast the average child's capabilities with our current "expert" or "knowledge-based" systems: the first task of the expert-system builder is to determine whether the essential knowledge of the problem domain can be expressed in a few hundred rules or assertions. If not, or if the knowledge has no sharp boundaries but trails off in all directions, the problem domain cannot be handled by our current AI technology. A modest increase in the speed of our systems would yield a proportionate increase in the number of rules that can be handled; that kind of improvement would be valuable, but these systems still are many orders of magnitude too small to handle the amount of knowledge needed for general-purpose common sense.

Note that the problem is not an inability to *store* enough information. A single video disk can hold the text of several encyclopedias, but in its raw form the knowledge just sits there waiting for someone to look at it. The real problem is the machine's inability to search through this vast body of knowledge in order to find the small collection of statements that are relevant to the problem at hand. A simple associative memory is not enough, since the relevant information may take many unanticipated forms. For example, if a human hears about a fire starting at a child's birthday party, he immediately thinks of the candles on the cake, paper decorations, excited kids knocking things over, and so on. This information just seems to pop up; everything else that we know about fires and birthdays stays out of the way. That is the ability our machines lack: they can store a large amount of knowledge, but they cannot find what they need when they need it.

The traditional (serial) AI answer to this problem has been to build complex indexing structures to help our programs find what they need, or to accompany the raw information with carefully hand-written programs that know just how and when to use each bit of knowledge. But effective indexes and specialist programs are hard to write, and they tend to be brittle: instead of using a piece of knowledge wherever and whenever it might be applicable, the builders of these systems try to anticipate how the knowledge might be used and index it accordingly. If they guess wrong, a potentially useful piece of knowledge simply does not come into play.

If there were enough cycles available, the problem would go away; we could simply scan every item in memory looking for the information we need. All of the complexity—the need for extensive indexing and for search-guiding heuristics—comes from our desire to avoid doing an exhaustive search of the whole memory. On a serial machine, the time to do a simple exhaustive search grows linearly with the size of the data base; on a parallel machine, of the type described below, it is possible to let the number of processing elements grow linearly with the size of the memory, while the search time remains nearly constant. This sounds very expensive, but remember that the number of memory calls needed to hold the knowledge is growing linearly anyway; to add some processing power to the memory is just to increase the cost by a constant factor, which may be large or small depending on the kind of processing we are talking about.

A second area in which we humans overpower our machines is in our ability to do certain kinds of simple deductions. Most of the information that we so effortlessly "find" is not really there in any explicit way; it must be computed from other information by a process of logical inference. If I tell you that some animal named Clyde is an elephant, you suddenly appear to know a great deal about him. You know, with a moderate degree of certainty, how many eyes he has, what those eyes are for, and what it means when they are closed. You know whether I can carry Clyde around in my pocket. You know that Clyde could be a male or a circus star in addition to being an elephant; but that he could not also be a cabbage. It is safe to assume that your mind has not looked up the fact that Clyde is not a cabbage, or that no elephant is a cabbage, in some table of known facts. Instead, you deduced this from some notion about elephants being animals, cabbages being plants, and these two sets being disjoint.

The point is that you do deductions like this very quickly and without any apparent effort, despite the fact that there are very many paths of inference that must be explored before we find the one that leads to the conclusion we want. Our best theorem-proving programs on our fastest serial machines choke when faced with a few thousand assertions. Even if we specialize our system for following "is-a" chains, the branching of these chains in a real knowledge base can easily produce so many paths of inference that a serial machine would be overwhelmed. And yet we humans have no trouble doing these simple inferences in a branching, tangled network of knowledge comprising millions of relations and entities.

Once again, we see that the problem would be very simple if we had an unlimited number of processing cycles to devote to it. To see if an elephant can be a cabbage, we just examine every category in which (directly or by a simple chain of deductions) an elephant belongs and every category in which a cabbage belongs, and we see whether any of these categories are labeled as mutually exclusive.

Finally, there is the problem of recognition. Whether the domain is vision, speech understanding, or some symbolic form of recognition such as medical diagnosis, the central problem is fundamentally the same: we have a set of observed features and we want to find the stored description in our memory that best matches this set of features. People are very good at this, and it does not seem to make the task harder if the number of stored descriptions that must be considered is very large. Our machines are forced either to scan every possible hypothesis to see how well it matches—simple but very time-consuming—or to use some sort of cleverness to limit the set of possibilities. Once again, the cleverness that allows us to avoid the exhaustive search is very hard to implement and tends to be brittle. In a massively parallel machine, each of the stored descriptions has some associated machinery that can, in effect, determine how well its particular hypothesis matches the observed set of features; all of the descriptions examine themselves at once, and a winner emerges.

4.2. NETL

The NETL system [9] is an example of a massively parallel architecture that attempts to handle large amounts of knowledge with something like a human's flexibility and speed. NETL is basically an active semantic network memory consisting of *nodes*, which represent noun-like concepts, and *links*, which represent the relationships between these concepts. Each node contains a few bits of memory, called *marker bits*. The number of marker bits per node is something like 16. (See Figure 1–1.)

When a new relationship is learned by the system, an unused link is chosen, is told what type of relationship it represents, and is wired up to the appropriate nodes by private-line connections. In any practical implementation, a path through some sort of switching network would be created rather than an actual physical wire, but it is essential that all the paths be able to carry independent signals at one time. The long-term knowledge in the system is represented by the

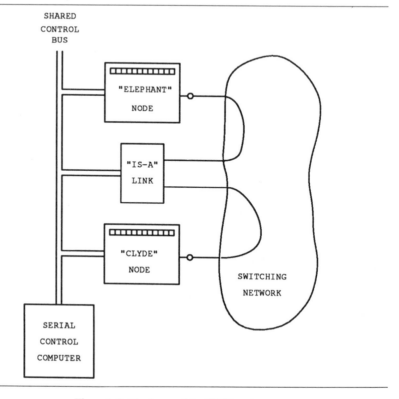

SHARED
CONTROL
BUS

"ELEPHANT"
NODE

"IS-A"
LINK

"CLYDE"
NODE

SWITCHING
NETWORK

SERIAL
CONTROL
COMPUTER

Figure 1–1. Hardware of the NETL system.

pattern of interconnection of the nodes and links, rather than by a pattern of pointers that sit in a static memory until some processor decides to look at them. This technique of storing knowledge as a variable pattern of active connections has been dubbed "connectionism" by Jerry Feldman [10].

The hardware elements representing the nodes and links receive their commands over a shared, party-line bus from a central controller, a serial computer of the conventional sort. Thus, the whole system functions as an SIMD machine; the NETL hardware functions as a sort of "smart memory" with some unusual abilities for search and simple inference. The hardware nodes can perform various Boolean operations on their marker bits, in response to commands broadcast by the controller. Commands can be executed conditionally, depending on the state of a node's marker bits. For example, a command might order all nodes with markers 1 and 2 on to turn on marker 3, or to report their identities to the controller. The hardware links can also respond to simple commands. For example, all of the links in the system might be ordered to sense whether one of the nodes they are connected to has marker 1 on and, if so, to set marker 1 in the other attached node. This would have the effect of propagating marker 1 from any node it is on to all of the neighboring nodes that are connected by links of any kind. All of the links that meet the specified conditions would execute the command at once—hence the need for private-line connections between nodes and links.

By passing these markers from node to node through the network, along only certain specified types of links, the system can very quickly perform certain types of search and inference. In just a few cycles, it can mark all of the purple objects represented in memory, or all of the vegetables. If it marks purple objects with marker 1 and vegetables with marker 2, it can then in a single cycle intersect these two sets by telling all nodes with both markers 1 and 2 to set marker 3. This intersection set can be used in subsequent processing or can be read out, one item at a time, by the controller. Thus, a NETL machine can intersect explicitly stored sets in constant time; to intersect two large sets on a serial machine requires that at least one of the lists be scanned, looking for members of the other, so time grows linearly. In fact, people who build AI knowledge bases have lavished a lot of cleverness on the problem of avoiding large set-intersections whenever possible; for NETL, such operations are so quick that there is no reason to avoid them. There is nothing magic about this; we have simply replaced a linear-time search using constant hardware with a constant-time search using a linear amount of hardware.

A particularly useful type of link is the "is a" link that ties individuals to classes, and classes to their super-classes. These links form a type hierarchy (or rather a type graph, because the paths can branch in both directions). An example of such a type hierarchy is shown in Figure 1–2. The arrows in this diagram correspond to the link units in Figure 1–1; the dots correspond to node units. In this case, the links say that Clyde is an elephant, an elephant is a mammal, and so on.

The class nodes in an "is a" hierarchy are not just labels; each of these nodes is attached to a bundle of information that is meant to be inherited by every member of the class that the node represents. For example, the Elephant node has a Color link to Gray; this says that every elephant is gray (unless this is overruled by the presence of an exception). Now, if we want to know the color of Clyde, we just put marker 1 on the Clyde node and propagate it up the branching chain of "is a" links to mark all of the classes from which Clyde is supposed to inherit properties. Then we ask all of these marked nodes whether any of them has a Color link attached to it. In just a few cycles we have in effect searched all of Clyde's superiors to determine his color.

If we want to know whether an elephant can be a cabbage, we mark the superior classes of elephant with marker 1, mark the superiors of cabbage with marker 2, and then see whether there is a "disjoint sets" link running between any member of set 1 and any member of set 2. In this case, we would find such a link between Animal and Vegetable.

These set-marking and set-intersection operations are also useful in recognition tasks. If we are trying to identify a four-legged green animal in the Everglades, we simply mark all of the four-legged things, all the animals, all the

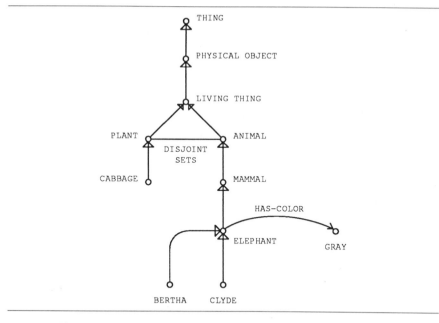

Figure 1-2. Fragment of a NETL network describing Clyde the Elephant.

green things, and all the Everglades things with different markers; then we ask the nodes with all four markers to identify themselves. If none step forward, we might ask whether any node has three out of the four markers, because the animal may not really belong in the Everglades or the green coloring might be paint. This gives us a simple Boolean kind of recognition. We are matching the features against all the descriptions stored in memory, rather than trying to be clever about which matches we will consider.

A simple marker-passing system like NETL does have some very definite limitations, however. Although some operations are sped up by very large factors, others are beyond the power of the simple parallel hardware and must be done sequentially on the serial control computer. These limitations are explored in [11]. In general, NETL is only good at finding things that are already represented in some form in its memory and at performing inferences by following chains of links. NETL cannot do generate-and-test in parallel, and is not capable of arbitrary theorem-proving in parallel. The net effect of this is that NETL provides a very flexible "active memory" system, providing quick access not only to the explicitly stored knowledge but also to some of its straightforward implications, but this architecture does *not* provide a way of speeding up general-purpose processing.

Through its use of massive parallelism and the integration of some very simple processing power with every item in the memory, NETL is able to duplicate *some* of the human abilities that have proven to be so difficult to match on serial machines. It can find information, intersect sets, and perform simple inferences in a very large knowledge-base without slowing down as the amount of knowledge grows. No clever programming or special heuristics are needed; each new item of knowledge becomes fully functional as soon as it is wired into the memory. NETL's power in this area suggests that we may be on the right track in trying to replace *some* uses of clever programming with massively parallel brute force.

The NETL architecture has been simulated, but no NETL machine has yet been built. A preliminary design study [12] has been done for a million-element NETL machine. This study suggests that such a machine would be only a few times more expensive than a serial machine with enough primary memory to hold the same amount of information in the form of a simple list of assertions. The MIT Connection Machine [13] is designed as a flexible vehicle for implementing massively parallel connectionist systems of many kinds and will be an excellent vehicle for NETL if a very large (million processor) version is built.

4.3. Value-Passing Parallelism

In many kinds of recognition, and in some areas of planning, the Boolean marker-passing parallelism of NETL is not enough. Although NETL can quickly locate any description in memory that exhibits a particular set of discrete features, it cannot go into memory and find the best-scoring match for a set of features when those scores must be computed arithmetically. In many cases a recognition system is not looking for a mere conjunction of features, but must take into account how much each feature counts as evidence for various hypotheses, how sure we are that an observed feature is correct, whether the presence of one feature modifies the strength of another, how well each hypothesis matches the system's expectations, and so on.

For this kind of recognition, we can use a massively parallel active memory system in which each connection carries some numerical weight and in which the processing elements can accumulate and compare various sets of incoming continuous values. In such a system, each observed feature could vote for the hypotheses that it supports, with various strengths for each vote; if we are lucky, a single winner will emerge with a score much larger than its competitors. Systems of this kind have been studied most intensively by Feldman, Ballard, and their colleagues at the University of Rochester [14].

4.4. Hopfield Networks

In some situations the simple network of evidence links from observed features to possible identifications is not enough. Often the features and objects constrain one another in complex patterns: an eye helps us to identify a face, which in turn helps us to identify an ear or a mouth. As soon as we allow the links in a value-passing network to form directed loops, we have a problem: the network is likely to oscillate rather than settling into some stable solution state.

John Hopfield and his colleagues at Caltech and Bell Laboratories have investigated a restricted class of networks that allow for complex interconnection patterns, but in which one can guarantee stable, nonoscillating behavior [15]. Hopfield's networks feature binary-valued (on/off) nodes with symmetrical weights between them. A positive weight between two nodes indicates that the nodes reinforce one another—if one is on, the other one prefers to be on as well. A negative weight indicates that the nodes inhibit one another and prefer not to be on at the same time.

Usually it is impossible to satisfy all of these preferences at once. The goal is to minimize the weighted sum of unsatisfied weights over the entire network, a measure that Hopfield calls the *energy* of the network. With symmetrical weights, a unique energy value can be assigned to any state of the units in the network. In a typical application, we might force some units to assume particular values and then try to find the configuration of all the other units that gives the lowest total energy consistent with these values. It is possible to search for low-energy states by a sort of (inverted) hill-climbing algorithm: we visit the nodes in some random order, and for each of them we add up the total incoming activation from connecting nodes that are on; we then compare this total to a threshold and set the node's new state accordingly. By applying this operation repeatedly, visiting each unit in the net work several times, we can be guaranteed that the network will move steadily downhill in energy space and will eventually reach a minimum, though it may only be a local minimum.

Such networks have obvious applications in recognition: the incoming sensory data force some of the units into particular states, and the network then tries to find an overall solution that matches these inputs while observing a variety of internal constraints. Hopfield and Tank have also studied the use of these networks to find good (but not optimal) solutions to problems such as the Traveling Salesman problem [16]. Several groups are currently working on parallel hardware to implement (or simulate) Hopfield nets.

4.5. The Boltzmann Machine

All of the active memory approaches discussed so far require the user to put in the connections and weights explicitly. This usually leads to the use of a *local representation*: there is a direct association between individual concepts or pieces of knowledge and pieces of hardware in the machine. This means that if a piece of hardware breaks, the knowledge associated with it is lost. In a system with millions of processing elements, some of the elements will always be broken, so a more robust representation would be desirable. An idea that has surfaced repeatedly in AI, and that has been advocated by many neuroscientists, is to use some sort of *distributed* or "holographic" representation, in which a concept is associated not with any single processing element, but with some total state of activation of all the units in a module. Each of these concepts would differ from all the others by a fairly large number of unit-states, so if one or a few units malfunction, the system still be in the same state as before. Such distributed-representation systems thus have an inherent reliability that would be very valuable if we wanted to build them out of wafer-scale silicon (flaws and all) or out of neurons.

The problem with such distributed systems is that it is very difficult to build the knowledge into them by hand. Since a piece of information does not reside in any particular place, but is spread around among many processing elements, it is necessary to adjust a large number of elements in order to get any new information into the system. In the early 1960s, researchers thought that they had found a way to make neural networks that could develop their own internal representation just by seeing examples of the desired input/output behavior. These learning networks were called *perceptrons* [17]. Unfortunately, the bubble burst: Minsky and Papert [18] showed that these simple perceptrons could not do much, and for many years nobody was able to extend the learning results to more complex networks.

The Boltzmann Machine [19] is a massively parallel memory architecture that can learn from examples, even in multilayer networks. Like perceptrons and Hopfield networks, the Boltzmann machine is inspired by some ideas about how to compute with networks of neuron-like elements. A Boltzmann machine is basically a Hopfield network with one essential difference: whenever a unit is making a decision about which state to assume next, we deliberately inject some random noise into the decision. Instead of being harmful, this random input helps to shake the system out of locally optimal configurations so that it can seek out the globally best solutions. (The name "Boltzmann" refers to the 19th century physicist Ludwig Boltzmann, who developed some concepts in statistical mechanics that are useful in analyzing stochastic networks of this sort.)

The surprising property of these networks is that it is possible to derive a very simple relationship between any given weight and the global behavior of the network, even if the network is very complex. We can present the network with a set of examples of a desired input/output mapping, and can decide how to adjust each weight in order to improve the fit between the network's current behavior and the desired behavior. Gradually, the network's performance improves.

This learning behavior has been demonstrated on simulated networks with a few hundred units [20]. In these simulations the network is not merely storing and reproducing the examples it has seen; rather, it makes use of the available nodes and links to develop internal representations that capture certain regularities in the training data. Because of this, the network is able to produce appropriate outputs for cases that are similar, but not identical, to the cases it was trained on. The internal representations are distributed and fault-tolerant: a transient or hard error in any given unit will not usually change the global behavior of the network.

These learning results for small networks are encouraging. However, the current Boltzmann learning techniques are slow, requiring hundreds or thousands of presentations of the training data as we change the weights by small amounts. As we scale up the networks to attack more interesting problems, the learning becomes even slower. We are investigating a number of approaches for speeding up the learning, including the so-called "back propagation" learning algorithm [21].

At present this must be regarded as highly speculative research. If we can solve the speed-of-learning problem, we could end up with a "recognition box" or memory system that can learn from examples, that can find best matches even in the presence of noise or variation in the input, and that uses an inherently reliable internal representation that is well-suited to large-scale integration. This could help to eliminate some of the fundamental weaknesses of present-day AI that I described earlier. The study of active memory networks may even give us some insight into what the cerebral cortex is doing. However, it must be emphasized that we still have much to learn in this area and that we must make more progress in increasing the speed of learning before we can tackle any large-scale practical applications.

5. SUMMARY

We have examined three basic approaches to the use of parallel processing in AI. In the first approach, we try to find opportunities for concurrent processing in general purpose programs of the sort that are currently popular in AI. In most of these programs, the opportunities for concurrency do exist, but they are rather limited.

In the second approach, we adopt a restricted coding style, giving up some flexibility and perhaps efficiency in exchange for a uniform program structure that offers much greater opportunities for parallel processing. This approach is generating a lot of excitement in the research community. The most important open question is whether these restricted languages will prove to be useful for many kinds of problems within AI or only for a few specialized tasks.

In the third approach, we attempt to apply massive amounts of parallel processing not to arbitrary programs, but rather to a specific set of memory-related tasks that play a pivotal role in AI. This approach offers the greatest amount of potential parallelism and may allow us to replace much of the clever programming of current AI systems with a sort of massively parallel brute force. In my opinion, this is the approach that offers the greatest hope for fundamental advances in what AI can accomplish, but this hope will only be realized if we can develop faster learning procedures that are suited to very large-scale networks.

ACKNOWLEDGMENTS

The author's research is supported by the Defense Advanced Research Projects Agency (U.S. Department of Defense); DARPA Order No. 4976, monitored by the Air Force Avionics Laboratory under contract F33615-84-K-1520. The views and conclusions contained herein are those of the author and should not be interpreted as representing the official policies, either expressed or implied, of the sponsors or the U.S. Government.

REFERENCES

1. R. H. Halstead, Jr., "Implementation of Multilisp: Lisp on a Miltiprocessor," *1984 ACM Symp. on Lisp and Functional Programming*, ACM, 1984.
2. L. D. Erman, F. Hayes-Roth, V. R. Lesser, and D. R. Reddy, "The Hearsay-II Speech Understanding System." *Computing Surveys* 12, June 1980.
3. L. D. Erman, P. E. London, and S. F. Fickas, "The Design and an Example Use of Hearsay-III," *Proc., IJCAI-81*, 1981.
4. P. M. Kogge, "Function-Based Computing and Parallelism: A Review," *Parallel Computing* 2(3): 243–254, November 1985.
5. C. L. Forgy, *OPS5 User's Manual*. Tech. Rep. CMU-CS-81-135, Computer Science Dept., Carnegie-Mellon University, Pittsburgh, PA, 1981.
6. C. L. Forgy, "Rete: A Fast Algorithm for the Many Pattern/Many Object Pattern Match Problem," *Artificial Intelligence* 19, September 1982.
7. S. J. Stolfo, "Five Parallel Algorithms for Production System Execution on the DADO Machine," *Proc. AAAI-84*, 1984.
8. C. L. Forgy, A. Gupta, A. Newell, and R. Wedig, "Initial Assessment of Architectures for Production Systems," *Proc., AAAI-84*, 1984.
9. S. E. Fahlman, *NETL: A System for Representing and Using Real-World Knowledge*. Cambridge, MA: MIT Press, 1979.
10. J. A. Feldman, "Connectionist Models and Their Applications: Introduction," Cognitive Science, (*Special Issue*) 9:1, 1985.
11. S. E. Fahlman, "Three Flavors of Parallelism," *Proc. Fourth Nat'l Conf. Can. Soc. for Computational Studies of Intelligence*, Saskatoon, Saskatchewan, May 1982.
12. S. E. Fahlman, "Design Sketch for a Million-Element NETL Machine," *Proc. Nat'l Conf. on Artificial Intelligence*, Stanford, CA, August 1980.
13. W. D. Hillis, *The Connection Machine*. Cambridge MA: MIT Press, 1985.
14. J. A. Feldman, and D. H. Ballard, "Connectionist Models and Their Properties," *Cognitive Science* 6:205–254, 1982.
15. J. J. Hopfield, "Neural Networks and Physical Systems with Emergent Collective Computational Abilities," *Proc. Nat'l Acad. Sci. U.S.A.* 79:2554–2558, 1982.
16. J. J. Hopfield, and D. W. Tank, "Neural Computation of Decisions in Optimization Problems," *Biological Cybernetics* 52:141–152, 1985.
17. F. Rosenblatt, *Principles of Neurodynamics*. New York: Spartan Books, 1962.
18. M. Minsky, and S. Papert, *Perceptrons*. Cambridge, MA: MIT Press, 1969.
19. S. E. Fahlman, G. E. Hinton, and T. J. Sejnowski, "Massively Parallel Architectures for A.I.: Netl, Thistle, and Boltzmann Machines," *Proc. Nat'l Conf. on Artificial Intelligence*, Washington DC, Aug. 1983.
20. D. H. Ackley, G. E. Hinton, and T. J. Sejnowski, "A Learning Algorithm for Boltzmann Machines." *Cognitive Science* 9:147–169, 1985.
21. D. E. Rumelhart, G. E. Hinton, and R. J. Williams, "Learning Internal Representations by Error Propagation." In D. E. Rumelhart, J. L. McClelland, and the PDP research group (eds.), *Parallel Distributed Processing: Explorations in the Microstructure of Cognition*. Cambridge, MA: Bradford Books, 1986.

2. PARALLEL COMPUTING USING MULTILISP

ROBERT H. HALSTEAD, JR.

1. INTRODUCTION

Programs differ from one another in many dimensions. In one such dimension, programs can be laid out along a spectrum with predominantly symbolic programs at one end and predominantly numerical programs at the other. The differences between numerical and symbolic programs suggest different approaches to parallel processing. This chapter explores the problems and opportunities of parallel symbolic computing and describes the language Multilisp, used at MIT for experiments in parallel symbolic programming.

Much of the attention that has been focused on parallel processing has been concerned with numerical applications. High-performance numerical computers have been designed using varying degrees of concurrency [1-4]. Programming tools for these computers range from compilers that automatically identify concurrency in Fortran programs [5] to languages featuring explicit parallelism following a "communicating sequential processes" model [3, 6]. Numerical computation emphasizes arithmetic: the principal function of a numerical program may be described as delivering numbers to an arithmetic unit to calculate a result. Numerical programs generally have a relatively data-independent flow of control: within broad limits, the same sequence of calculations will be performed no matter what the operand values are. Inner

This research was supported in part by the Defense Advanced Research Projects Agency and was monitored by the Office of Naval Research under contract number N00014-83-K-0125.

loops of numerical programs may contain conditionals, and overall control of a program generally includes tests of convergence criteria and such, but most numerical programs have a relatively predictable control sequence, compared with the majority of symbolic programs. Matrices and vectors are common data structures in numerical programs, a fact exploited by single instruction stream, multiple data stream (SIMD) [7] techniques in many numerically oriented supercomputers.

In contrast, symbolic computing emphasizes rearrangement of data. Partly because of this, heavily symbolic programs are more likely to be written in a language such as Lisp [8–11] or Smalltalk [12] than in Fortran. The principal function of a symbolic program may be broadly stated as the reorganization of a set of data so that the relevant information in it is more useful or easier to extract. Examples of primarily symbolic algorithms include sorting, compiling, data-base management, symbolic algebra, expert systems, and other artificial intelligence (AI) applications. The sequence of operations in symbolic programs is often highly data-dependent and less amenable to compile-time analysis than in the case of numerical computation [13]. Moreoever, there does not appear to be any simple operation style, comparable to vector operations in numerical programs, that can easily be exploited to increase performance with a SIMD type of architecture. Some operations, such as procedure calling, pointer following, and even tree search, occur frequently in symbolic programs, but it is not obvious how SIMD parallelism can help very efficiently with these.

The structure of symbolic computations generally seems to lend itself less well to analysis of loops—the major focus in parallelizing numerical computation—and favors recursions on composite data structures, such as trees, lists, and sets, as the major source of concurrency. Programming languages such as Qlisp [14] and Multilisp [15–17] include constructs to take advantage of these sources of concurrency.

This chapter explores parallel symbolic computing from the vantage point of the Multilisp project. We begin with an overview of Multilisp and then consider some examples illustrating how Multilisp's future construct can help expose concurrency in manipulating composite data structures. We close by discussing the requirements of parallel programming "in the large" and suggesting some important directions for research in parallel symbolic computing.

2. OVERVIEW OF MULTILISP

Multilisp is a version of the Lisp-like programming language Scheme [9] extended to allow the programmer to specify concurrent execution. Multilisp shares with Scheme two properties that distinguish them from the more common members of the Lisp family. The first is exclusive reliance on lexical scoping, which promotes modularity. The second is "first-class citizenship" for procedures: procedures in Scheme and Multilisp may be passed freely as arguments, returned as values of other procedures, stored in data structures, and treated in the same way as any other kind of value.

Multilisp includes the usual Lisp side-effect primitives for altering data structures and changing the values of variables. Therefore, control sequencing beyond that imposed by explicit data dependencies may be required in order to ensure determinate execution. In this respect, Multilisp parts company with many concurrent Lisp languages [18–21], which include only a side-effect-free subset of Lisp.

The default in Multilisp is sequential execution. This allows Lisp programs or subprograms written without attention to parallelism to run, albeit without using the potential concurrency of the target machine. Concurrency can be introduced into a Multilisp program by means of the future construct. The form (future X) immediately returns a *future* [22, 23] for the value of X and creates a task to concurrently evaluate X, allowing concurrency between the *computation* of a value and the *use* of that value. When the evaluation of X yields a value, that value replaces the future; we say that the future *resolves* to the value. Any task that needs to know a future's value will be suspended until the future resolves.

We say that a task T *examines*, or *touches*, a future when it performs an operation that will cause T to be suspended if the future is not yet resolved. Most operations, *e.g.*, arithmetic, comparison, type checking, *etc.*, touch their operands (any operation that is *strict* in an operand touches that operand). However, simple transmission of a value from one place to another, *e.g.*, by assignment, passing as a parameter to a procedure, returning as a result from a procedure, building the value into a data structure, does *not* touch the value. Thus, many things can be done with a future without waiting for its value.

In Multilisp, future is the *only* primitive for creating a task; there is a one-to-one correspondence between tasks and the futures whose values they were created to compute. Every task ends by resolving its associated future to some value.

future is related to the idea of "lazy evaluation" often used in designs for graph-reduction architectures [19, 24, 25]. In lazy evaluation, an expression is not evaluated until its value is demanded by some other part of a computation. When an expression is encountered in a program, it is not evaluated immediately. Instead, a *suspension* is created and returned, and evaluation of the expression is delayed until the suspension is touched (in the Multilisp sense). A suspension is much like a future: the only difference between future and lazy evaluation is that future does not wait for the suspension to be touched before beginning evaluation of the expression. Multilisp has a delay primitive that implements lazy evaluation exactly—it returns a future and does not begin evaluation of the expression until the future is touched—but delay by itself does not express any concurrency.

Although future induces some patterns reminiscent of those found in graph-reduction architectures, in other ways future creates a style of computation much like that found in dataflow architectures [26–28]. Every task suspended waiting for a future to resolve is like a dataflow operator waiting for an operand to arrive. As in the case of dataflow, each such task will become eligible to proceed as soon as all its operands become available. When a task proceeds, it will eventually resolve another future, reactivating other suspended tasks in a pattern very reminiscent of the flow of data tokens in a dataflow graph. Futures thus offer access to an interesting mixture of styles of parallel computation.

A complete Multilisp implementation including a parallel, incremental garbage collector [15] exists on Concert [29, 30], an experimental multiprocessor under construction in the author's laboratory. The Concert multiprocessor, when fully built, will comprise 32 MC68000 processors and a total of about 20 megabytes of memory. (As of this writing, the largest part of Concert that has been available for Multilisp is a 28-processor section of the eventual Concert machine.) Concert can be described most concise as a shared-memory multiprocessor, although its organization includes various local paths from processors to nearby memory modules, which enable it to provide a higher overall bandwidth between processors and memory if most memory accesses are local.

3. EXAMPLE PROGRAMS IN MULTILISP

An idea of what programming with futures is like may be gained by considering some example Multilisp programs. We consider two simple examples: binary search trees and Quicksort. Both examples are sequential programs to which futures have been added. Thus each example really involves two programs: one without future and another identical to the first except for the use of future. Each of these programs can then be executed by Concert Multilisp and the resulting behavior studied. In a later section, we describe the Concert Multilisp implementation in more detail and analyze some of the performance figures; however, the effect of different uses of future in our example programs is illustrated best by giving some performance figures, so it is useful to briefly examine Multilisp performance before beginning with the examples.

3.1. Performance Measurement Methodology

When a sequential (*i.e.*, future-less) Multilisp program P_S is executed on one processor, it will take some period of "real computing" time T_C to finish. If a parallel program P_P identical to P_S except for some uses of future is executed on one processor, it will take time $T_C + T_F$, where T_F is the time cost of the added future constructs. If P_P is executed on a multiprocessor with N processors, we may hope that the time T_N that it takes will be less than $T_C + T_F$. However, the total *processor time* taken on N processors is NT_N, which will certainly not be less than $T_C + T_F$, since all the work done in the uniprocessor case must also be done in the multiprocessor case. Typically, in fact, $NT_N > T_C + T_F$. The difference $NT_N - (T_C + T_F)$ represents multiprocessing losses that do not occur in the uniprocessor case. The losses fall into several categories: T_I, the idle time caused by insufficient parallelism in the program; T_A, the extra memory access latency due to contention for shared memory and/or due to accessing data in more "remote" locations than in the uniprocessor case; and several categories of excess computation due to synchronization, of which the major ones are T_S, the cost of more frequent suspension of tasks caused by touching unresolved futures, and T_L, the cost of waiting for locks on shared data structures.

Progress toward the goal of efficient parallel symbolic computing is, of course, measured simply in terms of T_N—the time a multiprocessor takes to perform a computation. But a deeper understanding of the differences between programs, and the possible effects of various changes in the Multilisp implementation, can be gained by examining the various components of T_N. It is useful to examine the amount of processor time that goes into each of these components, not only as totals over an entire program execution, but also as it varies over time while the program is running. Often, a program will show good parallelism (*i.e.*, low idle time) during one phase of its execution but large amounts of idle time during other phases. Such behavior is not easily discernible from looking at the totals.

In principle, we should be able to account for all the extra time represented by $NT_N - (T_C + T_F)$ in one of the four categories T_A, T_S, T_L, and T_I, so $NT_N = T_C + T_F + T_A + T_S + T_L + T_I$. However, precise measurement of these quantities poses some practical difficulties. T_C and T_F can be determined by running programs on one processor. T_I and T_L can be measured fairly directly on a multiprocessor. However, T_A tends to distribute itself throughout the computation, so that its most noticeable effect is to stretch out T_C, T_F, and all the other times we might measure directly. T_S is also somewhat challenging to measure: given that some suspension and activation of tasks occurs anyhow, it is difficult to determine just by looking at a multiprocessor execution of a parallel program which suspensions and activations are "excess" in the sense that they would not have occurred in the uniprocessor case. Therefore, it is sometimes difficult to know whether to charge a particular operation, such as a context switch, to T_F or T_S.

Multilisp has been instrumented to provide a breakdown of execution time in a slightly different way, as $NT_N = T'_C + T'_F + T_O + T_I$. T'_C is like the "real computing" time T_C except that it includes the part of T_A that stretches out memory accesses made during "real computing." Through the indirect means of measuring T_A currently available in Concert Multilisp, T_A does not appear to be a large fraction of NT_N, so this approximation is acceptable. T'_F counts time directly attributable to use of future. T'_F unfortunately includes a small amount of time that belongs to T_S; therefore, it may be greater than T_F. Moreover, T'_F, like T'_C, also includes some part of T_A, which can again make T'_F larger than T_F. Once again, the magnitude of these discrepancies does not appear to be major in Concert Multilisp. T_O, the "multiprocessor overhead" term, includes lock-waiting time and context-switching time that should definitely be charged to T_S. Therefore, it includes T_S (except for a small part of T_S that is charged to T'_F), T_L, and (because many of these operations access shared memory) part of T_A. Finally, T_I counts all the time a processor has no task to work on. Some of this time represents a genuine shortage of executable tasks in the system, and some of it simply represents "short-term unemployment" as a processor searches for an executable task that is available elsewhere (as a result of some imbalance in the

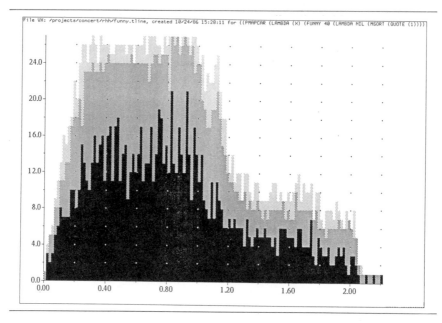

Figure 2–1. An example parallelism profile from Concert Multilisp.

distribution of work). A more detailed discussion of processor time accounting is not appropriate at this point, since our immediate goal is to document the behavior of certain parallel programs, not dissect the Concert Multilisp implementation.

Figure 2–1 displays statistics gathered from actual execution of an arbitrarily selected program on Concert Multilisp. The program was executed on 27 processors; the twenty-eighth is reserved as a network server. The passage of time is measured along the abscissa; the ordinate indicates the number of processors engaged in a particular kind of activity. Black areas on the graph represent processors whose time is currently being charged to T'_C. The area of dark gray corresponds to T'_F, and light gray and white correspond to T_O and T_I, respectively. Note that samples are taken only at intervals of one-sixtieth of a second. Although this might seem too long a sampling interval, processing in Concert Multilisp is slow enough in absolute terms (due to its use of a layer of interpretation) that only 30 to 100 primitive Multilisp operations usually occur within one sixtieth of a second.

As discussed above, it can be difficult to know whether to color the rectangle on a parallelism profile corresponding to a particular operation light or dark gray because we can't tell whether that operation should be charged to T_F or T_S. Nevertheless, we can count the total number of operations of a particular type (*e.g.*, context switches) that occur during execution of a program, and compare these numbers for the uniprocessor and multiprocessor cases. We can then apportion the total observed cost of, say, context switching in the multiprocessor case between T_F and T_S so that T_F is charged for the number of context switches that occur on one processor and T_S is charged for the rest. This approach does not help us refine the parallelism profiles, because it does not tell us which context switches to charge to which category, but it does help us refine summary statistics about a program execution as a whole.

Applying this analysis to our example programs leads to the following conclusions about Concert Multilisp performance.

- T_L is quite small. T_L was never more than 6% of T_O in any of the program executions reported here and was only a tiny fraction (at most 0.8%) of NT_N.
- T_A is significant, but not overwhelming. We have only indirect measurments of this, but it appears never to have exceeded 13% of NT_N. The creation and manipulation of futures uses shared-memory accesses especially intensively, absorbing a proportionately larger share of T_A than "real computing" does; however, there are many individual variations, and it is difficult to make a general statement stronger than this.
- T_F is equal to approximately 8 milliseconds per future created (these 8 ms include the time to create and resolve the future, as well as to schedule the associated task) plus 0.6 milliseconds per reference to a resolved future.
- T_S is equal to approximately 6 milliseconds per reference to an unresolved future (this consists mainly of the cost of suspending and re-activating the referencing task).

On the whole, the most significant variable not plotted on the parallelism profiles is T_A, the increase in shared-memory access time due to multiprocessing. In some of our tests, this consumed performance equivalent to an average of up to 3.5 out of 27 processors. However, T_A seems to affect the overhead components T'_F and T_O the most strongly, so we can have reasonable confidence that the black areas of the parallelism profiles reflect almost entirely "real computing" rather than memory access delays. This gives us confidence in the significance of the parallelism profiles presented in the following sections.

3.2. Binary Tree Insertion

Our first example program manipulates sets represented as binary trees. The precise nature of the elements of these sets is not important—they could be integers, ordered pairs, character strings, or whatever—but we assume that they are totally ordered by the Lisp predicate elt <, so (elt < A B) returns true if and only if the element A precedes the element B in the total order. The existence of the total order allows us to arrange the N elements of a set for lookup in $O(\log N)$ time by any of a variety of well-known techniques. Possible uses of such a set are to collect integers or character strings with certain properties in common, or to record pairs of values from the domain and range of some function.

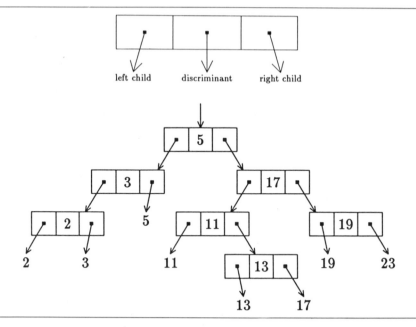

Figure 2-2. Structure of search trees manipulated by Program 2-1. (a) An interior node of a search tree. (b) A search tree with integers as leaf nodes.

Our example program uses binary trees built out of *nodes* as suggested by Figure 2-2. Each leaf node of a tree is an actual set element, and each interior node is a triple as shown in Figure 2-2(a). A Lisp function leaf? distinguishes between the two types of nodes: (leaf? X) returns true if X is a leaf node and false if X is an interior node. Each interior node has left and right children which are other nodes, and a *discriminant* equal to the largest element stored in the left subtree of that node, as shown in Figure 2-2(b). A Lisp function (make-node L D R) makes and returns a new interior node whose left child is L, whose discriminant is D, and whose right child is R. Given an interior node N, (left-child N), (discriminant N), and (right-child N) return, respectively, the left child, discriminant, and right child of N.

A Multilisp procedure to insert an element elt into a tree tree is shown in Program 2-1. This is a "nondestructive" insert—it copies the tree nodes to be modified and returns a new tree, rather than performing side effects on existing nodes. Except for its two uses of future, Program 2-1 is the straightforward Lisp procedure for insertion into this kind of tree. The case of inserting into an initally empty tree has to be treated specially. In this case, insert just returns elt—a single leaf node—as the resulting tree. If tree is not empty, then it may be leaf or an interior node. If it is a leaf, insert returns an interior node with elt and tree as children in the proper order. If tree is an interior node, insert determines whether

```
(defun insert (elt tree)
  (if (empty-tree? tree)
     elt
     (if (leaf? tree)
        (if (elt< tree elt)
           (make-node tree tree elt)
           (make-node elt elt tree))
        (if (elt< (discriminant tree) elt)
           (make-node (left-child tree)
                      (discriminant tree)
                      (future (insert elt (right-child tree))))
           (make-node (future (insert elt (left-child tree)))
                      (discriminant tree)
                      (right-child tree))))))
```

Program 2–1. Insert routine for search trees, using future. In addition to the procedures discussed in the text, this program uses two standard Lisp special forms [8]. (defun f (v_1 v_2 ...) body) defines a procedure f whose formal parameters are $v_1; v_2, \ldots$, and whose value is the value of the expression body. (if X Y Z) returns the value of Y if X evaluates to true; otherwise the value of Z is returned.

elt belongs in the left or right subtree of tree, and returns a new interior node with the same discriminant and suitable left and right children.

The use of future in Program 2–1 allows insert to return even before the insertion has been completed. If future were not used, then an insert applied to an interior node would not return until its recursive call to insert had returned; thus the new tree would be constructed in a bottom-up order, and no result would be returned until the new tree had been completely constructed. Using future, however, insert can construct a new node and return it without waiting for completion of recursive calls to insert. If tree is an interior node, insert makes a new node that points to a future that will resolve to the value of the recursive call to insert. Consequently, the result of an insertion develops in more of a top-down fashion, as shown in Figure 2–3.

To insert three new elements A, B, and C into some tree T, we could write

(insert C (insert B (insert A T)))   2.1

A naive analysis might conclude that no concurrency is available in this expression, due to data dependencies: the insertion of B requires the result of inserting A, and so on. Yet with futures we find that some concurrency is available. For example, if T were the tree of Figure 2–2(b), and A, B, and C were 7, 4, and 29, respectively, then the insert of B could begin as soon as the insert of A returns, and the insert of C need only await the return of the insert of B and the resolution of the first future created during A's insertion. The remaining work for the three insertions can then proceed in parallel.

The fallacy in the naive analysis is in treating structured values such as binary trees as indivisible units. In fact, many (if not most) operations on structured

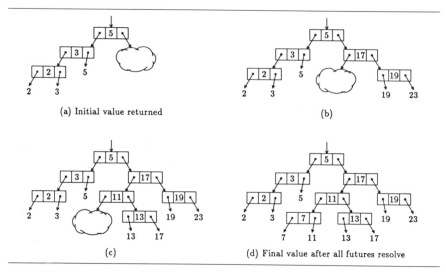

(a) Initial value returned   (b)

(c)   (d) Final value after all futures resolve

Figure 2-3. Top-down behavior of insert using future. (a) through (d) depict successive stages resulting from inserting 7 into the tree shown in Figure 2–2(b). The cloud-like shapes represent unresolved futures.

values require only partial information about their operands. Futures give us a way to represent partially computed values, so they can be released for use while they are still being computed. As illustrated by our example, this can expose concurrency not easily accessible using conventional fork-join control structures. This is especially significant in symbolic computing, where operations on structured data are the norm, and where opportunities to use the kinds of loop-and-flow-analysis techniques that are well known [5] are often much more limited than in the case of numerical computing.

It is of course possible to select values for A, B, and C in (2.1) such that futures will yield relatively little concurrency (e.g., $A = 7$, $B = 9$, and $C = 10$). In this case the lack of concurrency is due to real data dependencies: all three insertions are operating in the same region of the tree. Even in this case there will be some concurrency as the insertions of A, B, and C follow each other down the tree, but each insertion will be prevented from completely finishing until the previous one has finished most of its work. future cannot remove *actual* data dependencies, but can remove *apparent* dependencies by allowing structured values to be computed piecemeal.

To gauge the impact of using futures in Program 2–1, the program was tested on Concert by successively inserting long lists of random numbers into an initially empty tree. The test was essentially to evaluate the expression

$$(\text{insert } v_n \ (\text{insert } v_{n-1} \ \ldots \ (\text{insert } v_1 \ empty\text{-}tree) \ \ldots \ ))$$

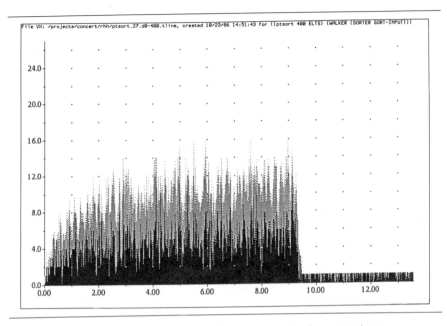

Figure 2–4. Parallelism profile for Program 2–1 using fast comparisons.

and then walk the resulting tree to wait for all futures to be resolved; $v_1, v_2, \ldots, v_n$ are the n numbers inserted into the tree.

Figure 2–4 shows the parallelism profile obtained by successively inserting 400 random integers into a tree. Several features are apparent in the figure. We might expect the available parallelism to be much less than 27, because we expect the parallelism to be on the same order as the average depth of the tree, and 400 randomly chosen numbers are likely to form a tree whose average depth is around nine. Indeed, Figure 2–4 shows parallelism that grows rapidly at first, as the initially empty tree grows in depth, and then more slowly, finally approaching the vicinity of nine.

Figure 2–4 also shows a large sequential "tail" emanating from the right of the computation. Although the set of insertions is in a certain sense "finished" when the final insert returns, some "mopping-up" computation, to resolve the last few unresolved futures, remains. The only way to *know* within a Multilisp program that computation of the final tree is complete is to walk the entire data structure, touching every element. When the walk finishes, completion of the task can be reported. To add a minimum of confusion to the parallelism profile, the walk operates sequentially, rather than exploring tree branches in the obvious parallel way. However, Figure 2–4 demonstrates that the resulting reported completion time is quite pessimistic: all computation due to insertions ended after 9.4 seconds, even though the walk did not finish until 4.2 seconds later. Although the

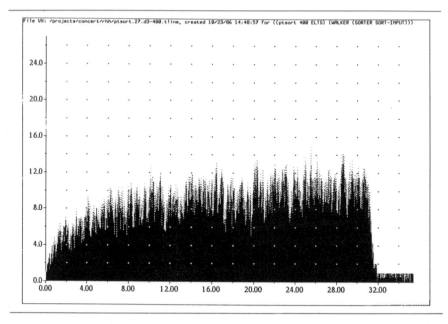

File VX: /projects/concert/rhh/ptsort.27.d3-400.tline, created 10/23/86 14:48:57 for ((ptsort 400 ELTS) (WALKER (SORTER SORT-INPUT)))

Figure 2–5. Parallelism profile for Program 2–1 using slow comparisons.

walk is needed for a conservative report of the result, an actual use of insert in practice would not be followed by a walk, but by some other computation that could begin as soon as the final insert had returned; the remaining computation due to insert would proceed concurrently with the use of the tree, just as it proceeds (to a small extent) in parallel with the walk in Figure 2–4.

Finally, the magnitude of overhead $(T'_F + T_O)$ in Figure 2–4 is notable. Only 50% of processor busy time is going into "real computing" (T'_C); 44% of the busy time is going into T'_F. Because 3327 futures are created (and resolved) during execution of the program, the marginal increase in T'_F for each future is 12.6 milliseconds. This is a heavy cost, but we can hope to reduce it in a well-desinged "Multilisp machine" through suitable processor design. As an approximate way of obtaining the parallelism profile that would be observed if future were cheaper, the comparison routine elt< was made artificially slow, lengthening T'_C by about a factor of five. (This change also models the probably more realistic situation in which the items to be compared have a more expensive comparison operation than numbers do.) The resulting parallelism profile is shown in Figure 2–5. This change has had little effect on the ratio of processor busy to idle time, but a much larger fraction (85%) of the total busy time is now represented by T'_C. (Also, it can be noted that the final tree walk makes a proportionally smaller contribution, because its operation was not slowed down.)

The purpose of this example is to illustrate the character of futures in a relatively simple setting, rather than to illustrate the best in parallel tree management schemes. Program 2–1 can be improved in many ways. At the superficial level, we can certainly extend it to cope with "insertion" of an item that is already in the tree. We can also add the delete and lookup routines that would be desired in many applications.

More serious for some applications than the lack of these features is the fact that Program 2–1 does not necessarily produce balanced search trees. If insertions are performed in some unfortunate order (*e.g.*, strictly increasing), the result of inserting K items can be a "tree" of depth K that takes $O(K^2)$ time to build. Various schemes for building balanced search trees, such as 2–3 trees and AVL trees, are known [31–33]. These schemes can be adapted using future to yield parallelism, but the results can be disappointing, for reasons that are instructive. Balanced tree schemes generally try to maintain rough equality at each node N between the number of nodes in the subtrees headed by the children of N. The common sequential algorithms for insertion into balanced trees first find the place where the new leaf node will be added and then work back up the tree toward the root, rearranging the structure as needed to ensure the proper balance. Thus, the final shape of the tree, even near the root, may be determined only after the location of the new leaf node has been determined.

Unfortunately, the concurrency in Program 2–1 comes from releasing information about the structure of the resulting tree even before an insertion has progressed all the way to a leaf node. Every recursive invocation of Program 2–1 ends by specifying the left and right children of some newly created node. One of the children may be specified as a future, so its *value* may not be known, but its *identity* is known. In the case both 2–3 trees and AVL trees, there are certain points where it can be seen that any tree reorgnization resulting from an insertion cannot propagate above that point. But at other points, even the *identities* of the child nodes cannot be fixed without additional information that will be generated as the insertion progresses. At such points, construction of a new node must be delayed until it becomes clear what its children should be. This delays the top-down evolution suggested by Figure 2–3 and therefore reduces the opportunities for parallelism. Balanced-tree schemes are not necessarily unsuitable for parallel execution, but different algorithms that operate in a more top-down manner, perhaps by accepting a more relaxed standard of balance for search trees, are needed.

3.3. Quicksort

Although Program 2–1 offers a simple and perhaps surprising example of the power of future, we see that insert by itself cannot use up a large parallel processor. Program 2–2, discussed next, uses future in a way that produces much more parallelism. The porcedure qs sorts a list l of numbers using the Quicksort algorithm: the procedure partition uses the first element elt of l to devide the rest of l into two lists, one containing only elements less than elt, and the other containing only elements greater than or equal to elt. Each of these lists is recursively sorted using qs, and the results, along with the partitioning element elt, are appended in the proper order to form the result. To avoid the overhead of an explicit append operation, qs takes an additional argument rest, which is the list that should appear after the list of sorted elements of I. The top-level procedure qsort accordingly supplies nil as the initial value for rest.

Where to put the future operators is not immediately obvious. Every use of future in Program 2–2 gains a significant amount of parallelism. The one use of future in the procedure qs allows the sorting of the left and right sublists returned by partition to occur in parallel. future works well here because this argument will not be touched inside the sort—it will simply be built in at the end of the sorted list.

The uses of future in partition are more interesting, and distinguish this Quicksort program from those that have been studied on other parallel processing systems [34, 35]. partition is designed to get some results back to its caller as soon as possible even while the partitioning is still continuing. Therefore, the recursive call to partition the cdr of the argument lst is enclosed within a future; otherwise, no value could be returned from partition until the recursive calls to partition had gone all the way to the end of lst and then returned.

```
(defun qsort (I) (qs I nil))
(defun qs (I rest)
  (if (null I)
    rest
    (let ((parts (partition (car I) (cdr I))))
      (qs (left-part parts)
        (future (cons (car I) (qs (right-part parts) rest)))))))
(defun partition (elt lst)
  (if (null lst)
    (bundle-parts nil nil)
    (let ((cdrparts (future (partition elt (cdr lst)))))
      (if (elt< (car lst) elt)
        (bundle-parts
          (cons (car lst) (future (left-part cdrparts)))
          (future (right-part cdrparts)))
        (bundle-parts
          (future (left-part cdrparts))
          (cons (car lst) (future (right-part cdrparts))))))))
(defun bundle-parts (x y) (cons x y))
(defun left-part (p) (car p))
(defun right-part (p) (cdr p))
```

Program 2–2. Quicksort using future. The input and output are represented as *lists*. A list is a sequence of *elements*, represented as a chain of conscells such that the car of the list contains the first element of the list, and the cdr is a list of the remaining elements. The empty list, *i.e.*, the list with no elements, is represented by nil. (cons X Y) builds a conscell whose car is X and whose cdr is Y. (car X) returns the car of the cons cell X; thus (car (cons A B)) always gives the value of A. (cdr X) returns the cdr of the conscell X. (null X) returns true if X evaluates to the value nil, else (null X) returns nil. (let ((var_1 val_1) (var_2 val_2) . . .) *body*) evaluates *body* in an environment where each var_i has been bound to the value of the corresponding expression val_i (free variables in the let-expression are evaluated in the surrounding environment). The procedures bundle-parts, right-part, and left-part were open-coded in the version of the program executed on Concert, reducing somewhat the number of procedure calls required.

This use of future (as well as the future in qs) resembles the use of future in Program 2–1: it allows the present task to continue its business (and return a value) without waiting for a potentially lengthy child computation to finish. The remaining uses of future in partition are different, but are needed to avoid throwing away the parallelism purchased with this first use. partition returns a "bundle" (represented as a conscell) containing the two sublists it produces. While building this bundle, it refers to cdrparts, a future for the bundle obtained by recursively partitioning the cdr of the argument lst. The first element of lst is consed onto the correct sublist of cdrparts, depending on whether this first element is greater than the discriminant element elt. However, since cdrparts starts its life as a future, even the simple operation of trying to select one of its component sublists may block, delaying the return from partition and largely negating the parallelism obtained by placing the recursive call to partition within a future. This problem is solved by also placing all expressions selecting the right or left sublists of cdrparts within futures, enabling partition to create and return a result bundle logically containing sublists that have not been fully (or even partially) computed yet. This use of future around a completely trivial computation purchases parallelism by allowing the parent task to continue even though the child may immediately block.

Since partition can return a bundle of two sublists before the partitioning of its argument has completed, the sorting of the sublists can begin before the production of the sublists has ended. This sorting will, in general, involve further partitioning, followed by further sorting, *etc*. The net result is that a large amount of concurrent activity, at many levels of recursion, quickly comes into being. This contrasts with other parallel implementations of Quicksort, where the partitioning is a sequential process, and sorting of the sublists cannot begin until the partitioning has finished. (In fairness, it should be noted that this program, which copies its argument list during partitioning, is subtly different from the usual Quicksort program, which updates the list of argument values in place. Thus Program 2–2 may incur some extra overhead in order to make extra parallelism available. Nevertheless, its structure shows some of the new ways in which futures can help expose parallelism.)

Figure 2–6 shows the parallelism profile that results from applying Program 2–2 to the same list of 400 random integers used earlier to generate Figures 2–4 and 2–5. It is interesting to compare Figures 2–4 and 2–6, since both programs— Quicksort and tree insertion—are ways to obtain sorted lists of items. Figure 2–6 shows the much greater degree of parallelism available in Quicksort: almost every processor is busy almost all the time. The small area of idle time along the top of the graph is shown by other measurements to be composed almost entirely of "short-term unemployment" of processors that have finished their current task and need to obtain their next task from another processor. However, this idle time results not from a lack of tasks but from maldistribution—tasks are available for execution but processors are momentarily idle until they locate a runnable task.

Figure 2–6 shows two other features also seen in Figure 2–4: the sequential

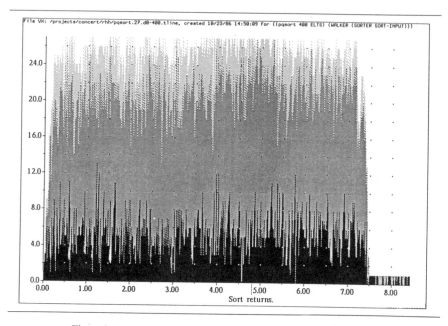

Figure 2–6. Parallelism profile for Quicksort using fast comparisons.

"tail" at the right and the large amount of overhead. The tail has the same cause as in Figure 2–4—to ensure that the sort has completely finished, the entire output list must be touched. But Quicksort makes partial information about the sorted list available much sooner. In fact, the first element of the list becomes available after only 4.8 seconds, as indicated by the legend "Sort returns" in Figure 2–6.

The overhead in Figure 2–6 is even greater than in Figure 2–4, representing 79% of all processor busy time. Despite this, the computation in Figure 2–6 finishes more quickly—a testament to the greater parallelism available. Nevertheless, the extremely small task size in Program 2–2—especially in the last four uses of future in partition—takes its toll in overhead cost: the number of futures created during the excution traced in Figure 2–6 is 10,231, three times as many as in Figure 2–4. As before, we can simulate the effect of less expensive futures by artificially prolonging the comparison operation elt <. The resulting parallelism profile is shown in Figure 2–7, which shows even less idle time than Figure 2–6, and a much smaller proportion of overhead.

An unsurprising lesson from these examples is that small task granularity increases the proportion of busy time that goes into overhead. The challenge is to find a way to increase granularity without sacrificing opportunities for parallelism. Because most of the futures in Program 2–2 are created by partition, a good way to increase granularity and reduce the number of futures created is to unfold partition as shown in Program 2–3, so that a set of three futures is created for every *two* elements of lst, instead of *every* element. This resulting program only

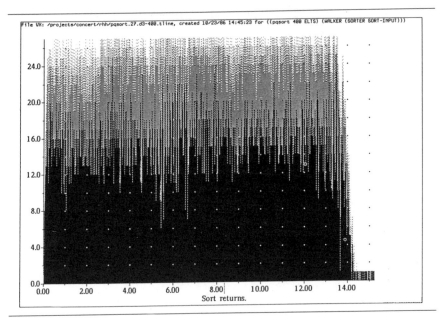

Figure 2-7. Parallelism profile for Quicksort using slow comparisons.

```
(defun partition (elt lst)
  (if (null lst)
    (bundle-parts nil nil)
    (if (null (cdr lst))
      (if (elt< (car lst) elt)
        (bundle-parts lst nil)
        (bundle-parts nil lst))
      (let ((cdrparts (future (partition elt (cddr lst)))))
        (let ((lpart (future (left-part cdrparts)))
              (rpart (future (right-part cdrparts))))
          (if (elt< (cadr lst) elt)
            (setq lpart (cons (cadr lst) lpart))
            (setq rpart (cons (cadr lst) rpart)))
          (if (elt< (car lst) elt)
            (setq lpart (cons (car lst) lpart))
            (setq rpart (cons (car lst) rpart)))
          (bundle-parts lpart rpart))))))
```

Program 2-3. Unfolded partition routine (cddr X) is equivalent to (cdr (cdr X). (cadr X) is equivalent to (car (cdr X). (setq v X) assigns the value X to the variable v.

creates 5068 futures to sort the same 400-element list. Its parallelism profile is shown in Figure 2-8 for normal-speed comparisons and in Figure 2-9 for sloweddown comparisons. Comparison with Figures 2-6 and 2-7 reveals a significant decrease in overhead, which translates into much faster execution: the sort in Figure 2-8 completes in 5.4 seconds and uses 32% of the busy time for "real

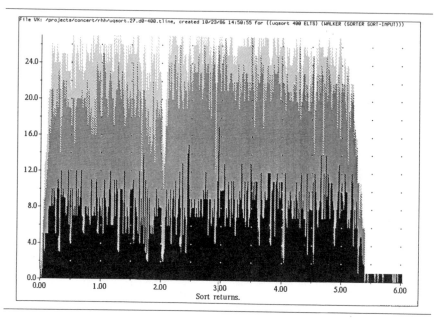

Figure 2–8. Parallelism profile for Qucksort with unfolded partition using fast comparisons.

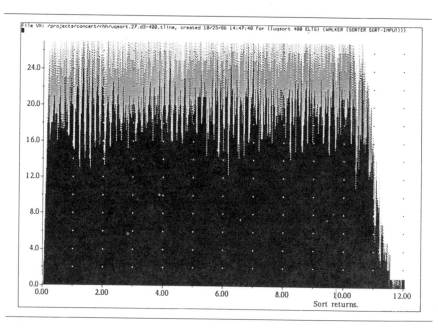

Figure 2–9. Parallelism profile for Quciksort with unfolded partition using slow comparisons.

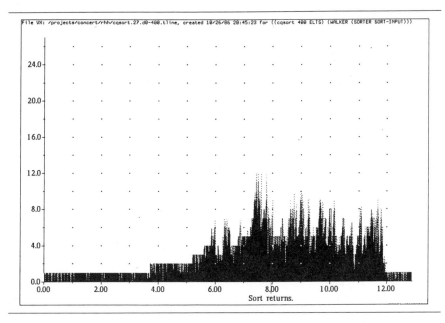

File VX: /projects/concert/rhh/cqsort.27.d0-400.tline, created 10/26/86 20:45:23 for ((cqsort 400 ELTS) (WALKER (SORTER SORT-INPUT)))

Figure 2–10. Parallelism profile for Qucksort with future-less partition using fast comparisons.

computing" (T'_c), compared with 7.5 seconds and 21% for Figure 2–6. Processor utilization is essentially unaffected by the change.

Even after unfolding, the futures created by partition are a considerable expense. Nevertheless, they have great value. This value is illustrated by comparing Figures 2–6 and 2–8 with Figure 2–10, which is the "classic" parallel Quicksort with no futures in partition (but still a future in qs). Figure 2–10 shows a long sequential phase, as the initial list of elements to sort is partitioned, followed by phases where the parallelism builds, as more and more sublists are available for sorting in parallel. Since the first partition does not generally divide the list precisely in half, the recursive sorts do not all finish at the same time. This explains why the concurrency in the right half of Figure 2–10 is sporadic, rather than building to one synchronized climax. Clearly, the removal of the futures in partition has reduced overhead greatly, but the reduction in available parallelism is even greater. Figure 2–11 profiles the classical Quicksort using slowed-down comparisons. It is not radically different from Figure 2–10 but is shown for comparison with Figures 2–7 and 2–9.

Figures 2–12 and 2–13 illustrate the effect of one final variant of partition—including the first future shown in partition in Program 2–2, but omitting the four subsequent futures surrounding the left-part and right-part operations. Comparing Figures 2–6 and 2–12 clearly shows the contribution made by these four futures. Figure 2–12 looks much like the classic Quicksort execution shown in Figure 2–10, indicating that little parallelism has been purchased with the

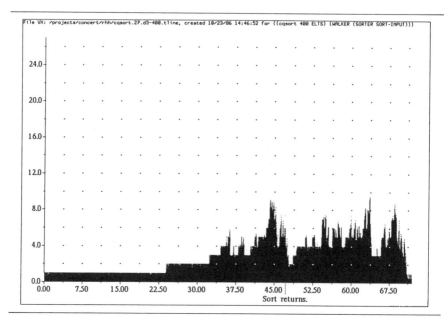

File VX: /projects/concert/rhh/cqsort.27.d3-400.tline, created 10/23/86 14:46:52 for ((cqsort 400 ELTS) (WALKER (SORTER SORT-INPUT)))

Figure 2-11. Parallelism profile for Qucksort with future-less partition using slow comparisons.

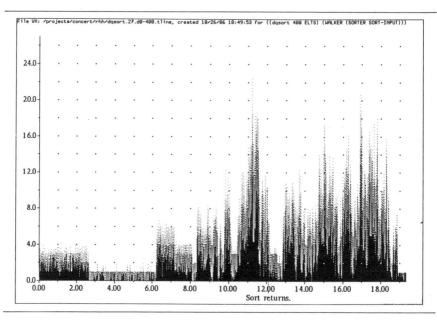

File VX: /projects/concert/rhh/dqsort.27.d0-400.tline, created 10/26/86 18:49:53 for ((dqsort 400 ELTS) (WALKER (SORTER SORT-INPUT)))

Figure 2-12. Parallelism profile for Quicksort with one future in partition using fast comparisons.

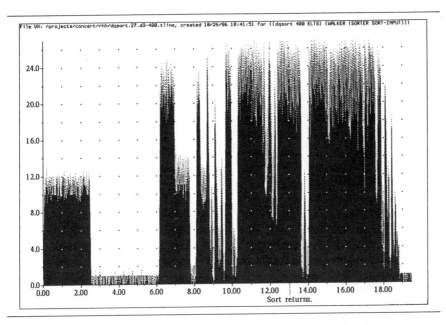

File VX: /projects/concert/rhh/dqsort.27.d3-400.tline, created 10/26/86 18:41:51 for ((dqsort 400 ELTS) (WALKER (SORTER SORT-INPUT)))

Sort returns.

Figure 2–13. Parallelism profile for Quicksort with one future in partition using slow comparisons.

added futures. In fact, the execution shown in Figure 2–12 takes *longer* than that in Figure 2–10, because the small increase in parallelism in Figure 2–12 has been more than offset by the increase in overhead for futures. The one future in partition allows a parent activation of partition to continue without waiting for its child activation to finish, but after the parent performs its comparison, it quickly blocks in a left-part operation awaiting a value from the child. The child, in turn, will not produce a value until it receives a value from *its* child, and so on. Therefore, this version of partition is effectively sequential even though it uses future. The one piece of concurrency available in this version is that a parent can do its comparison in parallel with the execution of its child. When comparisons are fast, as in Figure 2–12, little parallelism is exposed; however, this effect does explain the added concurrency evident at several points on Figure 2–12 (*e.g.*, at the beginning) when it is compared with Figure 2–10. When comparisons are slow, as in Figure 2–13, many more nested activations of partition can be executing concurrently, leading to a parallelism profile with a dramatically different appearance.

Interestingly, the versions of Quicksort used to generate Figures 2–6, 2–8, 2–10, and 2–12 are all correct, in the sense that they produce the right answer, but they differ widely in their performance characteristics. Thus, even after a program has been debugged to produce the correct answer, its performance may still need "debugging." This situation is not unknown in the world of sequential programming, but performance tuning is likely to be even more crucial in the parallel world. (As a historical footnote, the need for the last four futures in partition that make the difference between Figures 2–12 and 2–6 was only discovered after much trial and error and floundering around by the author, trying to understand why putting the first future in partition was not having the dramatic effect expected. Good "rules of thumb" for future insertion have since been codified and even implemented as an automatic future inserter for side-effect-free Lisp programs [36], but it is still far from trivial to visualize the precedence constraints enforced by the use of future in a large program and to predict the resulting degree of parallelism. Better tools for presenting this information to the programmer are badly needed.)

3.4. Summary

Our two examples illustrate two ways future can be used to generate concurrency: running a lengthy subcomputation as a child process so the parent can return without waiting for it to finish, and isolating a subcomputation that might block waiting for another future so the parent can continue. In both cases, using future allows a parent to return quickly even if the child's return is delayed, but the cases differ according to the *reason* for the child's delayed completion, which is due in one case to lengthy computation performed by the child and in the other to the child's becoming blocked on a future.

At a higher level, we can see other programming structures that can be implemented using future. One example is the kind of "pipelining" that occurs in Program 2–1, as successive insertions follow each other down the tree. Another instance of pipelining occurs in Quicksort, where activations of partition called by activations of qs at different levels will chase after each other, one activation of partition hungrily gobbling up values produced by a previous one. A different kind of structure, more closely related to conventional fork-join scenarios, is evident in the use of future for the recursive call to qs in Program 2–2. These calls execute independently in parallel, and their results are joined together at the end to be passed back to the caller.

Finally, the two examples illustrate some different points in multiprocessor operating space. Tree insertion has larger task granularity than Quicksort and consequently suffers less from overhead for futures. On the other hand, parallelism in tree insertion is clearly limited by algorithm, whereas parallelism in Quicksort appears to have been limited by Concert. It would be facile to draw from this contrast the general conclusion that finer granularity—and hence greater overhead—are inevitably linked to higher degrees of parallelism. However, there is probably some truth in the general statement, if qualified by the observation that for some algorithms a given level of parallelism can be achieved at much coarser levels of granualarity than for other algorithms.

4. PARALLEL PROGRAMMING IN THE LARGE

Although our example programs are simple, they show how futures can be used to expose concurrency in dealing with composite data structures by providing a representation for partially computed data. They also show the importance of algorithms that are able to release partial information about their results as soon as possible. However, applications for parallel computing are generally large programs, not 20-line programs such as Quicksort or tree insertion. Therefore, a useful system for applying parallel computation to real problems must support powerful ways of combining pieces together into large programs, not just techniques for making small subprograms use concurrency. Constructs such as future, which help us easily glue programs together in concurrent ways, are only part of what we need. We also need to have adequate control over the allocation of resources (notably processors) to the execution of various parts of a program— in effect, we need control over the focus of attention of a parallel computer as it executes a program. Other aids for the development and structuring of large programs include support for debugging, exception handling, data abstractions, and atomic modification of mutable data objects. Except for the last item, all of these are also important in sequential programming, but parallel programming brings some new dimensions to them.

4.1. Scheduling

Algorithms may have opportunities for concurrency at any of several levels of granularity, ranging from short sequences of primitive operations to large program modules. These opportunities are multiplicative: if the application of medium- or fine-grain parallelism within a module is sufficient to occupy m processors, and, furthermore, n of these modules can be executed in parallel, then mn processors can be used efficiently to execute the program as a whole (unless contention for shared resources imposes a smaller limit). Thus opportunities for concurrency should be exploited at all levels if execution on a highly parallel machine is desired.

Concurrency, however, arises from a variety of program structures. One way to write a concurrent program is to start with a suitably chosen sequential program and then relax some of the precedence constraints in that program to produce opportunities for executing some operations concurrently. This *mandatory work* style of parallel programming is supported by future, as well as by the fork-join constructs of other languages. A concurrent program written in the mandatory work style executes precisely the same set of operations as its sequential counterpart; only the scheduling of operations is different. Language constructs, such as future and fork-join, may differ in their effectiveness at relaxing precedence constraints, and may therefore be more or less useful in support of the mandatory work style, but the basic equivalence between the sets of operations performed by sequential and mandatory work parallel programs remains.

The mandatory work style contrasts with the *speculative* approach, where parallelism is obtained by eagerly spawning tasks before it is certain that their values will be needed. A characteristic that is particularly prevalent in AI programs, but can also be found elsewhere [16], is the existence of multiple techniques to solve a class of problems. For any particular problem, some of the techniques may work very quickly, while others may fail altogether. It is therefore desirable to be able to start using several techniques in parallel, but be able to terminate execution of the extra techniques when one of the techniques produces an answer.

Compared to speculative parallelism, mandatory work parallelism is especially nice because scheduling is less critical and, except for process management overhead, no extra operations are performed during parallel execution. Assuming the original sequential algorithm is efficient, the mandatory work approach represents a kind of lower bound: it may be possible to increase concurrency beyond that available in a mandatory work program by adding speculative operations, but these operations represent an overhead that is only justified if the increase in parallelism outweighs the extra work done.

Scheduling of mandatory operations is not usually critical because all mandatory operations must be done eventually, so *any* mandatory operation that is ready to be performed may be executed with assurance that it will not be wasted work. In fact, Concert Multilisp uses an *unfair* scheduler, which is perfectly legal in the case of mandatory work and helps solve some resource allocation problems that are very hard to solve using a fair scheduler [15]. (For utmost efficiency, mandatory operations on the "critical path" of a computation should be treated as "more mandatory" than others and always included in the set that get scheduled, but in practice the precedence graphs of most parallel programs seem to have a "bushy" enough structure that this is not a major concern.)

Acceptable scheduling is much more difficult in the presence of speculative parallelism. Usually, some speculative tasks have a higher potential payoff than others. Low-payoff speculative tasks should not be executed in preference to mandatory tasks or high-payoff speculative tasks. The only time to execute speculative tasks is when processing resources would otherwise go idle: speculative tasks should not take resources away from more important tasks.

To exploit concurrency at all levels and from all sources, both mandatory work and speculative parallelism should be used, and therefore both need to be supported by parallel programming languages; however, tools for expressing speculative parallelism cannot replace good constructs for mandatory work parallelism. The latter is "higher quality" parallelism and should always be exploited as fully as possible before resorting to speculative parallelism.

Multilisp's future construct is a fairly effective tool for exposing mandatory work parallelism, but future does not give information needed to properly schedule speculative tasks. One idea on how to do this is to associate a *sponsor* [37] with each task. The sponsor answers questions from the scheduler regarding the importance of its task relative to others. Although sponsors are a *mechanism* that can be used for scheduling speculative tasks, the *policy* implemented by the sponsors remains an issue. In some cases, the scheduling of tasks could be dictated by associating numerical priorities with tasks, but the general question of what tools to give the programmer for use in specifying the scheduling of speculative tasks remains an interesting question for research.

4.2. Data Abstractions and Mutable Objects

An important characteristic of a language for parallel computing is whether it allows the writing of nondeterminate programs—programs that may produce different results for different (legal) orders of execution. Multilisp and Qlisp, by including side effects, allow nondeterminism, whereas "functional languages" [26, 38, 39] forbid side effects and ensure determinate execution. Issues relating to determinancy are discussed elsewhere [9, 15]; a capsule summary of the debate is that potentially nondeterminate programs can be very hard to debug and verify but that the language restrictions needed to ensure determinacy are substantial and rule out many familiar and useful program structures. Multilisp allows side effects and hence permits these program structures. To help control the resulting solfware engineering problems, Multilisp supports side-effect-free expression of many computations and, through the "first-class citizenship" of Multilisp procedures, supports the construction of data abstractions within which side effects can be compartmentalized, reducing their contribution to program complexity.

Correct implementation of first-class citizenship for procedures, in combination with lexical scoping, requires the use of garbage-collected heap storage for procedure environments. Once this expense is incurred, however, procedures can be used as data abstractions. The nonlocal variables of a procedure, found in the lexically enclosing environment, can be considered as the underlying state variables of a data abstraction implemented by the procedure. Operations on this data abstraction can be performed by calls to the procedure. As with other implementations of abstract data types, the underlying state variables can be protected from access except through the channels provided by the abstraction [9].

Although it does include side effects, Lisp is superior to most other common programming languages in that it includes a side-effect-free subset with substantial expressive power. This subset is part of Multilisp; thus it is possible to write significant bodies of Multilisp code that are completely free side of effects. Furthermore, where side effects are used, as in maintaining a changing data base, they can be encapsulated within a data abstraction that synchronizes concurrent operations on the data. The data abstraction can ensure that the data are accessed according to the proper protocol.

Multilisp thus supports a programming style in which most code is written without side effects, and data abstractions are used to encapsulate data on which side effects may be performed, to present a reasonable interface to the exterior. A programmer's aim in using this style should be to produce a program whose side effects are compartmentalized carefully enough that any module may safely be invoked in parallel with any other. If this style is followed, the difficulties caused by the presence of side effects will be isolated to small regions of the program and should therefore be reduced to manageable proportions.

4.3. Debugging and Exception Handling

Debugging and exception handling are closely related topics. The need for debugging is often revealed by the occurrence of some run-time exception not anticipated by the programmer. At times, however, a programmer may anticipate the possible occurrence of an exception such as an end-of-file on read or an attempt to divide by zero. In such cases, the ability to flexibly specify a handler for an exception can be an important program-structuring tool.

The occurrence of exceptions in a parallel environment presents an interesting problem: if a task has been created to calculate the value of some future and is unable to complete due to the occurrence of an exception, what value should be given to the future? Before the occurrence of the exception, the procedure that created the future may have returned and the future itself may have been distributed to many other tasks, some of which may already have become suspended waiting for the future's value. If the occurrence of an exception causes the future never to receive a value, then these tasks will never resume execution, and nontermination of the program containing them is a likely result. On the other hand, what meaningful value do we give a future created by an expression such as (future (/ 3 0)), which has been asked to perform a division by zero? Multilisp's solution to this problem involves *error values* [17, 40]. If the evaluation of an expression X in (future X) cannot complete normally, the future can resolve to an error value. An exception will be raised in any task that touches an error value. In this way, the consequences of an exception that occurs while calculating a value propagate back through all users of the value. This propagation mirrors the popping of stack frames that occurs when "unwinding" a sequential computation after an exception.

Program debugging also takes on new dimensions in a parallel environment. Broadly speaking, debugging is concerned with two properties of programs: correctness and performance. Correctness rightly takes first place—a fast program is of little use if it produces incorrect results! Nevertheless, the reason for using parallel processing in the first place is to improve performance, so it is important for a programmer to be able to find and remove any obstacles to maximum performance (such as unnecessary data dependencies). To do this programmers need good tools for visualizing the operation of concurrent programs. As illustrated by the Quicksort example, the factors affecting the performance of a program in a parallel environment are more complex and subtle than in the sequential case; thus debugging for performance is an activity that should not be taken for granted in parallel programming.

An alternative to the explicit use of futures, in a side-effect-free dialect of Lisp, would be to simply cause every expression to return a future. This would ensure the availability of the maximum amount of parallelism, but at the cost of significant execution time overhead. An initial investigation [36] suggests that a compiler may be able to do a good job of locating the most desirable places to put future operators in side-effect-free procedures to maximize concurrency while minimizing overhead.

5. DIRECTIONS FOR RESEARCH IN PARALLEL SYMBOLIC COMPUTING

The critical research questions in parallel symbolic computing may be grouped into three areas: (1) programming languages and programming environments, (2) algorithm and application development, and (3) implementation and architecture. The first area encompasses most of the questions addressed in this article. A programming language for parallel symbolic computing must support both the mandatory work and speculative flavors of parallelism. Its associated programming environment must include debugging tools to help in finding both correctness and performance bugs. Furthermore, the language must support the construction of reasonably modular programs, and the constructs for obtaining concurrency must fit nicely within the modular structure of programs. A final major decision point in language design concerns the degree of nondeterminacy that can exist in program behavior.

The development of programming languages and environments should always be guided by the needs of application programs. Because few parallel symbolic application programs exist, research in programming languages for parallel machines must be complemented by the development of parallel application programs. Some of these programs should be of significant size: although "toy" examples such as Programs 2–1 and 2–2 can help increase insight into parallel language constructs, the ultimate application of parallel computers will be to much more complex programs, and it is well known that the engineering of large programs is qualitatively different from that of small programs. Language research and application development can reinforce each other: language ideas can suggest new application programming strategies, and the requirements of application programs can suggest areas where language design decisions should be reexamined.

Both language design and application program requirements should influence the architecture of systems for parallel computing. Language constructs may require clever implementation algorithms or special hardware support for efficient execution. Application programs provide the invaluable service of helping focus the design of implementations and architectures by indicating how much effect the efficient implementation of each language feature has on "bottom-line" performance. Thus, application programs are not just useful for calibrating language design decisions: they also serve an important role as benchmarks to help evaluate proposed architectures.

Of course, *all* of these aspects of design interact; the art of the desirable in language design must be balanced against the art of the possible. Also, as we learn more about parallel computing, old decisions will be seen in a new light and sometimes modified. Nevertheless, we must make substantial progress on language definition and application development before we can have any very solid objective grounds for evaluating proposed architectures for parallel symbolic computing. Developing the grounds for such evaluation is the principal research goal of the Multilisp project.

ACKNOWLEDGMENTS

This research could not have progressed as far as it has without the Concert multiprocessor [29, 30], which serves as the implementation vehicle for Multilisp. Many people have contributed to making Concert a reality; particularly noteworthy contributions were made by Tom Anderson, Jeff Arnold, Sharon Gray, Dan Nussbaum, Peter Nuth, Randy Osborne, Pete Osler, Doug Robinow, Tom Sterling, and Gautam Thaker. The collaboration of the Advanced Technology Department of Harris Corporation's Government Systems Sector has also been vital. The Concert Multilisp implementation itself exists only as a result of the outstanding efforts of Juan Loaiza.

REFERENCES

1. W. J. Bouknight, *et al.*, "The Illiac IV System," *Proc. of the IEEE 60(4):*369–388; 1972.
2. B. J. Smith, "A Pipelined Shared Resource MIMD Computer," 1978 *Int Conf. on Parallel Processing*, Aug, 1978, pp. 6–8.
3. C. L. Seitz, "The Cosmic Cube." *Comm. of the ACM 28(1):*22–33, 1985.
4. J. Beetem, M. Denneau and D. Weingarten, "The GF11 Supercomputer," *12th Annual Symp. on Computer Architecture*, Boston, MA, June 1985, pp. 108–115.
5. D. Kuck, Y. Muraoka, and S.-C. Chen, "On the Number of Operations Simultaneously Executable in Fortran-Like Programs and Their Resulting Speedup," *IEEE Trans. on Computers C-21(12):*1293–1310, 1972.
6. C. A. R. Hoare, "Communicating Sequential Processes," *Comm. of the ACM 21(8):*666–677, 1978.
7. M. J. Flynn, "Very High-Speed Computing Systems," *Proc. of the IEEE 54(12):*1901–1909, 1966.
8. G. Steele, *et al.*, *Common Lisp Reference Manual*, Bedford, MA: Digital Press, 1984.
9. H. Abelson and G. Sussman, *Structure and Interpretation of Computer Programs*, Cambridge, MA: MIT Press, 1984.
10. D. Weinreb and D. Moon, *Lisp Machine Manual*, Cambridge, MA: Symbolics Corp., 1984.
11. J. McCarthy, *et al.*, *LISP 1.5 Programmer's Manual*, Cambridge, MA: MIT Press, 1965.
12. A. Goldberg and D. Robson, *Smalltalk-80: The Language and its Implementation*. Reading, MA: Addison-Wesley, 1983.
13. G. Lee, C. Kruskal, and D. Kuck, "An Empirical Study of Automatic Restructuring of Non-numerical Programs for Parallel Processor," *IEEE Trans. on Computers C-34(10):*927–933, 1985.
14. R. P. Gabriel and J. McCarthy, "Queue-Based Multi-Processing Lisp," *ACM Symp. on Lisp and Functional Programming*, Austin, TX, Aug. 1984, pp. 25–43.
15. R. Halstead, "Multilisp: A Language for Concurrent Symbolic Computation," *ACM Trans. on Prog. Languages and Systems*, Oct. 1985, pp. 501–538.
16. R. Halstead, "Parallel Symbolic Computing," *IEEE Computer 19(8):*35–43, 1986.
17. R. Halstead and J. Loaiza, "Exception Handling in Multilisp." 1985 *Int'l. Conf. on Parallel Processing*, St. Charles, IL, Aug. 1985, pp. 822–830.
18. D. Friedman and D. Wise, "Aspects of Applicative Programming for Parallel Processing," *IEEE Trans. on Computers C-27 (4):*289–296, 1978.
19. R. Keller and F. Lin, "Simulated Performance of a Reduction-Based Multiprocessor," *IEEE Computer 17 (7):*70–82, 1984.
20. R. Keller, "Rediflow Multiprocessing," *Proc. COMPCON Spring 84*, San Francisco, CA, Feb. 1984, pp. 410–417.

21. S. Cohen, R. Rosner, and A. Zidon, *Paralisp Simulator.* (reference manual), Research Rep. 83–2, Computer Science Dept., Hebrew University, Jerusalem, Israel, Jan. 1983.
22. H. Baker and C. Hewitt, "The Incremental Garbage Collection of Processes," MIT Artifical Intelligence Laboratory Memo 454, Cambridge, MA, Dec. 1977.
23. P. Knueven, P. Hibbard, and B. Leverett, "A Language System for a Multiprocessor Environment," *Fourth Intl. Conf. on the Design and Implementation of Algorithmic Languages,* Courant Institute of Mathematical Studies, New York, NY, June 1976, pp. 264–274.
24. P. Henderson and J. H. Morris, "A Lazy Evaluator," *Proc. 3rd ACM Symp. on Principles of Prog. Languages,* 1976, pp. 95–103.
25. D. Turner, "A New Implementation Technique for Applicative Languages," *Software—Practice and Experience 9(1):*31–49, 1979.
26. Arvind, K. Gostelow, and W. Plouffe, *An Asynchronous Programming Language and Computing Machine,* University of California, Irvine, Report TR114a, 1978.
27. J. Gurd, C. Kirkham, and I. Watson, "The Manchester Prototype Dataflow Computer," *Comm. ACM 28(1):*34–52, 1985.
28. J. B. Dennis, "Data Flow Supercomputers," *IEEE Computer 13(11):*48–56, 1980.
29. R. Halstead, T. Anderson, R. Osborne, and T. Sterling, "Concert: Design of a Multiprocessor Development System," *13th Annual Symp. on Computer Architecture,* Tokyo, Japan, June 1986, pp. 40–48.
30. T. Anderson, *The Design of a Multiprocessor Development System.* Tech. Rep. TR-279, MIT Laboratory for Computer Science, Cambridge, MA, Sept. 1982.
31. A. V. Aho, J. E. Hopcroft, and J. D. Ullman, *The Design and Analysis of Computer Algorithms.* Reading, MA: Addison-Wesley, 1974, pp. 145–169.
32. C. Ellis, "Concurrent Search and Insertion in 2-3 Trees," *Acta informatica 14:*63–86, 1980.
33. C. Ellis, "Concurrent Search and Insertion in AVL Trees," *IEEE Trans. on Computers C-29:*811–817, 1980.
34. J. Deminet, "Experience with Multiprocessor Algorithms," *IEEE Trans. on Computers C-31 (4):*278–288, 1982.
35. P. Moller-Nielsen and J. Staunstrup, *Experiments with a Multiprocessor.* Tech. Rep. PB-185, Computer Science Dept., Aarhus University, Aarhus, Denmark, Nov. 1984.
36. S. Gray, *Using Futures to Exploit Parallelism in Lisp,* S. M. Thesis, MIT, Cambridge, MA, Dec. 1985.
37. D. Theriault, *Issues in the Design and Implementation of Act 2.* Tech. Rep. AI-TR 728, MIT Artificial Intelligence Laboratory, Cambridge, MA, June 1983.
38. W. Ackerman and J. Dennis, *VAL—A Value-oriented Algorithmic Language,* LCS TR-218, Laboratory for Computer Science, MIT, Cambridge, MA, 1979.
39. J. McGraw, *et al., SISAL—Streams and Iteration in a Single-assignment Language,* Language Reference Manual (version 1.0), Lawrence Livermore National Laboratory, Livermore, CA, July 1983.
40. C. Wetherell, "Error Data Values in the Data-Flow Language VAL," *ACM Trans. on Prog. Languages and Systems 4(2):*226–238, 1982.

3. EXECUTION OF COMMON LISP PROGRAMS IN A PARALLEL ENVIRONMENT

PATRICK F. McGEHEARTY and EDWARD J. KRALL

1. INTRODUCTION

To assess how much faster Lisp programs would run on large multiprocessor systems, several application kernels were modified for parallel execution and simulation of their behavior. The kernels exhibited speed-ups ranging from one to 850 times faster, suggesting that the technique is of no value to a few programs, of great value to a few programs, and of moderate value to most programs. The modifications were originally done manually but now are accomplished by a program. Further manual editing may yield even more parallelism.

The effective parallelism obtained is measured by means of simulation. These results are combined with results previously published [7, 8] to identify areas of research needed for parallel execution of Lisp programs with minimal programmer intervention.

2. REQUIREMENTS FOR "SAFE" PARALLEL EXECUTION

Unlike many languages, Lisp contains a viable "pure function" subset. Moreover, applications written in Lisp are typically composed of many functions that are "pure." Such functions can be rendered into parallel routines without fear of destroying the meaning of the program.

Unlike the functional languages, however, Lisp also supports applications that are not pure, which make use of "blackboards," global data structures, and side effects in order to be useful. These side effects must be carefully handled to ensure correct parallel program execution.

2.1. The Detection of Side Effects

Much of the effort in converting a program in Lisp (or any other language) to run in parallel comes in determining which parts may execute simultaneously without interference. Two cases were studied: the restricted case of executing side-effect-free functions in parallel, as well as the more general case (programs with side effects). Given a "black box" model of computation, a side-effect-free function may be viewed as a computational entity that accepts certain values as input parameters and returns one or more values through the well-isolated interface of the function call. As such, the black box operates independently of its implementation—it is behavior, not structure, that is important. Whether the function is implemented as software, firmware, or hardware, nothing in the calling environment is altered, except the values returned through the function call interface.

A side effect is therefore a change to the calling environment not associated with the function-call interface. Note that this definition is usually weakened somewhat to exclude changes in internal addresses, memory allocation, timers, etc., which are beyond the access of the program. The definition is usually extended to include *call by name* and read-write *call by reference* parameter passing.

For the purposes of research and implementation, there are two types of side-effect phenomena in Lisp: (1) functions that by their nature cause side effects, and (2) functions that make use of global or free variables. Side-effecting functions include *rplaca*, *rplacd*, *set*, and the Input/Output functions. Functions that use free variables have the potential for their computation being affected from any other part of the computation that uses those variables. In addition, any function that touches the property list of symbols (such as *get* and *putprop*) implicitly references globally available data. Moreover, any function that calls a side-effecting function is considered side effecting.

Three answers may occur when performing side-effect analysis on a function: (1) no side effects exist, (2) side effects exist, and (3) don't know. Only functions in the first category may be executed in parallel. Algorithms exist that correctly use overlaping execution with side effects, but these typically require hand-crafting, with the addition of critical sections, semaphores, locks, or other synchronization mechanisms.

Static syntactic analysis should approach 100% accuracy in identifying the presence of global variables and side-effecting functions if they exist, but will be less accurate in establishing the absence of global variables or the lack of side-effecting functions.

In this determination, however, "don't know" may be the most common answer. Certain constructs are so suspicious (*(setq x (format ...))* or *(eval ...)*) that they are flagged as side-effecting without further analysis. Others, such as *setq* require further consideration. If a global variable is used as the assignee, then *setq* will cause side effects. The use of a local variable as the assignee of a *setq* encapsulates the side effect to the scope of the local variable. Hence, the function itself acts as a black box and can be executed in an applicative and parallel fashion.

The determination of the existence of side effects is a transitive phenomenon: if *foo* calls *bar*, and *bar* is known to have side effects, then *foo* also is considered side-effecting. This is, again, a somewhat conservative approach, but it is necessary to guarantee deterministic execution and consistent results.

2.2. Obtaining Parallelism

After functions have been identified as safe candidates for parallel execution, some mechanism must be supplied for creating a separate task for their execution and observing the degree of parallelism obtained. The *future* construct from Multilisp [6] is the primary construct for specifying parallel execution. The *future* is a form that spawns a new task for the evaluation of a given Lisp form. For example,

```
(setq x (future (addl y)))
(setq z x)
```

spawns a task to evaluate *(add1 y)*, assigns to *x* a pointer to the future of *(add1 y)*, and continues execution in line. When *(add1 y)* completes, the value of *x* becomes a pointer to the value of *(add1 y)*. If some task needs the value of *x* before the future is completed, that task will suspend itself. However, if only a reference to *x* is needed (as in the subsequent assignment), the task is NOT blocked; instead *z* is set to point to the future also.

Note that the word *future* is used in two senses: as the name of the function that spawns the tasks, and as the (uncompleted) value of the spawned task. When it is necessary to distingush between the two, the value of the task spawning will be termed the future-object. In the example above, if *x* were inspected before the value was available, then something like the following might be seen:

```
< *-FUTURE-*: (future (add1 y))>
```

Two other forms are used in the study: *touch* and *pmapcar*. The function *touch* will return the value of its argument, blocking if necessary on an as-yet undetermined *future*. The function *pmapcar* is also built from futures. It is the analog of *mapcar*:

```
(pmapcar fn'(1 2 3 4 5))
```

will spawn tasks to evaluate (fn 1), (fn 2), . . . , (fn 5) simultaneously, and return the list of values (or their futures).

2.3. The Insertion Process

Because the *future* is a data-structuring concept, and because it behaves like a function call, it is not only easy for the programmer to use, but it is also easy for a preprocessor to insert *futures* in a program to be parallelized. The program analyzer, "FutureLisp Insertion Program" (FLIP), transforms a serial Lisp program into a parallel one by inserting *futures* in the application kernels, by means of an algorithm and heuristics that take into account not only the legality of such insertion, but also its effectiveness. Consider the following example:

```
(defun rewrite-args (1st)
   (cond ((null 1st) nil)
      (t (cons (FUTURE (rewrite (car 1st)))
         (rewrite-args (cdr 1st))))))
```

It is known that rewrite is side-effect-free; hence, the *future* can be inserted on the first argument of cons.

However, guaranteeing freedom from side effects is only a necessary condition for insertion of *futures*. The candidate function must also satisfy two other criteria:

1. The work being done by the spawned task must exceed some threshold value determined by the process scheduling overheads.
2. The work remaining the spawning task until the future value is needed must also exceed the scheduling overhead.

For example, consider the following function:

```
(defun test (x)
   ( + (sin x) (cos x)))
```

One may insert *futures* indiscrimanately as follows:

```
(defun test1 (x) ( + (future (sin x))
               (future (cos x))))
```

Such insertion on the second argument of the addition is pointless—the mainline task must block while it waits for the completion of computation of both arguments. A better transformation is

```
(defun test2 (x)
   ( + (future (sin x))
      (cos x)))
```

Now, after spawning the (sin x) process, the mainline will compute the (cos x) coincidentally with the computation of (sin x). The parallelism is now useful provided that (sin x) and (cos x) take longer to compute than a task takes to be spawned.

Sharon Gray at MIT has developed a program for inserting *futures* in code that is already known to be side-effect-free [5].

3. MEASUREMENT TOOLS

Several tools were developed to measure the parallel execution of Lisp programs. Since a multiprocessor was not readily available, a compiler-emulator system was built to approximate the behavior of parallel Lisp programs on a multiprocessor. The emulator models program execution at the instruction level by implementing a conventional multiple-processor, shared-memory architecture. It generates a trace of events related to task scheduling and timing, such as task start, task end, and task blocking (waiting for a value to be generated by another task). These trace events are used by a postprocessing program to determine a running average degree of parallel execution and the overall average number of processors in use.

3.1. The "FutureLisp" Emulator

FutureLisp extends Common Lisp by implementing several primitives, including *future* and *pmapcar* to support parallel execution. To study the effect of these primitives and their architectural implications, an instruction level emulator was developed for a parallel Lisp architecture, with a compiler to generate assembly language code for the architecture, and a run-time system to provide a distributed scheduling system.

The *future* primitive returns a future-object as a place-holder for the value to be computed. It also creates a new task to compute the value required. When a task requires the value of a future-object, a flag is checked to see if the value has been computed. If so, it is used; otherwise, the requesting task waits. Other tasks are allowed to use the processor until the *future* operation has completed. The run-time system provides scheduling and intertask communication support.

The architecture assumes a number of conventional serial processors connected in a shared memory structure. Each processor has a fast private memory to keep a copy of code, static data, and strictly local data such as its evaluation stack. It also has a memory bank for potentially sharable data. Any processor may access the sharable data memory of any other processor. Only one processor may access a given memory bank during a given memory cycle. If several processors request access, they are queued, to be serviced over cycles. Otherwise, no interconnection interference or collisions are modeled.

The primitive operations of each processor in this architecture are similar to those in a Lisp machine, such as PUSH (on stack), CAR (off stack), or CONS (top two elements on stack). This type is architecture was chosen to simplify the compiler design. For the purposes of this study, the instruction set could just as easily been a conventional register-oriented architecture. Note that the total overhead for creating a *future* and using its value is modeled as approximately 30 emulated memory cycles.

For this study, hardware limitations on parallelism are minimized. A rapid task scheduler is modeled by the emulator, and the interconnection delay between processors and memories is assumed to be zero. In addition, enough processors are provided by the emulator so that tasks are not delayed due to a lack of processors. This approach was selected to emphasize software limits on parallelism. In the following sections, any lack of parallelism stems from software limits in the application code rather than hardware limits, except for the assumption of a conventional multiple-processor architecture.

An earlier version of this study [8] used a more primitive Future Lisp emulator. That version used a less-precise modeling technique for measuring task interactions with the more optimistic assumption that a *future* operation required about ten primitive operations. These differences result in some differences in the performance results presented in the next section, but no differences in the conclusions presented here.

4. SAMPLE APPLICATION KERNELS

A number of sample programs were used to assess the potentials of obtaining automatic parallel execution. Two of these, Mandelbrot and TAK, are small programs, that are intended to exercise the primitives essential to parallel execution. Two others, EMY and REWRITE, are kernels of major programs in artificial intelligence (AI), intended to represent the computation of those programs. All timing results are presented in terms of memory cycles, which correspond to the cycle time of the shared memory. If this cycle time is one microsecond, then each processor would have (to within an order of magnitude) the performance of a LMI Lambda or Symbolics 3600.

4.1. Mandelbrot

The Mandelbrot program determines, for each of a set of points on a square grid in the complex plane, whether the point is in the Mandelbrot set [2]. Thus, Mandelbrot can be considered a representative kernel of a class of numerical algorithms. The determination for a single point is iterative, but independent of all other points. In the sequential version of the program, the determination for each point is done inside of a double loop. The outer loop controls which row in the grid is being evaluated, and the inner loop controls which element within the row is being evaluated. Given an assumption that at least 40 instructions should be performed by a parallel task to justify its creation overhead, the smallest computation that is suitable for execution as a separate task is the determination of whether a single point is or is not in the Mandelbrot set. Since each such determination is independent of the others, this unit of computation could be surrounded by a *future*.

To obtain experimental results, a grid of 50 × 50 points was selected, with an iteration limit of 50. Without *futures*, the program takes 3.18 million cycles

Memory Cycles	Active Processors	Each * = 2 Active Processors
000	18	*********
5,000	17	********
10,000	18	*********
15,000	17	********
20,000	16	********
25,000	14	*******
30,000	17	********
35,000	21	**********
40,000	24	************
45,000	27	**************
50,000	30	***************
55,000	32	****************
60,000	32	****************
65,000	30	***************
70,000	32	****************
75,000	33	****************
80,000	34	*****************
85,000	35	*****************
90,000	38	*******************
95,000	40	********************
100,000	42	*********************
105,000	42	*********************
110,000	40	********************
115,000	8	****
120,000	1	.
125,000	1	.

Figure 3–1. Mandelbrot—one *future* case.

(Mcycles). Figure 3–1 shows the parallel execution profile with a single *future*. The y-axis is simulated time, and the x-axis is average number of executing tasks during a time window. With a total run length of 0.125 Mcycles, the speed-up is approximately 25.

Because 2500 tasks were created and executed, this speed-up is disappointing. Careful consideration of program behavior shows that the problem is the rate at which tasks are created. On average, a delay of 40 cycles occurs between each task start-up, due to task creation time and loop overhead. In the first 5000 cycles, about 160 tasks are started and about 140 have already completed. Since the longest task takes 1250 cycles and some tasks take only 600 cycles, only 20 tasks are started before some tasks complete. Variation in the length of each task causes the variation in the number of active tasks.

Because the program is operating on a square grid, the iteration can easily be set up as a loop computing each point on a row, within a loop computing each row. There will now be a task for each row, each of these starting 50 subtasks in parallel. The average number of running tasks should rise to 50 times 25 or 1250. Figure 3–2 shows the parallel execution profile of the Mandelbrot program with two *futures*.

The graph shows a peak of 1115 tasks, with an average speed-up of approximately 500. The remaining sequential start-up time for the 50 rows and 50 points in each column is responsible for lost performance in the first half of the

Memory Cycles	Active Processors	Each * = 50 Active Processors
000	15	.
400	106	**
800	285	******
1,200	490	*********
1,600	692	*************
2,000	907	******************
2,400	1102	**********************
2,800	1115	***********************
3,200	1031	*********************
3,600	897	******************
4,000	703	**************
4,400	453	*********
4,800	244	*****
5,200	107	**
5,600	25	*
6,000	2	.
6,400	1	.

Figure 3–2. Mandelbrot—50 × 50 two *futures* case.

computation. The declining activity in the second half of the computation is due to differing compleltion times for the different points.

A fairly simple transformation program for obtaining automatic parallelism finds the two locations for inserting *futures* that were used here. A more advanced program might even use three or four levels of *futures* to speed the start-up further. Because very substantial amounts of speed-up were obtained with minimal overhead, it seems that programs similar to the Mandelbrot program, such as low-level image analysis, can be automatically converted to effective parallel execution.

4.2. TAK

TAK is a six-line program used in the Gabriel benchmarks [4]; it is intended to test the efficiency of Lisp implementations in calling recursive functions. For the purposes of this report, TAK provides opportunity for rapidly increasing parallelism provided that efficient primitives for small-grain task computation are available. Each recursive call to TAK spawns four more calls to TAK, three of which can execute in parallel. Thus, the potential parallelism of TAK grows exponentially with the call depth. Because the benchmark requires a call depth of 18 to complete, massive parallelism is available. However, a typical recursive call has fewer than ten instructions at each level of recursion. If the overhead of creating a separate task is large, then the effective speed-up will be poor. Therefore, TAK requires an efficient implementation of the parallelism primitives.

TAK requires 1.113 Mcycles to execute without *futures*. Figure 3–3 shows the results of *futures* on each of the three arguments to the recursive call to TAK.

The total processing time more than triples, increasing to 3.83 Mcycles in the parallel execution of TAK. The overhead of creating tasks exceeds the useful

Memory Cycles	Active Processors	Each * = 20 Active Processors
000	63	***
500	293	***************
1000	481	*************************
1500	470	************************
2000	490	*************************
2500	643	**********************************
3000	551	****************************
3500	531	***************************
4000	542	****************************
4500	617	********************************
5000	569	*****************************
5500	561	****************************
6000	443	**********************
6500	411	*********************
7000	486	************************
7500	310	****************
8000	77	****
8500	42	**
9000	19	*
9500	18	*
10,000	18	*
10,500	9	*
11,000	14	*
11,500	8	*

Figure 3–3. Tak with three *futures*.

computation. However, most of these task creations occur in parallel, allowing completion in 11,900 cycles, for an effective speed-up factor of approximately 94 using 691 processors. Therefore, even with fine-grain parallelism, significant speed-up is possible.

4.3. EMY

EMY is an implementation of the inference kernel of the EMYCIN expert system [1]. It represents approximately 600 lines of Lisp code. It was discussed in detail in [7]. Briefly, it uses backward chaining reasoning to answer queries against its data base. During the process of making deductions, it updates a global data base to save conclusions for use by other rules. These frequent operations on a shared data base or "blackboard" prevent much parallel operation without use of synchronization primitives. Note that the blackboard model of execution is used in other AI programs such as Hearsay [3].

The insertion tool, FLIP, found one location for inserting a *future* in the EMY program. The effective speed-up obtained was negligible. The lack of speed-up reflects the small granularity of parallel tasks between operations on the shared data base. These results are particularly noteworthy, because the EMY program has been shown to allow significant speed-up (by a factor of 16 for one data set) when synchronized operations are allowed on the global data base. At the current time, it is not well understood how to insert synchronization automatically around the access to a shared data structure.

Memory Cycles	Active Processors	Each * = 10 Active Processors
000	41	****
10,000	93	*********
20,000	61	******
30,000	32	***
40,000	29	***
50,000	36	****
60,000	48	*****
70,000	83	********
80,000	133	*************
90,000	158	****************
100,000	180	******************
110,000	241	************************
120,000	317	********************************
130,000	367	**************************************
140,000	306	*******************************
150,000	82	********
160,000	1	.
170,000	1	.
180,000	1	.
190,000	1	.
200,000	1	.
210,000	1	.

Figure 3–4. REWRITE with one *future*.

4.4. REWRITE

REWRITE is a simple theorem prover developed by Boyer and Moore to evaluate Lisp implementations; it is also included in the Gabriel benchmarks [4]. It represents approximately 100 lines of Lisp code and 350 lines of data, consisting of 104 lemmas. It was written with the intent of providing behavior that was representative of the much larger Boyer and Moore Theorem Prover. Theorem-proving is an important part of the planning section of many AI programs. REWRITE, like most benchmarks, fails to mimic completely the behavior of the actual theorem prover. It provides, however, a useful first approximation. As it is shown in the Gabriel benchmarks, there are two places in the code that use global variables to return extra values from a function. To allow parallel execution, the code was changed to pass the extra values back as part of the function. After this change, most of the program is free of side effects, allowing automatic parallel execution.

Figure 3–4 shows the results of executing REWRITE on the selected theorem with one *future* automatically inserted. Sequential execution requires 17.0 Mcycles, while the parallel version requires an elapsed time of 0.215 Mcycles. A speed-up of approximately 79 was obtained for this example. The speed-up obtained depends on the complexity of theorem to be proved. More complex theorems yield more opportunities for parallel execution, with corresponding greater speed-ups. Similar results should be obtained from programs similar to theorem provers.

The long tail of near sequential execution occurred when the tautology checker was doing a final check on the theorem to be proved. An important operation in this process was of the form "if case A is true, then check case B". Because it is known (whereas the automatic inserter cannot know) that case A will normally be true, both case A and case B can be executed in parallel. Since each case is recursive in nature, a significant additional speed-up is obtained. With this change, the parallel execution time reduces to 0.161 Mcycles for a speed-up of 105, an improvement of 33% over the version with one *future*.

4.5. Summary of Results

Table 3–1 summarizes the results of each experiment. The Mandelbrot program is listed in both the 1-*future* and 2-*future* form. Speedups based on automatic syntactic insertion of parallel constructs ranging from 1 to 500 have been observed. These results imply that the amount of parallelism to be obtained is strongly dependent on the application selected. In all but the most simple programs, human analysis of program behavior yields better than the current automatic tools.

5. CONCLUSIONS

5.1. Style

Programming style is a major determinant of the effectiveness of these mechanical parallelizing techniques. The EMY program achieved no gain in performance due to frequent reading and writing of global data structures. Note, however, that EMY with hand-coded parallelism displays a very reasonable speed-up of about an order of magnitude. The Mandelbrot program achieved massive parallelism because a well-defined separable unit of computation was encapsulated in a function. TAK and REWRITE achieved their parallel execution by having recursive functions with several arguments, each requiring substantial computation. Other programming styles may be expected to aid or hinder automatic parallel execution in similar ways.

5.2. Implications

The approach adopted here—automatic syntactic insertion of parallel constructs—has potential both for research into parallel execution of some Lisp programs and also for "real" Lisp application programming. Software engineering theorists have stressed that an applicative, non-side-effecting style of

Table 3–1. Summary

Program	Parallel Time (Mcycles)	Sequential Time (Mcycles	Parallel Factor
Mandelbrot-1	0.126	3.18	25
Mandelbrot-2	0.0064	3.18	500
TAK-3	0.012	1.113	94
EMY	0.066	0.065	1
REWRITE	0.215	17.0	79

programming produces clearer and safer code. This code can also be run in parallel with the same clarity and safety.

The requirements of many applications, however, force a blackboard model for efficient operation. Automatic syntactic insertion of parallel constructs will be hindered to the degree that the blackboard permeates the program design. This style of programming shows that the automatic parallelization by syntactic preprocessors is not a panacea for all programs, but can be an effective part of a total solution.

5.3. Approach to a Solution

A more complete solution would include: (1) syntactic preprocessors for modifying existing programs, (2) interactive analyzers to guide programmers in modifying existing programs for parallel execution, and to guide them in the initial construction of new applications, and (3) research into semantic analyzers to allow automation of the parallel execution of a broader class of programming styles.

REFERENCES

1. B. Buchanan, and E. Shortliffe, *Rule-Based Expert Systems*. Reading, MA: Addison-Wesley, 1984.
2. A. K. Dewdney, "Mandelbrot Sets" (in the column "Computer Recreations"), *Scientific American*. July 1985.
3. C. Forgy, A. Gupta, A. Newell, and R. Wedig, "Parallelism in artificial intelligence problem solving: A case study of Hearsay II," *IEEE Trans. on Computers, C-26:*98–111, 1977.
4. R. Gabriel, *Performance and Evaluation of Lisp Systems*. Cambridge, MA: Press, 1985.
5. S. Gray, *Using futures to exploit parallelism in Lisp*, Master's thesis, MIT, Cambridge, MASS., Feb. 1986.
6. R. Halstead, "Implementation of Multilisp: Lisp on a multiprocessor," *ACM Symp. on Lisp and Functional Programming*, Austin, TX, Aug. 1984.
7. E. Krall, and P. McGehearty, "A case study of parallel execution of a rule-based expert system," *Int'l. J. Parallel Programming*, XV: 1, February 1986.
8. P. McGehearty, and E. Krall, "Potentials for parallelism of common Lisp programs." *Proc. Sixth Int'l. Conf. on Parallel Processing*, Aug. 1986.

4. QLISP

RICHARD P. GABRIEL and JOHN McCARTHY

1. INTRODUCTION

As the need for high-speed computers increases, the need for multiprocessors becomes more apparent. One of the major stumbling blocks to the development of useful multiprocessors has been the lack of a good multiprocessing language—one that is both powerful and understandable to programmers.

Among the most compute-intensive programs are artificial intelligence (AI) programs, and researchers hope that the potential degree of parallelism in AI programs is higher than in many other applications. In this chapter we propose multiprocessing extensions to Lisp. Unlike other proposed multiprocessing Lisps, this one provides only a few very powerful and intuitive primitives rather than a number of parallel variants of familiar constructs.

This language is called Qlisp.

2. DESIGN GOALS

1. Because Lisp manipulates pointers, this Lisp dialect will run in a shared-memory architecture;
2. Because any real multiprocessor will have only a finite number of central processing units (CPU's), and because the cost of maintaining a process along with its communications channels will not be zero, there must be a means to limit the degree of multiprocessing at run-time;
3. Only minimal extensions to Lisp should be made to help programmers use the new constructs;

4. Ordinary Lisp constructs should take on new meanings in the multiprocessing setting, where appropriate, rather than proliferating new constructs;
5. The constructs should all work in a uniprocessing setting (for example, it should be possible to set the degree of multiprocessing to 1 as outlined in point 2).

3. QLET

The obvious choice for a multiprocessing primitive for Lisp is one that evaluates arguments to a lambda-form in parallel. **QLET** serves this purpose. Its form is:

$$(\textbf{QLET } prop \ ((x_1 \ arg_1)$$

$$\vdots$$

$$(x_n \ arg_n))$$
$$body)$$

Prop is a propositional parameter which is evaluated before any other action regarding this form is taken; it is assumed to evaluate to one of: ( ), **EAGER**, or something else.

If *prop* evaluates to ( ), then the **QLET** acts exactly as a **LET**. That is, the arguments $arg_1 \ldots arg_n$ are evaluated as usual and their values bound to $x_1 \ldots x_n$, respectively.

If *prop* evaluates to non-( ), then the **QLET** will cause some multiprocessing to happen. Assume *prop* returns something other than ( ) or **EAGER**. Then processes are spawned, one for each arg_i. The process evaluating the **QLET** goes into a wait state: When all of the values $arg_1 \ldots arg_n$ are available, their values are bound to $x_1 \ldots x_n$, respectively, and each form in the list of forms, *body*, is evaluated.

Assume *prop* returns **EAGER**. Then **QLET** acts exactly as above, except that the process evaluating the **QLET** does not wait: It proceeds to evaluate the forms in *body*. But if in evaluating the forms in *body* the value of one of the arguments is required, arg_i, the process evaluating the **QLET** waits. If that value has been supplied already, it is simply used.

To implement **EAGER** binding, the value of the **EAGER** variables could be set to an "empty" value, which could either be an empty memory location, like that supported by the Denelcor HEP [5], or a Lisp object with a tag field indicating an empty or pending object. At worst, every use of a value would have to check for a full pointer.

We will refer to this style of parallelism as **QLET** *application*.

3.1. Queue-Based

The Lisp is described as "queue-based" because each spawned process is placed on a global queue of processes. Processes are assigned to processors. Each processor is assumed to be able to run any number of processes, much as a time-sharing system does, so that regardless of the number of processes spawned, progress will be made. We will call a process running on a processor a *job*.

The ideal situation is that the number of processes active at any one time will be roughly equal to the number of physical processors available.[1]

The purpose of *prop*, then, is to control the number of processes spawned. Simulations show a marked dropoff in total performance as the number of processes running on each processor increases, *assuming that process creation time is non-zero.*

3.2. Example of QLET

Here is a simple example of the use of **QLET**. The point of this piece of code is to apply the function **CRUNCH** to the n_1th element of the list L_1, the n_2th element of the list L_2, and the n_3th element of the list L_3.

```
(QLET T ((X
          (DO ((L L₁ (CDR L))
               (I 1 (1+ I))
               ((= I N₁) (CAR L)))))
         (Y
          (DO ((L L₂ (CDR L))
               (I 1 (1+ I))
               ((= I N₂) (CAR L)))))
         (Z
          (DO ((L L₃ (CDR L))
               (I 1 (1+ I))
               ((= I N₃) (CAR L)))))
    (CRUNCH X Y Z))
```

3.3. A Real Example

The⁄is an example of a simple, but real, Lisp function. It performs the function of the traditional Lisp function, **SUBST**, but in parallel:

```
(DEFUN QSUBST (X Y Z)
       (COND ((EQ Y Z) X)
             ((ATOM Z) Z)
             (T
              (QLET T ((Q (QSUBST X Y (CAR Z)))
                       (R (QSUBST X Y (CDR Z))))
               (CONS Q R)))))
```

4. EXCESSIVE PARALLELISM

The most straightforward possibilities for achieving effective parallelism occur when only *AND-parallelism* is required. AND-parallelism occurs when there are some number of tasks, each of which must be performed, with minimal interdependence between them. However, since Lisp programming is recursive,

AND-parallelism alone is not always possible, and there is still the problem of avoiding too much parallelism. For example, **QSUBST** will generate parallelism in computing the arguments of a single **CONS**. It is straightforward to avoid excessive parallelism if the program can determine how big a computation will be. If it is going to be too small, the **QLET** propositional parameter can be set to be ( ), or control can be given to a version of the program that has no parallelism. In general, efficiency will not be very sensitive to how the parallelism is arranged to occur, provided that amount of bookkeeping to determine when to introduce parallelism is small, and this will be true if parallelism is avoided for small computations.

There are at least two ways of doing this. First, it may be trivial to determine how big the computation is. Consider computing $n!$. In order to do the computation recursively, we generalize it to computing the product of the numbers from m to n:

```
(DEFUN FACT (N)
 (LABELS
 ((MULT
   (LAMBDA (N M)
    (COND ((= N M) M)
          (T
           (LET ((H (FLOOR (+ N M) 2)))
            (* (MULT N H) (MULT (+ H 1) M)))))))
 (MULT 1 N)))
```

If $|n-m|$ is small enough, we can call a function that multiplies them nonrecursively. Otherwise, we split the range in half and compute the products of the halves in parallel. This immediately generalizes to computing any commutative operation applied to elements indexed by the numbers from m to n, because $|n-m|$ provides an estimate of the size of the problem, which can be used to determine whether parallelism is worthwhile.

In this example it might be better to put the parallelism in the bignum multiplication code rather than in the overall structure of the program. The point is that it is immediately decidable whether the computation is too small to do in parallel.

Second, perhaps the size of the computation can be computed by a linear scan of the arguments of the function. When the time required to compute the function is much larger than the time taken by the scan, this approach can be used to decide whether to compute the argument values in parallel.

From this point of view, **QSUBST** presents the most difficult case: The time required to determine the size of the computation is as large as the time required to do the computation. Here one might as well gamble on parallelism if the program is really going to have to do substitutions with no advance estimate of the size of the expressions.

However, if an operation of substitution or something of similar characteristics is going to occur frequently in a program, it may be worthwhile to include a size estimate as part of the data structures involved. An extreme would be to use a modified **CONS** that includes a size as well as the two pointers. We suspect that this is rarely worthwhile and that it will be more common to use data structures that contain size estimates sparingly.

5. QLAMBDA CLOSURES

In some Lisps (Common Lisp, for example) it is possible to create *closures*: function-like objects that capture their definition-time environment. When a closure is invoked, that environment is reestablished.

QLET application, as we saw above, is a good means for expressing parallelism that has the regularity of, for example, an underlying data structure. Because a closure is already a lot like a separate process, it could be used as means for expressing less regular parallel computations.

(**QLAMBDA** *prop* (*lambda-list*) . *body*)

creates a closure. *Prop* is a propositional parameter which is evaluated before any other action regarding this form is taken. It is assumed to evaluate to either ( ), **EAGER**, or something else. If *prop* evaluates to ( ), then the **QLAMBDA** acts exactly as a **LAMBDA**. That is, a closure is created; applying that closure is exactly the same as applying a normal closure.

If *prop* evaluates to something other than **EAGER**, the **QLAMBDA** creates a closure that, when invoked, is run as a separate process. Creating the closure by evaluating the **QLAMBDA** expression is called *spawning*; the process that evaluates the **QLAMBDA** is called the *spawning process*; and the process that is created by the **QLAMBDA** is called the *spawned process*. When a closure running as a separate process is invoked, the separate process is started, the arguments are evaluated by the spawning process, and a message is sent to the spawned process containing the evaluated arguments and a return address. The spawned process does the appropriate lambda-binding, evaluates its body, and finally returns the results to the spawning process. We call a closure that will run or is running in its own process a *process closure*. In short, the expression (**QLAMBDA** non-( ) ...) returns a process closure as its value.

If *prop* evaluates to **EAGER**, then a closure is created which is immediately spawned. It lambda-binds empty binding cells as described earlier, and evaluation of its body starts immediately. When an argument is needed, the process either has had it supplied or it blocks. Similarly, if the process completes before the return address has been supplied, the process blocks.

5.1. Value-Requiring Situations

Suppose there are no further rules for the timing of evaluations than those given, along with their obvious implications; have we defined a useful set of primitives? No. Consider the following situation:

(**PROGN** (**F** X) (**G** Y))

If **F** happens to be bound to a process closure, then the process evaluating the **PROGN** will start the process evaluating (**F** X), wait for the result, and then move on to evaluate (**G** Y), throwing away the value **F** returned. If this is the case, it is plain that there is not much of a reason to have process closures.

Therefore, we make the following behavioral requirement: If a process closure is invoked in a value-requiring context, the calling process waits; and if a process closure is invoked in a value-ignoring situation, the caller does not wait for the result, and the callee is given a void return address.

For example, given the following code:

(LET ((F **(QLAMBDA** T (Y) **(PRINT** (∗ Y Y)))))
    (F 7)
    (PRINT (∗ 6 6)))

there is no *a priori* way to know whether you will see 49 printed before or after 36.[2]

To increase the readability of code we introduce two forms, which could be defined as macros, to guarantee a form will appear in a value-requiring or in a value-ignoring position.

(WAIT *form*)

will evaluate *form* and wait for the result;

(NO-WAIT *form*)

will evaluate *form* and not wait for the result. For example,

(PROGN

  (WAIT *form₁*)

  form₂)

will wait for *form₁* to complete.

5.2. Invoking a Process Closure

Process closures can be passed as arguments and returned as values. Therefore, a process closure can be in the middle of evaluating its body, given a set of arguments when it is invoked by another process. Similarly, a process can invoke a process closure in a value-ignoring position and then immediately invoke the same process closure with a different set of arguments.

Each process closure has a queue for arguments and return addresses. When a process closure is invoked, the new set of arguments and the return address is placed on this queue. The body of the process closure is evaluated to completion before the set of arguments at the head of the queue is processed.

We will call this property *integrity*, because a process closure is not copied or disrupted from evaluating its body with a set of arguments: Multiple invocations of the same process closure will not create multiple copies of it.

6. CATCH AND QCATCH

So far we have discussed methods for spawning processes and communicating results. Are there any ways to kill processes? Yes, there is one basic method, and it is based on an intuitively similar, already-existing mechanism in many Lisps.

CATCH and **THROW** are a way to do non-local, dynamic exits within Lisp. The idea is that if a computation is surrounded by a **CATCH**, then a **THROW** will force return from that **CATCH** with a specified value, terminating any intermediate computations.

(CATCH *tag form*)

will evaluate *form*. If *form* returns with a value, the value of the **CATCH** expression is the value of the *form*. If the evaluation of *form* causes the form

(THROW *tag value*)

to be evaluated, then **CATCH** is exited immediately with the value *value*. **THROW** causes all special bindings done between the **CATCH** and the **THROW** to revert. If there are several **CATCH**'s, the **THROW** returns from the **CATCH** dynamically closest with a tag **EQ** to the **THROW** tag.

6.1. CATCH

In a multiprocessing setting, when a **CATCH** returns a value, all processes that were spawned as part of the evaluation of the **CATCH** are killed at that time. Consider:

```
(CATCH 'QUIT
      (QLET T ((X
                  (DO ((L L₁ (CDR L)))
                      ((NULL L) 'NEITHER)
                      (COND ((P (CAR L))
                             (THROW 'QUIT L₁)))))
               (Y
                  (DO ((L L₂ (CDR L)))
                      ((NULL L) 'NEITHER)
                      (COND ((P (CAR L))
                             (THROW 'QUIT L₂))))))
        X))
```

This piece of code will scan down L_1 and L_2 looking for an element that satisfies P. When such an element is found, the list that contains that element is returned, and the other process is killed, because the **THROW** causes the **CATCH** to exit with a value. If both lists terminate without such an element being found, the atom NEITHER is returned.

Note that if L_1 and L_2 are both circular lists, but one of them is guaranteed to contain an element satisfying P, the entire process terminates.

If a process closure was spawned beneath a **CATCH** and if that **CATCH** returns while that process closure is running, that process closure will be killed when the **CATCH** returns.

6.2. QCATCH
(**QCATCH** *tag form*)

QCATCH is similar to **CATCH,** but if the *form* returns with a value (no **THROW** occurs) and there are other processes still active, **QCATCH** will wait until they all finish. The value of the **QCATCH** is the value of *form*. For there to be any processes active when *form* returns, each one had to have been invoked in a value-ignoring setting, and therefore all of the values of the outstanding processes will be duly ignored.

If a **THROW** causes the **QCATCH** to exit with a value, the **QCATCH** kills all processes spawned beneath it.

We will define another macro to simplify code. Suppose we want to spawn the evaluation of some form as a separate process. Here is one way to do that:

```
((LAMBDA (F) (F) T)
 (QLAMBDA T ( ) form))
```

A second way is:

```
(FUNCALL (QLAMBDA T ( ) form))
```

We will chose the latter as the definition of:

```
(SPAWN form)
```

Notice that **SPAWN** combines spawning and invocation.

Here are a pair of functions that work together to define a parallel **EQUAL** function on binary trees:

```
(DEFUN EQUAL (X Y)
 (QCATCH 'EQUAL
  (EQUAL-1 X Y)))
```

EQUAL uses an auxiliary function, **EQUAL-1**:

```
(DEFUN EQUAL-1 (X Y)
 (COND ((EQ X Y))
       ((OR (ATOM X)
            (ATOM Y))
        (THROW 'EQUAL ( )))
       (T
        (SPAWN (EQUAL-1 (CAR X) (CAR Y)))
        (SPAWN (EQUAL-1 (CDR X) (CDR Y)))
        T)))
```

The idea is to spawn off processes that examine parts of the trees independently. If the trees are not equal, a **THROW** will return a ( ) and kill the computation. If the trees are equal, no **THROW** will ever occur. In this case, the main process will return T to the **QCATCH** in **EQUAL**. This **QCATCH** will then wait until all of the other processes die off; finally it will return this T.

6.3. THROW

THROW will throw a value to the **CATCH** above it, and processes will be killed where applicable. The question is, when a **THROW** is seen, exactly which **CATCH** is thrown to and exactly which processes will be killed?

The processes that will be killed are precisely those processes spawned beneath the **CATCH** that receives the **THROW** and those spawned by processes spawned beneath those, and so on.

The question boils down to which **CATCH** is thrown to. To determine that **CATCH**, find the process in which the **THROW** is evaluated and look up the process-creation chain to find the first matching tag.

In a code fragment like

(QLAMBDA T ( ) **(THROW** *tag values*))

the **THROW** is evaluated within the **QLAMBDA** process closure, so look at the process in which the **QLAMBDA** was created to start searching for the proper **CATCH**. Thus, if a process closure is invoked with a **THROW** in it, the **THROW** will be to the first **CATCH** with a matching tag *in the process chain in which the* **QLAMBDA** *was created*, not in the current process chain. Thus we say that **THROW** throws dynamically by creation.

7. UNWIND-PROTECT

When **THROW** is used to terminate a computation, there may be other actions that need to be performed before the context is destroyed. For instance, suppose that some files have been opened and their streams let-bound. If the bindings are lost, the files will remain open until the next garbage collection. There must be a way to gracefully close these files when a **THROW** occurs. The construct to do that is **UNWIND-PROTECT**.

(**UNWIND-PROTECT** *form cleanup*)

will evaluate *form*. When *form* returns, *cleanup* is evaluated. If *form* causes a **THROW** to be evaluated, *cleanup* will be performed anyway. Here is a typical use:

(**LET** ((F (**OPEN** "FOO . BAR")))
 (**UNWIND-PROTECT** (**READ-SOME-STUFF**) (**CLOSE** F)))

In a multiprocessing setting, when a cleanup form needs to be evaluated because a **THROW** occurred, the process that contains the **UNWIND-PROTECT** is retained to evaluate all of the cleanup forms for that process before it is killed. The process is placed in an unkillable state, and, if a further **THROW** occurs, it has no effect until the current cleanup forms have been completed.

Thus, if control ever enters an **UNWIND-PROTECT**, it is guaranteed that the cleanup form will be evaluated. Dynamically nested **UNWIND-PROTECT**'s will have their cleanup forms evaluated from the inside-out, even if a **THROW** has occurred.

To be more explicit, recall that the **CATCH** that receives the value thrown by a **THROW** performs the kill operations. The **UNWIND-PROTECT** cleanup forms are evaluated in unkillable states by the appropriate **CATCH** *before* any kill operations are performend. This means that the process structure below that **CATCH** is left intact until the **UNWIND-PROTECT** cleanup forms have completed.

7.1. Other Primitives

One pair of primitives is useful for controlling the operation of the processes as they are running; they are **SUSPEND PROCESS** and **RESUME-PROCESS**. The former takes a process closure and puts it in a wait state. This state cannot be interrupted, except by a **RESUME-PROCESS**, which will resume this process. This is useful if some controlling process wishes to pause some processes in order to favor some process more likely to succeed than these.

A use for **SUSPEND-PROCESS** is to implement a general locking mechanism, which will be described later.

This completes the definition of the extensions to Lisp. Although these primitives form a complete set—any concurrent algorithm can be programmed with only these primitives along with the underlying Lisp—a real implementation of these extensions would supply further convenient functions, such as an efficient locking mechanism.

The remainder of this chapter will describe some of the tricks that can be done in this language.

8. RESOURCE MANAGEMENT

We have mentioned that we assume a shared-memory Lisp, which implies that many processes can be accessing and updating a single data structure at the same time. In this section we show how to protect these data structures with critical sections to allow consistent updates and accesses.

The key is closures. We spawn a process closure, which is to be used as the sole manager of a given resource, and we conduct all transactions through that closure. The following example illustrates this method.

Suppose we have an application where we will need to know for very many n whether $\exists\ i.\ s.t.\ n = \text{Fib}(i)$, where **Fib** is the Fibonacci function. We will call this predicate *Fib-p*. Suppose further that we want to keep a global table of all of the Fibonacci argument/value pairs known, so that *Fib-p* will be a table lookup whenever possible. We can use a variable, *V*, which has a pair—a cons cell—as its value with the CAR being i and the CDR being n, and $n = \text{Fib}(i)$, such that this is the largest i in the table. We imagine filling up this table as needed, using it as a cache, but the variable *V* is used in a quick test to decide whether to use the table rather than Fibonacci function to decide *Fib-p*.

We will ignore the details of the table manipulation and discuss only the variable *V*. When a process wants to find out the highest Fibonacci number in the table, it simply will do (**CDR** *V*). If a process wants to find out the pair $(i\ .\ \text{Fib}(i))$, it had better do this indivisibly because some other processes might be updating *V* concurrently.

We assume that we do not want to **CONS** another pair to update *V*—we will destructively update the pair. Thus, we do not want to say:

. . .

(**SETQ** *V* (**CONS** *arg val*))

. . .

Here is some code to set up the *V* handler:

(**SETQ** *V-HANDLER* (**QLAMBDA** T (CODE) (CODE *V*)))

The idea is to pass this process closure a second closure which will perform the desired operations on its lone argument; the *V* handler passes *V* to the supplied closure.

Here is a code fragment to set up two variables, I and J, which will receive the values of the components of *V*, along with the code to get those values:

```
(LET ((I ()) (J ()))
 (*V-HANDLER* (LAMBDA (V)
              (SETQ I (CAR V))
              (SETQ J (CDR V)))))
```

Because the process closure will evaluate its body without creating any other copies of itself, and because all updates to *V* will go through *V-HANDLER*, I and J will be such that J = Fib(I).

The code to update the value of *V* would be:

```
. . .

(*V-HANDLER* (LAMBDA (V)
              (SETF (CAR V) arg)
              (SETF (CDR V) val)))

. . .
```

If the process updating *V* does not need to wait for the update, this call can be put in a value-ignoring position.

8.1. Fine Points

If the process closure that controls a resource is created outside of any **CATCH** or **QCATCH** that might be used to terminate subordinate process closures, then once the process closure has been invoked, it will be completed. If this process closure is busy when it is invoked by some process, then even if the invoking process is killed, the invocation will proceed. Thus requests on a resource controlled by this process closure are always completed. Another way to guarantee that a request happens is to put it inside of an **UNWIND-PROTECT**.

9. LOCKS

When we discussed **SUSPEND-PROCESS** and **RESUME-PROCESS** we mentioned that a general locking mechanism could be implemented using **SUSPEND-PROCESS**. Here is the code for this example:

```
(DEFMACRO GET-LOCK ( )
 '(CATCH 'FOO
  (PROGN
   (LOCK
    (QLAMBDA T (RES) (THROW 'FOO RES)))
   (SUSPEND-PROCESS))))
```

When **SUSPEND-PROCESS** is called with no arguments, it puts the currently running job (itself) into a wait state.

```
1  (LET ((LOCK
2        (QLAMBDA T (RETURNER)
3          (CATCH LOCKTAG
4               (LET ((RES (QLAMBDA T ( ) (THROW 'LOCKTAG T))))
5               (RETURNER RES)
6               (SUSPEND-PROCESS))))))
```

```
 7   (QLET T ((X
 8                (LET ((OWNED-LOCK (GET-LOCK)))
 9                  (DO ((I 10 (1– I)))
10                      ((= I 0)
11                       (OWNED-LOCK) 7))))
12             (Y
13                (LET ((OWNED-LOCK (GET-LOCK)))
14                  (DO ((I 10 (1– I)))
15                      ((= I 0)
16                       (OWNED-LOCK) 8))))))
17       (LIST X Y))
```

The idea is to evaluate a GET-LOCK form, which in this case is a macro, that will return when the lock is available; at that point, the process that called the GET-LOCK form will have control of the lock and, hence, the resource in question. GET-LOCK returns a function that is invoked to release the lock.

Lines 7–17 are the test of the locking mechanism: The **QLET** on line 7 spawns two processes; the first is the **LET** on lines 8–11; the second is the **LET** on lines 13–16. Each process will attempt to grab the lock, and when a process has that lock, it will count down from 10, release the lock, and return a number—either 7 or 8. The two numbers are put into a list that is the return value for the test program.

As we mentioned earlier, when a process closure is evaluating its body given a set of arguments, it cannot be disrupted—no other call to that process closure can occur until the previous calls are complete. To implement a lock, then, we must produce a process closure that will return an unlocking function, but which will not actually return!

GET-LOCK sets up a **CATCH** and calls the LOCK function with a process closure that will return from this **CATCH**. The value that the process closure throws will be the function we use to return the lock. We call LOCK in a value-ignoring position so that when the lock is finally released, LOCK will not try to return a value to the process evaluating the GET-LOCK form. The **SUSPEND-PROCESS** application will cause the process evaluating the GET-LOCK form to wait for the **THROW** that will happen when LOCK sends back the unlocking function.

LOCK takes a function, the RETURNER function, that will return the unlocking function. LOCK binds RES to a process closure that throws to the **CATCH** on line 3. This process closure is the function that we will apply to return the lock. The RETURNER function is applied to RES, which throws RES to the catch frame with tag FOO. Because (RETURNER RES) appears in a value-ignoring position, this process closure is applied with no intent to return a value. Evaluation in LOCK proceeds with the call to **SUSPEND-PROCESS**.

The effect is that the process closure that will throw to LOCKTAG—and which will eventually cause LOCK to complete—is thrown back to the caller of GET-LOCK, but LOCK does not complete. No other call to LOCK will begin to execute until the **THROW** to LOCKTAG occurs—that is, when the function OWNED-LOCK is applied. Hence, exactly one process at a time will execute with this lock.

The key to understanding this code is to see that when a **THROW** occurs, it searches up the process-creation chain that reflects dynamically scoped **CATCH**'s. Because we spawned the process closure in GET-LOCK beneath the **CATCH** there, the **THROW** in the process closure bound to RETURNER will throw to that **CATCH**, ignoring the one in LOCK. Similarly, the **THROW** that RES performs was created underneath the **CATCH** in LOCK, and so the process closure that throws to LOCKTAG returns from the **CATCH** in LOCK.

9. Reality

As mentioned earlier, a real implementation of Qlisp would supply an efficient locking mechanism, and the details of a realistic locking protocol will be discussed later. We have tried to keep the number of primitives down to see what would constitute a minimum language.

10. KILLING PROCESSES

We have seen that a process can commit suicide, but is there any way to kill another process? Yes; the idea is to force a process to commit suicide. Naturally, everything must be set up correctly. We will show a simple example of this "bomb" technique. Here is the entire code for this example:

```
 1   (DEFUN TEST ( )
 2    (LET ((BOMBS ( )))
 3     (LET ((BOMB-HANDLER
 4          (QLAMBDA T (TYPE ID MESSAGE)
 5            (COND ((EQ TYPE 'BOMB)
 6,                  (PRINT '(BOMB FOR ,ID))
 7                   (PUSH '(,ID . ,MESSAGE) BOMBS))
 8                  ((EQ TYPE 'KILL)
 9                   (PRINT '(KILL FOR ,ID))
10                   (FUNCALL
11                    (CDR (ASSQ ID BOMBS)))
12                   T)))))
13      (QLET 'EAGER ((X
14                     (CATCH 'QUIT (TESTER BOMB-HANDLER 'A)))
15                    (Y
16                     (CATCH 'QUIT (TESTER BOMB-HANDLER 'B))))
17       (SPAWN
18        (PROGN (DO ((I 10. (1- I)))
19                   ((= I 0)
20                    (PRINT '(KILLING A))
21                    (BOMB-HANDLER 'KILL 'A ( )))
22                 (PRINT '(COUNTDOWN A ,I)))
```

```
23              (DO ((I 10. (1– I)))
24                  ((= I 0)
25                   (PRINT '(KILLING B))
26                   (BOMB-HANDLER 'KILL 'B ( )))
27                  (PRINT '(COUNTDOWN B ,I)))))
28      (LIST X Y)))))
29  (DEFUN TESTER (BOMB-HANDLER LETTER)
30         (BOMB-HANDLER 'BOMB LETTER
31                        (QLAMBDA T ( ) (THROW 'QUIT LETTER)))
32         (DO ( )(( )) (PRINT LETTER)))
```

First we set up a process closure that will collect bombs and explode them. Line 2 defines the variable that will hold the bombs. A bomb is an ID and a piece of code. Lines 3–12 define the bomb handler. It is a piece of code that takes a message type, an ID, and a message. It looks at the type; if the type is BOMB, then the message is a piece of code. The ID/code pair is placed on the list, BOMBS. If the type is KILL, then the ID is used to find the proper bomb and explode it.

Lines 13–28 demonstrate the use of the bomb-handler. Lines 14 and 16 are CATCH's that the bombs will kill back to. Two processes are created, each running TESTER. TESTER sends a bomb to BOMB-HANDLER, which is a process closure that will throw back to the appropriate CATCH. Because the process closure is created under one of two CATCH's, the THROW will kill the intermediate processes. The main body of TESTER is an infinite loop that prints the second argument, which will either be the letter A or the letter B.

The QLET on line 13 is eager. Unless something kills the two processes spawned as argument-calculation processes, neither X nor Y will ever receive values. But because the QLET is eager, the SPAWN on line 17 will be evaluated. This SPWAN creates a process closure that will kill the two argument processes.

The result of TEST is (LIST X Y), which will block while waiting for values until the argument processes are killed.

The killing process (lines 18–27) counts down from 10, kills the first argument process, counts down from 10 again, and finally kills the second argument process.

To kill the argument process, the BOMB-HANDLER is called with the message type KILL and the name of the process as the ID. The BOMB-HANDLER kills a process by searching the list, BOMBS, for the right bomb (which is a piece of code) and then FUNCALLing that bomb.

Because a process closure is created for each call to TESTER (line 31), and because one is spawned dynamically beneath the CATCH on line 14 and the other beneath the CATCH on line 16, the BOMB-HANDLER will not be killed by the THROW. When the process that is printing A is killed, the corresponding THROW throws A. Similarly for the process printing B.

The value of TEST is (A B). Of course there is a problem with the code, which is that the BOMB-HANDLER is not killed when TEST exits.

11. EAGER PROCESS CLOSURES

We saw that EAGER is a useful value for the propositional parameter in **QLET** applications, that is, in constructions of this form:

(QLET *prop* $((x_1\ arg_1)$

$\vdots$

$(x_n\ arg_n))$

$.\ body)$

But it may not be certain what use it has in the context of a process closure.

When a process closure of the form:

(QLAMBDA 'EAGER (*lambda-list*) . *body*)

is spawned, it is immediately run. And if it needs arguments or a return address to be supplied, it waits.

Suppose we have a program with two distinct parts: The first part takes some time to complete and the second part takes some large fraction of that time to initialize, at which point it requires the result of the first part. The easiest way to accomplish this is to start an eager process closure, which will immediately start running its initialization. When the first part is ready to hand its results to the process closure, it simply invokes the process closure.

Here is an example of this overlapping of a lengthy initialization with a lengthy computation of an argument:

(LET ((F **(QLAMBDA** 'EAGER (X)
[Lengthy Initialization]
**(OPERATE-ON** X))))
(F [Lengthy computation of X]))

There are other ways to accomplish this effect in this language, but this is the most flexible technique.

12. SOFTWARE PIPELINING

Multiprocessing programming languages must support the styles of programming that are natural to the programmer, and they must be able to express all of the forms of concurrency that exist. In this section we will introduce a style of programming, called *software pipelining*, which can produce speed-ups in sequential code under certain circumstances. Moreover, sequential code can be easily transformed into pipelined code.

Pipelining is a technique used in computer architectures to increase the execution speed of programs. The idea is that while one instruction is being executed the next instruction in the instruction stream can be decoded. Thus, the execution of one instruction can overlap the execution of another. This is possible because the execution of an instruction can be broken up into independent stages. These stages are implemented as separate pieces of hardware that perform the steps in each stage.

There are several complications with this scheme as far as the hardware is concerned. First, if the second instruction requires a result from the first instruction, and if the result is not ready for use from the first instruction when the second instruction wants to use it, then the pipeline "blocks." This delay can cause the throughput of the pipeline to decrease and sometimes this decrease can be significant.

Second, if the first instruction is a conditional jump, then perhaps the address to which control will pass might not be known when the second instruction is being fetched. This will result in a pipeline blockage also. This type of complication is similar to the first—simply consider the address from which the next instruction is to be fetched as a result of the current instruction. Normally this address—the program counter or PC—is implicitly known to be the next sequential PC after that of the current instruction.

The effect of pipelining is that programs that are not inherently parallel can enjoy some degree of parallelism and, hence, can run faster on a pipelined architecture than on the same architecture without pipelining. There is a window of instructions such that if one instruction within that window depends on the result of a second instruction within that window, then we might expect the pipeline to block. This window is certainly no larger than the length of the pipeline, and this window slides along the stream of executed instructions. For most pipelined computers the window is smaller than the length of the pipeline.

The hope is that the window is small enough and the dependencies within that window are rare enough there will not be a significant slowdown from the ideal situation, which is a program with no dependencies within any window.

Software pipelining is the adaptation of the idea of hardware pipelining to Qlisp. We will see that often programs can be pipelined when they cannot be made fully parallel, and we will also see that dependencies between stages of a software pipeline can be implemented using a locking mechanism with certain characteristics.

There are two sorts of parallelism in Qlisp: (1) the true parallelism that derives from the parallel evaluation of arguments in a **QLET**, and (2) the unstructured concurrency of process-closure invocation, particularly when the invocation is in a value-ignoring situation. In the latter case, a number of processes are created and messages are passed among them, causing some pattern of concurrent activity.

Software pipelining is a subspecies of the latter type of parallelism, but it is structured subspecies. Suppose that there is a computation that is inherently sequential and which must be performed repeatedly. In fact, suppose that this computation takes a certain set of arguments and that we intend to stream sets of arguments to that computation at the fastest possible rate. If that computation is expressed as a process closure, then the second set of arguments cannot be processed until the first set has been completely processed. To apply software pipelining to that computation, we break up that computation into stages such that the amount of information that needs to passed from one stage to the next is manageable; each stage is a process closure. Because each stage will be smaller than the entire original computation, the second set of arguments can enter the computation sooner after the first set than in the original computation.

An example of an inherently sequential computation is one that performs some actions on a shared resource, such as a global structure.

12.1. Simple Example

We will present a simple example of a computation along with a pipelined implementation of it. This example is designed to explain the concept of software pipelining; it is not an example of a computation that requires software pipelining—much better speed-ups can be achieved with true parallelism or even with a reformulation of the algorithm than with pipelining.

The example is polynomial evaluation: Given a polynomial, $P(x)$, and a value, v, for x, produce $P(v)$. Let

$$P(x) = 5x^4 + 4x^3 + 3x^2 + 2x + 1,$$

then using Horner's rule we have that,

$$P(x) = (((5x + 4)x + 3)x + 2)x + 1$$

We can define four functions—F_1, F_2, F_3, and F_4—such that

$$P(x) = F_4(x, F_3(x, F_2(x, F_1(x)))),$$

as follows:

(DEFUN F_1 **(X)**
          (+ (* 5 X) 4))
(DEFUN F_2 **(X V)**
          (+ (* V X)3))
(DEFUN F_3 **(X V)**
          (+ (* V X) 2))
(DEFUN F_4 **(X V)**
          (+ (* V X) 1))

These functions define stages of the computation of P. Each stage is largely independent of the others aside from the values x and v which are passed as arguments, and each stage does about the same amount of computation as the

others. Given these definitions, the pipelined version of the original polynomial
evaluation function can be written:

```
(DEFUN HORNER-STREAM ()
 (QCATCH 'HST
  (LABELS ((P1 (QLAMBDA T (X)
                  (P2 (+ (* 5 X) 4) X)
                  T))
           (P2 (QLAMBDA T (X V)
                  (P3 X (+ (* V X) 3))
                  T))
           (P3 (QLAMBDA T (X V)
                  (P4 X (+ (* V X) 2))
                  T))
           (P4 (QLAMBDA T (X V)
                  (+ (* V X) 1)))))
 (P1 x₁)(P1 x₂)(P1 x₃)...)))
```

The **QCATCH** will kill all of the processes when HORNER-STREAM is
exited, but only after each of the process closures, P1–P4, has finished its last
computation. **LABELS** is a construct for defining mutually recursive functions,
and each one of P1–P4 is bound to a process closure. P1 corresponds to F_1, P2
corresponds to F_2, P3 corresponds to F_3, and P4 corresponds to F_4. The next
stage of each pipe is called in a value-ignoring position.

The ellipsis [...] is a sequence of invocations of P1 for various arguments.
Each process, P1–P4, is presumed to be running on different processors.

Imagine a stream of arguments to P1, $v_1...v_n$. Suppose v_1 is passed to P1 and
then immediately v_2 is passed. P1 cannot process v_2 until v_1 has been processed; as
soon as $5x+4$ has been passed on to P2, P1 can accept v_2 and so on. When P4 is
processing the final stage of the computation of $P(v_1)$, P3 can be processing the
third stage of $P(v_2)$, P2 can be processing the second stage of $P(v_3)$, and P1 can be
processing the first stage of $P(v_4)$.

The straightforward code for P is:

```
(DEFUN HORNER ()
 (LABELS ((P1 (LAMBDA (X)
                (+ 1 (* X (+ 2 (* X (+ 3 (* X (+ 4 (* 5 X)))))))))))
 (P1 x₁)(P1 x₂)(Pl x₃)...)))
```

Using a simple performance simulator for Qlisp [2], when 40 requests are
streamed through HORNER and HORNER-STREAM, HORNER-STREAM
is approximately 3.8 times faster than HORNER, compared with the theoretical
maximum of 4.0.

Of course, there are better ways to speed up this particular program, but the
technique is the important point. The technique enables speed-ups in sequential

code, and these speed-ups can achieved by applying the software pipelining technique rather than by discovering the, possibly clever parallel algorithm.

12.1.1. *Discussion*

There are several things to note about this example and the technique. First, the amount of computation per process closure is quite small, and the performance of the pipeline will depend on the function-call overhead in HORNER-STREAM, which is not present in HORNER. Note that because process-closures are invoked to move control from one stage of the pipe to the next, function-call overhead is, in reality, message-passing overhead.

Second, the software pipelining style of programming is very much like that used in continuation-passing style. With continuation passing, an additional function—the continuation—is passed as an argument to each function. When a function computes a value, it applies the continuation to that value in a tail-recursive position rather than returning to its caller. With software pipelining, the continuation for each stage of the pipe is the next stage of the pipe, if there is one.

The last stage of a pipeline can either invoke some other process, or else that stage could invoke a continuation that had explicity passed to it.

Third, this example does not contain any global or special variables. For this technique to be useful, it ought to be possible to use it in the presence of global variables. Of course, heavy use of globals will diminish the performance advantages, much as instruction dependencies limit the effectiveness of a pipeline in a computer.

12.2. Global Variable Example

In the simple example of polynominal evaluation, all of the information that is passed among the stages is passed from one stage to the next as arguments. Therefore, we can say that all of the information flow is in the forward direction—each stage can only receive information from the preceding stages. With global variables it is possible for this information to be passed in the backward direction.

One use of global variables is for one invocation of a function to communicate with a later invocation. The first function can store some value in a variable whose extent is indefinite—a global variable. A later invocation of that function (or some other function) can read that value and act on it.

Global variables are used quite often to record a *state* for a function. In Lisps that do not support closures, a programmer will often construct a closure equivalent by packaging the code for a function with an explicit environment, which is simply a set of global variables. In a closure, maintaining an environment—a state—is simply an example of one function invocation communicating with a later one.

In the instruction stream in a computer, an early instruction can write some value into a memory location or a register, and a later instruction can read and use that value. When this happens within the pipeline window, as we discussed earlier, the pipeline may block, and performance may be lost.

Similarly, we can define a software pipeline in which later stages of the pipe can communicate with earlier stages—early arguments to the pipeline can influence the behavior of the pipeline on later arguments.

To handle global variables, we use vectors in place of variables and a locking mechanism to keep reads and writes of the global variables straight. We will demonstrate the technique with a variant of the polynomial example:

$$P(x) = 5x^4 + 4x^3 + 3x^2 + + Qx + 1$$

Q is a global variable, and let us assume that after each evaluation of P, Q is incremented. Thus, the HORNER code should become:

```
(DEFUN HORNER ()
 (LABELS
 ((P1 (LAMBDA (X)
      (LET ((ANS (+ 1 (* X (+ Q (* X (+ 3 (* X (+ 4 (* 5 X)))))))))))
        (SETQ Q (1 + Q))
        ANS))))
  ... ))
```

In this new version of HORNER, an early invocation of the code will communicate with a later invocation by changing the value of Q.

For the sake of the example, we will stipulate that the global variable, Q, must be updated after the computation of the value of the polynomial has been completed, though there is no apparent reason for this in the code. This will allow us to see how a variable might be handled at various stages in the pipeline.

Because there are four stages in the pipe, we will substitute a 4-long vector for Q. We will call an index into this vector a 'slice of Q.' Each slice is associated with one complete flow of control through the pipeline. That is, each time a value is passed through the pipe in order to evaluate the polynomial once, a slice of Q is assigned to that computation.

To allocate the slice, we will create a lock for each slice of Q. In fact, there will be a 4-long vector that holds the locks. Earlier we showed that locks could be implemented with only those primitives described earlier. However, Qlisp directly supports a more streamlined locking mechanism.

In Qlisp, locks are first-class and can be passed around as any other Lisp object can. Locks can be created, gotten, and released. One interesting aspect of Qlisp locks is that they can be *named*. Most of the time anonymous locks are sufficient, and such locks are granted in the order in which requests are received. A lock is a Qlisp structure with several fields: the owner field, the request-queue field, and the *name* field. Locks are created and pointers to them are passed exactly as with other Lisp objects. To request a lock, a process must have a pointer to it; if a process requests a lock and it already has an owner, then that requestor is put in the queue for that lock. If there is no owner, then the name of the lock comes into play.

When a lock is owned by a certain process, that process might wish to pass the lock to a particular process. To do this, the owner sets the name of the lock to some particular value.

A lock that has a name can only be granted to a process that asks for that lock by its name. If several processes request a named lock, then the first process that asks for that lock by its name gets it. If a request for a named lock is placed, and the lock has no name (at that time), the request is granted regardless of what name was supplied by the requestor.

Named locks will solve a difficult problem in pipelines with global variables. This is the new code for HORNER-STREAM:

```
1   (DEFUN HORNER-STREAM ()
2   (QCATCH 'HST
3    (LABELS ((P1 (LET ((N 0)
4                        (ID (NCONS ()))
5                        (NEXT-ID (NCONS ()))))
6                   (QLAMBDA T (X)
7                    (LET ((LOCK (GET-LOCK (LOCK N))))
8                    (P2 X (+ (* 5 X) 4) LOCK N ID NEXT-ID)
9                    (SETQ ID NEXT-ID)
10                   (SETQ NEXT-ID (NCONS ()))
11                   (SETQ N (REMAINDER (1 + N) 4))
12                   T))
13          (P2 (QLAMBDA T (X V LOCK N ID NEXT-ID)
14               (P3 X (+ (* V X) 3) LOCK N ID NEXT-ID)
15               T))
16          (P3 (QLAMBDA T (X V LOCK N ID NEXT-ID)
17               (P4 X (+ (* V X)(GET-Q N ID)) LOCK N ID NEXT-ID)
18               T))
19          (P4 (QLAMBDA T (X V LOCK N ID NEXT-ID)
20               (LET ((ANS
21                      (+ (* V X) 1)))
22               (SETF (ASET *QAR* N) (1 + (AREF *QAR* N)))
23               (SET-LOCK-NAME LOCK NEXT-ID)
24               (RELEASE-LOCK LOCK)
25               ANS))))))
26           . . .)))
```

where GET-Q is defined as:

```
27   (DEFUN GET-Q (N ID)
28   (LET ((LOCK (GET-NAMED-LOCK ID (PREVIOUS-LOCK N))))
29    (LET ((Q (AREF *QAR* (PREVIOUS-INDEX N))))
30    (SETF (AREF *QAR* N) Q)
31    (SET-LOCK-NAME LOCK ())
32    (RELEASE-LOCK LOCK)
33    Q)))
```

where *QAR* holds the slices of Q.

N is a variable that is local to process P1 and whose values circulate among 0–1–2–3–0. ... As each new argument arrives at P1, the proper slice of Q and the correct lock are selected by this N. When control is passed onto P2, the second pipe stage, N is incremented (mod 4).

ID and NEXT-ID are variables that are local to process P1; ID is the name to be used for the current lock, and NEXT-ID is the name for the next lock. These two variables are initialized on lines 4 and 5. **NCONS** takes one argument and returns a list containing that argument as its sole element. The idiom (**NCONS** ()) is frequently used to create a unique pointer for use as a name.

There are four locks used to control access to the four slices of Q. Each of the four locks—one for each stage—is initially given a null name.

The lock for the Nth slice of Q is grabbed at line 7, so that no other process has access to that slice of Q until it is released with **RELEASE-LOCK**. Each time a lock is grabbed at line 7, it has no name. The lock, along with the values of N, ID, and NEXT-ID, is passed from stage to stage.

A process executing in stage P4 wants the next process in line to get a hold the value of Q it just wrote—no other process should be able to get to it first. Therefore, we want to name the lock in such a way that this inevitable. Consider the environments of the processes in question. From within stage P4, ID is the current name and NEXT-ID is the name of the next process in line behind the one currently in P4 (lines 9 and 10). Thus, the value of NEXT-ID in stage P4 is EQ to the value of ID in stage P3.

At line 23, the name of the lock for the Nth slice of Q is set to NEXT-ID. Because the process in stage P4 has had control of this lock since that process started in stage P1, no other process can have control of it, and now that that the lock's name has been set, there is exactly one process that can get a hold of it the process that asks for that name, which is the process right behind the one in stage P4.

The process in stage P3 asks for the value of Q, using GET-Q, at line 17. In GET-Q at line 28, the lock with ID as its name is requested. This will result in the process in stage P3 getting lock right after the process in stage P4 is through with it. In GET-Q, after the value for Q writen into the Nth slice of Q has been copied into the $(N + 1)^{st}$ *(mod* 4) slice of Q (line 30), the name of the lock is set to () (line 31), and the lock is released. Now any other process can grab this lock.

The worst case is that reference to Q in P3 will need to wait until stage P4 of the previous computation has released that slice; this will happen quite frequently. Also, the amount of computation that goes into each stage is quite low compared with the amount computation that goes into maintaining the locks. The result is that HORNER-STREAM is slower than HORNER on 40 computed values by factor of approximately 1.7.

There are two factors that could improve the performance of pipelines that communicate among stages with global variables: (1) the frequency of interaction between pipe stages using global variables could be decreased; and (2) the amount of computation per pipe stage could be increased.

The frequency of global variable use as a determiner of the performance of a pipeline is obvious. The amount of computation per stage as compared with the amount of computation needed to maintain the locks can be shown to be determiner of performance by modifying HORNER and HORNER-STREAM so as to increase the amount of computation per pipe stage.

```
(DEFUN HORNER-STREAM ()
 (QCATCH 'HST
  (LABELS ((P1 (LET ((N 0)
                     (ID (NCONS ()))
                     (NEXT-ID (NCONS ()))))
                (QLAMBDA T (X)
                 (LET ((LOCK (GET-LOCK (LOCK N))))
                  (P2 X (+ (* (DELAY 5) X) (DELAY 4))
                        LOCK N ID NEXT-ID)
                  (SETQ ID NEXT-ID)
                  (SETQ NEXT-ID (NCONS ()))
                  (SETQ N (REMAINDER (1+ N) 4))
                  T))
           (P2 (QLAMBDA T (X V LOCK N ID NEXT-ID)
                (P3 X (+ (* V X) (DELAY 3)) LOCK N ID NEXT-ID)
                T))
           (P3 (QLAMBDA T (X V LOCK N ID NEXT-ID)
                (P4 X
                    (+ (* V X) (DELAY (GET-Q N ID))) LOCK N ID NEXT-ID)
                T))
           (P4 (QLAMBDA T (X V LOCK N ID NEXT-ID)
                (LET ((ANS
                       (+ (* V X) (DELAY 1))))
                 (INCR-GLOBAL N)
                 (SET-LOCK-NAME LOCK NEXT-ID)
                 (RELEASE-LOCK LOCK)
                 ANS))))))
   ...)))
```

where DELAY is a macro defined as:

```
(DEFMACRO DELAY (FORM)
        '(DO ((I *DELAY* (1- I)))
             ((ZEROP I) ,FORM)))
```

We can similarly modify HORNER. With *DELAY* set to 20, HORNER-STREAM is faster than HORNER over 20 polynomial evaluations by a factor of approximately 2.2.

12.3. Comparison with Other Techniques

Qlisp is essentially an asynchronous language—we assume several Central Processing Units (CPU's) attached to a single address space, where each CPU can run several jobs (or processes) at once in a time-shared mode. We do not assume that there is any explicit control of the scheduling of processes outside of those implied by the language (locks and flow of data and control).

Because of this, Qlisp supports a style of parallism that is quite different from both systolic arrays and systolic-array-like mechanisms like the Bagel [Shapiro 1983]. There is no network or grid of processors, and data/control is not shunted from one processor to the next. Therefore, the use of locks is necessary to control access to globals.

Moreover, within each stage of a pipeline it is possible to use the full power of Qlisp to achieve local speed-ups—each stage can exploit a high degree of parallelism within it. This is not readily performed with any of the systolic-array-like techniques.

The examples we have shown have been coded using the underlying Qlisp mechanisms without using any macros or other structuring. The code in each stage of the pipes presented, along with the actions to deal with global variables within those stages, is so stylized that macros are easily written to support software pipelining. This would shorten and simplify the unreadable code we have been using for expository purposes.

The Qlisp programming environment supports a suite of such macros, and here is how the second version of HORNER-STREAM is actually written:

```
(DEFUN HORNER-STREAM ()
        (PIPELINE FOO ((Q 0))
                ((STAGE (X) X ( + (* 5 X) 4))
                (STAGE (X V) X ( + (* V X) 3))
                (STAGE (X V) X ( + (* V X) (GLOBAL-REF Q)))
                (STAGE (X V) ( + (* V X) 1)
                                (SETF (GLOBAL-REF Q)
                                        (1 + (GLOBAL-REF Q)))))
                ...))
```

In this formulation, each stage simply invokes the next; the form for a stage in the pipe is:

(**STAGE** < *formal arguments* > . < *arguments to next stage* >)

There is also a formulation in which pipe stages are explicitly named and can be invoked by name. This allows one to write a pipeline that is a directed graph.

Software pipelining is also similar to stream processing, in which one process supplies a stream of values to another. Software pipelining is different in that it is useful for introducing concurrency to an existing serial program by breaking it up into a stream with several stages. Thus, it is not only a technique that is useful for thinking about programs as processes that produce or consume a sequence of values, but it is also useful for thinking about increasing the running speed of a program.

This viewpoint allowed us to introduce software pipelining into programs which use global variables to enable early invocations of a program to communicate with later invocations.

13. GEOMETRIC CONTROL STRUCTURES

In this section we will introduce a style of programming called *gemoetric control structuring*.

Systolic arrays have been used extensively in numeric analysis computing. The idea is that a network of computers organized as an array can be programmed to perform operations—typically on arrays—by streaming data from several computers in the array to a single computer. That single computer performs some operation on the data and passes along its value to some other computer.

The advantage of this style of programming is that geometric intuition about the structure of a computation can be brought to bear by the programmer to produce an effective and clear program. If there is a multiprocessor whose interconnection structure corresponds to the program structure, then there may be a performance advantage as well.

13.1. Motivation for Geometric Control Structures

The key observation about systolic arrays is that the control structure corresponds very closely to the geometry (or topology) of the problem. Process closures were used to define software pipelining; process closures can also be used to define any hierarchical or heterarchical control structure.

13.2. Data-Structure-Resident Closures

The key is to allocate processes within a data structure. If this data structure is global, then each process within the data structure is able to access other processes—that is, any process can invoke any other process that it is able to access through the data structure.

An example might be a two dimensional array, which could correspond to some physical aspect of the problem the programmer wishes to solve. If the solution to the problem requires that each element in the array have an associated process, which performs some computation, then the programmer can store a process closure in each element in the array. These process closures can incorporate communications capabilities to other elements in the array, perhaps limited to nearby neighbors.

Once the problem is solved in its own terms, attention can be turned towards laying down the data structure of process closures on the physical structure of the multiprocessor. Perhaps the multiprocessor is itself a rectangular array and the mapping is simple. Perhaps not. The key is to solve the problem without much concern for the geometry of the underlying hardware, leaving the matching of the software architecture to the hardware architecture until later.

Software pipelining can be a seen as a simple example of this idea, with the underlying data structure being a simple list. Systolic arrays can be viewed this way with some sort of grid as the underlying data structure.

14. CONCLUSIONS

We have presented a new language for multiprocessing. A variant of Lisp, this language features a unique and powerful diction for parallel programs. Parallel constructs are expressed elegantly, and the language extensions are entirely within the spirit of Lisp.

Multiprocessors that support shared memory among processors are important, and even some or all of the nodes in a distributed system should be multiprocessors of this style. To achieve maximum performance we will need to pull every trick in the book, from coarse-grained down to fine-grained parallelism. This language is a step in the direction of achieving that goal by allowing programmers to easily express parallel algorithms.

NOTES

1. Strictly speaking this is not true. Simulations show that the ideal situation depends on the length of time it takes to create a process and the amount of waiting the average process needs to do. If the creation time is short, but realistic, and if there is a lot of waiting for values, then it is better to use some of the waiting time creating active processes, so that no processor will be idle. The ideal situation has no physical processor idle.

2. We can assume that there is a single print routine that guarantees that when something is printed, no other print request interferes with it. Thus, we will not see 43 and then 96 printed in this example.

REFERENCES

1. R. P. Gabriel, and L. M. Masinter, *Performance of Lisp Systems. Proc. 1982 ACM Symp. on Lisp and Functional Programming*, Aug. 1982.
2. R. P. Gabriel, and J. M. McCarthy, "*Queue-based Multiprocessor Lisp.*" *Proc. 1984 ACM Symposium on Lisp and Functional Programming*, Aug. 1984.
3. R. P. Gabriel, *Performance and Evaluation of Lisp Systems*. Cambridge, MIT Press, 1985.
4. R. Halstead, "MultiLisp." *Proc. 1984 ACM Symp. on Lisp and Functional Programming*, Aug. 1984.
5. B. J. Smith, *A Pipelined, Shared Resource MIMD Computer. Proc. Intl. Conf. on Parallel Processors*, 1978.
6. G. L. Steele, Jr., and G. J. Sussman, "The Revised Report on SCHEME: A Dialect of LISP." AI Memo 452, MIT Artificial Intelligence Laboratory, Cambridge, MA, Jan. 1978.
7. G. L. Steele, Jr., et al. *Common Lisp Reference Manual*. Digital Press, 1984.
8. G. J. Sussman, and G. L. Steele, Jr., *SCHEME: An Interpreter for Extended Lambda Calculus*. Tech. Rep. 349, MIT Artificial Intelligence Laboratory, Cambridge, MA, Dec. 1975.

5. RESTRICTED AND-PARALLEL EXECUTION OF LOGIC PROGRAMS

DOUG DeGROOT

1. INTRODUCTION

One of the most exciting and promising aspects of logic programming is its richness of parallel execution models. The challenge is to find cost-effective, robust implementation techniques for these parallel execution models. A fairly large number of techniques have been proposed so far, and more are continually being proposed. Although these models possess many unique features, most are based on one form or another of either AND-parallelism or OR-parallelism as a result of the fact that the program-execution search-spaces of logic programs are naturally expressed as AND-OR search trees [2].

In logic programming, given a predicate (procedure or goal) to prove (solve), there are generally several clauses that can be used to prove the predicate, with each clause requiring the proof of several additional predicates (subgoals). Because any one *or* another of the different clauses may be used to prove the predicate, attempting these proofs in parallel is called *OR-parallelism*. Once a particular clause has been selected for a proof attempt, all subgoals within the clause must be solved for the clause to succeed. Executing these subgoals in parallel—the first *and* the second *and* so on—is called *AND-parallelism*.

OR-parallelism is generally believed to be easier to implement than AND-parallelism. When a given predicate must be solved, separate, independent processes may be activated in parallel to solve this predicate, one process for each clause that defines this predicate. Although each process must receive its own copy of the activation environment, once activated, a process need not communicate with any other process. Any variable bindings made by this process are private bindings. Additionally, backtracking is totally eliminated. The major cost then clearly is that of replicating or sharing the activation environment [3].

With OR-parallelism, the amount of execution parallelism that will be exhibited for a given application depends entirely on the amount of nondeterminism in the program, or, specifically, the number of clauses that can be attempted per goal. The more there are, the greater the parallelism that may result. However, when little nondeterminism exists, and there are many such applications for which this is true, little parallelism will be exhibited by OR-parallel execution models.

Additionally, OR-parallel models attempt to find all solutions (actually, all proofs of all solutions) to a problem, even though only one may be needed. In such cases, the time to produce the first answer may not be shorter than that of sequential execution, although such performance should be rare. AND-parallel execution models, instead of focusing on producing all possible answers, attempt to produce the first answer as quickly as possible before perhaps then going on to produce another. The amount of parallelism exhibited by AND-parallel models is thus independent of the amount of nondeterminism in the program. However, unlike OR-parallelism, AND-parallelism involves the parallel execution of goals, which may be (and usually are) highly interdependent. Consequently, significant amounts of communication between parallel processes may be required, thereby raising the cost of the parallelism achieved. To keep the communication costs down to acceptably low levels, the amount of potential AND-prarallelism may need to be reduced. Several significant AND-parallel execution models have been proposed that do in fact result in reduced AND-parallelism [1, 4, 8, 9]. One of these is described here.

2. PARAMETER PASSING IN LOGIC PROGRAMMING

The data objects in logic programming are called *terms* [10]. Terms are defined recursively as follows. First, integers, characters, strings, and various other atomic symbols are all terms. Variables are terms, where a variable is an object without any value but which may receive a value during execution, including the value of some other variable. If t_1 through t_n are all terms and f is a functor, where functors are alphanumeric symbols, then $f(t_1, \ldots, t_n)$ is also a term and also called a structured term or simply a structure. It should be noticed, for the purposes of this chapter, that in particular, structured terms can contain variables within them. Atomic symbols and structured terms containing no variables are called *ground* terms; structured terms containing one or more variables and variables themselves are called *nonground* terms. In the remainder of this chapter, terms will be classified as either (1) ground, (2) nonground, nonvariable, or (3) variable.

In Prolog, clauses can be called with actual parameters of any of the three types and can return values of any of the three types. During execution of a clause, any variables passed directly as arguments or passed within a nonground, structured term may be assigned values, either ground or nonground.

For example, consider the clause:

$f(X) :- g(X), h(X).$

When f is called, the actual parameter passed in as the formal parameter X may be a variable. In normal sequential Prolog execution, subgoal g first begins execution with this variable as its actual parameter. Suppose g succeeds and returns with some particular value bound to (assigned to) X. Then h begins execution with this new value of X as its actual parameter. If h succeeds with this value, the clause succeeds, and f returns with this value of X. If h fails with this value, execution backtracks to g, and g attempts some other proof. If g succeeds, a new value for X is returned, and h tries this new value. The execution behavior of the two subgoals in this example is that of g's acting essentially as a producer of values for X and h's acting as a consumer of the values. For the clause (and hence f) to succeed, both subgoals must succeed with the same value for X. This should be obvious since both g's and h's single formal parameter is clearly identical.

As noted before, the value of X returned by g can be any of the three types of terms defined above. If g returns a ground value, h cannot affect the value. If g returns a nonground, structured term, h cannot affect the structure of the term, but it can assign values to any of the variables in the term. And if g returns a variable value, h can assign any value whatsoever to X. So clearly, either g or h can assign a value to X, and if g assigns a nonground value to X, h can modify that value. But the values that h can assign to X are limited by the values g first assigns to X—g and h must "agree" in some sense on the value assigned to X. If g and h execute in parallel, each must be made to "see" the actions of the other so that whatever values they produce are guaranteed to agree. If g and h do execute in parallel and assign two values to X that do not agree, we say that a *binding conflict* has occurred. As will be shown, preventing binding conflicts is the central execution problem of AND-parallelism.

3. AND-PARALLELISM

As previously described, AND-parallelism involves the simultaneous execution of two or more subgoals in a single clause. If all subgoals execute in parallel, full (maximal) AND-parallelism results. Unfortuantely, full AND-parallelism can lead to several severe performance and semantic problems, as will be shown below.

For example, consider the following clause:

$f(X) :- g(X), h(X).$

Assume f is called with X bound to a variable and that both g and h begin execution in parallel. Because X is bound to a variable, both g and h may assign any value whatsoever to X. If they assign two values that do not agree, a binding conflict occurs, and even though they have both succeeded, they have not succeeded with values that agree; consequently, the clause f cannot succeed.

If both g and h produce one answer each, the chance may be small that these answers will agree. To solve this problem, one approach is to simply have both g and h each produce the entire set of all their possible answers instead of just one answer each. The intersection of these two sets can then be computed (using unification instead of equality), and the result can then be returned as the value for f. Notice that both subgoals execute in parallel with no interaction between them. By considering the clause

$$f(X, Z) :\text{-} \ g(X, Y), h(Y, Z).$$

it can be seen that it is really a relational join operation that must be executed to combine the result sets rather than intersection, but again using unification instead of equality.

Note that in this approach each goal, and hence each clause activation, returns as its answer the entire set of all possible solutions. Thus the answer to a query will be the set of all possible solutions, not just one possible solution as in Prolog. Clearly the time to produce all possible answers to a query could be considerable compared to the time required to produce just one answer. And if just one answer (any answer) will do, this parallel execution scheme could result in a much worse performance than sequential execution. Additionally, the total memory requirements for storing the solution sets may be significantly greater than those of Prolog.

To solve this performance problem, the joins can be computed dynamically as subgoals return answers. As soon as one member of the join is produced, it is sent back to the parent goal immediately. Thus the solution set of each goal is returned incrementally in a pipelined fashion instead of all at once. Accordingly, the time to produce the first answer will most likely be significantly reduced, especially if demand-driven execution techniques are used instead of data-driven techniques [7].

Because the join techniques treat all subgoals as independent computations whose separate answers are collected and "combined" into an overall solution, no computational information is passed from one subgoal to another, and thus no binding information is shared. For example, consider the following clauses:

$$p(X, Y, Z) :\text{-} \ \text{non-zero}(Y), \text{div}(X, Y, Z).$$

$$f(X) :\text{-} \ \text{write ('enter number: '), read}(X), g(X).$$

Here, full AND-parallel execution can lead to great amounts of wasted computation, machine checks, or other undesirable results. Furthermore, infinite loops can easily occur. These and several other problems [2] make full AND-parallelism impractical except in certain very restricted cases.

Full AND-parallelism has been studied extensively by Pollard [11]. He uses the join techniques to define an execution model based on full AND-parallelism, which he calls the "reconciliation" model.

4. RESTRICTED AND-PARALLELISM

Another approach to AND-parallelism is to ensure that goals do interact with each other when they share terms that can result in bindings. This way, when one goal binds a shared variable, all other goals having access to that variable will "see" the binding. One straightforward way to accomplish this is to force sequential execution of all goals sharing a particular variable; goals not sharing variables can execute in parallel. If this simple scheme is followed, no binding conflicts can occur because a variable is never shared by two simultaneously executing goals.

A simple technique for accomplishing this form of restricted AND-parallelism is described below. The technique uses a model consisting of several components, only three of which are described here: (1) the typing algorithm, (2) the independence algorithm, and (3) the execution graph expressions.

4.1. Typing Algorithm

As previously described, terms can be classified into three types: ground, variable, and nonground, nonvariable. A numeric type code is assigned to each as follows: 1 = ground; 2 = nonground, nonvariable; 3 = variable.

Every term represented in memory contains the appropriate type code (these type codes are in addition to the data-element type codes, such as integer, list, variable, and so on [13]). Terms are typed recursively at all levels. See Figure 5–1 for examples.

All terms appearing in the source code can be typed at compile-time. Terms created during run-time will have their types codes set during run-time as follows. First, when a clause is invoked, during unification, variables assume the type code of the term to which they become bound. All parameters of type 2 (nonground, nonvariable) are detected and "flagged." The goals in the clause body then execute. If successful, then before returning from the clause, all the 'flagged' terms are inspected to see if they have become ground as a result of executing the clause body.

How is this check performed? One way is to simply scan through the entire term looking for a variable. If one is found, the term is still nonground and thus still of type 2. If no variable is found, the term has become ground, and so its type code is accordingly set to 1. Clearly, however, scanning through entire terms on every clause exit can be phenomenally expensive. A potential solution is to merely examine the type codes of all top-level components of the terms. If they all have type codes of 1 (ground), then they contain no variables, and therefore neither does the overall term; its type code can thus be set to 1 as well. If any component is not of type 1, that component is assumed to contain a variable, and thus the overall term must remain of type 2. Although this approach is clearly much faster,

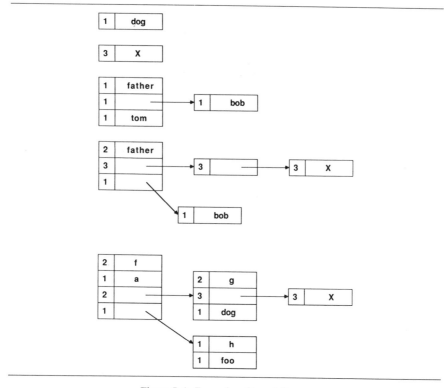

Figure 5-1. Examples of typed Terms.

it may occasionally fail to detect that a term has become ground and so mistakenly keep the type code set to 2 instead of changing it to 1. So the typing algorithm is only an approximation algorithm; it may occasionally mistype a term as nonground when in fact it has become ground. Initial indications are that such events will be rare. But, in any event, if the typing algorithm does err, it errs on the side of safety, for it is much better to assume a ground term is nonground than to assume a nonground term is ground.

4.2. Independence Algorithm

The independence algorithm is used to determine when two terms are independent. Two terms are said to be independent when they contain no variable in common. Two goals can execute in parallel if the parameters of one are all independent from the parameters of the other, for, if so, the two goals share no variables, and hence no binding conflicts can occur. The independence algorithm is illustrated in Figure 5-2.

Note that the independence algorithm assumes that two terms are interdependent of each other if they cannot in fact be proven to be independent. Two type-2

```
function Independent (term1, term2): boolean;
begin
 if ground(term1) or ground(term2) then
  independent:=true
 else if variable(term1) and variable(term2)
  and (address(term1) ≠ address(term2)) then
   independent:=true
 else {assume} independent:-false;
end; {independent}
```

Figure 5-2. The independence algorithm.

terms (nonground, nonvariable terms) are automatically assumed to be inter-dependent, since to prove them independent would require complete traversals of the two terms in order to compare all the variables of one to all variables of the other; clearly this operation is infeasible. Instead, the independence algorithm simply assumes they are interdependent. Similarly, any variable and any type-2, term are assumed to be interdependent for similar reasons.

It can be seen then that the independence algorithm is also an approximation algorithm. However, as will be argued later, it is expected that the independence algorithm will be correct more than enough to allow a parallel-processing system to remain fully loaded.

4.3. Execution Graph Expressions

Six types of execution graph expressions are defined:

1. G, where G is any goal
2. $(SEQ\ E_1 \ldots E_n)$
3. $(PAR\ E_1 \ldots E_n)$
4. $(GPAR\ (V_1 \ldots V_k)\ E_1 \ldots E_n)$
5. $(IPAR\ (V_1 \ldots V_k)\ E_1 \ldots E_n)$
6. $(IF\ B\ E_1\ E_2)$

Expressions of type 1 are simply goal expressions; so any goal is considered an execution graph expression. A *SEQ* expression indicates that the following n execution graph expressions E_1 through E_n are all to execute sequentially. Similarly, a *PAR* expression says that the n subexpressions are all to execute in parallel. A *GPAR* expression tests its k variables, and if all are *ground*, the n subexpressions can all execute in parallel; if at least one of the k variables is not ground, then the n subexpressions must execute sequentially. Similarly, an *IPAR* expression tests to see if the k variables are all mutually independent; if so, then the n subexpressions E_1 through E_n can execute in parallel. If any two are interdependent, then the n subexpressions must execute sequentially. An *IF* expression tests a Boolean expression B; if B is true, then the subexpression E_1 executes; if B is false, E_2 executes. In addition, *IPAR* and *GPAR* tests can be combined, as in the following example:

$(GPAR\ (X)\ IPAR\ (X,Y)\ f(X,Y)\ \ g(X,Z)$

In such expressions, all tests must succeed for the subexpressions to execute in parallel; if any test fails, the subexpressions must execute sequentially.

The *IPAR* tests use the independence algorithm, while the *GPAR* tests simply check the type codes of the variables to ensure that they are all type 1 (*ground*). These tests are very simple and could be implemented in microcode straightforwardly. Consequently, the *IPAR* and *GPAR* tests are very "cheap."

5. EXECUTION GRAPHS OF LOGIC PROGRAMMING CLAUSES

The execution behavior of a logic programming clause can be represented with an execution graph that represents the data dependencies of the execution. Using the left-to-right ordering of subgoals in a clause, we say that one subgoal precedes another if the first is to the left of the other. Additionally, the head of the clause precedes all subgoals. One subgoal is dependent on a preceding subgoal if the two subgoals share a common variable and if before execution of the first subgoal, the shared variable is nonground. In such a case, the preceding goal must execute first, and then upon completion, the dependent subgoal may be able to execute. In this way, binding conflicts can be prevented.

For example, consider the following clause:

$f(X)$:-$g(X)$, $h(X)$, $k(X)$.

Suppose a call to f of the form $f(Z)$ is made, where Z represents an unbound variable. Clearly, f precedes g, h, and k. Additionally, because all subgoals share the variable X with f, and because Z, the actual parameter, is nonground, g, h, and k are all dependent on f. When f is, entered, Z is still nonground, and so g begins execution first since it is the leftmost subgoal sharing X.

When g returns, two conditions are possible: (1) X is still nonground, and (2) X is ground. In the first case, because X is still nonground, k becomes dependent on h, and h executes first. When h returns, no matter what the value of X, k can begin execution. In the second case, if g returns a ground value of X, h and k can execute in parallel because neither is dependent on the other (and, of course, clearly because no binding conflicts can now occur).

Consider the case now in which a call is made to f of the form $f(dog)$, where the actual parameter is ground. Then none of the subgoals are dependent on the other, and so all three can execute in parallel. Figure 5-3 illustrates these three cases. Figure 5-3(a) illustrates the execution graph that results when f is called with a ground argument. Figures 5-3(b) and 5-3(c) illustrate the two possible execution graphs that result when f is called with a nonground argument. In both cases, because the argument is nonground, subgoal g must execute first. If g returns with a ground result, the execution graph shown in Figure 5-3(b) results; if g returns a nonground result, the execution graph of Figure 5-3(c) must occur. It is important to notice that a single logic programming clause can result in more than one execution graph. Each of the different execution graphs expresses different amounts of parallelism. Because the determination of the proper execution graph is data-dependent, compile-time analysis cannot determine which execution graph to use for any given call. (Actually, a compile-time analysis approach is discussed below.)

When a clause is called, the only way to determine which execution graph can be used, and therefore how much parallelism can be exhibited, is to examine at run-time whether the actual parameters are ground or nonground, and if nonground, whether or not they are independent. Clearly, the terms can be scanned in their entirety [2] or a typing algorithm such as that described in Section 4.1 can be used. Notice that the arguments must be examined upon every clause invocation and upon almost every return in order to continually update the information needed to determine which execution graph can be used.

Consider now the following execution graph expression:

$(GPAR\ (X)\ g(X)$
$\qquad (GPAR\ (X)\ h(X)\ k(X)).$

Suppose we equate this graph to the clause for f above. Then when a call to f is made with a ground argument, the $GPAR(X)$ test succeeds, and thus the two following subexpressions can be executed in parallel. The first subexpression invokes $g(X)$; the second expression retests X with the $GPAR\ (X)$ test, finds X is ground, and so begins parallel execution of $h(X)$ and $k(X)$. The result is the execution graph of Figure 5-3(a). Suppose a call to f is made with a *nonground* argument; then the initial $GPAR(X)$ test fails, and the two following subexpressions are executed sequentially. First $g(X)$ executes; when it completes, the second subexpression begins. This second expression tests X again with the $GPAR(X)$ test; if it finds X is now ground, $h(X)$ and $k(X)$ begin executing in parallel. Thus the execution graph of Figure 5-3(b) is achieved. If the test fails, X is still *nonground*, and so $h(X)$ and $k(X)$ must execute sequentially, thereby achieving the execution graph of Figure 5-3(c). The single execution graph expression above then represents the three possible execution graphs for the clause. This is significant, because it is not necessary to construct these graphs dynamically at run-time.

However, the graph expression makes a redundant test in the case when f is called with a ground argument. This results in a slight performance penalty. But because the $GPAR$ test is so very simple—the type code of the argument is checked to see if it is 1—the performance penalty is extremely small.

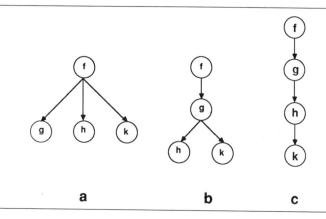

Figure 5–3. Execution graphs.

Other execution graph expressions are possible for the clause:

$f(X)$:- $g(X)$, $h(X)$, $k(X)$.

Some of the more obvious are:

1. $(SEQ\ g(X)\ h(X)\ k(X))$
2. $(PAR\ g(X)\ h(X)\ k(X))$
3. $(GPAR(X)\ g(X)\ h(X)\ k(X))$

The first of these always executes the three subgoals sequentially, achieving execution Figure graph 5–3(c). The second always results in execution graph Figure 5–3(a), even though this may not be correct. The third achieves either graph 5–3(a) or 5–3(c), depending on whether f is called with a ground or nonground argument. Clearly, the execution graph expression

$(GPAR\ (X)\ g(X)$
$\qquad(GPAR\ (X)\ h(X)\ k(X))$

is maximal in that it can achieve any of the three possible execution graphs.

Significant work has been done recently to develop a capability to determine as much as possible at compile-time what types of arguments can be passed to a clause and what types of results it will return [1, 6]. This compile-time analysis might yield results such as stating that upon successful return from a call to g, the result will always be ground. If so, then the maximal graph expression would become:

$(GPAR\ (X)\ g(X)$
$\qquad(PAR\ h(X)\ k(X))$.

The second *GPAR* test could be omitted. And if it could be determined that f will always be called with a ground argument, then the maximal graph expression would become:

$(PAR\ g(X)\ h(X)\ k(X))$.

Unfortunately, clauses are frequently called with several types and combinations of arguments, and they frequently return several types and combinations of results. Consequently, it is impossible to compile a maximal graph expression that does not contain any *GPAR* or *IPAR* tests. In such cases, the worst-case invocation and exit conditions can be assumed, and then the best graph expression for these cases can be compiled. Although these expressions will not contain any tests, they also may not always be able to achieve maximal parallelism. How much worse these expressions will be from optimal parallelism remains an open research problem.

Consider another example:

$f(X, Y):- p(X),\ q(Y),\ s(X,Y),\ t(Y)$.

This clause can be compiled into the execution graph expression

$(GPAR\ (X,Y)$
$\qquad (IPAR\ (X,Y)\ p(X)\ q(Y))$
$\qquad (GPAR(Y)\ s(X,Y)\ t(Y)))$.

If X and Y are both ground upon entry, the execution graph of Figure 5–4(a) is achieved. This particular example points out the fact that whenever $GPAR(X,Y)$ is true, $(IPAR(X,Y))$ is also true. Thus $GPAR$ is a stronger test than $IPAR$. If X and Y are not both ground upon entry into f but are independent, then the execution graph of either Figure 5–4(b) or 5–4(c) is achieved, depending upon whether Y is ground after execution of the *IPAR* subexpression. The execution graphs of Figure 5–4(d) and 5–4(e) result when X and Y are neither ground nor independent upon entry to f.

6. RESTRICTIONS ON THE AND-PARALLELISM

The AND-parallel execution model presented here actually restricts AND-parallelism in several ways —some intended and some not. First of all, subgoals are prevented from executing in parallel when they share one or more variables; this is done to prevent binding conflicts and to avoid having to collect all answers and "reconcile" their differing sets. This restriction is desirable and is efficiently achieved by the model.

In addition, several other restrictions may occur, which are not desirable. First, as pointed out previously, the typing algorithm is only an approximation

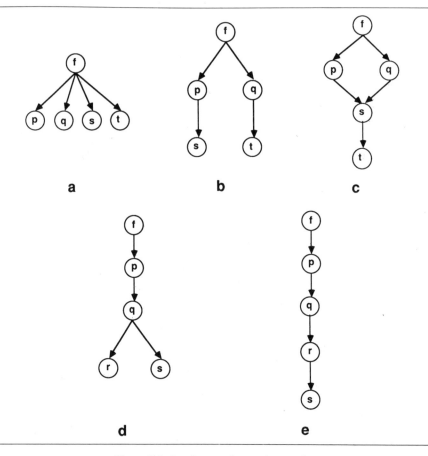

Figure 5–4. Another set of execution graphs.

algorithm. It may occasionally fail to detect that a nonground term has become ground. The following example illustrates one way in which this may occur:

p(t(h(X))) :- f(X).
f(5).

When this type of error occurs, a *GPAR* test will fail because the term will still be mistakenly typed as nonground. So the typing algorithm, due to its approximation approach, may occasionally restrict parallelism unnecessarily by leading to false *GPAR* tests.

The independence algorithm may also unnecessarily restrict parallelism due to its assumption that two type-2 terms or one type-3 term and one type-2 term are always interdependent. To prove otherwise would require full traversals of the two terms; this is clearly unacceptable.

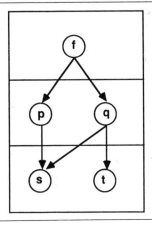

Figure 5–5. Layered execution of graph expressions.

Finally, the execution graph expressions also impose certain restrictions on the AND-parallelism. For example, reconsider the last clause of the previous section:

$f(X, Y) :- p(X), q(Y), s(X,Y), t(Y)$.

Suppose X and Y are independent upon entry to f but that neither is *ground*. Additionally, suppose Y is *ground* upon return from q. Then the execution graph of Figure 5–4(b) is achieved. Notice however that even though the final subgoal, $t(Y)$, is dependent only upon $q(Y)$, it must wait for $p(X)$ to complete execution as well, due to the fact that the second *GPAR* subexpression cannot begin execution until after the first *IPAR* subexpression has completely finished. The result is a kind of layered execution, as illustrated in Figure 5–5. Other AND-parallel models allow $t(Y)$ to begin execution immediately after $q(Y)$ completes, irrespective of the progress of the other, nonrelated goals [2, 9]. These models appear very costly to implement, however. To gain the efficiency of the model proposed here, as in [8], the graph expressions used, by their nature, restrict the AND-parallelism to a certain extent.

There is one additional way in which the proposed model can restrict the amount of AND-parallelism and in a way that is believed to be highly desirable. This restriction is described in the next section.

7. A PARALLEL EXECUTION MODEL
In this section, an abstract architectural model is described which can be used to implement the AND-parallelism model based on the execution graph expressions. The architecture is assumed to consist of a number of distinct processing elements, each with its own local memory and an ability to communicate with all other processors in the system. Each processing element is assumed to have access to the entire logic program to be executed.

Within each processing element are a sequential stack and a parallel stack. The sequential stack contains goals and graph expressions that must be executed sequentially; the parallel stack contains goals and graph expressions that can be executed in parallel. By definition, elements of the parallel stack can be executed in any order, by any processor. Elements in the sequential stack must be executed sequentially, in order. Initially, all stacks of all processors are empty. When a logic programming query is entered into the system, it is compiled into an execution graph expression and placed on the sequential stack of one of the processors.

Each processor treats all work on the sequential stack as its own; because this work must be performed sequentially, no benefit is gained by sending elements on this stack out to other processors. Work on the parallel stack may however be shared with other processors. The central execution loop of the processors works as follows. A processor looks at its sequential stack for its next piece of work. If one is found, it is either a goal or a graph expression. If it is a goal, it is simply executed. If it is an expression, the expression is evaluated. If the expression is a *GPAR* or *IPAR* that succeeds, or simply a *PAR* expression, the subexpressions can all be executed in parallel, and so they are placed on the parallel stack. A failing parallel test or a *SEQ* expression results in its subexpressions being placed on the sequential stack.

If a processor finds that it has no work on either its sequential or parallel stack, it may send a request to the other processors for work to do. A processor receiving a request to help from an idle processor checks to see if it has work on its parallel stack, and, if so, it can send one or more of these elements to the requesting processor. A processor completing a piece of work that it obtained from another processor sends the results back to the originating processor. Manuel de Hermenegildo has worked out an extensive execution model for such a system [8].

The point of interest here is that once a processor's parallel stack becomes sufficiently full, where "sufficiently" is defined as a system parameter, the processor may switch modes so that it treats *IPAR*, *GPAR*, and *PAR* expressions as if they were *SEQ* expressions. In such an event, the processor no longer decomposes expressions into their constituent parts. Instead, the processor assumes it will execute the entire expression itself well before running out of work on its parallel stack to ship out to volunteering processors. The result will be increased cache-hit ratios, lessened overhead in managing and reintegrating the results of more subexpressions, and fewer instruction pipeline interruptions. Switching modes in this manner is a conscious attempt to restrict the amount of AND-parallelism detection during run-time.

This conscious attempt to restrict parallelism is prompted by the following views. First, the ideal system state is to have all processors busy doing useful work. During such times, maximal system performance is being achieved. Second, when maximal system parallelism has been achieved, it no longer benefits system performance to continue decomposing work into smaller and smaller units. In fact, this may easily prove harmful to performance due to the overhead

```
qksort([Head|Tail],SortedList)  :-
  split(T,H,Smaller,Bigger),
  qksort(Small,SortedSmaller),
  qksort(Big,SortedBigger),
  append(SortedSmaller,SortedBigger,SortedList).
qksort([],[]).

split([H|T],E,[H|S],B)  :- H ≤ E, split(T,E,S,B).
split([H|T],E,S,[H|B])  :- split(T,E,S,B).
split([],E,[],[]).

append([],L,L).
append([H|T],L,[H|R]) :- append(T,L,R).
```

```
qksort([Head|Tail],SortedList)  :-
  (SEQ split(T,H,Smaller,Bigger)
    (PAR qksort(Small,SortedSmaller),
     qksort(Big,SortedBigger))
  append(SortedSmaller,SortedBigger,SortedList).

qksort([],[]).

split([H|T],E,[H|S],B)  :-
  (SEQ H ≤ E
   split(T,E,S,B)).
split([H|T],E,S,[H|B])  :- split(T,E,S,B).
split([],E,[],[]).

append([],L,L).
append([H|T],L,[H|R]) :- append(T,L,R).
```

Figure 5–6. A Quicksort program and its execution graph.

costs. Accordingly, maximal system parallelism is differentiated from maximal program parallelism. What is required from a parallel execution model is the ability to find enough program parallelism to achieve maximal system parallelism; finding maximal program parallelism is necessary only when less parallelism exists in the program than the system can exhibit.

However, this may be rare. The nature of logic programming and most parallel logic programming schemes is that the granularity of the tasks tends to become rather small rather quickly. For example, consider a typical Quicksort logic program, as shown in Figure 5–6. If a call to Quicksort is made to sort the list of numbers (5, 3, 2, 1, 4, 8, 7, 6, 9), almost 20 Quicksort tasks might be created, with an additional large number of split and append tasks. Whether this is good depends on when the call to Quicksort is made. If made at a time when all processors are busy, the system is already maximally parallel; creating these additional tasks will not result in increased parallel execution. If we adopt the rather normal view that a certain significant amount of time is required to create a task and to reintegrate its results [8], then task creation that does not result in increased parallelism should be avoided whenever possible.

If the call to quicksort is made when the system is idle or at least nearly so, then it may indeed prove beneficial to create some of these additional tasks and distribute them across the system in order to increase system performance. But how many should be created? All possible tasks, or just enough to bring the system to maximal parallelism? Although the latter clearly appears better, it requires the ability to turn parallel decomposition off and on. Such a capability is present in the model presented, and for just such a reason.

The issue is far from clear, however. Clearly there is a certain nontrivial cost associated with creating a task and reintegrating its results. Furthermore, additional costs are associated with interprocessor communications for volunteering to help and shipping out work elements and receiving results. If the amount of increased performance that results from farming out a piece of work is not greater than that lost by the overhead associated with doing so, it is not worth trying to obtain the increased parallelism. For example, suppose a call to quicksort is made to sort a list of only two or three elements. Clearly such a list can be sorted more quickly on a single processor than by decomposing the list and sending out a subtask to sort a single element list. Consequently, sometimes it may clearly be desirable to restrict parallelism even when idle processors exist. The guiding principle should be that when a piece of work is sent out, the increase in parallelism and performance should be far greater than the cost of shipping that work out. Determining the size of a piece of work is difficult and little understood, however. Because it is a data-dependent determination, compile-time analysis may prove ineffective. Efficient run-time mechanisms for making these determinations are yet to be explored.

The restricted AND-parallelism model presented here assumes that a great many typical logic programs will contain sufficiently more program parallelism than system parallelism, even for fairly large parallel computer systems. In such cases, many logic programming clauses will be decomposed at the top levels and find their way across the system. These top-level tasks will tend to involve substantial computations, and therefore the tasks shipped out will increase performance more than the overhead will reduce it. Additionally, because the detection of parallelism can be turned off once the system becomes fully loaded and turned back on when idle spots turn up, the system will be able to keep itself load-balanced with minimal costs. The total amount of interprocessor communication should therefore be low, thereby allowing cheaper interprocessor communication networks. All these assumptions remain to be validated.

If these assumptions prove to be correct for a large number of applications, the benefit is that more than enough parallelism can be easily found to achieve near maximal system parallelism. Finding maximal program parallelism is unnecessary. As a result, the loss of program parallelism due to the approximations of the typing and independence algorithms and to the limited expressability of the graph expressions becomes much less serious if not totally irrelevant. The efficient implementation of this scheme then becomes one of its greatest virtues, as demonstrated by de Hermenegildo [8].

8. SUMMARY

Although logic programming enjoys a great many ways of being executed in parallel, most techniques involve either OR-parallelism or AND-parallelism. Considerable work is being performed in both areas. AND-parallelism, however, seems to possess certain characteristics that promise more robust parallelism over a larger number of application domains. Within the area of AND-parallelism, several major approaches are being pursued, with various forms of restricted AND-parallelism receiving most of the attention. In these approaches, the parallelism is restricted so that tasks that cooperate to produce a single answer do not execute in parallel until no danger of creating binding conflicts exists.

A particular model of restricted AND-parallelism has been presented. This model consists of a typing algorithm, an independence algorithm, and an execution-graph expression language, each of which has been described. The model results in several forms of parallelism restriction, some of which are explicit and some implicit. A given parallel execution model was described, which could be used for implementing the restricted AND-parallelism model. This execution model attempts to achieve large-grained parallelism with demand-driven distribution of subgoals. Several of the promises and problems associated with this model have been discussed.

REFERENCES

1. J-H. Chang, A. Despain, and D. DeGroot, "AND-Parallelism of Logic Programs Based on Static Data Dependency Analysis," *Proc. 30th IEEE Computer Society Intl. Conf., 1985*, pp. 218–226.
2. J. Conery, *Parallel Execution of Logic Programs*, Norwell, MA: Kluwer Academic Press, 1986.
3. J. Crammond, "A Comparative Study of Unification Algorithms for OR-Parallel Execution of Logic Languages," *IEEE Trans. on Computers*, Vol C-34(10): 911–917, 1985. (Special Issue on Parallel Processing, Doug DeGroot, ed.).
4. D. DeGroot, "Restricted And-Parallelism," *Proc. Int'l Conf. on Fifth Generation Computer Systems*, OHMSHA, Tokyo, 1984, pp. 471–478.
5. D. DeGroot, "Alternate Graph Expressions for Restricted And-Parallelism." *Proc. COMPCON, Spring 85*, IEEE, 1985, pp. 206–210.
6. D. DeGroot, and J Chang, "A Comparison of Two And-Parallel Execution Models," *Proc. AFCET Conf. on Hardware and Software Components and Architectures for the Fifth Generation*, Paris, France, March 5–7, 1985.
7. D. DeGroot, "Logic Programming and Parallel Porcessing: A Tutorial," 1985, unpublished.
8. M. de Hermenegildo, "An Abstract Machine for Restricted and-Parallel Execution of Logic Programs," *Proc. 3rd Int'l Conf. on Logic Programming*, E. Shapiro, New York: Springer-Verlag, 1986, pp. 25–39.
9. Y-J. Lin and V. Kumar, "A Parallel Execution Scheme for Exploiting And-Parallelism of Logic Programs," *Proc. 1986 Int'l Conf. on Parallel Processing*, K. Hwang, S. Jacobs, and E. Swartzlander, IEEE, pp. 972–975.
10. J. Lloyd, *Foundations of Logic Programming*. New York: Springer-Verlag, 1984.
11. G. H. Pollard, *Parallel Execution of Horn Clause Programs*. Ph.D. Thesis, University of London, Imperial College of Science and Technology, London, England, 1981.
12. Y-W. Tung, *Parallel Processing Model for Logic Programming*. Ph.D. Thesis, Dept. of Electrical Engineering, University of Southern California, May 1986.
13. D. Warren, An Abstract Prolog Instruction Set. Tech. Note 309, SRI International, Menlo Park, CA, October 1983.

6. PARLOG: PARALLEL PROGRAMMING IN LOGIC

KEITH CLARK and STEVE GREGORY

1. INTRODUCTION

Parlog is a logic programming language in the sense that nearly every procedure can be read as a definition of a relation in first-order predicate logic. Parlog differs from Prolog in incorporating parallel evaluation. It incorporates both AND-parallelism and OR-parallelism. This chapter is an updated and shortened version of [4]. A more-detailed account of the language can be found in [16].

The Chapter assumes some familiarity with the general concepts of logic programming and with Prolog. For introductory reading we suggest [24, 26] or the books [7, 9, 22].

2. PARLOG AND-PARALLELISM

The AND-parallelism of Parlog is a generalization of that of our earlier Relational Language described in [3], which was itself a derivative of IC-Prolog [8]. Parlog also has many features, in common with the languages Concurrent Prolog (CP) [36] and Guarded Horn Clauses (GHC) [38], which are both derivatives of the Relational Language. There are, however, significant differences between these three languages, which we outline in the final section of this chapter.

This research was supported by the Science and Engineering Research Council under grant GR/B/97473.

In Parlog, the attempt to find a solution to each condition of a parallel conjunction becomes a separate concurrent process. The shared variables of the conditions (the calls) are the communication channels between the processes. Because of mode declarations, which restrict the unification between a call and an invoked clause to "input matching" on certain arguments, usually only one process will be able to bind each shared variable. This process is called the *producer* process for the variable. Any other (consumer) process needing the value of the shared variable suspends until the variable is bound by the producer of the variable. Suspension waiting for a value of a shared variable is the means of process synchronization in Parlog.

2.1. Example: Parallel Conjunction with Shared Variables

We introduce the special characteristics of Parlog AND-parallel evaluation through a simple example.

Suppose we have the parallel conjunction

prod1(x), prod2(y), merge-consumer(x, y, z).

with **merge-consumer** defined by the program

mode merge-consumer(list1?, list2?, merged-list^).

merge-consumer([u|x], y, [u|z]) < − merge-consumer(x, y, z).
merge-consumer(x,[v|y], [v|z]) < − merge-consumer(x, y, z).
merge-consumer([ ], y, y).
merge-consumer(x, [ ], x).

We use the convention that variables are names beginning with a lower-case letter. So **u, v, x, y** and **z** are variables. The term **[u|x]** is the pattern of a list with head element **u** followed by a tail list **x**.

The **merge-consumer** program is a complete definition of the relation **merge-consumer(list1, list2, merged-list)**: **merged-list** is an arbitrary interleaving of **list1** and **list2**.

Each clause is implicitly universally quantified with respect to each variable. The first clause covers the case when **merged-list** begins with the item at the head of **list1**. Its logical reading is:

For all **u, x, y,** and **z,**
a list of the form **[u|z]** is an arbitrary interleaving of a list of the form
[u|x] and a list **y** if **z** is an arbitrary interleaving of **x** and **y**.

We leave the reader to check the correctness of the other clauses.

2.2. Mode Declarations

The mode declaration for the program constrains the unification between any **merge-consumer** call and the clauses of the program.

An argument annotated with a '?' in the mode declaration for a relation signifies that a nonvariable term appearing in that argument position in the head of a clause can only be used for input matching. Thus, in a call to **merge-consumer**, the first clause can only be used if the first argument of the call is a substitution instance of the pattern **[u|z]**, and the third clause can only be used if the first argument of the call is the empty list **[ ]**. The second and fourth clauses have similar constraints with respect to the second argument of the call.

A '^' annotation in the mode declaration means that a nonvariable term appearing in that argument position in the head of a clause can be used for output unification against the corresponding argument in the call. So, a call to **merge-consumer** can have any term as its third argument.

The Parlog mode declarations express constraints on the unification between call and clause head similar to the mode constraints of DEC-10 Prolog. The difference is that, in DEC-10 Prolog, the attempt to use a clause when a mode constraint is not satisfied is always considered an error. In Parlog, if an input mode is not satisfied, the attempt to use the clause is suspended.

An input mode is not satisfied if an argument **a** of the call is not yet a substitution instance of the corresponding term **t** in the head of the clause but **a** *would* unify with **t** with a substitution that binds one or more variables of **a** to nonvariable terms. These variables in **a** must be given nonvariable bindings by *other* processes, that is, via the unification with other calls. When this occurs, the attempt to use the clause is resumed. Of course, if one of the variables in **a** is given a nonvariable value that does not unify with **t**, the attempt to use the clause fails.

Returning to the example, in the parallel conjunction

: prod1(x), prod2(y), merge-consumer(x, y, z).

the mode declaration for **merge-consumer** means that this call cannot bind either of the shared variables **x** and **y**. Therefore, **prod1** and **prod2** should have modes

mode prod1(list1 ^), prod2(list2 ^).

and be defined such that their evaluation will eventually generate nonvariable bindings for their variable output arguments, **x** and **y**, respectively. Until one of these producer processes generates a nonvariable binding for its output argument, the **merge-consumer** process is suspended because each of its clauses will be suspended on an input match.

2.3. Nondeterministic Evaluation

The four **merge-consumer** clauses represent alternative evaluation paths for the **merge-consumer** process.

Initially, the evaluation of the **merge-consumer** call is a concurrent attempt to apply each clause to the call. Each clause is then suspended waiting for one of the two producer processes to generate a nonvariable binding for either **x** or **y**. Let us suppose that the **prod1** process binds **x** to the term [2|**x1**]. The input match constraint on the first **merge-consumer** clause is now satisfied because [2|**x1**] is a substitution instance of the term [**u**|**x**]. The clause can therefore be used to reduce the call

merge-consumer([2|x1], y, z)

to the recursive call

merge-consumer(x1, y, z1)

and at the same time the output variable z of the top-level call is bound to [2|**z1**]. The **merge-consumer** process must now again suspend because it has been reduced to another **merge-consumer** call that cannot proceed until there is a nonvariable binding for either **x1** or **y**. It must wait until either the **prod1** process generates a binding for **x1** or the **prod2** process binds **y**.

2.4. Stream Communication

We can think of the **2** as the first message of the list or *stream* of messages that will be sent by the **prod1** process to the **merge-consumer** process. [2|**x1**] is the first approximation to this stream of messages where **x1** represents the rest of the message stream. The second message will be given when **prod1** generates another partial list binding for the variable **x1**, say the binding [3|**x2**]. A subsequent empty list binding [ ] for the variable **x2** would signal the end of the message stream. By binding its output variable **z** to the partial list [2|**z1**], the **merge-consumer** process is passing the first received message through to its output stream.

2.5. Time-Dependent Computation

For each **merge-consumer** call of the recursive **merge-consumer** process, there is a concurrent attempt to use each of the clauses. As soon as the input match constraint for a clause is satisfied, that clause can be used. The merging of the message streams sent by the two producer processes will partly depend upon the rate at which the two processes send messages. If **prod1** sends three messages before **prod2** sends its first message, these three messages will usually be the first three on the **merge-consumer** output stream. If the two producers both send messages while the **merge-consumer** process is being reduced to its recursive call, then either message may be passed through to the output stream. This is because the input match constraints of both recursive clauses will be satisfied. (The program as written does not guarantee that the merging of the message streams will be fair.)

2.6. Committed Choice Nondeterminism and Guards

When a clause is used to reduce a call, there is *no* backtracking on the choice of the clause. As a logic programming language, the distinguishing feature of Parlog is that its operational semantics incorporates the *committed choice* nondeterminism of Dijkstra's guarded commands [11] and Hoare's (CSP) [21]. Indeed, it was the elegant use of this concept in CSP that inspired us to incorporate it into the Relational Language [3], and hence into Parlog.

In general, the attempt to find a solution to some call **R(. . . .)** invokes an OR-parallel search for a clause that can be used to evaluate the call, from among all of the program clauses for **R**. (We shall see later that we can constrain this parallel search and even force a Prolog-style sequential search for the clause to be used, but the default is a parallel search.) A *candidate* clause for the reduction is one which "read-only matches" with the call on all its input arguments *and* which has a successfully terminating guard. The *guard* is an optional initial conjunction of conditions in the body of the clause, separated from the rest of the conditions by a ':'.

2.6.1. *Example: Guarded Clauses*

Suppose we replace the first clause for **merge-consumer** by the pair of clauses

```
merge-consumer([u|x], y, [u|z]) < − accept(u):
    merge-consumer(x, y, z).
merge-consumer([u|x], y, z) < − reject (u):
    merge-consumer(x, y, z).
```

The conditions **accept(u)** and **reject(u)** which precede the ':' in the clauses are guards. Now the first clause can only be used to pass a message through to the **merge-consumer** output stream if a message **u** has been sent by the **prod1** producer *and* the condition **accept(u)** is true for the transmitted message. The second clause is used if the message is to be rejected. This clause causes the process to recurse without passing the message through. (The output is just **z**, the output stream of the recursive call.) With this modification the program now describes the relation

merge-consumer(list1, list2, merged-list): merged-list is an arbitrary interleaving of **list2** with the sublist of **list1** which are the "accept" elements; all other elements of **list1** are "reject" elements.

2.7. Test Role of Guards

A guard can only *test* values of variables obtained by input matching. It cannot generate a binding for any variable in an input argument of the call. However, the evaluation of a guard may generate bindings for local variables of the clause (i.e., variables not appearing in the head) and for variables that appear in output arguments of the head of the clause.

Any candidate clause for a call can be used to reduce the call to the conjunction of conditions constituting the body of the clause. If this is a parallel conjunction, the process forks into several component processes that may communicate via bindings for a new set of shared variables in the body of the clause. The evaluation *commits* to the use of one of the candidate clauses. Usually this will be the first clause to become a candidate clause.

2.8. Bindings to Call Variables Made Only on Commitment

At the point of commitment, the output unification for the output arguments of the call is performed. (Thus, for the **merge-consumer** call of our example query, the output [u|z] of the first of the above guarded clauses will only be transmitted to the call if and when the input match with [u|x] succeeds and the **accept** guard succeeds.) Because the evaluation of a guard is not allowed to generate bindings for any variables in the input arguments of the call, no variables in a call will be bound until there is a commitment to use some candidate clause. As there is no backtracking on the choice of the candidate clause, bindings made to variables in the call are never retracted. This property considerably simplifies the implementation of Parlog and is the main reason why Parlog has this "commit then bind" style of nondeterminism rather than the Prolog "bind, fail, and rescind bindings" style of nondeterminism.

2.9. Minimal Guards for Maximum Parallelism

Because the evaluation of a call may commit to the use of any candidate clause, we must use the guard and the matching terms for the input arguments of a clause to ensure that if the input matches succeed and the guard is true, then either (1) a solution to the matched call can be found using that clause, or (2) no solution can be found using any other clause. We cannot rely on the failure to find a solution to the call using the chosen clause to automatically invoke a backtracking attempt to use an alternative clause as we can in Prolog.

We can trivially ensure that each candidate clause has the required property by making the guard of each clause contain its entire conjunction of conditions. However, because output bindings are not made until the guard computation terminates, and other processes may be suspended waiting for the output bindings, this tactic will considerably reduce the amount of overlapped computation. To achieve the greatest degree of parallelism, we must keep the guards as simple as possible.

2.10. Logical Reading of Programs

In Parlog we can write logic programs that behave as a set of communicating, forking, nondeterministic processes. The programs define a set of relations over message streams (or any other incrementally constructed data structure), and each process computes some instance of the relation its program defines. Which instance is computed will generally depend on the rate of progress of the processes with which it communicates.

This is exactly the logical property of many concurrent communicating systems. The program for each process in the system constrains the process so that its observed history of communications with other processes satisfies some relation. For example, the history of file retrievals of a filestore manager must correspond to some interleaving of the sequence of requests sent by each user. This guarantees that a later file retrieval request from a user will not be answered before an earlier request from that user.

In imperative programming languages, the relation that the communications of a process must satisfy is often heavily disguised by the highly procedural nature of the code. In Parlog, the relation that must be satisfied by the process can nearly always be determined by a straightforward logical reading of its program. This is because each program has a dual interpretation: a logical interpretation as a set of statements about a relation, and an imperative interpretation as a description of a communicating forking process. Both interpretations are important and should be kept in mind. The former enables us to write correct programs, the latter, efficient programs.

2.11. Cooperating Construction of Binding Terms

One of the elegant features of Prolog is the "logical variable." This is the ability to have the evaluation of some condition **C** bind a variable **x** to a term **t**, which contains variables that are bound by the evaluation of some other condition **C′**. **C** and **C′** have, in effect, cooperated in the construction of **t′**, the final value of **x**. The style of programming that this allows is one of the most important features of Prolog and the logic programming approach to computation (see, for example, [39]).

A cooperating construction of the final term binding for a shared variable can also be programmed in Parlog. Indeed, it is a much more powerful device in Parlog and related parallel logic languages than it is in Prolog. In Prolog, the communication is in one direction only, from **C** to **C′**. In Parlog, because the calls can be evaluated concurrently, the process **C** which binds **x** to **t** can suspend, waiting for a "back communication" from the consumer of the binding, **C′**. The back communication occurs when **C′** binds some variable in **t**.

2.12. Example: Back Communication

Suppose that our original **merge-consumer** program is modified so that the two recursive clauses become:

```
merge-consumer([(k, v)|x], y, [(k, v)|z]) < −
     check(k, v), merge-consumer(x, y, z).
merge-consumer(x, [(k, v)|y], [(k, v)|z]) < −
     check(k, v), merge-consumer(x, y, z).
```

The program now only accepts messages that are pairs of the form **(k, v)**, and there is an extra call **check(k, v)** in each clause. Our modified program now defines the relation

merge-consumer(list1, list2, merged-list): merged-list is an arbitrary interleaving of **list1** and **list2** which are lists of pairs of elements of the form **(k, v)** such that **check(k, v)** is true.

Let us also suppose that **check** has the mode declaration

mode check(key?, value⌢).

accepting a given key argument and returning a value associated with that key.

The behavior of the **merge-consumer** process is now subtly different. It still accepts a message on either input stream and passes it through to its output stream, but it also further instantiates the message as it passes through. The producer processes of the streams feeding into **merge-consumer** generate messages comprising a key **k** paired with a variable **v**. When a producer has generated such a message pair it *may* suspend waiting for the variable of the pair to be given a value. If it does, we not only have cooperating construction; we also have back communication.

3. PARLOG PROGRAMMING

3.1. Syntax and Semantics of Relation Definitions

Each Parlog procedure comprises a *single* mode declaration and a sequence of guarded clauses.

The *mode declaration* takes the form

mode R(ml, . . . ,mk).

Each **mi** of the mode declaration is '**?**' or '**⌢**', optionally preceded by an argument identifier that has no semantic significance.

A '**?**' in a mode declaration specifies that a nonvariable term **t** in that argument position in the head of a clause for **R** can only be used for input matching against the corresponding argument **a** of the call. The match succeeds only if there is a substitution **s** such that **ts** is identical to **a**.

A '**⌢**' signifies that a nonvariable term **t** in that argument position in the head of a clause can be used for output unification. This succeeds only if the call argument unifies with **t**.

A *guarded clause* is a clause of the form

R(t1, . . . ,tk) < − < guard conditions >: < body conditions >.

where the '**:**' signals the end of the guard and **t1, . . . ,tk** are argument terms.

3.1.1. *Logical Reading*

The logical reading of a guarded clause is:

For all term values of the variables of the clause,
   R(t1, . . . ,tk) is true if
   all of the guard conditions and the body conditions are true.

A relation definition is read as the conjunction of all of its clauses.

3.1.2. *Search for a Candidate Clause*

A clause **C** is a *candidate* for a call **G** if the head of **C** input matches with **G** on all input arguments and **C** has a successfully terminating guard.

The clauses for a relation are separated from one another by either a '.' or a ';' operator. These define the order in which the clauses are tried in order to find a candidate clause for some call to the relation.

All clauses in a '.' -separated group are to be tried in parallel.

A ';' indicates that the clauses following the ';' should be tried only if all of the preceding clauses are found to be non-candidate clauses.

A clause is a *non-candidate* if it fails to match the call on one of its input arguments or it has a terminating and failing guard.

If a clause is suspended in its input matching or in its guard evaluation, because it is waiting for some other process to bind a variable in the call, it is not classed as a noncandidate clause. Thus, if one of the clauses preceding a ';' is suspended, the search for a candidate clause does not move past the ';'.

In testing a clause for candidate status, the input matching and the guard evaluation proceed in parallel, but all of the output unification is deferred. In general, the first candidate clause to be found is the one that is used to solve the call. The evaluation *commits* to that clause. There is no backtracking on the choice of clause. At commitment all of the output unification is done: the terms in the output argument positions in the head of the chosen clause are unified with the corresponding arguments in the call. It is an error if the guard evaluation of a clause attempts to bind a variable of the call made accessible via an input match.

3.1.3. *Example Search Control*

A definition of the form

Clause 1;
Clause 2.
Clause 3;
Clause 4.

specifies that **Clause1** should be tried first. If it fails to input match the call or has a failing guard, then **Clause2** and **Clause3** are to be tried in parallel. Finally, if both of these clauses fail to input match or have failing guards, then **Clause4** should be tried. The later clauses are not tried if **Clause1** suspends during the test for candidate status. They are tried only when it is known that **Clause1** definitely is not a candidate clause. The final '.' has no control significance. We shall use '.' as a terminator of definitions, queries, and mode declarations.

The guard and body conditions are conjunctions of calls to single-solution relations, including primitive relations of Parlog such as the set constructors. The conjunctions are built up using either ',' or '&' as conjunction operators. The ',' is the parallel conjunction and the '&' is the sequential conjunction.

(C1, C2)

signals that the combined conjuncts **C1** and **C2** are to be evaluated in parallel.

(C1 & C2)

indicates that **C2** is to be evaluated only when the evaluation of **C1** successfully terminates

3.1.4. *Example: Program 1—List Partition*
The following program is a recursive definition of the relation

partition (pivot, list, less-list, greater-list): less-list is the subsequence of elements on **list** less than **pivot** and greater-list is the subsequence of **list** greater than or equal to **pivot**.

mode partition (pivot?, list?, less-list ˆ, greater-list ˆ)

partiton (u, [v|x1], [v|y1], z) < −v < u: partition (u, x1, y1, z).
partition (u, [v|x1], y, [v|z1]) < −u = < v: partition (u, x1, y, z1).
partitiin (u, [ ], [ ], []).

We leave the reader to check that the program is a correct and complete description of the relation under its logical reading. Remember that the Parlog convention to distinguish constants from variables is that all unquoted names beginning with a lower-case letter are variables.

3.1.5. *Imperative Interpretation*
The '.' operators mean that in trying to solve a **partition** call all clauses will be tried in parallel to find a candidate clause. The **v < u** and **u = < v** conditions are guards. The mode declaration means that the third clause is a candidate only if the second argument of the call is given and is the empty list [ ]. The first clause is a candidate only if the second argument of the call is a partial list structure (if input matches [v|x1] and u and v are sufficiently determined so that the guard can be evaluated and found to be true. Similar conditions apply to the second clause.

For this program there is never more than one candidate clause. If the second argument of the call is not yet sufficiently determined to enable the input matches with [ ] or [v|x1] to succeed, each clause is suspended waiting for some other process to supply the requisite data even if the second argument is given as a partial list structure of the form **[v|x1]**, the first and second clauses will suspend until both **u** and **v** are sufficiently determined so that the guards can be evaluated.

When the candidate clause is found, the output unification for its third and fourth arguments is performed. If it is one of the recursive clauses the **partition** call is reduced to a new **partition** call to which the same mode constraints apply. The call will therefore suspend until some other process binds the tail **x1** of the input list to the empty list **[ ]** or to a term of the form **[v1|x2]** that gives the head of this tail list.

Because only one clause can be a candidate, using the ';' operator between clauses will not affect which clause is selected. It will just limit the number of OR-processes generated during the evaluation of the program in exchange for a slightly slower selection of the candidate clause (on a parallel architecture). The ';' operator allows the Parlog programmer to make these trade-offs.

3.1.6. Example: Program 2—Quicksort
The following is a recursive definition of the relation

sort(list, sorted-list): sorted-list is an ordered permutation of **list**,

which behaves as a parallel Quicksort algorithm. The program uses the above **partition** relation and an auxiliary relation

append (list1, list2, appended-list): appended-list comprises the sequence of elements on **list1** followed by those on **list2**.

As syntactic sugar we have highlighted each variable in a clause in the position where it will be given a value. This emphasizes the "dataflow" through the shared variables. The highlighting has no semantic significance.

```
mode sort(list?, sorted-list^),
     append(list1?, list2?, appended-list^).
sort([hd|tail], sorted-list) < −
     partition (hd, tail, list1, list2),
     sort(list1, sorted-list1),
     sort(list2, sorted-list2),
     append (sorted-list1, [hd|sorted-list2], sorted-list).
sort([ ], [ ]).
append([hd|tail], list2, [hd|a tail]) < −
     append(tail, list2, atail).
append([ ], list2, list2).
```

Note that all the conditions in the body of the recursive clause for **sort** are joined by the parallel conjunction operator ','. This means that as soon as this clause is used to reduce some sort call with input argument a nonempty list (or nonempty partial list), the process evaluating the call forks into four concurrent processes. Because of the mode declarations, the variables **list1** and **list2** become one-way communication channels between the **partition** process and the two recursive **sort** processes and the variables **sorted-list1** and **sorted-list2** become one-way communication channels between the two **sort** processes and the **append** process. The first **sort** process will suspend (because of the read-only constraint on its first argument) until the **partition** process finds an element **e** on its **tail** argument less than the pivot element **hd**. At that point, this recursive **sort** process itself forks into four processes with their own local communication channels and **e** as its pivot element. Similarly, the second **sort** process forks into four processes as soon as the **partition** process has found an element on **tail** greater than or equal to **hd**.

The **append** process is constrained by the supply of the stream of elements on the channel **sorted-list1**. As and when they are sent from the first **sort** process, it passes them through to the output stream **sorted-list**. When the **append** process terminates on reaching the end of the **sorted-list1** input stream, its output stream **sorted-list** is identified with append's second input argument **[hd|sorted-list2]** via the output unification of the second **append** clause. This has the effect of immediately placing all elements that have already been generated by the second **sort** process onto **sorted-list**. Any further elements put onto **sorted-list2** by this process are then put directly onto **sorted-list**.

3.2. Constraining the Parallelism

As with the **partition** program, the OR-parallel search for a candidate clause for each **sort** and **append** call can be replaced by a sequential search by using ';' operators between the clauses. Again, this will not affect the choice of the candidate clause since there is always only one candidate for any **sort** or **append** call in the declared modes.

The degree of forking of each **sort** process can usefully be constrained by using '**&**' operators. If we write the recursive clause as

```
sort([[hd|tail]], sorted-list) < −
    partition (hd, tail, list1, list2) &
    (sort(list1, sorted-list1), sort(list2, sorted-list2)) &
    append(sorted-list1, [hd|sorted-list 2], sorted-list).
```

the **sort** process does not immediately fork. The '**&**' following the **partition** call means that this process must terminate before there is a fork into two concurrent recursive **sort** processes. Finally, the '**&**' after the parallel conjunction means that the **append** process will only start when the recursive **sort** processes have both terminated. This yields a "fork and join" control. The join before the **append** means that elements on the **sorted-list** output are not passed through as soon as they are produced by the recursive processes. They are only piped through to **sorted-list** when both processes have terminated.

All parallelism can be removed by using ';' operators between clauses, and only the '&' operator between the calls of the recursive clause. The evaluation of a **sort** call will then be the same as in Prolog.

3.3. Back Communication

3.3.1. *Example: Program 3—Find and Retrieve*

The following program defines the relation

find-retrieve (pair, list-of-pairs): pair is of the form **(key, value)** and it is a member of **list-of-pairs**, which are ordered by their **key**.

mode find-retrieve (pair?, list-of-pairs?).

find-retrieve ((key, value), [(key, value1)|rem-list]) < −
  value = **value1.**
find-retrieve((key, value), [(key1, value1)|rem-list]]) < −
  key1 < key:
  find-retrieve ((key, value), rem-list).

We leave the reader to check that the clauses are true statements about the intended meaning of **find-retrieve**. Remember that '=' is read as a normal equality.

Although the program defines a list membership relation, its use is to retrieve a value for a given key. It will cooperate with some other process to construct a **(key, value)** pair that is on the list. The other process must generate the pair structure because the **find-retrieve** program performs an input match on its first argument, so the first argument must be a term of the form **(key, value)**. That process must also generate a nonvariable value for the **key** variable of this pair because this must be compared, in the input matching of the first clause and in the guard of the second clause, with the key of the first pair on the second argument, **list-of-pairs**. Notice that neither the input matching nor the guard requires the **value** variable of the input term **(key, value)** to be instantiated.

In fact, in normal use, the **value** variable of the input pair will *not* be given a value by the other process: it will be bound by the **find-retrieve** process when it finds the given key on its list of pairs. When it finds the key, the first clause becomes a candidate clause. The single body call of this clause is a unification **value = value1** that binds the variable **value** (if unbound) to the **value1** associated with the given key.

The explicit use of the unification '=' is essential. If we were to replace the first clause by

find-retrieve ((key, value), [(key, value)|rem-list]).

then both the search **key** and its associated **value** would have to be given in any call to the program. This is because the repeated use of a variable within the input argument terms of a clause is understood by Parlog as an implicit test that the values passed to the clause in these argument positions are identical. The use of the clause is not allowed to make them identical by binding variables.

4. METALEVEL PROGRAMMING IN Parlog

4.1. The Control Metacall Primitive

The metacall primitive of Parlog is a three-argument relation: **call (goal?, status ^, control?)**.

The first argument, **goal**, is a term denoting a call to a relation to be evaluated by the metacall. If this evaluation succeeds, the metacall will succeed with **status** bound to the constant **SUCCEEDED**. Output bindings to variables of **goal** are made in the same way as they would be if **goal** were being evaluated as a normal call. So they may be incrementally constructed, with the partially constructed terms communicated to another AND-parallel calls in the normal way.

The difference between the control and an ordinary call is the handling of the failure of **goal**. If the evaluation of **goal** fails, the metacall will still *succeed*, but with **status** bound to the constant **FAILED**. Any partially constructed output bindings for variables of **goal** generated by the evaluation up to the point of failure remain as bindings for these variables. This contrasts with the failure of an ordinary call, which causes failure of the guard from which the call was invoked, or the failure of the entire top-level process if it was part of that evaluation. The metacall is used precisely to avoid such a global failure of the computation.

The third argument will normally be an uninstantiated variable at the time of the call. If it is bound to the term **STOP** by another process, the evaluation of **goal** will be terminated with **status** bound to **STOPPED**. More generally, the **control** variable can be incrementally bound to a stream of control messages of the form

[SUSPEND, CONTINUE, SUSPEND, CONTINUE, . . . |STOP]

When the first **SUSPEND** message is sent, evaluation of the metacall is suspended and the **status** output variable is bound to

[SUSPEND|status1]

and when the **CONTINUE** is sent, **status1** is bound to

[CONTINUE|status2]

and so on. Thus, when the **control** is a stream of messages, the **status** report is also a stream of messages of the form

[SUSPEND, CONTINUE, SUSPEND, CONTINUE, . . . |result]

where the final **result** is **SUCCEEDED**, **FAILED** or **STOPPED**.

4.1.1. *Logical Reading*

Because the metacall always succeeds, the condition

call(goal, status, control)

is not logically equivalent to the condition

goal

Instead, it has the metalogical reading

call(goal, status, control):
either **status** is a message stream of the form
        [SUSPEND, CONTINUE, . . . |SUCCEEDED]
   and **control** is a message stream of the form
        [SUSPEND, CONTINUE, . . .]
   and **goal** is true
or **status** is a message stream of the form
        [SUSPEND, CONTINUE, . . . |FAILED]
   and **control** is a message stream of the form
        [SUSPEND, CONTINUE, . . .]
   and **goal** is false
or **status** is a message stream of the form
        [SUSPEND, CONTINUE, . . .|STOPPED]
   and **control** is a message stream of the form
        [SUSPEND, CONTINUE, . . . |STOP]
   and **goal** is true or false

The evaluation of **call(goal, status, control)** generates bindings for **status** and the variables of **goal** for which this metastatement holds.

4.1.2. *The Simple Metacall*

The general metacall primitive subsumes the simple single-argument form familiar to Prolog programmers. This evaluates its single argument **goal** and succeeds or fails depending on the evaluation of **goal**. It can be defined by the program

mode call(goal?).

call(goal) < −

call(goal, status, **control)** & status = SUCCEEDED.

During the evaluation of **call(goal)**, bindings to variables in **goal** are made public immediately. However, because of the added test **status** = SUCCEEDED, the call will succeed only if the evaluation of **goal** succeeds.

call(goal)

is logically and behaviorally equivalent to

goal

We can define a two-argument metacall that has the **status** output argument but lacks the **control** input. Like the three-argument form, it always succeeds, and bindings to variables in **goal** are made public as soon as they are made public by the program for **goal**.

mode call(?, ^).

call(goal, **status**) < −
    call(**goal**, status, **control**).

4.2. Defining Negation as failure

As in Prolog, negation as failure can be defined in Parlog by a metalogical program. The definition that is analogous to the Prolog defnition is

mode ˜ goal?.
˜ goal < −
    call(goal):**FAIL**;
˜ goal.

FAIL is a Parlog primitive that always fails. This form of negation as failure is given a logical justification in [2]. The justification requires that a successful evaluation of **goal** does not generate any bindings for its variables. This condition cannot be guaranteed in Prolog, but in Parlog we can use mode declarations to ensure that **goal** is a test-only evaluation. Then, the argument in [2] can be modified to justify the use of this negation as failure operator in Parlog.

4.3. Defining Sequential "and"

The sequential "and" ('**&**') can also be defined by a metalogical program. The conjunction **a & b** is evaluated by executing a call to **a** in parallel with a process which is input-suspended awaiting the result of **a**. If the result of **a** is SUCCEEDED, the second call **b** is called; otherwise the conjunction fails.

mode cond1? & cond2?, nextcall(status?,call?).

a & b < −
    call(a, status), **nextcall**(status, b).

nextcall(SUCCEEDED, b) < −
    call(b).

This means that sequential evaluation of calls need not be a primitive control facility of a Parlog implementation.

We can similarly dispense with sequential search for a candidate clause, and implement this using the metacall primitive. The details are given in [6].

4.4. Implementing a Unix-Like Shell

The control metacall primitive is an ideal tool for implementing a Unix-style operating system for a Parlog system in Parlog. We can define a shell program that accepts a stream of commands to initiate the evaluation of Parlog programs as foreground or background processes and to suspend, resume, or prematurely terminate background processes. The methods of programming such a shell are presented in [5], where the Parlog programs are also compared with similar Concurrent Prolog programs presented in [37]. Here, we give one simple example to illustrate the approach.

The example is a very elementary shell program that handles a stream of commands to run foreground and background processes. The following program for **shell(cmds?)** behaves as a process that consumes the stream of user commands **cmds** and invokes each as an auxiliary process using the **call** metacall. The commands are denoted by terms of the form **FG(proc)** (foreground) or **BG(proc)** (background), where **proc** is the Parlog call to be evaluated as the user process.

mode shell(cmds?).

```
shell([BG(proc)|cmds]) < −
     call(proc, status), shell(cmds).
shell([FG(proc)|cmds]) < −
     call(proc, status) & shell(cmds).
shell([]).
```

The first clause terminates the shell evaluation when the command stream is terminated. The second deals with a background command **BG(proc)** by invoking **proc** concurrently with the recursive **shell** invocation to process the next command. The third clause is similar but handles foreground commands. It waits for the command process to terminate successfully before recursing to accept the next command. This is because of the use of the sequential "and" ('&') in place of the parallel "and" (',').

Notice that, because of the use of the two-argument form of the metacall, the shell is protected from failure of a user process. If we had used the single-argument metacall, the shell would fail on failure of a user process.

5. CONCLUDING REMARKS

5.1. A Brief History of Parlog

As mentioned in the introduction, Parlog is a development of earlier work on IC-Prolog [8] and the Relational Language [3].

IC-Prolog began as an attempt to emulate in logic programming the corouting ideas of lazy Lisp [13, 20] and Kahn and MacQueen's extension to parallel evaluation [23]. In IC-Prolog, the equivalent of **data** and **var** tests were expressed by annotations on terms in clause heads, while producer-consumer communication was specified by annotations on variables in clause bodies. The use of annotations was inspired largely by the work of Schwarz [35].

IC-Prolog also featured guards, but their role was simply to delay communication; they did not have the effect of commitment. This meant that the implementation of pseudoparallel evaluation of calls had to provide for backtracking and undoing variable bindings on failure. The implementation of this was crude: on the failure of a process, all evaluation steps that took place after the choice point of the failed process were undone, even evaluation steps of other processes. It proved impossible to efficiently implement a more selective backtracking scheme.

IC-Prolog was quite well suited to problem-solving applications of logic programming [25], as was the similar experimental-logic programming language of [19]. In both of these, one could implement such algorithms as the sieve of Eratosthenes primes generator that require some form of nonsequential evaluation. However, we were dissatisfied with the overhead associated with process failure. Moreover, the global backtracking scheme appeared to be viable only in a single-processor implementation. For an efficient parallel implementation, the failure independence of processes seemed to be essential.

The desired property was attained by strengthening the role of guards so that they also had the effect of commitment, as in Dijkstra's guarded commands [11] and Hoare's CSP [21]. Our Relational Language incorporated this idea and also introduced more declarations as the means of imposing communication constraints on processes.

The communication constraints of the Relational Language were actually very strong. The language was designed to allow efficient implementation on a loosely coupled distributed architecture, so messages passed between processes were restricted to variable-free terms. The communication was unidirectional.

The major difference between Parlog and the Relational Language is the relaxation of the communication constraints to allow the cooperating construction of bindings of shared variables. We made this change when we started to explore the implementation of the Relational Language on the tightly coupled ALICE architecture [10], in which processes share a global memory of packets.

This change also prompted by a programming need, when we attempted to write a compiler for the Relational Language in itself. As shown by Warren [39], the use of the logical variable makes Prolog an elegant language for compiler writing; we wanted to use the same techniques in a parallel context. We were further convinced of the need to relax the communication constraints when the elegant use of two-way communication was demonstrated by Concurrent Prolog [36]. The language resulting from this change was named Parlog.

5.2. Implementations of Parlog

The first implementation of the language described in this paper is one that runs on top of a Prolog system [14]. This compiles Parlog programs to Prolog clauses and simulates AND-parallel evaluation by a breadth-first or depth-first scheduling strategy. Sequential Parlog programs can be run at a speed of up to 20% of that of the host Prolog implementation.

We have investigated the implementation of Parlog on abstract instruction sets designed for Prolog; in [15] we consider the suitability of McCabe's Abstract Prolog Machine [30] for this purpose. The same techniques have since adapted to Warren's abstract Prolog instruction set [40] by Moens and Yu [33].

Current implementation efforts are directed toward both parallel and conventional sequential machines. A fast, portable implementation of Parlog (in C) has been developed. This is centered on an abstract instruction set, the Sequential Parlog Machine [17], which is loosely based on Warren's Prolog machine [40], but was designed especially for the sequential implementation of Parlog. The SPM Parlog system is obtained from: The Secretary, Parlog Group, Department of Computing, Imperial College of Science and Technology, 180 Queen's Gate, London SW7 2BZ, England. Work has begun to extend this instruction set to multiprocessor operation.

Following a pilot implementation of Parlog on the parallel machine ALICE [10] in 1982, both Parlog and ALICE have developed substantially. Work has begun on a new compiler from Parlog to ALICE CTL (Compiler Target Language) [34], in association with the Alvey "Flagship" project. The principles of this compilation are explained in [16] and [27].

5.3. Applications of Parlog

The use of Parlog as a systems programming language was investigated in [5] and [12].

Parlog is an ideal language for programming runnable specifications of parallel systems. A specification written in Parlog can be evaluated in several different ways. By running it in the normal manner, the specified system is *simulated* and so exhibits a single evaluation history. The simulation can be controlled by discrete event-driven time, as considered in [1]. Alternatively, by combining Parlog with a backtracking facility, more than one of the possible nondeterministic evaluation histories can be obtained. This allows a user to *browse* through several possible evaluations to explore the behavior or to obtain all possible histories in order to *verify* that the specification satisfies certain properties. These topics are treated in [18].

Natural language processing is another application area for Parlog. Matsumoto [29] has rewritten a bottom-up parser, originally written in Prolog, as a parlog program. His original logic program is evaluated with a form of OR-parallelism, to explore alternative candidate parsings of a natural language sentence. This is achieved by a transformation into an AND-parallel Parlog program.

5.4. Related Work

5.4.1. *Concurrent Prolog*

Although Concurrent Prolog [36] and the single-solution component of Parlog have a great deal of common—both use guarded clauses, committed choice nondeterminism, and the ability to have variables in messages—there remain significant differences. The major difference is in the way the interprocess communication constraints are expressed. Mode declarations determine the communication constraints on Parlog processes. A clause invoked by a process can only perform read-only matches with terms in the input argument positions for its declared mode of use, and it is suspended if this constraint is not satisfied.

In Concurrent Prolog, programs do not have fixed modes of use. Read-only annotations on variables provide the communication constraint. For example, a read-only constraint on the use of some nonvariable term t in the head of a clause is usually specified by a read-only annotation which is placed on the corresponding variable in the call to the relation. A read-only annotated variable cannot be bound to a nonvariable. A different call to the relation might not have a read-only annotated variable in that argument position so the term t can then be used for output. That is, the mode of use is determined by the call.

The declared modes enable a Parlog compiler to check that no clause guard binds variables in the call (this was also illustrated in Section 2). In Concurrent Prolog this cannot be guaranteed, so that environments must be copied for each clause that is being tried to solve the call [28, 32]. In general, the copying of environments can be very complex and expensive, and is one reason why implementation of Concurrent Prolog is limited to the simpler variant, Flat Concurrent Prolog [31].

5.4.2. *Guarded Horn Clauses*

Another parallel logic programming language, Guarded Horn Clauses (GHC), has been designed by Ueda [38]. This is rather similar to Parlog in that there is no need to copy environments. The language uses a different communication constraint: a guard must not bind variables belonging to the environment of the invoking call; if it tries to make such a binding, the clause suspends. This constraint is essentially the same as the "safe guards" property of Parlog. A difference is that, in Parlog, an error occurs if it is not satisfied (rather than a suspension).

In general, GHC appears to require, each time a variable is to be bound, a run-time suspension test that determines whether a variable is global or local to a guard evaluation. This might prove to present a considerable constraint on the target architecture. This is not required in Parlog because of the insistence that a program pass a *compile-time* safety check. The run-time suspension test in Parlog is much simpler: it simply tests whether a variable is bound. For this reason, current implementation efforts at ICOT are limited to a simpler subset of GHC: Flat GHC.

ACKNOWLEDGMENTS

We are grateful to all the people who have read and commented on an earlier version of this paper.

REFERENCES

1. K. Broda and S. Gregory, "PARLOG for Discrete Event Simulation," *Proc. 2nd Int'l Logic Programming Conference*, Uppsala, Sweden, July 1984, pp. 301–312.
2. K. L. Clark, "Negation as Failure." In H. Gallaire and J. Minker (eds.), *Logic and Databases*. New York: Plenum Press, 1978.
3. K. L., Clark and S. Gregory, "A Relational Language for Parallel Programming." *Proc. 1981 ACM Conf. on Functional Programming Languages and Computer Architecture*, Portsmouth, NH, Oct. 1981, pp. 171–178.
4. K. L. Clark and S. Gregory, "PARLOG: Parallel Programming in Logic," *ACM Trans. on Programming Languages and Systems*, 8(1):1–49, 1986.
5. K. L., Clark and S. Gregory, "Notes on Systems Programming in PARLOG," *Proc. Int'l Conf. on Fifth Generation Computer Systems*, Tokyo, Japan, Nov. 1984, pp. 299–306.
6. K. L., Clark and S. Gregory, "Notes on the Implementation of PARLOG," *J. of Logic Programming* 2 (1):17–42, 1985.
7. K. L. Clark and F. G. McCabe, "*Micro-PROLOG: Programming in Logic*," Englewood Cliffs, Prentice-Hall, NJ: 1984.
8. K. L., Clark, F. G., McCabe, and S. Gregory, "IC-PROLOG Language features," in K. Clark and S-A. Tarnlund (eds.), *Logic Programming*. London: Academic Press, 1982, pp. 253–266.
9. W. F. Clocksin and C. Mellish, *Programming in Prolog*. New York: Springer-Verlag, 1981.
10. J. Darlington and M. J. Reeve, "ALICE: A Multi-Processor Reduction Machine." *Proc. 1981 ACM Conf. on Functional Programming Languages and Computer Architecture*, Portsmouth, NH, Oct. 1981, pp. 65–75.
11. E. W. Dijkstra, *A Discipline of Programming*. Englewood Cliffs, NJ: Prentice-Hall, 1976.
12. I. T., Foster, "Logic Operating Systems: Design Issues." *Proc. 4th International Logic Programming Conf.*, Melbourne, Australia, May 1987.
13. D. P. Friedman and D. S. Wise, "CONS Should Not Evaluate Its Arguments," In *Proc. 3rd Int'l Colloquium on Automata, Languages and Programming*. Edinburgh: Edinburgh University Press, 1976.
14. S. Gregory, "How to Use PARLOG." Unpublished report, Department of Computing, Imperial College, London, England, Aug. 1984.
15. S. Gregory, *Implementing PARLOG on the Abstract PROLOG Machine*. Research Rep. DOC 84/23, Department of Computing, Imperial College, London, England, Aug. 1984.
16. S. Gregory, *Parallel Logic Programming in PARLOG*. Reading, MA: Addison-Wesley, 1987.
17. S. Gregory, I. T. Foster, A. D. Burt, and G. A. Ringwood, *An Abstract Machine for the Implementation of PARLOG on Uniprocessors*. Research rep., Department of Computing, Imperial College, London, England, Jan. 1987.
18. S. Gregory, R. Neely, and G. A. Ringwood, "PARLOG for Specification, Verification and Simulation." *Proc. 7th Int'l Symp. on Computer Hardware Description Languages and Their Applications*, Tokyo, Japan, Aug. 1985, pp. 139–148.
19. A. Hansson, S. Haridi, and S-A. Tarnlund, "Properties of a Logic Programming Language." In K. L. Clark and S-A. Tarnlund (eds.): *Logic Programming*, London: Academic Press, 1982, pp. 267–280.
20. P. Henderson and J. H. Morris, "A Lazy Evaluator," *Proc. 3rd ACM Symp. on Principles of Programming Languages*, Jan. 1976, pp. 95–103.
21. C. A. R. Hoare, "Communicating Sequential Processes." *Comm. of the ACM*, 21(8): 666–677, 1978.
22. C. J. Hogger, *Introduction to Logic Programming*. London: Academic Press, 1984.

23. G. Kahn and D. B. MacQueen, "Coroutines and Networks of Parallel Processes," *Proc. of the IFIP Congress*, 77:993–998, 1977.
24. R. A. Kowalski, "Predicate Logic as Programming Language." *Proc. of the IFIP Congress*, 74: 569–574, 1974.
25. R. A. Kowalski, *Logic for Problem Solving*. New York: North Holland, 1979.
26. R. A. Kowalski, "Logic Programming," *Proc. IFIP Congress*, 83:133–145, 1983.
27. A. Lam, M. Y. C. and S. Gregory, "PARLOG and ALICE: A Marriage of Convenience," *Proc. of the 4th Int'l Logic Programming Con.*, Melbourne, Australia, May 1987.
28. J. Levy, "A Unification Algorithm for Concurrent Prolog," *Proc. 2nd Int'l Logic Programming Conference*, Uppsala, Sweden, July 1984, pp. 333–341.
29. Y. Matsumoto, "A Parallel Parsing System for Natural Language Analysis," *Proc. 3rd Int'l Logic Programming Conference*, London, England, July 1986.
30. F. G. McCabe, *Abstract PROLOG Machine—A Specification*. Research Report DOC 83/12, Department of Computing, Imperial College, London, England, June 1984.
31. C. Mierowsky, *Design and Implementation of Flat Concurrent Prolog*. M.Sc. thesis, Department of Applied Mathematics, Weizmann Institute of Science, Rehovot, Israel, Nov. 1984.
32. T. Miyazaki, A. Takeuchi, and T. Chikayama, "A Sequential Implementation of Concurrent Prolog Based on the Shallow Binding Scheme," *Proc. IEEE Symposium on Logic Programming*, Boston, MA, July 1985, pp. 110–118.
33. E. Moens and B. Yu, *Implementation of PARLOG on the Warren Machine*, Tech. Rep., Department of Computer Science, University of British Columbia, Vancouver, Canada 1985.
34. M. J. Reeve, "A BNF Description of the ALICE Compiler Target Language." Unpublished report, Department of Computing, Imperial College, London, England, March 1985.
35. J. Schwarz, *Using Annotations To Make Recursion Equations Behave*. Research rep. 43, Department of Artificial Intelligence, University of Edinburgh, Edinburgh, Scotland, 1977.
36. E. Y. Shapiro, *A Subset of Concurrent Prolog and Its Interpreter*. Tech. Rep. TR-003, ICOT, Tokyo, Japan, Feb. 1983.
37. E. Y. Shapiro, "Systems Programming in Concurrent Prolog," *Proc. 11th ACM Symp. on Principles of Programming Languages*, Salt Lake City, UT, Jan. 1984.
38. K. Ueda, *Guarded Horn Clauses*. Tech. Rep. TR-103, ICOT, Tokyo, Japan, June 1985.
39. D. H. D. Warren, "Logic Programming and Compiler Writing," *Software—Practice and Experience*, 10:97–125, 1980.
40. D. H. D. Warren, "An Abstract Prolog Instruction Set." Technical Note 309, SRI International, Menlo Park, CA, Oct. 1983.

7. DATA-DRIVEN PROCESSING OF SEMANTIC NETS

LUBOMIR BIC

1. INTRODUCTION

The use of semantic nets is a well-known approach to knowledge representation in Artificial Intelligence (AI). Even though there is not a precise, universally accepted definition of semantic nets, their common characteristics and advantages have been discussed extensively in the literature [1–3]. A semantic net consists of a collection of nodes interconnected by edges. Each node represents an object (physical object, set, relationship, event, logical entity) and each edge represents a binary relation. Usually, there is a finite set of such relations, e.g., "subset of," "element of," "agent," "consequence," etc.

The main attraction of semantic nets largely centers around two factors. First, they provide sufficient expressive power to encode facts or concepts that are encodable in any other formal system. Second, the structures constituting a net serve themselves as a guide for information retrieval: information most closely related to a node is found simply by following edges incident on that node.

There are two major problems with implementing systems based on semantic nets. The first is *efficiency* in implementation. Many operations require the examination of a significant portion of the nodes and links to derive an answer. For example, finding the set of objects with a certain property may require the examination of all nodes in a given set. Similarly, finding objects that lie in the intersection or union of two sets may require the traversal of many edges in

This work was supported by the NSF Grant DCR-8503589: The UCI Dataflow Databases Project.

the net. If such operations are performed sequentially by a single processor, the processing time grows linearly with the given problem size. Fortunately, many operations on semantic nets lend themselves well to parallel processing and, as a result, a number of special-purpose architectures have been designed for such applications. In this chapter, we describe an approach based on *data-driven* computation, which permits potentially very large numbers of asynchronous processing elements to cooperate in solving a given problem [4].

The second major deficiency of semantic nets has to do with *operations* performed on semantic nets. Most systems define only the meaning of nodes and edges constituting a semantic net, i.e., the *information* represented by that net. However, no precise definition of the rules or procedures governing the retrieval and modification of this information is usually given. The system typically assumes the existence of some *outside* agent—a program—that embodies the knowledge about how to interpret and use that information. To illustrate this problem, consider the rule of *property inheritance*, used in most semantic nets to reduce the amount of information stored with each node in a hierarchy. This rule states that a property associated with a given node in a hierarchy applies not only to that node itself but is inherited by all its descendants. In most implementations, the inheritance property is not recorded as part of the semantic net; instead, it is incorporated in the programs that use and manipulate the net. Since many other such rules are typically hidden in the interpreter, it is difficult for any user (other than perhaps the system's developer) to fully understand the functioning of the system and to assess its potential.

To alleviate this problem, it is necessary to devise some rigid formalism capable of describing not only the semantic net itself but also the operations that can be applied to extract information from or to modify the net. We have chosen a restricted form of *logic programming* for this purpose.

In the course of this chapter, we shall demonstrate how the virtues of the three fundamental concepts—semantic networks, logic programming, and data-driven computation—may be integrated into a knowledge-processing system capable of exploiting the potential of a highly parallel computer architecture.

1.1. Dataflow Systems and Semantic Nets

The importance of parallelism in solving AI problems has been recognized in recent years, and, as a result, efforts are being made to construct highly parallel computer architectures tailored specifically to AI applications. For an extensive literature survey the reader is referred to [5]. The main problem common to many such approaches is the lack of a suitable *model of computation* capable of exploiting the potential of a large number of processing elements. Many novel architectures claiming applicability to AI problems are based on the conventional von Neumann model of computation, which uses the concept of a program counter to control the order of instruction fetch and execution. Using this model, it is very difficult to divide computation into independent subtasks and to synchronize their progress. Only if the problem to be solved has a highly regular nature, for example, the application of a local averaging function to a digitized image, will it be possible to effectively use any significant number of processing elements. If, on the other hand, an architecture for the support of a wider range of problems is sought, it is essential that a suitable non–von Neumann *model* of computation is defined *first*. Only then should architectural requirements be analyzed and the design of a possible architecture to support that model be attempted.

The computational model proposed for the processing of semantic nets is based on the concept of dataflow, pioneered in the early 1970s by Jack Dennis [6], followed by a number of other researchers. This model abandons the sequential fetch/execute cycle of the von Neumann model by permitting asynchronous data-driven computation. A dataflow program is a directed graph consisting of operators interconnected by edges. Operand values are propagated along edges in the form of messages (also called tokens). Each operator will execute when and only when all its operands have arrived via the corresponding input edges; at that point, the operand messages are absorbed by the operator and output messages are created and placed on outgoing edges. Since each operator may potentially be mapped onto a distinct physical processing element, a high degree of parallelism is achieved.

The most important features of dataflow systems are the lack of (1) centralized *control*, and (2) centralized *memory*.

The lack of centralized control results from the fact that instructions or other atomic units of computation are triggered solely by the arrival of messages. Each node in the dataflow graph may actually be viewed as a logical processing element, communicating with other such processing elements via messages. The lack of centralized memory, on the other hand, results from the fact that data are not stored and accessed by operators but rather 'flow' along the edges of the dataflow graph.

The two characteristics are essential in exploiting massive parallelism at the architecture level. Each operator could conceptually be mapped onto a separate physical processing element. This is because synchronization of individual operations—a major problem in conventional systems—is accomplished implicitly through the exchange of messages. The lack of centralized memory then eliminates the problem of contention when fetching instructions and data.

The concept of dataflow is normally associated with high-speed numeric computation. The same principles, however, can be applied to exploiting high degrees of parallelism in symbolic computation. In this chapter, we describe a model of computation that does not view a semantic net simply as a passive data structure stored in memory and manipulated by a program. Instead, all computational power is incorporated into the nodes of the net itself. That is, the semantic net is not merely a *passive* representation of data; rather, it is a *dataflow graph* in that each node of the graph is an *active* component, capable of receiving, processing, and emitting messages traveling asynchronously along the graph edges.

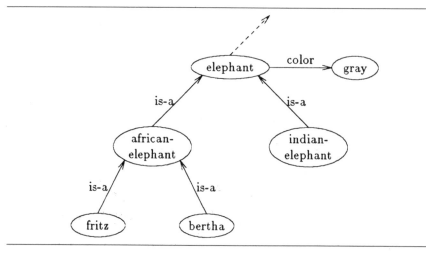

Figure 7–1. Simple semantic net.

Messages are the carriers of data (both intermediate values, exchanged among network nodes, and final results, returned to the user), as well as query information carried from the user into the net. Each given query is transformed into a collection of messages which are injected into the semantic net. According to well-defined rules, messages propagate through the net until the nodes satisfying the given query are located and their contents extracted from the net.

To illustrate these principles, consider the semantic net of Figure 7–1 which shows a portion of a "is-a" hierarchy. It divides *elephants* into *african* and *indian elephants* and includes two instances of the former—*fritz* and *bertha*. A property called *color* is associated with the node *elephant*; it carries the value *gray*. Assuming that the principles of property inheritance hold in this net, the *color gray* applies not only to the *elephant* node itself but to all nodes lower in the hierarchy, i.e., all elephants, including *fritz* and *bertha*, are gray. (We apologize to white elephants for this simplification.)

Inherited properties must be determined explicitly during execution. For example, it may be necessary to determine *fritz's color*. To accomplished that, a message carrying the necessary information for this query is injected into the node *fritz*, which checks if *color* is attached to it as a local property. If this is the case, the corresponding value is extracted; otherwise, the message is propagated along the *is-a* edge to the parent of *fritz*. This node, *african-elephant*, repeats the same check for the property *color* and, if unsuccessful, propagates the message to the next higher node in the hierarchy. Eventually, the desired property is found, or the root of the hierarchy is reached, indicating that the property does not apply to *fritz*.

On the surface, the above scheme resembles the marker propagation approach to processing of semantic nets proposed by Fahlman in NETL [7]. The two approaches, however, are significantly different. In NETL, waves of marker bits are pushed through the network in lock step under the supervision of a centralized controller. In the case of dataflow, each message carries sufficient information to permit any node receiving that message to determine how to process it and where to send it next. Hence, there is no need for any centralized control. In the above example, the message injected into *fritz* would carry the information that each receiving node should check locally for the property *color* and, if unsuccessful, propagate the message to its parent in the *is-a* hierarchy. In the next section we present a formalism, which permits us express such information in a systematic manner for a variety of possible queries to be processed against a semantic net.

1.2. Logic Programming and Semantic Nets

As explained above, we can search semantic nets using asynchronous messages propagated among the graph nodes. Thus, by designing an architecture supporting this type of processing, we can solve the performance problem pointed out earlier. We need, however, some well-defined formalism to conveniently express the operations (queries) to be performed on a given semantic net. In particular, we need to specify what information is to be carried by messages when they are injected into the net and what procedures are executed by nodes when receiving a message.

We have chosen a subset of predicate logic for this purpose. The main attraction of logic is that it permits different types of information, including facts, deductive rules, meta-information, as well as queries to be expressed in a uniform way [8, 9]. This implies that a single scheme can serve both as a language for representing knowledge and as a practical high-level query language, thus erasing the distinction between "knowledge (data) base" and "program."

Another important virtue of logic programming is that no rigid order of instruction execution is prescribed. Typically, there are many possible branches of computation that may be pursued at any given point. This makes logic programming inherently well suited to implementation on a highly parallel architecture.

A logic program is a set of *Horn clauses* of the form

$$p_0 := p_1, \ldots, p_n.$$

Each p_i is called a *literal* and has the form $p(t_1, \ldots, t_m)$, where p is a *predicate* symbol and $t_1, \ldots, t_m$ are *terms*. Terms may be constants, variables, or functors which are expressions of the form $f(t_1, \ldots, t_k)$, where f is a function symbol and $t_1, \ldots, t_k$ are terms. Terms containing no variables will be referred to as *ground terms*. Similarly, clauses containing no variables will be called *ground clauses*. The literal p_0 is called the *head* or *conclusion*, and p_1 through p_n form the *body* or *conditions* of the clause. A clause with an empty set of conditions is called an *assertion* and is used to represent explicit facts. A clause that contains both a head

---

```
(1) is-a(african-elephant, elephant).
(2) is-a(indian-elephant, elephant).
(3) is-a(fritz, african-elephant).
(4) is-a(bertha, african-elephant).
(5) color(elephant, gray).
(6) property(X, Y) :- color(X, Y).
(7) inherited-prop(X, Y) :- property(X, Y).
(8) inherited-prop(X, Y) :- is-a(X, Z), inherited-prop(Z, Y).
(9) :- inherited-prop(fritz, gray).
```

Figure 7-2. Sample logic program.

and a body can be interpreted as a *rule* that records *implicit* information. A clause with an empty conclusion is interpreted as a *query*, which the system tries to solve by unifying it with the head of some other clause.

Figure 7–2 shows a sample logic program. As is common in logic programming, identifiers beginning with a lower-case denote constants whereas those beginning with a capital denote free variables. The first five lines are assertions, recording the same information as the semantic net of Figure 7–1. Line 6 is a rule that states that *color* Y of a node X is a *property* of that node. Other possible properties could be defined in a similar manner. Lines 7 and 8 are rules defining the principle of property inheritance: An inherited property, Y, of an object X is either a local property of that object (line 7) or it is a property of an object, Z, found by following the *is-a* edge from the node X (line 8). Line 9 then shows a query, interpreted as "is *gray* an *inherited-property* of *fritz*?"

Deliyanni and Kowalski [10] demonstrated a strong relationship between semantic nets and logic programming. They proposed an *extended* form of semantic nets that permits the recording of deductive information as part of the net itself, rather than keeping it hidden in the programs that use and manipulate the net. A typical example that illustrates this type of information is the relationship "grand-parent"; instead of recording such a relationship explicitly for any two qualifying individuals, it may be recorded only once as a definition: x is the grandparent of y if there exists an individual, z, such that x is the parent of z and z is the parent of y. Assuming that the individual "parent" relationships are recorded explicitly in the knowledge base, a "grandparent" relationship may be deduced dynamically when needed. Similarly, the concept of property inheritance could be stated explicitly as part of the semantic net, rather than hiding it in the manipulation programs. Thus it could be added to or removed from the knowledge base as any other item of information, without having to change the basic interpreter.

The extended semantic nets have been shown to map onto a *subset* of logic programming defined by the following restrictions:

1. All predicates are binary, i.e., of the form $p(t_1, t_2)$. This restriction is not serious for two reasons. First, if knowledge is represented in the form of networks, the use of binary predicates is natural to the user, because each edge in the network represents a binary relationship between two nodes. Second, it has been shown that an n-ary predicate may be transformed into $n+1$ binary predicates with the addition of a new constant [10].
2. Terms may only be constants, variables, or immediately evaluable functions; they may not be structured. Within the context of semantic networks, terms need not be structured because they correspond to nodes. Although functional terms do occur in semantic networks, they are usually limited to simple arithmetic or logical operations applied to a given node or its immediate vicinity. They are immediately evaluable if their arguments are constants or bound variables.

1.3. Semantic Nets, Logic Programming, and Dataflow

As mentioned earlier, the approach described in this chapter attempts to integrate the virtues of semantic networks, logic programming, and data-driven computation. We consider a subset of logic programming, such that any program can be transformed into a semantic network form, similar to that of Deliyanni and Kowalski. For this subset we define a data-driven interpreter that permits the semantic nets to be processed in a highly parallel manner. This model is based on the principles of dataflow: each node of the semantic net is capable of communicating with other nodes via messages traveling asynchronously along the network edges. Extracting information from such an active network is then accomplished by an asynchronous propagation of messages. Queries are placed on one or more messages that are injected into specific nodes of the network. Each message is replicated into all possible directions, thus searching for data that satisfy the given query. The propagation of messages is governed by the rules of the logic program. In the next section we will elaborate on the basic principles of the model outlined above. More detail may be found in [11–13].

2. A DATA-DRIVEN MODEL OF COMPUTATION

2.1. Describing Semantic Nets as Logic Programs

A literal consists of a predicate name and a sequence of arguments. In the restricted form, all predicates are binary, and thus a given literal $e(v_1, v_2)$ may be transformed into a directed edge of the form:

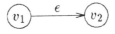

The arrowhead records the order in which the terms of the literal were given. This information must be preserved when the literal represents an asymmetric relation. As will be discussed later, the arrowheads do not prescribe the direction in which messages may flow through the network.

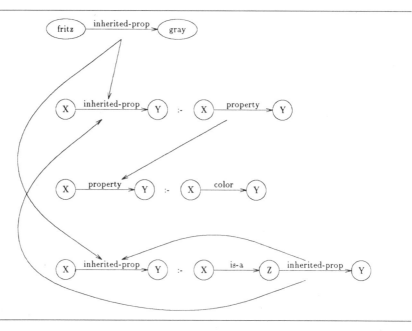

Figure 7–3. Goal structure of sample program.

Literals sharing the same term result in edges connected to one another via the corresponding node. Because many terms may be shared among different literals, networks of arbitrary complexity may result. Any semantic net may be described as a set of assertions containing only ground terms (i.e., terms without free variables.) Figure 7–1 shows the semantic net constructed from the five program assertions of Figure 7–2. Note that multiple occurrences of any ground term are mapped onto the same node of the semantic net.

Operations on semantic nets may be expressed as arbitrary sets of rules (logic programs), provided the two restrictions (see Section 1.2) are observed. Each such program may be transformed into a graphical form as follows: The head of each clause in the program is a binary predicate, and hence it may be viewed as a simple edge connecting two nodes. The body of each clause may be viewed as a graph consisting of one or more edges, similar to the semantic net. The only difference is that nodes in the semantic net are only ground terms, whereas nodes in the graph constructed from a general clause may represent variables. We will refer to graphs corresponding to clause bodies as *graph templates*.

All templates resulting from a given program are interconnected via pointers into a directed structure as follows: an edge points to all clauses whose heads are unifiable with that edge. This (possibly cyclic) collection of graphs will be referred to as the *goal structure*. Figure 7–3 shows the goal structure constructed from the program in Figure 7–2.

Finding a solution to a given template means binding constant values to variables of the template such that the template matches exactly some portion of the semantic net. The template is "unified" with the net. This unification must be performed for all edges constituting the template. If a given edge *e* cannot be unified directly, the goal structure is used to replace that edge by some other template pointed to by *e*.

For example, to solve the initial query of Figure 7–2, a match for the graph template

must be found. Because no direct match exists, the edge is replaced by the template

according to the goal structure. Note that the variables *X* and *Y* have been bound to the constants *fritz* and *gray*, respectively. No direct match is found for this template either, hence the substitution process continues by creating new templates according to the pointers of the goal structure. Eventually, the template

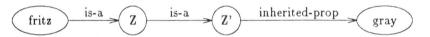

is created, for which a match exists in the semantic net if *Z* and *Z'* are bound to *african-elephant* and *elephant*, respectively. Hence the query is answered affirmatively.

Notation: To avoid drawing figures, we will use the notation $V_1 \overset{e}{\to} V_2$ to denote an edge labeled *e* between two nodes V_1 and V_2. Edges sharing a common node are joined to form connected sequences. For example, the last graph template above would be transcribed as *fritz* $\xrightarrow{\text{is-a}}$ Z $\xrightarrow{\text{is-a}}$ Z' $\xrightarrow{\text{inherited-prop}}$ *gray*.

2.2. Solving Goals Using Message Passing

In this section we describe in detail how the graph-matching process presented intuitively in the preceding section is carried out in a data-driven manner using message passing.

2.2.1. Subgoals Without Pointers

The sequence of literals constituting the body of a clause is usually referred to as a *goal*, whereas each of the individual literals is called a *subgoal*. We first consider subgoals without pointers to other clauses. In the graph representation, solving such a subgoal $e(V_1, V_2)$ corresponds to the following *graph-fitting* problem: determine possible bindings for the terms V_1 and V_2 such that the graph template $V_1 \xrightarrow{e} V_2$ matches some edge of the semantic net. Conceptually, this is accomplished by placing the graph template on an *activation message* and injecting it into specific nodes of the semantic net. From each of these nodes, the message is replicated along existing edges in an attempt to find a match. (If either V_1 or V_2 is a function, it is first evaluated, thus yielding a constant.) We can distinguish the following four cases:

1. Both nodes V_1 and V_2 are bound to ground terms v_1 and v_2, respectively. Because each of the nodes v_1 and v_2 can only occur once in the semantic net, the message is injected into one of these, say v_1. This node then replicates the message along all incident edges labeled e whose direction matches that of the template. If a node receiving the replicated message matches the second term v_2, the subgoal is solved successfully; otherwise there is no direct match for this pattern.

    The same result is obtained when the message is initially injected into v_2 from which it replicates in a search for v_1. This will be denoted by reversing the direction of the edge: $V_2 \xleftarrow{e} V_1$.

    For example, to verify that *bertha* is an *african-elephant* would result in a graph template of the form *bertha* $\xrightarrow{\text{is-a}}$ *african-elephant*. It could be injected in either of the two involved nodes, *bertha* or *african-elephant*, and propagate to the other along the *is-a* edge.
2. The node V_1 is bound to a ground term v_1 while the node V_2 is a free variable. As in the first case, the message is injected into the node v_1 from which it is replicated along all edges labeled e. This time, however, any node v_2 receiving the replicated message may bind to the variable V_2 and hence presents a solution to the given subgoal $p(V_1, V_2)$. For example, to determine all immediate parent nodes of *bertha* in the *is-a* hierarchy, the template *bertha* $\xrightarrow{\text{is-a}}$ Y would be used. It would be injected into the node *bertha* and propagate along all *is-a* edges emanating from *bertha*. In the above example, only one such node—*african-elephant*—would be found.
3. The node V_2 is bound to a ground term v_2 while the node V_1 is free. In this case, reversing the edge to $V_2 \xleftarrow{e} V_1$ yields a situation analogous to (2), where the first term is bound while the second is free. Therefore, the same approach can be taken. For example, to find all african elephants, would result in the graph template *african-elephant* $\xleftarrow{\text{is-a}}$ X. It would be injected into the node *african-elephant* and propagated against the arrowheads of all *is-a* edges, i.e., to the nodes *fritz* and *bertha*.
4. Both variables V_1 and V_2 are free. This case differs from the previous three in that there is no unique injection point for the message. Rather, any node of the semantic net is a potential binding for either variable, and hence the message must *conceptually* be injected into *all* nodes of the semantic net. Each of these

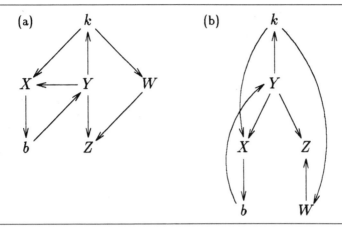

Figure 7-4. Conjunction of subgoals.

nodes binds the first variable V_1 to its own content and replicates the message along all edges labeled e in the same way as described in (2). In other words, the search is started in all nodes simultaneously. In an actual implementation, however, indexing on predicate names would be used. In this case, the message would not have to be replicated to all nodes of the semantic net but only to those connected to an edge labeled e. This could be viewed as injecting the message into specific edges instead of nodes and would drastically reduce the number of injected messages. (Note that edges are always constants because logic programming is limited to *first-order* predicate logic.)

2.2.2. Conjunctions of Subgoals Without Pointers

In this section we extend the scheme for solving individual subgoals presented above to cope with an arbitrary conjunction of subgoals, i.e., complete clause bodies. Any such conjunction corresponds to a directed graph template where the edges are labeled with the predicates and the nodes are labeled with the terms. For example, the graph template for

$$:- e_1(k, X),\ e_2(Y, k),\ e_3(k, W),\ e_4(Y, X),\ e_5(X, b),\ e_6(b, Y),\ e_7(Y, Z),\ e_8(W, Z).$$

is shown in Figure 7-4(a). (Edge labels are omitted for clarity.) Note that if a query produces a disconnected graph, then the query can actually be processed as multiple independent queries; one for each connected component. (This corresponds to AND-parallelism in logic programming terminology.) For now, we will assume that all predicates e_i correspond only to edges in the semantic net and do not point to any clause heads. In this case, satisfying a conjunction corresponds to the graph-fitting problem of finding all matches of the predicates and ground terms in the graph template to those in the semantic net such that bindings can be made between variables in the graph template and ground terms in the semantic net. Conceptually, the graph fitting process is as follows.

The graph template is placed in an activation message. If there is at least one ground term in the graph template, the activation message is injected into the matching node in the semantic net. If there are no ground terms in the graph template, we must index on a predicate to determine which nodes to inject with the message: Once an injection node has been chosen, say k in Figure 7–4(a), we face the problem that many different query edges may be incident on k. If k replicates the activation message on all such edges, then inconsistent binding may be produced that require reconciliation. For example, if k sends the same activation message to two different nodes that bind free variables Y and W, respectively, they may independently produce contridictory bindings for a third free variable Z. Finding solutions subsequently would require the extraction of consistent sets of bindings by a relational equi-join operation [14].

The production of inconsistent bindings can be avoided, however, by using a *depth-first spanning tree* of the graph template with k as the root. For the purpose of constructing the depth-first spanning tree, the direction of the graph edges is ignored. In such an *undirected* graph, any spanning tree partitions the graph edges into *tree-edges* and *back-edges*. Starting from the root k, the activation message can be replicated on all matching *tree-edges* such that any node at depth i is the *generator* for all immediately descendent nodes at depth $i+1$. Thus, matching of the query template to the semantic net proceeds from the root to the leaves. Back-edges always point from a given node v to one of its ancestors in the tree, i.e., to a node that lies on the path between the root and the node v. This guarantees that both nodes of a back-edge are bound to ground terms when that edge is being matched against the semantic net and thus the possibility of producing conflicting bindings is eliminated. Figure 7–4(b) shows one possible spanning tree for the graph template in Figure 7–4(a). Note that at any node with two or more descendant edges, the matching can proceed in parallel along both (all) edges. For example, in Figure 7–4(b), when node Y is bound, the matching can proceed in parallel along the paths $Y \rightarrow X \rightarrow b \rightarrow k$ and $Y \rightarrow Z \rightarrow W \rightarrow k$. The matching process continues until one of the following conditions occurs:

a. A node v_i is unable to bind itself to the corresponding node V_i (i.e., V_i is already bound to a term different from v_i), or, no edge incident on v_i matches the corresponding template edge e_i. In this case, a *reply message* is sent back to the parent node that indicates *failure*; no solution can be found along this path.

b. A leaf node or the last node of a back-edge has been reached, implying the detection of a match for a given branch of the graph template. At this point, a reply message is sent back to the parent node that indicates *success* and carries the binding just made (if any). As successful reply messages from other branches percolate from the leaves back to the root, larger reply messages are built, carrying a tree structure of all bindings made during the forward

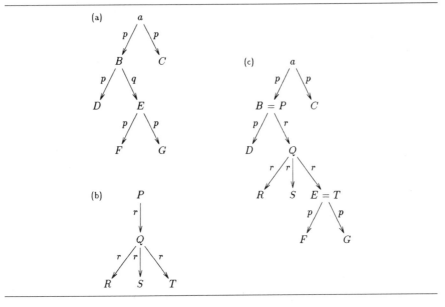

Figure 7-5. A dereference.

propagation. A successful reply message that reaches the root contains all possible solutions to the original goal.

The use of depth-first spanning trees in this model allows AND-parallelism without producing contradictory bindings by ensuring that all subqueries are independent, i.e., different tree branches do not share free variables. This means that backtracking is not necessary and a breadth-first search of the solution space can occur. The transformation of a goal or clause body into a depth-first spanning tree is easily accomplished with the well-known linear algorithm [15].

2.2.3. Goals with Pointers to Other Clauses
The scheme described so far only finds solutions that result from processing the given goal against the semantic net itself, i.e., the collection of all facts; no deductive steps involving clause substitutions were considered. We now extend the scheme to utilize all clauses that may contribute to solving the given goal. This process will be called *dereferencing*.

Suppose for a moment that the matching of a query tree to the semantic net is underway when such an edge (literal) is encountered. As discussed earlier, a clause body can be viewed as a graph template and, hence, transformed into a spanning tree in the same manner as an initial query. Thus, the edge representing the clause head can be replaced by the tree representing the clause body where the endpoints (variables) of the head are unified with the nodes (ground terms or variables) in the query tree. As an example, Figure 7–5(a) shows the query

:– $p(a, B)$, $p(a, C)$, $p(B, D)$, $q(B, E)$, $p(E, F)$, $p(E, G)$.

Figure 7–5(b) shows the clause body for

$q(P, T)$:– $r(P, Q)$, $r(Q, R)$, $r(Q, S)$, $r(Q, T)$.

Assume that p matches only assertions, but q has a pointer to the clause shown in Figure 7–5(b). The query tree results from the dereferencing is shown in Figure 7–5(c). The edge q in Figure 7–5(a) has been replaced by the tree in Figure 7–5(b) where B and P have been unified and E and T have been unified.

Note that any back-edges in the query tree would just be "carried-along" after the dereferencing. If there had been a back-edge from F to a, then this same back-edge would exist after dereferencing, even though the tree path between F and a may have changed. Also, if more than one clause head for predicate q could be unified, then an equal number of tree substitutions would occur, increasing the OR-parallelism. It is important to note that, in general, the variable names (identifiers) in the resultant query would have to be modified to avoid identifier collision. If D appeared in the clause body for predicate q in Figure 7–5(b), then identifier collision would occur after dereferencing.

The deductive process of clause substitution as described above is performed dynamically as execution progress. It is powerful enough to handle recursion, as illustrated by the following example.

We can now describe in more detail how the sample program in Figure 7–2 would be executed. The query to be processed is

:– inherited-prop (fritz, gray).

The initial activation message carries the graph template $fritz \xrightarrow{\text{inherited-prop}} gray$. Because it has two ground terms, it could be injected at either $fritz$ or $gray$; for now, we arbitrarily choose the former. The template is examined by $fritz$, which finds that no outgoing edge matches inherited-prop. There are, however, two pointers in the goal structure to other templates that can be tried instead (see Figure 7–3). The first leads to the template $fritz \xrightarrow{\text{property}} gray$, for which also no match is found by $fritz$. The second template, $fritz \xrightarrow{\text{is-a}} Z \xrightarrow{\text{inherited-prop}} gray$, on the other hand, matches the is-a edge emenating from $fritz$ and hence is propagated to the node african-elephant. This binds the variable Z and the same procedure is repeated: since no inherited-prop edge is found, the edge $african\text{-}elephant \xrightarrow{\text{inherited-prop}} gray$ is replaces (also unsuccessfully) by $african\text{-}elephant \xrightarrow{\text{property}} gray$ and, subsequently, by $african\text{-}elephant \xrightarrow{\text{is-a}} Z' \xrightarrow{\text{inherited-prop}} gray$. The is-a edge now matches and hence the template reaches the node elephant that binds to the variable Z'. After substituting the inherited-prop by property and subsequently by color, the match is successful.

3. IMPLEMENTATION ON A PHYSICAL ARCHITECTURE

3.1. Architectural Requirements

There are two main advantages of the data-driven model presented in the previous sections. The first is the total absence of *centralized control*. Each node of the semantic network may be viewed as an autonomous unit of computation—a logical processing element—whose execution is triggered solely by the arrival of a message. The second advantage is the absence of a *centralized memory*. Each node of the semantic network is at the same time a logical processing element and an item of information to which the appropriate procedure is applied. The absence of these two main bottlenecks makes the model suitable to implementation on a highly parallel architecture.

There are number of possible architectural schemes on which the proposed model could be implemented. We need to consider the following three major requirements:

1. Each node of the semantic net must be mapped onto a processing elememt (PE), that will perform the necessary message-processing and propagation operations on the node's behalf; the PE is the "incarnation" of all the nodes mapped onto that PE. Congruent with the model, there is no centralized controller to start or supervise the execution of individual PE's; rather, the operation of each PE is initiated through an interrupt triggered by the arrival of a message.
2. Nodes of the semantic net must be able to communicate with one another via logical connections corresponding to edges in the net. This implies that any two PE's holding logically connected nodes must be able to communicate with one another. This communication may be direct, if a physical link is provided, or indirect via intermediate PE's.
3. An interface to the outside world, i.e., the user communicating with the semantic net, must be provided. This must permit (a) the injection of messages carrying queries to be processed against the semantic net, and (b) the retrieval of results extracted from it.

There are many architectural schemes that would satisfy the above criteria. Unfortunately, there are no simple strategies or methodologies for designing novel architectures. Most of the decisions rest with the experience and the intuition of the computer architect. Typically, the first step is to consider a hypothetical abstract architecture that can be studied analytically or by simulation to determine its potential performance. Through a sequence of successive refinements during which the various physical constraints of actual hardware components are considered, the abstract machine is transformed into a physical machine for the selected computational model.

In the remainer of this chapter, we shall describe one possible architecture for the proposed data-driven model. The performance of this machine is currently being studied through simulation by our research group at the University of California, Irvine.

3.2. Mapping the Model onto a Physical Architecture

The architecture consists of a potentially large number (on the order of several hundreds) of PE's. Each PE is independent from any other: it executes its own instructions in a local random access memory. Despite the large number of PE's, the number of nodes in a semantic net will normally exceed the number of PE's. Therefore, each PE will have to be "multiplexed" among possibly many nodes. The assignment of nodes to PE's may be done statically or dynamically. In the first case, it may be viewed as a function f, which, given node n, yields a number f(n), ranging between 1 and p, where p is the number of PE's. f(n) designates the PE that will hold the node n. The advantage of a static mapping is less overhead during execution. The choice of the mapping function is, however, critical to performance. It must attempt to distribute the computational load evenly among all PE's. In the simplest case, this would mean assigning an equal number of nodes to each PE. In the semantic net, however, each node may not experience the same workload. In this case, a differing number of nodes may constitute an equal amount of work. Unfortunately, it may not be always possible to determine the behavior of a given application ahead of time, or the application may be such that the load in different parts of the net varies significantly over time. In this case, a dynamic mapping may be necessary, which changes the assignment of nodes to PE's depending on the current load in each node. In general, a static mapping is preferable in systems with a fine grain of parallelism, such as general dataflow programs, where each node is a simple arithmetic or logical operation. In the proposed model, the granularity of nodes is considerably higher. Furthermore, the net is not reloaded for each query but resides in the architecture for extensive periods of time during which many queries are processed. Therefore, we envision a mapping that evolves over time, i.e., reassigns portions of the net as more information about its typical usage is gathered.

Another critical decision is the *interconnection topology* of the architecture. Ideally, any two PE's holding two logically connected nodes should have a physical link. In that case, a fully connected network would be desirable. This, however, is not practical with the envisioned number of PE's and so a compromise must be made that reduces the number of physical connections yet permits the necessary exchange of messages. At the same time, redundant paths must be provided between any two PE's to guarantee a certain level of fault tolerance.

There are a large variety of possible interconnection topologies. We have chosen a mesh-connected array of $n \times n$ PE's with the edges wrapped around as shown in Figure 7–6. Visually, the PE's may be imagined as distributed over the surface of a torus. The main reasons for this choice were threefold:

1. This interconnection topology is easily extensible, because the number of connections per PE remains constant (four).
2. There are many possible routes between any two PE's; consequently, the failure of any one PE does not disable the communication between any other PE's; this is important to guarantee a graceful degradation of the system under hardware failures.

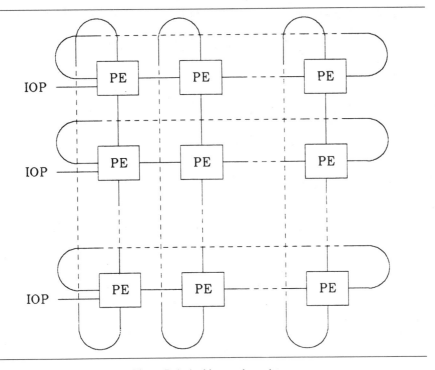

Figure 7–6. Architectural topology.

3. The routing algorithm is simple—to send a message from one node to another, the PE holding the sending node determines the i and j coordinates of the PE holding the receiving node. Based on that information and its own position within the array, it determines which of its four nearest neighbors has the shortest geometric distance to the destination PE and sends the message into that direction. This operation is repeated by each PE receiving the message until the final destination is reached.

This simple routing algorithm can easily be extended to account for communication under PE or link failure. As long as all PE's operate correctly, messages are routed along the path corresponding to the shortest geometric distance between the sender and the receiver. When a failed node is encountered, the algorithms must attempt to circumnavigate the failed node or group of nodes. The solution used in AGM in analogous to the "maze searching" algorithm, where the groups of failed nodes correspond to the maze "walls," working nodes are the "pathways", and the message to be delivered is the "mouse." Pictorially, the solution is to put one hand on the wall and follow the obstruction until the destination is reached or until the starting position is reached again. In the latter case, the destination is unreachable.

The complete message-routing algorithm may be summarized as follows:

1. Select the node with the shortest geometric distance to the destination (if equidistant, select the node with less communication traffic).
2. If the selected node is inoperable, select the node with the longer geometric distance; continue with rule 1.
3. If the node selected by rule 2 is also inoperable, follow the "maze" algorithm: remember the current position and proceed clockwise (or counterclockwise) around inoperable nodes until (a) a node with a shorter geometric distance than the starting position is reached (continue with rule 1); or (b) the same starting position is reached in this case, report failure): destination node is unreachable.

To permit users to communicate with the system, one or more input/output processors (IOP's) must be provided. In Figure 7–6 we show one IOP attached to each PE of one column; in an actual machine, the number and type of IOP's will depend on the given application domain. An initial query message to be injected into one of the semantic network nodes may be input through any of the available IOP's. The IOPs use the same routing algorithm as regular PE's. That is, based on the message destination, the IOP determines the i and j coordinates of the PE holding the destination node and sends the message in the appropriate direction. Output is handled in an analogous way. Each final result extracted from the net is routed to the IOP through which the initial query message was injected.

4. CONCLUSIONS

There is significant potential parallelism in the processing of semantic nets. The main problem, however, is to devise a scheme that would facilitate the exploitation of this parallelism at the architectural level. To accomplish that, the user must be able to express operations on the semantic net in a declarative manner, without having to explicitly specify where parallelism is to occur.It must be the system's responsibility to transform the user's specifications into low-level operations that could be executed by many cooperating asynchronous PE's.

In this chapter, we have described an approach that combines the concepts of semantic nets, logic programming, and data-driven computation to achieve the above goals. We considered a subset of logic programming as a formalism to express user queries in a nonprocedural manner. Any program written using this formalism may be transformed into a system of networks and network templates, in which processing a query may be viewed as a process of finding matches for given templates in the underlying nets. This matching process may be carried out in a highly parallel manner by implementing the underlying semantic net as a dataflow graph in which nodes may communicate with one another asynchronously by exchanging messages.

The main advantage of this approach is that the processing and propagation of messages is distributed throughout the network and is performed in a *data-driven* manner—each node of the network represents an independent unit of computation whose execution is triggered solely by the arrival of a message. This eliminates the need for *centralized control* and a *centralized memory*, which are the main limitations to high performance under the von Neumann model of computation. The data-driven model, on the other hand, permits many independent processing elements to be engaged simultaneously in the processing and forwarding of messages, which results in the following two major sources of parallelism:

1. *Intra request parallelism.* A message injected into the net is replicated into possibly many directions in the search of matches. Each node that receives a copy of that message may then process and forward it concurrently with other nodes. Thus the theoretical time complexity for finding all matches is proportional to the number of edges constituting that template.

2. *Interrequest parallelism.* Assuming a significant number of PE's in the underlying architecture, certain queries may be able to exploit only a small subset of these at any given time. This implies that the unused computational power of the idle PE's may be utilized to process other queries concurrently. A simple coloring scheme is sufficient to distinguish messages belonging to different templates and thus to permit their coexistence in the system.

REFERENCES

1. R. E. Fikes, and G. G. Hendrix, *A Network-Based Knowledge Representation and its Natural Deduction System.* IJCAI, 1977.
2. N. V. Findler, *Associative Networks.* New York: Academic Press, 1979.
3. W. A. Woods. "What's in a Link: Foundations for Semantic Networks." in *Representation and Understanding.* Bobrow and Collins (eds.), New York: Academic Press, 1975.
4. *IEEE Computer,* Special Issue on Dataflow Systems, V15(n2): Feb. 1982.
5. B. W. Wah, and G. Li, "A Survey of Special Purpose Architectures for AI," SIGART *Newsletter,* 96; 28–46, 1986.
6. J. B. Dennis, "First Version of Dataflow Procedure Language." Mac Tech. Memorandum 61, MIT, Cambridge, MA, 1975.
7. S. E. Fahlman, *NETL: A System for Representing Real-World Knowledge.* Cambridge, MA. MIT Press, 1979.
8. H. Gallaire, and J. Minker (eds.), *Logic and Data Bases.* New York: Plenum Press, 1978.
9. H. Gallaire, J. Minker, and J. M. Nicolas, "Logic and Databases: A Deductive Approach." *ACM Computing Surveys,* V16(n2): 1984.
10. A. Deliyanni, and R. Kowalski, "Logic and Semantic Networks," *Comm. of the ACM.* V22(n3): 184–192, 1979.
11. L. Bic, "A Data-Driven Model for Parallel Interpretation of Logic Programs," *Proc. Int. Conf. on Fifth Generation Computer Systems,* Tokyo, Japan, 1984.
12. L. Bic, "Processing of Semantic Nets on Dataflow Architectures." *Artificial Intelligence J.* V27: 1985.
13. L. Bic, and C. Lee, *A Data-Driven Model for a Subset of Logic Programming.* Tech. Rep. Dept. of ICS, University of California, Irvine, 1986.
14. S. Taylor, A. Lowry, G. Q. Maguire, and S. J. Stolfo, "Logic Programming Using Parallel Associative Operations," *1984 Symp. on Logic Programming,* pp. 58–68.
15. A. V. Aho, J. E. Hopcroft, and J. D. Ullman, *The Design and Analysis of Computer Algorithms.* Reading, MA: Addison-Wesley, 1974.

II. PARALLEL COMPUTERS

8. APPLICATION OF THE BUTTERFLY PARALLEL PROCESSOR IN ARTIFICIAL INTELLIGENCE

DONALD C. ALLEN and N. S. SRIDHARAN

1. INTRODUCTION

Given the inherent parallelism and great computational requirements of many artificial intelligence (AI) problems, it is only natural that parallel computers should be enlisted in the cause. The Butterfly parallel processor, developed by Bolt Beranek and Newman Inc. under a Defense Advanced Research Projects Agency (DARPA) contract, has proven useful in the development of tools and techniques for the AI environment and holds great promise for the development of parallel AI applications.

Continuing development of languages, software tools, and investigation into the inherent parallelism of problems will be required to fully realize the potential of parallel processing for AI. This chapter focuses on some of the ongoing efforts to increase our understanding of parallel computers and to develop a suitable environment for solving AI problems using parallel-processing techniques.

2. BUTTERFLY OVERVIEW

The Butterfly computer consists of from one to 256 processor nodes connected through a proprietary, high-performance switch network (Figure 8–1). Each processor node consists of an MC68020 microprocessor and an MC68881 floating-point coprocessor, with one megabyte of memory, expandable to four megabytes (Figure 8–2). The memory of the processor nodes collectively forms the shared memory of the machine, which is accessible to all nodes through the Butterfly switch network. Memory, switch bandwidth, and input/output (I/O)

Butterfly Switch

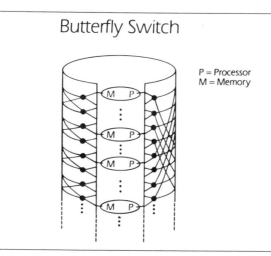

P = Processor
M = Memory

Figure 8–1. The Butterfly switch.

Processor Node

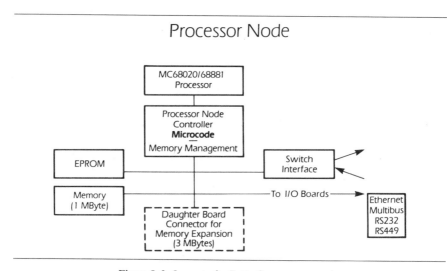

Figure 8–2. Layout of a Butterfly processor node.

capacity scale with the number of nodes to maintain system balance and prevent performance bottlenecks.

The shared memory is managed by the Chrysalis operating system, which provides a program execution environment where tasks are distributed among the nodes without concern for the physical location of related data. This simplifies programming mutliple processors for a broad range of applications. Furthermore, processor nodes are essentially identical, although they may have different memory and I/O configurations. The uniformity of the nodes and the transparent memory management make it easy to write application programs that are configuration-independent.

Besides the microprocessor and the memory, each node contains a microcoded coprocessor called the processor node controller (PNC), memory management hardware, an I/O bus, and an interface to the Butterfly switch network. The PNC is involved in all data transfers to and from the switch and all memory references for the MC68020. Because the PNC manages all memory references, it can guarantee that no other node can access data that are being manipulated locally. With these capabilities, we use the PNC to augment the 68020 instruction set with microcoded atomic multiprocessing primitives.

The Butterfly switch network is a key element of the Butterfly parallel processor [1]. It uses packet-switched networking techniques to implement processor-to-memory communication. Switching nodes are configured as a serial decision network with a topology similar to the fast Fourier transform (FFT). The FFT flow diagram contains a recurring X-shaped pattern known as a "Butterfly," hence the name. The switch is packaged in a modular fashion with each switch module consisting of a printed circuit board with 16 inputs and outputs. These modules each contain eight custom very large scale integration (VLSI) switch nodes that route messages within the switch.

The scalability of the Butterfly system, to a maximum configuration of 256 processors and one gigabyte of memory, is possible because of the Butterfly switch, which overcomes the expansion limitations of bus- and crossbar-based multiprocessor architectures. Busses have fixed bandwidth and, except for a narrow range of configurations, will therefore be either underutilized or overutilizgd. A small configuration that does not fully use the bus capacity wastes expensive resources, because each bus interface must operate at the needlessly high bus speed. A configuration that is too large for the bus capacity will exhibit poor performance due to bus saturation. In either case, cost/performance suffers.

Crossbars, on the other hand, are not limited by fixed capacity. Their bandwidth grows linearly with the number of nodes interconnected. However, the hardware complexity (and therefore cost) of a crossbar grows as the *square* of the number of nodes, in contrast with the linear cost-scaling characteristic of a bus. In a 100-node system, for example, the Butterfly switch would require about 500 wires, compared with 5000 for a crossbar. As the size of a configuration increases, the cost of the crossbar comes to dominate the cost of the system.

The Butterfly switch is an excellent compromise between the extremes represented by the bus and crossbar. The cost of the switch grows only slightly faster than linearly with the size of the system (for our implementation the switch cost is proportional to $N*\log_4 N$, where N is the number of processor nodes), whereas the bandwidth grows slightly less than linearly. These favorable scaling characteristics permit the construction of balanced and cost-effective Butterfly systems over a wide range of configurations.

The latency of the switch is minimal, making memory-reference transactions practical. Typical 68020 instructions take one to two microseconds to complete

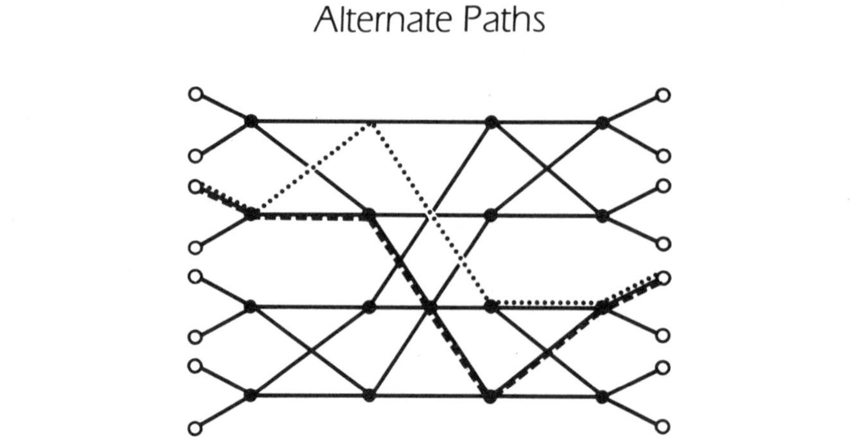

Alternate Paths

Figure 8–3. Alternate paths within the Butterfly switch.

when referencing operands in local memory. The same instruction will take five to six microseconds with its operand in any remote memory. In both cases we assume that the instruction itself was fetched from local memory.

There are as many paths through the Butterfly switch network as there are processors in the system. Data transfer for each path is 32 Mbits/second, thus the switch for a 16-processor system has a peak capacity of 512 Mbits/second, and a 64-node system transfers data at a peak 2048 Mbits/second.

The switching nodes use packet address bits to route the packet through the switch network from source to destination along the appropriate path between the two nodes. There is a path through the switch network from each processor node to every other node. However, because the path is not dedicated, it is possible for messages to collide, for example, when messages require the same switching node output port. When this type of situation occurs, one message is allowed through and the others are retransmitted after a short, randomized delay. This delay can be reduced by configuring a Butterfly system with an extra switch column so that an alternate path exists between each pair of processor nodes. If present, the alternate paths are automatically used for message retransmission. Alternate paths also provide redundancy in the event of a switching node failure. All systems with 16 or more processors are configured with an extra switch column. (Figure 8–3) [2].

The Butterfly I/O system may be distributed among the processor nodes with I/O boards attached to any node. There are several types of boards available: serial I/O, Multibus adapter, and VME interface, which attaches directly to the switch instead of a processor node.

The Butterfly system is programmed primarily in high-level languages: C, Fortran, and Lisp. Application programs run under the control of the Chrysalis operating system, which provides a Unix-like environment. The operating system contains utilities for accessing, controlling, and debugging programs; application libraries for managing system resources; and kernel functions for process support, memory management, and interprocess communications. In a typical application environment, programs are edited, compiled, and tested on a host front-end, such as a VAX, Sun Workstation, or Symbolics 3600. These programs are then downloaded, run, and debugged on the Butterfly system.

The Chrysalis operating system contains application libraries that manage many of the details required to use system resources, such as memory allocation and process set-up. The most significant of these is the Uniform System Library, which provides a programming methodology for the C and Fortran programmer that makes it very easy to simultaneously apply a single procedure to many elements of a complex data structure. The Uniform System creates an environment where all processors share a common address space and where tasks are dynamically assigned to the processor nodes. It facilitates processor management by providing configuration independence, dynamic load balancing, and an efficient generator mechanism to minimize scheduling overhead.

For symbolic processing and AI applications, a Common Lisp programming environment has been developed for the Butterfly system. This environment includes Butterfly Common Lisp, with multiprocessing extensions, together with user interface and program development facilities implemented on a front-end Lisp machine (the Symbolics 3600). Butterfly Common Lisp is a shared-memory multiprocessor Lisp that allows the concurrent evaluation of multiple Lisp expressions in the context of global, shared Lisp heap. This approach preserves the shared-memory quality that has always characterized Lisp, allowing data structures of arbitrary size and shape to be communicated by name. Copying, while optional, is not required, as in the case with loosely coupled multiprocessor Lisp systems employing multiple heaps.

3. THE BUTTERFLY SYSTEM AND AI APPLICATIONS

More than 100 Butterfly parallel processors have been installed. Several of these are being used for AI applications that involve the development of algorithms, tools, and techniques for tomorrow's applications. Currently, parallelism is being explored as a method for solving some of the most intractable problems associated with AI.

BBN Laboratories is implementing a continuous speech recognition algorithm on the Butterfly system to investigate how parallel processing can be used to achieve real-time speeds. An existing recognition algorithm, based on the use of probabilistic Hidden-Markov models of speech sounds, has been parallelized, achieving good performance and processor utilization.

The decomposition of the algorithm into tasks that match one word to a single frame of input speech provides a granularity that efficiently uses the processors. Running an algorithm using a 335-word vocabulary, 95% processor utilization was achieved on a 15-processor Butterfly system and 79% utilization on a 97-processor system.

Large-scale speech understanding is another possible AI application for parallel processing. Recent work, done by Henry Thompson at the University of Edinburgh, involves a system with a 60,000-word vocabulary that is capable of recognizing continuous speech. An inherently parallel technique, chart-parsing, is applied at the signal-processing level, at the phonetic level, at the phonemic level, at the word level, and at the sentence level. The project was designed as a parallel Lisp algorithm that was first tested in a serial environment. Linear speed-up was achieved when the algorithm was ported and run on the Butterfly system.

Connectionism is an AI paradigm that has recently received much attention. It derives its inspiration from neural networks, creating computing engines from complex interconnections of neuron-like elements. Each neural element has a number of input lines, an internal state, and a number of output lines. The element adds all the input signals with a weight-coefficient on each one of them. The sums, when added to the internal state, determine signals on the output lines and the modified internal state.

There are a large number of interesting algorithms that have been developed using the connectionist framework. They have been used for low-level vision processing, mobile object recognition, recognition of shapes around shapes, and natural language parsing. The University of Rochester is developing a connectionist-network interpreter on a 128-processor Butterfly system. An important goal of the university's work is to develop a parallel-processing programming environment for applications, including machine vision and control for robotic systems. The promise of parallelism is central to the future of connectionism. Without parallel processors, it would be an extremely unrealistic processing paradigm.

4. NATURAL LANGUAGE RESEARCH AT BBN LABORATORIES

BBN's natural-language work has traditionally used an augmented-transition network (ATN) parser, a formalism in which the English grammar (RUS) is described to a machine. RUS contains grammatical categories as nodes in a graph and arcs that describe transitions that a parser can take if it sees certain words or word categories. The RUS grammar is deterministic by design, and tries to get the best possible parse of a given input text as the first parse that it produces.

Grammar parser designers try to build in enough tests on transitions so that the selection is deterministic when several alternative transitions emanate from a given state. Since ATN-based English parsers do not backtrack, but instead select the best parse first, there can be no parallelism at the state-transition level. Because it insists on a left-to-right traversal of the input string, the RUS parser also does not support parallelism over the input string.

To explore and capitalize on the benefits of parallel processing, BBN had to develop a new parser that did not assume serial left-to-right processing and did not use a state-transition grammar. The production rules that the grammar uses were reworked in a formalism that identifies what constituents can be assembled together and under what conditions they form certain categories. The conditions required to recognize a certain category and the associated features are expressed in a logical formalism. The parser uses unification, which is a special operation in logic that tests constraints to the extent that information is available. There is no penalty if the information is not available in a particular time-order. Unification allows constraints to be tested in any order that information becomes available. The parser also permits the input string to be processed in any order: right to left, left to right, or randomly. The parser allows parallelism over the entire grammar and over the input string to produce all the possible parses of the input sentence.

With the new parser, the level of concurrency is sufficient to run on a 256-processor Butterfly system. Thus, the user is not limited by the way any finite-sized parallel algorithms are conceptualized. The parser, or the grammar interpreter, is coded in Butterfly Lisp.

This parallel parser was developed not, as might be expected, to increase the speed of the parsing process, but rather to invest the increased computing power in a parser with greater capability, e.g., greater coverage of the language and the ability to deal with ill-formed (ungrammatical) input.

In the latter case, the parser must accept an input string that does not satisfy any grammatical category, which relaxes the rules of the language. Handling ill-formed input requires major functional extensions that necessitate more processing than could be managed on a serial machine. BBN's unification-based parser produces a table of well-formed substrings that could be given to a module for managing nongrammatical input by relaxation rules.

An important issue in parallel programming involves the use of side effects. A side effect is a write or store operation that alters an existing value. Using side effects is problematic when there are multiple threads of control referencing and writing into a variable. Such activity needs to be carefully coordinated to prevent race conditions. Race conditions are the hardest errors to find because their symptoms are probabilistic; the program's behavior will vary from run to run, even when presented with the same inputs.

A possible approach to parallel programming, then, is to eliminate the use of side-effecting operations; this is known as purely applicative, or functional, programming. Experience indicates that, while program correctness is more easily achieved (and, in fact, proven), functional programs do not execute efficiently on today's parallel machines. An alternative methodology is to first develop, write, and debug an algorithm without the use of side effects. Once correct execution is achieved, side effects are carefully introduced to enhance performance.

For example, BBN Laboratories began with the parsing algorithms used for a simple, context-free (not natural) language parser as a formal definition of the problem and developed a range of about 16 different parsing algorithms using program transformations. Each of these is entirely parallel and written in an

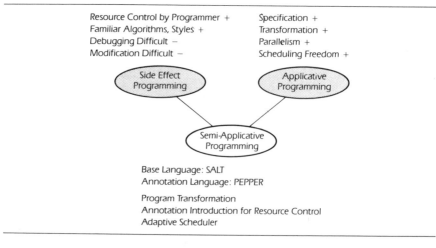

Resource Control by Programmer +   Specification +
Familiar Algorithms, Styles +   Transformation +
Debugging Difficult −   Parallelism +
Modification Difficult −   Scheduling Freedom +

Side Effect Programming   Applicative Programming

Semi-Applicative Programming

Base Language: SALT
Annotation Language: PEPPER

Program Transformation
Annotation Introduction for Resource Control
Adaptive Scheduler

Figure 8–4. Semi-applicative programming methodology using SALT and PEPPER

applicative, side-effect-free language called SALT. Annotations (PEPPER), which have a side-effecting implementation on a parallel machine, then were introduced. PEPPER annotations have been carefully selected so that they cannot alter the answer produced by the program, but only affect the time behavior [3] (Figure 8–4).

The (SALT and PEPPER) algorithms were rewritten in Lisp and tested on a VAX before being tested on the Butterfly computer. The final program had no logical bugs because the algorithm development process was systematic and correct. Although there have been some similar programs developed in the past, such systematic development has only been completed for very small algorithms like sorting, or finding a maximum, a minimum, or a GCD of two numbers. The parser developed at BBN is among the most complex algorithms developed using this methodology.

5. LISP ENVIRONMENT AND USER INTERFACE

As the previous discussion illustrates, AI is a rapidly emerging field and an increasingly important source of complex, compute-intensive applications. Furthermore, many of these problems are more easily solved in a parallel computational environment than with traditional serial methods.

The Butterfly parallel machine has an architecture that is suited for such AI applications, primarily because of its shared-memory capability. However, realizing the machine's potential in this domain requires a suitable AI programming environment. Such an environment is under development for the Butterfly. It includes support for both the Common Lisp and Scheme languages, with parallel extensions, and a user interface with program development facilities implemented on the Symbolics 3600.

Butterfly Lisp is a shared-memory, multiple-interpreter system [4]. It supports memory-sharing by providing a single Lisp heap, mapped identically by all interpreters. This approach has significant ease-of-programming and efficiency advantages over multiple-heap systems.

Butterfly Lisp uses the *future* mechanism (first implemented at MIT by Professor Robert Halstead and students in their Multilisp system) as its basic task-creating construct. Evaluating the form—(*future* < lisp-expression >)—causes the system to record that a request has been made for the evaluation of < lisp-expression > and to commit resources to that evaluation when they become available. Control returns immediately to the caller, passing back a new type of Lisp object called an "undetermined *future*."

The "undetermined *future*" may be manipulated as if it were an ordinary Lisp object: it may be stored as the value of a symbol, consed into a list, passed as an argument to a function, etc. If, however, it is subjected to an operation that requires the value of < lisp-expression > prior to its arrival, that operation will automatically be suspended until the value becomes available. *Future* provides an elegant abstraction for the synchronization required between the producer and consumer of a value, preserving and encouraging the applicative style integral to good Lisp programming.

Butterfly Lisp uses a parallel stop-and-copy garbage collector. When garbage collection becomes necessary, the machine suspends processing and all processors participate in the garbage-collection procedure, which typically takes less than a second [5]. The garbage collection times tends to be less than 10% of the total run-time so that overhead is comparable to the garbage-collection overhead of sequential machines.

The Symbolics 3600–based Butterfly Lisp User Interface provides interaction windows that are associated with tasks that are running on the Butterfly system. The windows may be selected, moved, resized, or folded into task icons. Each task can initiate an associated interaction window. Task output is directed to this window, and any input typed while the window is selected may be read by the task.

A Butterfly Lisp Mode provided for the Symbolic 3600's ZMACS editor connects evaluation commands to an evaluation service task running the Butterfly Lisp system. The Butterfly Lisp environment also includes a new performance analysis facility that allows users to display combined spawning and data dependency graphs for algorithms written in Butterfly Lisp (Figure 8–5). This facility graphically displays the evolution of an algorithm after it has been run on the Butterfly system. It allows the programmer to see the various threads of parallel control plotted on a time line. On the display, each horizontal bar represents a parallel task that was created by a *future*. The scheduling state of the task (waiting, queued, or running) is represented by different stipple patterns within the horizontal bars. In the queued state, the task is waiting in the system

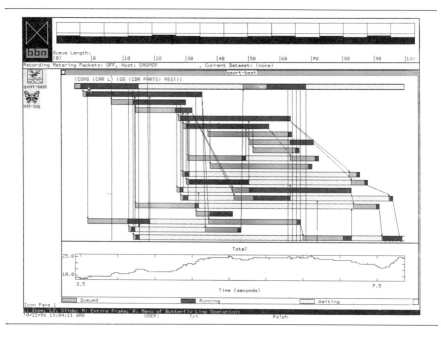

Figure 8–5. Display of combined spawning and dependency graphs.

scheduling queue to be assigned to a processor. In the running state, a processor is actively working on the task. Waiting indicates that the task has referenced the value of a *future* that is not yet determined. Arrows between tasks indicate causality relationships among them, e.g., *spawning, touching,* and *determination* events. A *spawning* operation occurs when one task creates another task by evaluating a *future* form. A *touching* event occurs when one task requires the undetermined value of another. This is shown by an arrow emanating from a task making the transition from running to waiting. Another arrow shows when the value is returned to the waiting task, indicating a *determination* event. The task bars will display the source expression that created them when selected by the mouse.

Instantaneous system-state information is displayed in an area at the top of the screen. This area contains a number of slices, each with crosshatching corresponding to the state of a particular processor—idle, running or garbage collecting. In addition, status is shown for the number of tasks waiting to be executed, effective processor utilization, and the rate of memory consumption.

6. EXPERT SYSTEMS TOOL KIT
An Expert Systems Tool Kit aids in the development of expert systems, shells, and prototypes on the Butterfly parallel processor [6]. Implemented entirely in

Common Lisp, it supports object-oriented programming, annotated slots (active values), and rule-system programming.

The object-oriented programming supported by the Butterfly Expert System Tool Kit emulates the Xerox Corporation's CommonLoops. In CommonLoops, an object is an instance of a class that is a member of a class hierarchy. Classes are represented as objects that are instances of metaclasses. New classes are defined by an extended version of the Common Lisp *defstruct* form. Objects respond to messages in a class-specific manner. This behavior is procedurally described as a *method* defined using an extension to the Common Lisp *defun* form.

Another programming methodology supported by the Expert Systems Tool Kit is called annotated slots. Similar mechanisms are called "active values" in systems such as Loops from Xerox or KEE from Intellicorp. The activity stems from an annotation explicitly placed on the slot. Annotated slots are used to invoke a function whenever the slot is read or written. A slot annotation causes a procedure to be run when the slot is accessed for retrieval or modification. Any slot on a CommonLoops object instance may be annotated.

A major objective of the Butterfly Expert Systems Tool Kit is to provide a programming environment that will allow users to quickly develop rule systems on the Butterfly system. A rule system defines rule structure, capabilities, and execution. A rule-system application solves problems in a specific area of knowledge that has been developed using a rule system. Butterfly Common Lisp, the object oriented programming facility, and the annotated slots capability are all part of the rule-system environment. The complete rule environment, however, includes additional architectural features, utilities, and programming conventions.

7. CONCLUSION

The promise of parallelism has been around for some time. But early attempts did not meet expectations because of hardware limitations. These limitations have been eliminated by the tremendous advances made in the design and manufacture of integrated circuits. As serial computers reach power and speed limitations and are faced with increasingly difficult engineering and scientific problems, parallel computers will be in great demand.

A growing number of companies, universities, and government agencies currently are exploring parallel computing. With this exploration has come the realization that there is considerably more parallelism in real-world problems than originally believed. Consequently, the number of application areas is expanding as the parallel nature of these problems becomes apparent. AI applications are typical of this trend. Expert systems, image processing, robotics, and natural language processing and learning may eventually yield to parallel AI techniques.

But much of the present work is directed at more fundamental issues such as the development of appropriate language constructs and software tools as well as exploring the inherent parallelism of various applications. In addition, further research and development into the best possible hardware architecture continues. BBN, for example, is working on the next generation of massively parallel computers—an 8000 processor system. Funded under a research contract from DARPA, the system will be capable of billions of instructions and floating-point operations per second. This future system will have several gigabytes of memory and an aggregate billion-byte-per-second distributed I/O capacity. The biggest challenge will be in learning to exploit the potential of such a machine. AI techniques will undoubtedly play a great role in the exploration.

REFERENCES

1. R. H. Thomas, R. Gurwitz, J. Goodhue, D. Allen, *Butterfly Parallel Processor Overview.* Cambridge, MA: BBN Laboratories Inc., Dec. 1986.
2. *April 16—July 15, 1984 Development of a Butterfly Multiprocessor Test Bed: The Butterfly Switch,* BBN Tech. Rep. No. 3, Rep. No. 5874, Cambridge, MA: Oct. 1985, pp. 15–21.
3. N. S., Sridharan, *Semi-Applicative Programming: Examples of Context-Free Recognizers in Distributed Artificial Intelligence,* In M. Huhns (ed.), *PITMAN Research Notes in AI.* London: (to be published).
4. D. C. Allen, "The BBN Multiprocessors: Butterfly and Monarch," *Proc. of the Princeton Conf. on Supercomputers and Stellar Dynamics,* N. Princeton, June 1, 1986 (to be published).
5. S. Steinberg, D. Allen, L. Bagnall, and C. Scott, "The Butterfly Lisp System," *Proc. of the August 1986 AAAI,* vol. 2. Philadelphia, PA, p. 730.
6. C. Quayle, A. Boulanger, D. Clarke, M. Thome, M. Vilain, and K. Anderson, *Parallel Expert Systems Execution Environment: A Functional Specification.* Rep. No. 6225, Cambridge, MA, BBN Laboratories Inc., Aug. 1986.

9. ON THE RANGE OF APPLICABILITY OF AN
ARTIFICIAL INTELLIGENCE MACHINE

DAVID ELLIOT SHAW

1. INTRODUCTION

As the focus of artificial intelligence (AI) research begins to move from small-scale "toy" problems to larger-scale "real world" applications, issues of computational efficiency have begun to attract growing attention. The ambitious performance goals of the Fifth Generation project in Japan, for example, and of the Strategic Computing program in the United States, are among the indications of the importance currently attached by many to the development of machines having vastly improved performance and cost/performance characteristics in various AI applications.

Several researchers [5, 10, 20, 32, 35, 45] have proposed machines intended to accelerate various operations relevant to one or more AI applications. The problem is complicated, however, by the fact that many integrated AI systems will ultimately require the performance of a number of *different* computationally intensive operations, ranging from the various signal-processing algorithms employed in low-level computer vision and speech understanding through a wide range of inferencing and knowledge-base management tasks that may be involved in high-level reasoning.

This research was supported in part by the Defense Advanced Research Projects Agency, under contract N00039-84-C-0165, in part by the New York State Center for Advanced Technology in Computers and Information Systems at Columbia University, and in part by an IBM Faculty Development Award.
An earlier version of this paper appeared in *Artificial Intelligence*, 32 (1987) 151–172.

The central goal of the NON-VON project is the investigation of massively parallel computer architectures capable of providing significant performance and cost/performance improvements by comparison with conventional von Neumann machines in a *wide range* of artificial intelligence and other symbolic applications. In this Chapter, we provide some evidence of NON-VON's range of applicability within the space of AI problems by summarizing certain performance projections, derived through detailed analysis and simulation, in three distinct AI task areas: rule-based inferencing, computer vision, and knowledge base management.

The chapter begins with a brief discussions of two approaches—one based on multiple specialized subsystems, the other on a single, more general machine—to the implementation of integrated systems that must perform a number of different AI tasks to satisfy the application at hand. The NON-VON machine family is then introduced in Section 3 as an example of the latter approach. The remainder of the Chapter summarizes the results of analytical and simulation studies conducted to predict NON-VON's performance on a number of tasks in each of the three areas under consideration.

In Section 4, we report the results of a detailed projection of the machine's performance in executing OPS5 production systems, based on data derived from Gupta and Forgy's investigation of six existing production system at Carnegie-Mellon University [16, 17]. In Section 5, we review 11 low- and intermediate-level computer-vision algorithms that have been developed and simulated for the NON-VON machine; performance projections are presented and compared with results and projections for other sequential and parallel machines. Section 6 presents the results of a projection of NON-VON's performance on certain AI-relevant database management benchmarks formulated by Hawthorn and DeWitt [19], using the analytical techniques employed by those researchers. In the final section we summarize our results and attempt to characterize the essential architectural and algorithmic principles that appear to be responsible for NON-VON's strong performance in these diverse AI application areas.

2. GENERALITY OF AI MACHINES

One possible approach to the realization of high performance in integrated AI systems involves the construction of a number of separate specialized hardware subsystems, each designed to execute a different function. A hypothetical robot system that has integrated speech, natural language, and vision capabilities, for example, might contain separate modules specialized for various types of two-dimensional image and acoustical signal processing, for rapid access to and manipulation of information from a domain-specific knowledge base, and for high-speed rule-based inferencing.

An alternative approach involves the development of a single architecture capable of providing better performance and cost/performance characteristics than a conventional von Neumann machine over a wide range of AI tasks. Although such a machine might not perform any one operation as quickly or cost-effectively as a special-purpose subsystem designed to perform only that operation, the design of a single, more general "AI machine" would, if feasible, seem to offer several potential advantages over the specialized subsystem approach:

1. *Greater flexibility.* The present state of the art makes it difficult to specify with any certainty the precise functions that should be implemented in special-purpose AI hardware. Adaptation, both to accommodate the novel require-ments of a new application and to incorporate experience gained over time with a given application, would presumably be considerably easier with a more general machine. Empirical support for this general principle is provided, for example, by the rather surprising lack of commercial success enjoyed by manufacturers of functionally specialized minicomputers during the 1970s by comparison with those supplying lower performance, but more generally applicable machines to the same specialized target markets.
2. *Improved machine utilization.* Except in applications in which several types of information processing can be effectively pipelined or otherwise overlapped, the special-purpose subsystem approach tends to result in systems in which only one of several hardware modules is performing useful work at any given time, resulting in a potentially significant cost/performance degradation. While there is no reason to expect a single "AI machine" to achieve perfect utilization of its hardware resources, the incorporation of hardware that proves useful in the performance of many tasks would seem likely to reduce the extent of such underutilization.
3. *Reduced communication costs.* In many applications, the specialized sub-system approach results in the need to transfer large amounts of data among the constituent subsystems at various times in the course of processing. These transfers may carry a significant time and/or interconnection cost, in some cases exceeding that associated with the processing itself. While a single, more general machine must still provide for system input and output functions and algorithmically intrinsic communication, this approach obviates the need for communication among a number of functionally specialized modules.

The NON-VON architecture represents an initial attempt to explore the possibilities for the development of machines of the second category. In particular, the central focus of the NON-VON project has been the development of a single machine having favorable performance and cost/performance characteristics over a relatively wide range of AI and other symbolic applications.

3. NON-VON ARCHITECTURE
The name NON-VON is used to describe a family of massively parallel machines that have been under investigation at Columbia University since 1980. The top-level organization of the current version of the general NON-VON architecture is shown in Figure 9–1. A number of distinct machine configurations have been defined and evaluated, however, based in part on the fact that some of the

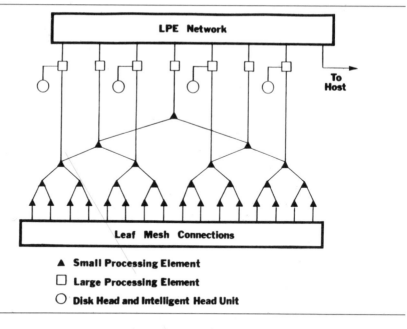

Figure 9–1. Organization of the General NON-VON Machine.

applications that have been investigated require only a subset of the subsystems comprised by the general NON-VON machine, and in part on the evolution of the architecture over time in response to experimental findings. An initial prototype, called NON-VON 1, embodying some, but not all of the features of the general machine architecture, has been operational at Columbia University since January, 1985. An overview of the NON-VON machine family is provided in [37].

Central to all members of the NON-VON family is a massively parallel *active memory*. The active memory is composed of a very large number (as many as a million in a full-scale "supercomputer" configuration, and between 4K and 32K in the low-cost configurations evaluated in this chapter) of simple, area-efficient *small processing elements* (SPE's), which are implemented using custom very large scale integrated (VLSI) circuits. The most recently fabricated active memory chip contains eight 8-bit processing elements; a detailed description of this chip can be found in [41]. Each SPE comprises a small local RAM, a modest amount of processing logic, and an *I/O switch* that permits the machine to be dynamically reconfigured to support various forms of interprocessor communication.

In the current version of the general NON-VON machine, the SPE's are configured as a complete binary tree whose leaves are also interconnected to form a two-dimensional orthogonal mesh. Each node of the active memory tree, with the exception of the leaves and root, is thus connected to three neighboring SPE's, which are called the *parent, left child,* and *right child* of the node in question. (Aspects of the chip-, board-, and system-level packaging of the active memory tree are discussed in [38]. Each leaf is connected to its parent and to its four mesh-adjacent SPE's, which are called its *north, south, east,* and *west* neighbors. In addition, the I/O switches may be dynamically configured in such a way as to support "linear neighbor" communication—specifically, communication between any pair of nodes that would be adjacent in an in-order enumeration [26] of the active memory tree.

NON-VON programs are not stored within the small RAM associated with each SPE, but instead are broadcast to the active memory by one or more large processing elements (LPE's), each based on an off-the-shelf 32-bit microprocessor (a Motorola 68020, in the current design) having a significant amount of local RAM. In the simplest NON-VON configuration, which was also the first to be implemented, the entire active memory operates under the control of a single LPE[2] which broadcasts instructions through a high-speed interface called the active memory controller for simultaneous execution by all enabled SPE's. This simple configuration thus restricts NON-VON's operation to what Flynn [11] has called the single instruction stream, multiple data stream (SIMD) mode of execution.

The current version of the general NON-VON design, however, provides for a number of LPE's, each capable of broadcasting an independent stream of instructions to some subtree of the active memory tree, as first described in [45]. Specifically, each SPE above a certain fixed level in the active memory tree is connected to its own LPE and active memory controller, which is capable of sending an independent instruction sequence to control the corresponding active memory subtree. The LPE's in the general machine are interconnected using a high-bandwidth, low-latency two-stage interconnection scheme called a root-point network [Shaw, 1985a]. The incorporation of a number of communicating LPE's gives the general NON-VON architecture the capacity for multiple instruction stream, multiple data stream (MIMD) and multiple SIMD (MSIMD) execution, multitasking applications, and multiuser operation. (Further discussion may be found in [37].)

The general NON-VON architecture also includes a secondary processing subsystem based on a bank of "intelligent" rotating storage devices. Specifically, each LPE at a particular, fixed level within the active memory tree is connected to a single-head Winchester disk drive, permitting high-bandwidth parallel I/O. Associated with each disk head is a small amount of logic capable of dynamically examining and performing certain simple computations (hash coding, for example) on the data passing beneath it. (Further discussion may be found in [35] and [36].)

Only a subset of the features of the general NON-VON architecture are in fact required to perform the benchmark tasks described in this chapter. The particular configuration assumed for each task will be described in the three sections in which the results themselves are presented.

One of the most important aspects of the NON-VON active memory is the highly efficient hardware support it provides for a set of associative processing primitives that have proven useful in a wide range of AI applications. The machine's very fine granularity allows processing elements to be associated with individual data elements, offering the user the capabilities of an unusually powerful and flexible content-addressable memory. Hardware features of the active memory support the massively parallel manipulation of data elements of arbitrary length. Large data elements may span more than one SPE, or several small ones may be packed within a single SPE. It is expected that systems software will ultimately hide the detailed mapping between processing elements and data elements from the programmer, allowing the user to deal with such abstractions as sets of "intelligent records," which may be thought of as capable of manipulating their own contents in parallel.

Among the hardware features provided within the SPE's to support these associative processing capabilities are

1. Logic allowing a string broadcast by the controlling LPE to be very rapidly matched against the contents of all SPE's in parallel. Using the special NON-VON string-matching instructions, a single-instruction inner loop for string matching (terminated by an "end-of-string" signal carried by a special control wire) may be implemented, allowing matching to occur at approximately 3 million bytes per second per SPE (in the most recently fabricated prototype chip). A large active memory should thus be capable of matching at an aggregate rate of more than a trillion bytes per second.

2. The inclusion of both eight-bit and one-bit registers and RAM, allowing sets of data elements to be conveniently marked and manipulated in parallel in various ways. Such operations are facilitated by the ALU, which provides highly efficient support for logical operations on one-bit flags.

3. A special one-bit register called the ENABLE flag. All SPE's in which the ENABLE flag is set to zero are *disabled*, and ignore all instructions until the subsequent execution of an ENABLE instruction, which "awakens" all SPE's. This mechanism, variants of which have been used in a number of other parallel machines, facilitates parallel operations on selected sets of data elements identified on the basis of some aspect of their contents.

4. A multiple match resolution instruction called RESOLVE, which may be used to mark a single member (the one which would occur first in an inorder traversal of the active memory tree) of a specified set of SPE's. Together with the REPORT instruction, which transfers data from a single enabled SPE to the controlling LPE, this technique may be used to sequentially enumerate the members of an arbitrary marked set of data elements in time linearly proportional to the cardinality of the set.

These associative processing mechanisms are employed in a number of the algorithms whose performance is reported in this paper. Further discussion of the use of NON-VON's active memory to support various associative processing techniques may be found in [36].

4. PRODUCTION SYSTEMS

After several decades of research on artificial intelligence, rule-based *production systems* have emerged as one of the most important and widely employed tools for the implementation of expert systems and other AI software. Although the modularity, perspicuity, and ease of modification and augmentation that are characteristic of rule-based systems offer a number of potential advantages in the execution of many large-scale AI tasks, their use in such applications is in some cases very costly in execution time. This poses particular problems in the case of real-time applications and other tasks characterized by severe and inflexible time constraints. The possibility of using parallel hardware to accelerate the execution of production systems is thus of considerable interest.

Forgy [12] considered the problem of executing production systems in parallel on the ILLIAC IV, but was forced to significantly modify the production system paradigm in order to obtain reasonable performance. Stolfo and Shaw [45] subsequently proposed a highly parallel machine called DADO, which was intended specifically for the execution of production systems; an early prototype of the DADO machine is presently operational. More recently, members of the DADO project have investigated a number of issues related to languages and algorithms for the parallel execution of production systems [44].

As a first step in evaluating NON-VON's performance in the domain of rule-based systems, we have implemented and analyzed an algorithm [22] for the parallel execution of production systems implemented using the language OPS5 [13], which was developed by researchers at Carnegie-Mellon University. OPS5 was chosen as the vehicle for our investigations into parallel execution of production systems for several reasons:

1. It is widely known and has been evaluated favorably by other researchers.
2. It has been used to build a large and successful commercial production system [31].
3. Static and dynamic characteristics of six substantial OPS5 production systems have already been measured [17].
4. Its speed can be increased significantly by parallel execution, despite the fact that the language was designed for sequential processing.

The NON-VON OPS5 algorithm may be regarded as a parallel version of Forgy's Rete Match [14] algorithm, which exploits the observation that firing an OPS5 production causes only a few changes to working memory and that these changes have few effects on the conflict set. This observation may be exploited, even on a sequential machine, if the production system is compiled into a dataflow graph, with state information saved at each node during execution. A change to working memory is entered into initial nodes of the graph. Consequent state changes then propagate through the graph, updating information stored in intermediate nodes. State changes in terminal nodes of the graph represent changes to the conflict set.

The execution cycle for an OPS5 production system has three phases: *match*, *select*, and *act*. In the Rete Match algorithm, the match phase has two steps. First, *intracondition tests* are executed to check that attributes in a working memory element satisfy the specified relational operators, and that variables occurring more than once in a condition element are bound consistently. Subsequently, *intercondition tests* are performed to verify consistent binding of variables across multiple condition elements in a production's left-hand side. The NON-VON OPS5 algorithm, which was implemented and tested by Bruce Hillyer using the NON-VON instruction-level simulator, achieves its performance and cost/performance advantages primarily by accelerating the execution of these two components of the match phase in the case of working-memory additions and by replacing them with a more highly parallel associative step in the case of working-memory deletions.

The NON-VON OPS5 algorithm is based on an algorithm by Gupta [16] (his Algorithm 3). This algorithm was designed for the DADO machine [45] in a prototype configuration consisting of 1023 identical "off-the-shelf" 8-bit microprocessors. The NON-VON algorithm assumes 33 LPE's (or 32 LPE's and one dedicated host machine), each of which is somewhat more powerful than a DADO PE, and 16K SPE's, which make possible a greater degree of associative parallelism. The 32 "non-host" LPE's are assumed to be attached at the fifth level of the active memory tree; the LPE's that would be associated with the first through fourth levels in a fully general NON-VON machine are not required for the execution of this algorithm. The high-bandwidth LPE network is also not required, and could be replaced with a simple bus without significantly degrading performance in the production systems application.

In the NON-VON OPS5 algorithm, intracondition testing is performed in the active memory using two massively parallel SIMD computation steps. The first step simultaneously evaluates individual terms of all condition elements. The second step determines the satisfaction of all condition elements in a single parallel communication step, requiring time proportional to the number of terms in the longest condition element.[3] The synchronous nature of SIMD execution was found not to limit the rate of processing in this phase.

The more limited potential for parallelism embodied in the intercondition testing step is captured using a MSIMD execution discipline, in which independent instruction streams are broadcast to 32 separate active memory subtrees by the 32 LPE's. Pure SIMD processing would have been a serious constraint during this portion of the execution because evaluation of the Rete dataflow graphs presents a high degree of data sensitivity. The use of active memory subtrees, on the other hand, significantly enhances the power of the LPE's by providing a fast associative search capability. The select and act phases, which have little inherent parallelism in OPS5, are performed sequentially by a single LPE (or by an attached host processor), although a modest speed-up is obtained by overlapping a portion of these computations with the subsequent match phase.

An experimental complier and run-time system for the execution of OPS5 on a one-LPE NON-VON has been written and tested on an instruction-level simulator. In order to predict the algorithm's performance when executing real production systems, its running time was calculated based on measurements obtained by Gupta and Forgy [17] of the static and dynamic characteristics of six actual production systems, which had an average of 910 inference rules each. By counting the number of NON-VON instructions, it has been possible to determine the number of clock cylces required for each of the SIMD processing steps under the assumptions implicit in Gupta and Forgy's data. By adding approximate overhead values for nonoverlapped execution in the LPE's,[4] we have been able to predict with reasonable accuracy the time required per production firing cycle,[5] and hence the rate of production system execution on NON-VON.

According to these calculations, the NON-VON configuration outlined above should require 1108 microseconds per production firing, yielding an execution rate of 903 productions per second. By way of comparison, A Lisp-based OPS5 interpreter executing the sequential Rete Match algorithm on a VAX 11/780 typically fires between 1 and 5 rules per second, while a Bliss-based interpreter executes between 5 and 12 productions per second [Gupta (personal communication)]. The NON-VON machine configuration assumed in these calculations would embody 2048 custom chips, each containing eight SPE's, and about 660 chips for the 33 LPE's. The hardware cost of such a system is projected to be somewhere between that of a VAX 11/780 and a DECSystem-2060. NON-VON's cost/performance ratio in executing OPS5 production systems is thus estimated to be approximately two orders of magnitude better than that of a conventional sequential machine in practice. Furthermore, our analysis suggests that the machine's relative performance advantage should increase as the production system becomes larger.

A detailed discussion of the assumptions underlying the above projections, and of the precise manner in which our results were derived, can be found in [22].

5. COMPUTER VISION

A number of operations performed by commerical and experimental image-understanding systems are extremely time-consuming when executed on a conventional sequential machine. For this reason, substantial efforts have already been made to develop special-purpose machines and algorithms adapted to various computer vision tasks. The machines described in the literature may, for the most part, be divided into four general architectural categories:

1. *Pipelined architectures* such as the NBS Pipelined Image Processing Engine [24] and the Cytocomputer [43], in which the task at hand is typically divided into a number of functions and each stage in the pipeline is configured by a control unit to perform one function.
2. *Mesh-connected architectures* [50] such as CLIP4 [8], MPP [34], and the ICL DAP [30], which are based on a rectangular array of (typically one-bit) processing elements, each connected to its nearest four or eight neighbors, and each corresponding to a either a single pixel or a small rectangular cell of pixels in the image.
3. *Multiprocessor architectures*, examples of which include PASM [46] and ZMOB [27], in which a number of general-purpose microcomputers cooperate to solve a given image-understanding task, communicating through some form of processor interconnection network.
4. *Hierarchical architectures*, including *cone* and *pyramid* machines [9, 18, 47, 49], in which the original image is progressively reduced through the application of successive transformations in a manner analogous to that apparently employed in the human visual system.

The general NON-VON architecture provides efficient support for most of the parallel vision algorithms typically executed on each of the last three classes of architectures; in addition, many of the algorithms executed on pipelined vision machines may be transformed into SIMD algorithms amenable to execution within NON-VON's active memory. While we expect NON-VON to prove highly useful for all levels of computer vision applications, from low-level signal processing and the extraction of primitive geometric properties through high-level object recognition and scene analysis, our work to date has concentrated largely on low- and intermediate-level computer vision tasks.

A number of image understanding algorithms have been developed and tested using a functional simulator, and in some cases, the NON-VON machine instruction level simulator. In particular, algorithms have been developed for:

1. Image correlation
2. Image histogramming
3. Image thresholding
4. Union, intersection, and difference of two binary images
5. Connected component labeling
6. Euler number of connected components
7. Component area
8. Component perimeter
9. Component center of gravity
10. Component eccentricity
11. The Hough transform
12. The "moving light display" problem

These tasks were chosen to span several levels of image-understanding applications, and to assess NON-VON's applicability to a number of different kinds of operations arising in the course of constructing integrated vision systems. Performance comparisons among machines is made more difficult by the fact that the figures reported in the literature are based on a number of different benchmarks. We have nonetheless attempted to compare NON-VON's performance on the above tasks with that of other (parallel and sequential) machines wherever possible. Our projections suggest that NON-VON should offer significant performance and cost/performance advantages over sequential machines for each of these tasks, and should in a number of cases improve on the best results reported in the literature for special-purpose vision architectures and other highly parallel machines.

Table 9–1 summarizes NON-VON's projected performance on some of the applications for which figures are available, or may be estimated, for other machines. In particular, the performance of a 32K-processor NON-VON machine[6] is compared with that of the CLIP4, with 9K processors, the ICL DAP, with 4K processors, and the Goodyear Aerospace MPP, with 16K processors, as well as with a conventional sequential machine, the DEC VAX 11/780. We were unable to find or estimate performance figures for these machines in the case of the Hough transform and the "moving light display" tasks. Our projections indicate, however, that a NON-VON configuration with 32K processing elements should be capable of executing a Hough transform with 1000 boundary points in approximately 1.1 milliseconds, and a moving-light-display task with 10 frame points in about 1.5 milliseconds.

Two hierarchical data structures that may be implemented naturally on the NON-VON machine are employed in the NON-VON algorithms for these tasks. The first is the *multiresolution pyramid* [48], which represents the original (binary or gray-scale) image at a number of different levels of detail, each containing one quarter of the number of pixels present at the next highest level of detail. Multiresolution pyramids are implemented on NON-VON by storing the

Table 9–1. Comparative Execution Times for Certain Vision Tasks[a]

Task	VAX	CLIP4	DAP	MPP	NON-VON
Image histogram	85.0[b]	512.0[b]	69.0	128.0	2.2
Image thresholding	85.0[b]	1.0[b]	0.062[b]	0.025	0.015
Image correlation	3000.0[b]	16.0[b]	16.0[b]	1.0	0.5
Connected component labeling	8000.0[b]	160.0[b]	160.0[b]	20.0[b]	12.5
Area	85.0[b]	4.0[b]	5.0[b]	0.5[b]	0.2
Moments	85.0[b]	4.0[b]	5.0[b]	1.0[b]	0.2
Perimeter	245.0[b]	8.0[b]	8.0[b]	0.5[b]	0.3
Center of gravity	340.0[b]	24.0[b]	24.0[b]	3.0[b]	0.6

[a] *All times in milliseconds*; image size: 128 × 128.
[b] Estimated.

original image in the (mesh-connected) leaf SPE's and the less detailed levels in the internal SPE's. The latter process is based on a straightforward mapping of the natural quartic-tree interpretation of the multiresolution pyramid onto the active memory's binary tree structure.

The second data structure used to represent images in the NON-VON machine is a variant of the *quadtree* called the *binary image tree*, which was originally proposed by Knowlton [25] as an encoding scheme for the compact transmission of image data. The original binary image is again stored in the leaf SPE's. Internal nodes, however, can take one of three values, which may be thought of as "black," "white," and "gray." An internal node has the value black if its two children are both black, white if its two children are both white, and gray otherwise. This data structure is used in most of the NON-VON algorithms that operate on binary image data.

A number of aspects of the NON-VON machine architecture, exploited as part of several frequently used algorithmic techniques, are responsible for the machine's performance and cost/performance advantages in computer vision applications. The simplest technique, which has also been employed on such machines as MPP and the ICL DAP, involves the use of ordinary content-addressable arithmetic and logical operations to perform a single operation in parallel on all pixels. This technique is illustrated in its simplest form by the algorithm for image thresholding, in which a gray-scale image is transformed to a binary image by setting all pixels whose intensities exceed a specified threshold value to one, and all other pixels to zero. A NON-VON machine of a size sufficient to store each pixel in its own PE is capable of thresholding an entire image in approximately 15 microseconds, independent of the size of the image, by broadcasting the threshold value to all pixels and executing a parallel comparison and assignment sequence.

Like a number of highly parallel machines developed by other researchers, NON-VON is thus able to achieve a very substantial speed-up over a conventional sequential machine on simple associative operations of the kind exemplified by image thresholding. The same general technique is used in the NON-VON algorithm for image histogramming [23], in which the bounds of a given intensity range are compared in parallel with all pixel values to identify those pixels whose values fall within a given intensity range. (Histogramming is often performed prior to the conversion of a gray-scale image to a binary image in order to choose an appropriate threshold value.)

Unlike the massively parallel mesh-connected machines, however, the tree-structured connections embedded in the NON-VON active memory permit a major reduction in the time required to determine the number of pixels falling within each histogram bin. In the NON-VON algorithm, this quantity is computed through an $O(\log n)$ level-by-level addition procedure, where n is the number of pixels in the image. The running time of the algorithm is further reduced, however, by pipelining this computation for successive intensity ranges, resulting in an $O(b + \log n)$ algorithm, where b is the number of histogram bins.

The NON-VON histogram algorithm is easily modified to produce a cumulative or normalized histogram.

A different use of the active memory tree is illustrated by Ibrahim's connected component algorithm for NON-VON [23]. The algorithm begins by constructing the binary image tree representation of the original image data, which requires time logarithmic in the number of pixels. It will be recalled that the binary image tree includes explicit representations of black rectangles of various sizes from the original image. The connected component algorithm enumerates all of these black rectangles (using the RESOLVE and REPORT instructions) one by one in order of decreasing size (or equivalently, of increasing tree level).

As each such rectangle R_i is enumerated, it is assigned a new component number if not already labeled. Any rectangle R_j that is adjacent to R_i is then assigned the same label, as are all other rectangles previously assigned the same component number as R_j. (Note that this last operation requires only a single broadcast and assignment step, independent of the number of rectangles having the same component number as R_j.) Because only one pass through the set of black rectangles in the binary image tree is required, Ibrahim's algorithm executes in time proportional to the number of rectangles, which in most images is much smaller than the number of pixels. (Details of this and other geometric NON-VON algorithms may be found in [23].)

The importance of NON-VON's mesh connections in computer vision applications is illustrated by such low-level signal processing operations as image correlation and various types of two-dimensional filtering. The NON-VON algorithms for these operations rely on a considerable amount of communication among adjacent and nearly-adjacent neighbors in the mesh. Although Ibrahim [23] has developed techniques to perform such operations on a "pure" tree machine that tend to minimize the need for such communication, NON-VON's mesh connections make possible a considerable increase in performance.

Other vision algorithms make use of the MSIMD execution capabilities of the general NON-VON architecture to partition a problem into a number of subproblems, each of which is solved in a different active memory subtree. In many cases, several forms of parallelism are exploited in the same algorithm. Although work on high-level image understanding on the NON-VON machine is still in its earliest phases, our experience with the parallel execution of production systems suggests that significant opportunities exist for accelerating such applications as well.

6. KNOWLEDGE BASE MANAGEMENT

A number of "real world" AI applications require the construction and manipulation of large *knowledge bases*. Such applications tend to be characterized by the need to access the same data in a number of different ways, often in conjunction with some form of inferencing. The need to flexibly access and deductively manipulate large knowledge bases has led a number of researches to construct logic-based and knowledge-oriented database systems [15, 35, 51], whose primitive operations are based on the relational model of data [2]. In addition, many knowledge base systems that do not make explicit use of relational data structures or access primitives nonetheless employ equivalent or closely analogous representation formalisms and operations at some level.

Unfortunately, knowledge base management systems tend to rely heavily on such "difficult" operations as the relational join, whose execution may be extremely time consuming on a sequential machine, particularly in the case of large databases. Several researchers [32, 35] have thus proposed using special hardware supporting the rapid execution of such database primitives in constructing systems designed for AI applications. Algorithms for a number of database primitives have been developed for the NON-VON machine, including:

1. Select
2. Project
3. Join
4. Union
5. Intersection
6. Set difference
7. Aggregation
8. Various statistical operations

To evaluate NON-VON's applicability to the kinds of database operations most relevant to AI applications, a detailed analysis was performed of the machine's projected performance on a set of benchmark queries formulated by Hawthorn and DeWitt [19]. These authors presented an analysis of the predicted performance of a number of database machine architectures (specifically, RAP [33], CASSM [3], DBC [1], DIRECT [6], CAFS [4], and associative disks [28, 29, 42]) on three relational database queries.

In evaluating NON-VON, we used the same three queries and similar techniques for performance analysis and for the adjustment of machine configuration to control for hardware cost. In particular, we assumed a NON-VON configuration having 4K SPE's (512 8-processor chips), 16 disk drives, and a single LPE—a configuration comparable in each relevant dimension to that of the other machines considered in the Hawthorn and DeWitt analysis.

Hawthorn and DeWitt's first query was a simple relational selection operation. Their analysis predicted that all six of the architectures they examined would have roughly comparable performance on this query. Our analysis, using the same techniques, predicted that NON-VON should achieve a slightly, but not significantly, faster performance on this simple selection query. The lack of a significant performance difference between NON-VON and the six database machines evaluated by Hawthorn and DeWitt is attributable to the fact that all seven machines are capable of the kinds of simple associative processing techniques required to achieve close to the maximum performance permitted by

Table 9–2. Query 1, Hawthorn and DeWitt (Simple Relational Selection)

	Response Times in Seconds	
	Best	Worst
Associative Disks, CAFS	0.089	0.267
CASSM	0.156	0.334
DBC	0.095	0.273
DIRECT	0.066	0.490
RAP	0.066	0.493
NON-VON	0.042	0.267

Table 9–3. Query 2, Hawthorn and DeWitt (Relational Join)

	Response times in seconds	
	Best	Worst
Associative Disks	5.04	5.90
DBC	5.04	5.90
CASSM	15.50	15.83
DIRECT	2.37	3.24
RAP	7.06	14.18
CAFS	14.48	14.81
NON-VON	0.21	0.67

the aggregate disk transfer rate of their (cost-normalized) banks of disk drives. It is on the more demanding queries frequently found in AI-oriented applications that NON-VON is able to offer a greater relative advantage. Table 9–2 summarizes our results and those of Hawthorn and DeWitt for the first sample query. The second query, which may have more immediate relevance to complex knowledge base management applications, involves a relational join operation. On this query, NON-VON achieves a performance improvement of approximately an order of magnitude over the six database machines evaluated by Hawthorn and DeWitt, as indicated in Table 9–3.

There are three reasons for NON-VON's surprising speed, even by comparison with DIRECT, which is the fastest of the database machines on this query. The first is that DIRECT stores entire records in its cache when processing, whereas NON-VON projects over those attributes that are of interest, discarding the rest. Second, DIRECT reads data from one of its eight (faster) disk drives, whereas NON-VON loads one of the argument relations in parallel through all 16 heads of its (slower) drives. (Unlike NON-VON, DIRECT would not benefit greatly from the use of parallel disk transfers; DeWitt and Hawthorn [7] estimate that parallel disk input would improve the join performance of architectures like DIRECT by only 4%.) Third, DIRECT performs a sequential search through one of the argument relations for each tuple of the other relation it

Table 9-4. Query 3, Hawthorn and DeWitt (Aggregation)

	Response times in seconds	
	Best	Worst
Associative Disks	1.6	2.2
CAFS	1.6	2.2
CASSM	0.6	0.8
RAP	0.8	1.5
DBC	0.7	1.8
DIRECT	0.2	0.5
NON-VON	0.05	0.27

considers, in contrast with NON-VON's associative matching, followed by fast enumeration of responders using RESOLVE and REPORT instructions.

The final query considered by DeWitt and Hawthorn involved an aggregation operation in which the tuples in the argument relation were divided into groups according to the values of two attributes, and the sum of the values of a third attribute was computed separately for each group. Using associative processing techniques (both internal and external), together with the capability for fast addition provided by the active memory's tree connections, NON-VON again achieved significant performance improvements over the other architectures evaluated by Hawthorn and DeWitt. Although the authors did not explicitly present the times required by the machines they studied for this query, a graph is provided from which these times were estimated. Comparative results for this query are presented in Table 9-4.

Further details of the assumptions and analysis underlying the results presented above may be found in [21].

7. CONCLUSIONS

It is dangerous to attempt to draw firm conclusions about the range of applicability of a novel computer architecture over a wide range of applications on the basis of a relatively small number of benchmark tasks. Based on our research to date, however, it would appear that the general NON-VON architecture may offer significant performance and cost/performance advantages over both conventional and, in a number of cases, special-purpose machines in at least three superficially disparate AI task areas.

In particular, we have presented a number of algorithms, analytic performance projections, and simulation results suggesting that NON-VON is capable of rapid and cost-effective performance on a number of tasks in the areas of production system execution, low- and intermediate-level image understanding, and knowledge-base management. Although the extent of NON-VON's relative advantage over conventional sequential machines differs for different AI tasks, performance and cost/performance advantages of as much as two to three orders of magnitude have been predicted in many cases.

Different aspects of the NON-VON architecture appear to be responsible for the machine's advantages in different problem areas. It is nonetheless possible to identify a relatively small number of features, several of which are typically operative in the case of any single application, to which the machine's advantages may be attributed:

1. The effective exploitation of an unusually high degree of parallelism, which is made possible by the very fine granularity of the active memory.
2. The extensive use of broadcast communication, high-speed content-addressable matching, and other associative processing techniques.
3. The use of the active memory tree to execute algebraically commutative and associative operations (such as sum and maximum) in logarithmic time.
4. The exploitation of other physical and logical interconnection topologies to support a number of problem-specific communication functions.
5. The capacity for SIMD, MIMD and MSIMD execution, and for a mixture of synchronous and asynchronous execution within a single algorithm.
6. The simplicity and cost-effectiveness with which the machine can be implemented using currently available technology.

Although not all of these architectural features are relevant to every AI application, each is exploited in different ways in a number of different algorithms. While it is difficult to rigorously explicate the intuitive notion of computational generality, NON-VON would seem to have many of the properties of a rather general AI-oriented machine having a number of widely applicable architectural features, as opposed to an amalgam of special-purpose subsystems, each performing a fixed, application-specific task.

In closing, it is worth noting that NON-VON's strong performance on any given AI task is probably of less interest than the *range* of diverse AI tasks that would appear to be efficiently executable within a single machine. Although there is still insufficient evidence to adequately evaluate the extent to which the NON-VON architecture might serve as the basis for a high-performance "general AI machine," the work described in this chapter might be regarded as an early, preliminary step toward the ultimate development of such machines.

ACKNOWLEDGMENTS

Bruce Hillyer was directly responsible for implementing, simulating, and analyzing most of the data-base management and production-system algorithms discussed in this chapter. The NON-VON image understanding work we have described is largely attributable to Hussein Ibrahim and John Kender. More generally, the author wishes to acknowledge the direct and indirect contributions of the NON-VON hardware implementation team, under the direction of Ted Sabety; of Dong Choi, who was responsible for much of the simulation software used to obtain the results we have reported, and of the other Ph.D. students and research staff members associated with the NON-VON project, without whose efforts this work would not have been possible.

NOTES

1. To maximize circuit yield, each SPE was fabricated with only 32 bytes of local RAM in the current working prototype; in a production version of the machine, however, each SPE would probably contain the maximum amount of local RAM supported by the instruction set, which is 256 bytes.
2. The prototype now in operation uses a VAX 11/750 in place of the Motorola 68020.
3. This can be improved to time logarithmic in the number of terms in the longest condition element with a worst-case 50% decrease in memory utilization, using techniques closely related to the allocation schemes for database records described by Shaw and Hillyer [40].
4. The figures given for host and LPE processing are estimates, unlike the SPE figures, which are derived from actual code.
5. We have assumed that the only actions in the right-hand sides of productions are additions, deletions, and modifications of working-memory elements. The right-hand side of a production expressed in OPS5 can in fact cause arbitrarily large amounts of I/O and can call any function written in Lisp, but the time consumed by such operations does not provide any information about the performance of the production system inferencing engine.
6. The cost of such a NON-VON configuration is estimated to be on the order of that of a DECSystem-2060.

REFERENCES

1. J. Banerjee, R. I. Baum, D. K. Hsiao, and K. Kannan, "Concepts and Capabilities of a Database Computer," *ACM Trans. on Database Systems*, no. 3. (4): 1978.
2. E. F. Codd, "Relational Completeness of Data Base Sublanguages," In R. Rustin (ed.) *Courant Computer Science Symposium 6:* Data Base Systems, New York: Prentice-Hall, 1972.
3. G. P. Copeland, G. J. Lipovski, and S. Y. W. Su, "The Architecture of CASSM: A Cellular System for Nonnumeric Processing," *Proc. First Annual Symp. on Computer Architecture*, 1973.
4. G. F. Coulouris, J. M. Evans, and R. W. Mitchell, "Towards Content Addressing in Databases," *Computer Journal*, 15(2): 1972.
5. M. F. Deering, "Hardware and Software Architectures for Efficient AI," *AAAI-84, Proc. of the Natl. Conf. on Artificial Intelligence*, 1984, pp. 73–78.
6. D. J., DeWitt, "DIRECT—A Multiprocessor Organization for Supporting Relational Database Management Systems," *IEEE Trans. on Computers*, C-28(6), June 1979.
7. D. J. DeWitt, and P. B. Hawthorn, "A Performance Evaluation of Database Machine Architecture," *Journal of Digital Systems*, 1982.
8. M. J. B. Duff, "A Large Scale Integrated Circuit Array Parallel Processor," *Proc. IEEE Conf. on Pattern Recognition and Image Processing*, 1976, pp. 728–733.
9. C. R. Dyer, "A VLSI Pyramid Machine for Hierarchical Parallel Image Processing," *Proc. IEEE Conf. on Pattern Recognition and Image Processing* 1981, pp. 281–386.
10. S. E. Fahlman, "Preliminary Design for a Million-Element NETL Machine," Tech. Rep. Department of Computer Science, Carnegie-Mellon University, Pittsburgh, PA, 1980.
11. M. J. Flynn, "Some Computer Organizations and their Effectiveness," *IEEE Trans. on Computers*, vol. C-21, Sept. 1972.

12. C. L. Forgy, "Note on Production Systems and Illiac IV," Tech. Rep. Department of Computer Science, Carnegie-Mellon University, Pittsburgh, PA, July 1980.
13. C. L. Forgy, "OPS5 Users' Manual." Tech. Rep. CMU-CS-81-135, PA, Dept. of Computer Science, Carnegie-Mellon University, Pittsburgh, PA, 1981.
14. C. L. Forgy, "Rete: A Fast Algorithm for the Many Pattern/Many Object Pattern Match Problem," *Artificial Intelligence*, 19 (1), Sept. 1982.
15. H. Gallaire, and J. Minker (eds.) *Logic and Data Bases.* New York: Plenum Press 1978.
16. A. Gupta, "Implementing OPS5 Production Systems on DADO," *Proc. of the 1984 Intl Conference on Parallel Processing*, Aug. 21–24, 1984.
17. A. Gupta, and C. L. Forgy, "Measurements on Production Systems," Tech. Rep. Computer Science Department, Carnegie-Mellon University, Pittsburgh, PA, 1983.
18. A. R. Hanson, and E. M. Riseman, "Processing Cones: A Computational Structure for Image Analysis," In S. Tanimoto and A. Klinger (eds.), *Structured Computer Vision*, New York: Academic Press, 1980.
19. P. B. Hawthorn, and D. J. DeWitt, "Performance Analysis of Alternative Database Machine Architectures," *IEEE Trans. on Software Engineering*, SE-8(1):61–75, 1982.
20. W. D. Hillis, "The Connection Machine," AI Memo No. 646, Artificial Intelligence Laboratory, MIT, Cambridge, MA, Sept. 1981.
21. B. K. Hillyer, D. E. Shaw, and Nigam, A. "NON-VON's Performance on Certain Database Benchmarks," Tech. Rep. Department of Computer Science, Columbia University, New York, NY, 1984.
22. B. K. Hillyer, and D. E. Shaw, "Execution of Production Systems on a Massively Parallel Machine," Tech. Rep. Department of Computer Science, Columbia University, New York, NY, Sept. 1984.
23. H. A. H. Ibrahim, *Image Understanding Algorithms on Fine-Grained Tree-Structured SIMD Machines.* Ph.D. thesis, Department of Computer Science, Columbia University, New York, NY, Oct. 1984.
24. E. Kent, M. Shneier, and R. Lumia, "NBS Pipelined Image Processing Engine," *Workshop on Algorithm-Guided Parallel Architectures For Automatic Target Recognition*, Leesburg, VA, July 1984.
25. K. Knowlton, "Progressive Transmission of Gray-Scale and Binary Pictures by Simple, Efficient, and Lossless Encoding Schemes," *Proc. of the IEEE*, 68(7): July 1980.
26. D. E. Knuth, *The Art of Computer Programming, Vol. 1: Fundamental Algorithms.* Reading, MA: Addison-Wesley, 1969.
27. T. Kushner, A. U. Wu, and A. Rosenfeld, "Image Processing on ZMOB," *IEEE Trans. on Computers*, 31(10): October 1982.
28. G. G. Langdon, "A Note on Associative Processors for Data Management," *Trans. on Database Systems*, 3(2): June, 1978.
29. C. S. Lin, D. C. P. Smith and J. M. Smith, "The Design of a Rotating Associative Memory for Relational Database Applications," *Trans. on Database Systems*, (1): March 1976.
30. P. Marks, "Low Level Vision Using an Array Processor," *Computer Graphics and Image Processing*, 14:287–292 1980.
31. J. McDermott, "R1: A Rule-Based Configurer of Computer Systems," Tech. Rep. CMU-CS-80-119, Computer Science Department, Carnegie-Mellon University, April 1980.
32. T. Moto-oka, and K. Fuchi, "The Architectures in the Fifth Generation Computers," In R. E. A. Mason (ed.), *Information Processing 83*, Sept. 1983.
33. E. A. Ozkarahan, S. A. Schuster, and K. C. Smith, *A Data Base Processor*, Tech. Rep. CSRG-43, Computer Systems Research Group, University of Toronto, Ontario, Canada, 1974.
34. J. L. Potter, "Image Processing on the Massively Parallel Processor," *Computer*, 16(1): Jan. 1983.
35. D. E. Shaw, *Knowledge-Based Retrieval on a Relational Database Machine.* Ph.D. thesis, Department of Computer Science, Stanford University, Stanford, CA, 1980.
36. D. E. Shaw, "The NON-VON Supercomputer," Tech. Rep. Department of Computer Science, Columbia University, New York, NY, Aug. 1982.
37. D. E. Shaw, "SIMD and MSIMD Variants of the NON-VON Supercomputer," *Proc. of COMPCON Spring '84*, San Francisco, CA, Feb. 1984.
38. D. E. Shaw, "Applications of VLSI Technology in a Massively Parallel Machine," *Circuits, Systems and Signal Processing*, 1985a (to appear).
39. D. E. Shaw, *The Rootpoint Interconnection Network.* Tech. Rep. Computer Science Department, Columbia University, New York, NY, 1985a (in preparation).

40. D. E. Shaw and B. K. Hillyer, "Allocation and Manipulation of Records in the NON-VON Supercomputer." Tech. Rep. Computer Science Department, Columbia University, New York, NY, 1982.
41. D. E. Shaw, and T. M. Sabety, "An Eight-Processor Chip for a Massively Parallel Machine," Tech. Rep. Computer Science Department, Columbia University, New York, NY, July 1984.
42. D. L. Slotnik, "Logic Per Track Devices," In F. Alt (ed.), *Advances in Computers*, Vol. 10. New York: Academic Press 1970.
43. S. R. Sternberg, "Biomedical Image Processing," *Computer*, 16(1): Jan. 1983.
44. S. J. Stolfo, "Five Algorithms for PS Execution on the DADO Machine," Tech. Rep. Computer Science Department, Columbia University, New York, NY, AAAI-84, *Proc. of the Natl. Conf. on Artificial Intelligence*, Aug. 1984.
45. S. J. Stolfo, and D. E. Shaw, "DADO: A Tree-Structured Machine Architecture for Production Systems," *Proc. Natl. Conf. on Artificial Intelligence*, 1982.
46. H. J. Siegel, L. J. Siegel, F. C. Kemmerer, P. T. Mueller, H. E. Smalley, and S. D. Smith, "PASM: A partitionable SIMD/MIMD System for Image Processing and Pattern Recognition," *IEEE Trans. on Computers*, 30(12): Dec. 1981.
47. S. Tanimoto, "A Pyramidal Approach to Parallel Processing." Tech. Rep. Computer Science Department, University of Washington, Scatter, WA, January 1983.
48. S. Tanimoto and A. Klinger, *Structured Computer Vision*. New York: Academic Press, 1980.
49. L. Uhr, "Recognition Cones, and Some Test Results." In A. R. Hanson and E. M. Riseman (eds.), *Computer Vision Systems*. New York: Academic Press, 1980.
50. S. H. Unger, "A Computer Oriented Towards Spatial Problems," *Proc. of the IRE*, 1958, p. 1744.
51. G. Wiederhold, "Knowledge and Database Management," *Software Magazine*, 1(1): p. 63–73, 1984.

10. LOW-LEVEL VISION ON WARP AND THE APPLY PROGRAMMING MODEL

LEONARD G. C. HAMEY, JON A. WEBB, AND I-CHEN WU

1. INTRODUCTION

In computer vision, the first, and often most time-consuming, step in image processing is *image-to-image* operations. In this step, an input image is mapped into an output image through some local operation that applies to a window around each pixel of the input image. Algorithms that fall into this class include: edge detection, smoothing, convolutions in general, contrast enhancement, color transformations, and thresholding. Collectively, we call these operations low-level vision. Low-level vision is often time-consuming simply because images are quite large—a typical size is 512×512 pixels, so the operation must be applied 262,144 times.

Fortunately, this step in image processing is easy to speed up, through the use of parallelism. The operation applied at every point in the image is often independent from point to point, and also does not vary much in execution time at different points in the image. This is because at this stage of image processing, nothing has been done to differentiate one area of the image from another, so that all areas are processed in the same way. Because of these two characteristics, many parallel computers achieve good efficiency in these algorithms, through the use of *input partitioning* [1].

In this chapter, we discuss a particular parallel computer, called the Warp machine, which has been developed for image and signal processing, and describe its use at this level of vision. We also define a language called Apply, which is specifically designed for implementing these algorithms. Apply runs on the Warp machine and also in C under Unix. The same Apply program can be compiled either to run on the Warp machine or under Unix, and it runs with good efficiency in both cases. Therefore, the programmer is not limited to developing his programs just on Warp, although they run much faster (typically 100 times faster) there; he can do some development under the more generally available Unix system.

We consider Apply and its implementation on Warp to be a significant development for image processing on supercomputers in general. The programmer of a supercomputer usually makes a substantial commitment to the particular supercomputer he is using because he cannot expect that his code will run efficiently on any other computer. This limits the use of supercomputers, because such a great investment in coding is required that only truly committed users will make this investment. With Apply however, the programmer can recompile his code for other machines. Right now, only Unix systems and Warp run Apply programs. But since we include a definition of Apply as it runs on Warp, and because most parallel computers support input partitioning, it should be possible to implement it on other supercomputers as well. Once this is done, the Apply programmer will be able to port his code easily to many different computers, lengthening the lifetime of his code and lessening the commitment he must make to a particular computer.

Apply also has implications for benchmarking of new image-processing supercomputers. Currently, it is hard to compare these computers, because they all run different, incompatible languages and operating systems, so the same program cannot be tested on different computers. Once Apply is implemented on different supercomputers, it will be possible to test their performance on an important class of image operations, namely low-level vision.

Apply is not a panacea for these problems; it is an application-specific language, which is potentially machine-independent. It cannot be used for all vision algorithms, and even some low-level vision algorithms cannot be efficiently expressed in it as it is currently defined.

We begin by reviewing the structure of the Warp machine, and then discuss our early work on low-level vision, where we developed the input partitioning method on Warp. Then we define and discuss Apply. Following this, we describe how Apply might be implemented on other computers.

1.1. Warp Machine Overview

This is a brief overview of Warp; more detail is available elsewhere [2–4]. Warp has three components—the Warp processor array (Warp array), the interface unit (IU), and the host, as depicted in Figure 10–1. The Warp array performs the computation-intensive routines, for example, low-level vision routines. The IU handles the input/output (I/O) between the array and the host and generates addresses and control signals for the Warp array. The host executes the parts of the application programs that are not mapped onto the Warp array and supplies the data to and receives the results from the array.

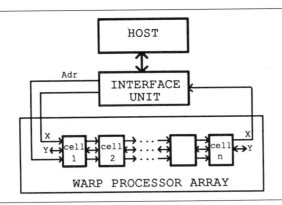

Figure 10–1. Warp machine overview.

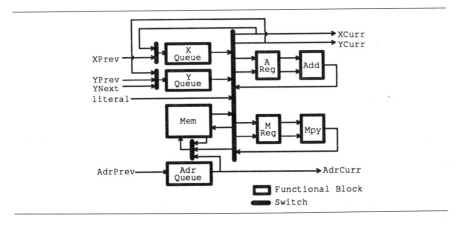

Figure 10–2. Warp cell data path.

The Warp array is a programmable, one-dimensional systolic array with identical cells called Warp cells. Data flow through the array on two data paths (X and Y), while addresses and systolic control signals travel on the Adr path (as shown in Figure 10–1).

Each Warp cell is implemented as a programmable horizontal microengine, with its own program memory and microsequencer. A Warp cell has a 32-bit-wide data path, as depicted in Figure 10–2. The data path consists of two 32-bit floating-point processing elements: one multiplier and one ALU, a 4K-word memory for resident and temporary data, a 128-word queue for each communication channel, and a 32-word register file to buffer data for each floating-point unit. All these components are interconnected through a crossbar switch as shown in Figure 10–2.

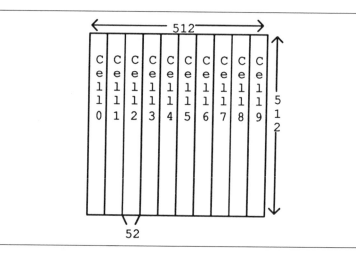

Figure 10–3. Input partitioning method on Warp.

The host consists of a VME-based work station (currently a Sun 3/160), which serves as the master controller of the Warp machine, and an "external host," so named because it is external to the work station. The work station provides a Unix environment for running application programs and the external host provides a high data transfer rate for communicating with the Warp array. The external host consists of three *stand-alone* 68020-based processors, which run without Unix support to avoid operating-system overheads. Two of the stand-alone processors are *cluster processors* responsible for transferring data to and from the Warp array, while the third one is a *support processor* that controls peripheral devices (e.g., the camera and the monitor) and handles interrupts originating in the clusters and Warp array.

The first two ten-cell machines used wire-warp technology. Production Warp machines are implemented with PC boards; the 19-inch rack is able to host the IU and up to 24 Warp cells. For the PC board version, each cell has increased local memory (32K-words) enlarged queues, and several other improvements [5].

2. LOW-LEVEL VISION ON WARP

We map low-level vision algorithms onto Warp by the input partitioning method. On a Warp array of ten cells, the image is divided into ten regions, by column, as shown in Figure 10–3. This gives each cell a tall, narrow region to process; for 512×512 image processing, the region size is 52 columns by 512 rows. To use technical terms from weaving, the Warp cells are the "warp" of the processing; the "weft" is the rows of the image as it passes through the Warp array.

The image is divided in this way using a series of macros called GETROW PUTROW, and COMPUTEROW. GETROW generates code that takes a row of an image from the external host, and distributes one-tenth of it to each of ten cells. The programmer includes a GETROW macro at the point in his program where he wants to obtain a row of the image; after the execution of the macro, a buffer in the internal cell memory has the data from the image row.

The GETROW macro works as follows. The external host sends in the image rows as a packed array of bytes—for a 512-byte-wide image, this array consists of 128 32-bit words. These words are unpacked and converted to floating-point numbers in the interface unit. The 512 32-bit floating-point numbers resulting from this operation are fed in sequence to the first cell of the Warp array. This cell takes one-tenth of the numbers, removing them from the stream, and passes through the rest to the next cell. The first cell then adds a number of zeros to replace the data it has removed, so that the number of data received and sent are equal.

This process is repeated in each cell. In this way, each cell obtains one-tenth of the data from a two of the image. As the program is executed, and the process is repeated for all rows of the image, each cell sees an adjacent set of columns of the image, as shown in Figure 10–3.

We have omitted certain details of GETROW—for example, usually the image row size is not an exact multiple of ten. In this case, the GETROW macro pads the row equally on both sides by having the interface unit generate an appropriate number of zeros on either side of the image row. Also, usually the area of the image each cell must see to generate its outputs overlaps with the next cell's area. In this case, the cell copies some of the data it receives to the next cell. All this code is automatically generated by GETROW.

PUTROW, the corresponding macro for output, takes a buffer of one-tenth of the row length from each cell and combines them by concatenation. The output row starts as a buffer of 512 zeros generated by the interface unit. The first cell discards the first one-tenth of these and adds its own data to the end. The second cell does the same, adding its data after the first. When the buffer leaves the last cell, all the zeros have been discarded and the first cell's data have reached the beginning of the buffer. The interface unit then converts the floating-point numbers in the buffer to zeros and outputs it to the external host, which receives an array of 512 bytes packed into 128 32-bit words. As with GETROW, PUTROW handles image buffers that are not multiples of ten, this time by discarding data on both sides of the buffer before the buffer is sent to the interface unit by the last cell.

During GETROW, no computation is performed; the same applies to PUTROW. Warp's horizontal microword, however, allow input, computation, and output at the same time. COMPUTEROW implements this. Ignoring the complications mentioned above, COMPUTEROW consists of three loops. In the first loop, the data for the cell are read into a memory buffer from the previous cell, as in GETROW, and at the same time the first one-tenth of the output buffer is discarded, as in PUTROW. In the second loop, nine-tenths of the input row is passed through to the next cell, as in GETROW; at the same time, nine-tenths of the output buffer is passed through, as in PUTROW. This loop is unwound by COMPUTEROW so that for every nine inputs and outputs passed through, one output of this cell is computed. In the third loop, the outputs computed in the second loop are passed on to the next cell, as in PUTROW.

There are several advantages to this approach to input pointing:

- Work on the external host is kept to a minimum. In the Warp machine, the external host tends to be a bottleneck in many algorithms; in the prototype machines, the external host's actual data rate to the array is only about one-fourth of the maximum rate the Warp machine can handle, even if the interface unit unpacks data as they arrive. Using this input partitioning model, the external host need not unpack and repack bytes, which it would have to do if the data were requested in another order.
- Each cell sees a connected set of columns of the image, which is one-tenth of the total columns in a row. Processing adjacent columns is an advantage because many vision algorithms (e.g., median filter [6]) can use the result from a previous set of columns to speed up the computation at the next set of columns to the right.
- Memory requirements at a cell are minimized, because each cell must store only one-tenth of a row. This is important in the prototype Warp machines, since they have only a 4K-word memory on each cell.
- The image is processed in raster order, which has for a long time been a popular order for accessing data in an image. This means that many efficient algorithms, which have been developed for raster-order image processing, can be used.
- An unexpected side effect of this I/O model was that it made it easier to debug the hardware in the warp machine. If some portion of a Warp cell is not working, but the communication and microsequencing portions are, then the output from a given cell will be wrong, but it will keep its proper position in the image. This means that the error will be extremely evident—typically a black stripe is generated in the corresponding position in the image. It is quite easy to infer from such an image which cell is broken!.

3. INTRODUCTION TO APPLY

The Apply programming model is a special-purpose programming approach that simplifies the programming task by making explicit the parallelism of low-level vision algorithms. We have developed a special-purpose programming language called the Apply language, which embodies this parallel programming approach. When using the Apply language, the programmer writes a procedure that defines the operation to be applied at a particular pixel location. The procedure conforms to the following program model:

It accepts a window or a pixel from each input image.
It performs arbitrary computation, usually without side effects.
It returns a pixel value for each output image.

The Apply compiler converts the simple procedure into an implementation which can be run efficiently on the Warp supercomputer or on a uni-processor machine in C under Unix.

3.1. The Apply Language

The Apply language is designed for programming image-to-image computations where the pixels of the output images can be computed from corresponding rectangular windows of the input images. The essential feature of the language is that each operation is written as a procedure for a single pixel position. The Apply compiler generates a program that executes the procedure over an entire image. No ordering constraints are provided for in the language, allowing the compiler complete freedom in dividing the computation among processors. As a consequence of this, however, Apply does not allow the output of the computation at one pixel location to be used as the input for the same computation at a nearby pixel, as is done in several low-level vision operators, such as uniform smoothing (see FLWL2 [7]) or median filter [6]. Provision for limited feedback is an area for future research.

Each procedure has a parameter list containing parameters of any of the following types: *in, out* or *constant*. Input parameters are either scalar variables or two-dimensional arrays. A scalar input variable represents the pixel value of an input image at the current processing co-ordinates. A two-dimensional array input variable represents a window of an input image. Element (0, 0) of the array corresponds to the current processing coordinates.

Output parameters are scalar variables. Each output variable represents the pixel value of an output image. The final value of an output variable is stored in the output image at the current processing coordinates.

Constant parameters may be scalars, vectors, or two-dimensional arrays. They represent precomputed constants that are made available for use by the procedure. For example, a convolution program would use a constant array for the convolution mask.

The reserved variables ROW and COL are defined to contain the image coordinates of the current processing location. This is useful for algorithms that are dependent in a limited way on the image coordinates.

Figure 10–4 is a grammar of the Apply language. The syntax of Apply is based on Ada [8]; we chose this syntax because it is familiar and adequate, and because we do not wish to create yet another new language syntax, nor do we consider language syntax to be an interesting research issue. However, as should be clear, the application dependence of Apply means that it is not an Ada subset, nor is it intended to evolve into such a subset.

<u>procedure</u>	::=	PROCEDURE <u>function-name</u> (<u>function-args</u>) IS <u>variable-declarations</u> BEGIN <u>statements</u> END <u>function-name</u>;
<u>function-args</u>	::=	<u>function-arg</u> , <u>function-args</u>
	|	<u>function-arg</u>
<u>function-arg</u>	::=	<u>var-list</u> : <u>parameter-source</u> <u>type</u>
	|	<u>var-list</u> : IN <u>type</u> BORDER <u>const-expr</u>
<u>var-list</u>	::=	<u>variable</u> , <u>var-list</u>
	|	<u>variable</u>
<u>parameter-source</u>	::=	IN
	|	OUT
	|	CONST
<u>var-declarations</u>	::=	<u>var-list</u> : <u>type</u> ; <u>var-declarations</u>
	|	Empty
<u>type</u>	::=	ARRAY (<u>dimension-list</u>) OF <u>elem-type</u>
	|	<u>elem-type</u>
<u>dimension-list</u>	::=	<u>range</u> , <u>dimension-list</u>
	|	<u>range</u>
<u>range</u>	::=	<u>int-expr</u> .. <u>int-expr</u>
<u>elem-type</u>	::=	<u>sign</u> <u>object</u>
	|	<u>object</u>
<u>sign</u>	::=	SIGNED
	|	UNSIGNED
<u>object</u>	::=	BYTE
	|	INTEGER
	|	FLOAT
<u>statements</u>	::=	<u>statement</u> ; <u>statements</u>
	|	<u>statement</u> ;
<u>statement</u>	::=	<u>assignment-stmt</u>
	|	<u>if-stmt</u>
	|	<u>for-stmt</u>
<u>assignment-stmt</u>	::=	<u>scalar-var</u> := <u>expr</u>
<u>scalar-var</u>	::=	<u>variable</u>
	|	<u>variable</u> (<u>subscript-list</u>)
<u>subscript-list</u>	::=	<u>int-expr</u> , <u>subscript-list</u>
	|	<u>int-expr</u>

Figure 10–4. Continued.

<u>expr</u>	: :=	<u>expr</u> + <u>expr</u>
	|	<u>expr</u> - <u>expr</u>
	|	<u>expr</u> * <u>expr</u>
	|	<u>expr</u> / <u>expr</u>
	|	(<u>expr</u>)
	|	<u>pseudo-function</u> (<u>expr</u>)

<u>if-stmt</u>	: :=	IF <u>bool-expr</u> THEN
		 <u>statements</u>
		 END IF

	|	IF <u>bool-expr</u> THEN
		 <u>statements</u>
		 ELSE
		 <u>statements</u>
		 END IF

<u>bool-expr</u>	: :=	<u>expr</u> < <u>expr</u>
	|	<u>expr</u> <= <u>expr</u>
	|	<u>expr</u> = <u>expr</u>
	|	<u>expr</u> >= <u>expr</u>
	|	<u>expr</u> > <u>expr</u>
	|	<u>expr</u> /= <u>expr</u>
<u>for-stmt</u>	: :=	FOR <u>int-var</u> IN <u>range</u> LOOP <u>statements</u> END LOOP

Figure 10–4. Grammer of the Apply language.

Apply is strongly typed and does not allow assignment of integer expressions to floating variables or floating expressions to integer variables. Mixed expressions are also disallowed. An integer expression may be explicitly converted to floating by means of the pseudofunction FLOAT and a floating expression can be converted to integer by using the pseudofunction INTEGER.

Variable names are alpha-numeric strings of arbitrary length, commencing with an alphabetic character. Case is not significant, except in the preprocessing stage, which is implemented by the *m4* macroprocessor [9].

Parameter variables refer to images, so they can be only one or two dimensional; function variables can be of any dimension. Both the C and Fortran forms of array indexing (with brackets or commas separating dimensions) are allowed. BYTE, INTEGER, and FLOAT refer to (at least) 8-bit integers, 16-bit integers, and 32-bit floating-point numbers. BYTE values are converted implicitly to INTEGER within computations. The actual size of the type may be larger, at the discretion of the implementor.

Some restrictions in the current implementation of the Apply result from limitations in the W2 compiler [10] for the prototype Warp machine.

There are no Boolean *and*, *or*, or *not* operations.
There may not be any *for* loops inside of *if* statements.

$$\begin{vmatrix} 1 & 2 & 1 \\ 0 & 0 & 0 \\ -1 & -2 & -1 \end{vmatrix} \qquad \begin{vmatrix} 1 & 0 & -1 \\ 2 & 0 & -2 \\ 1 & 0 & -1 \end{vmatrix}$$

Horizontal   **Vertical**

Figure 10–5. The Sobel convolution masks.

```
procedure sobel (inimg  : in array (-1..1, -1..1) of byte    -- 1
                          border 0,
                 thresh : const float,
                 mag    : out float)
is                                                           -- 2
   horiz, vert : integer;                                    -- 3
begin                                                        -- 4
   horiz := inimg(-1,-1) + 2 * inimg(-1,0) + inimg(-1,1) -   -- 5
           inimg(1,-1) - 2 * inimg(1,0) - inimg(1,1);
   vert := inimg(-1,-1) + 2 * inimg(0,-1) + inimg(1,-1) -    -- 6
           inimg(-1,1) - 2 * inimg(0,1) - inimg(1,1);
   mag := sqrt(FLOAT(horiz)*FLOAT(horiz)                     -- 7
               + FLOAT(vert)*FLOAT(vert));
   if mag < thresh then                                      -- 8
      mag := 0.0;                                            -- 9
   end if;                                                   -- 10
end sobel;                                                   -- 11
```

Figure 10–6. An Apply implementation of thresholded Sobel edge detection.

For loops must have constant integer lower and upper bounds.
There are no structured variables, only scalar variables and arrays.
There is no facility for writing functions that invoke other functions.

We except these limitations will be lifted in the future, once Apply is implemented on the printed-circuit-board version of Warp.

3.2. An Implementation of Sobel Edge Detection

As a simple example of the use of Apply, let us consider the implementation of Sobel edge detection. Sobel edge detection is performed by convolving the input image with two 3×3 masks. The horizontal mask measures the gradient of horizontal edges, and the vertical mask measures the gradient of vertical edges. Diagonal edges produce some response from each mask, allowing the edge orientation and strength to be measured for all edges. Both masks are shown in Figure 10–5.

An Apply implementation of Sobel edge detection is shown in Figure 10–6. The lines have been numbered for the purposes of explanation, using the comment convention. Line numbers are not a part of the language.

Line 1 defines the input, output, and constant parameters to the function. The input parameter **inimg** is a window of the input image. The constant parameter **thresh** is a threshold. Edges which are weaker than this threshold are supressed in the output magnitude image **mag.** Line 3 defines **Horiz** and **vert**, which are internal variables used to hold the results of the horizontal and vertical Sobel edge operator.

Line 1 also defines the input image window. It is 3×3 window centered about the current pixel processing position, which is filled with the value 0 when the window lies outside the image. This same line declares the constant and output parameters to be floating-point scalar variables.

The computation of the Sobel convolutions is implemented by the straight forward expression on lines 5 through 7. These expressions are readily seen to be a direct implementation of convolutions in Figure 10–5.

3.3. Border Handling

Border handling is always a difficult and messy process in programming kernel operations such as Sobel edge detection. In practice, this is usually left up to the programmer, with varying results—sometimes borders are handled in one way, sometimes another. Apply provides a uniform way of resolving the difficulty. It supports border handling by extending the input images with a constant value. The constant value is specified as an assignment. Line 1 of Figure 10–6 indicates that the input image **inimg** is to be extended by filling with the constant value 0.

If the programmer does not sepcify how an input variable is to be extended as the window crosses the edge of the input image, Apply handles this case by not calculating the corresponding output pixel.

We plan to extend the Apply language with two other methods of border handling: extending the input image by replicating border pixels, and allowing the programmer to write a special-purpose routine for handling border pixels.

4. APPLY ON WARP

The implementation of Apply on Warp employs straightforward raster processing of the images, with the processing divided among the cells as described in Section 2. The Sobel implementation in Figure 10–6 processes a 512×512 image on a ten-cell Warp in 330 milliseconds, including the I/O time for the Warp machine.

5. APPLY ON UNIPROCESSOR MACHINES

The same Apply compiler that generates Warp code also can generate C code to be run under Unix. We have found that an Apply implementation is usually at least as efficient as any alternative implementation on the same machine. This efficiency results from the expert knowledge, that is built into the Apply implementation but which is too verbose for the programmer to work with explicitly. (For example, Apply uses pointers to move the operator across the image, instead of moving data.) In addition, Apply focuses the programmer's attention on the details of his computation, which often results in improved design of the basic computation.

The Apply implementation for uniprocessor machines relies upon a subroutine library, which was previously developed for this purpsoe. The routines are designed to efficiently pass a processing kernel over an image. They employ data buffering, which allows the kernel to be shifted and scrolled over the buffer with a low constant cost, independent of the size of the kernel. The Sobel implementation in Figure 10–6 processes a 512×512 image on a Vax 11/785 in 30 seconds.

6. APPLY ON OTHER MACHINES

Here we briefly outline how Apply could be implemented on other parallel machine types, specifically bit-serial processor arrays and distributed-memory, general-purpose processor machines. These two types of parallel machines are very common; many parallel architectures include them as a subset or can simulate them efficiently.

6.1. Apply on Bit-Serial Processor Arrays

Bit-serial processor arrays [11] include a great many parallel machines. They are arrays of large numbers of very simple processors, which are able to perform a single-bit operation in every machine cycle. We assume only that it is possible to load images into the array such that each processor can be assigned to a single pixel of the input image, and that different processors can exchange information locally, that is, processors for adjacent pixels can exchange information efficiently. Specific machines may also have other features that may make Apply more efficient than the implementation outlined here.

In this implementation of Apply, each processor computes the result of one pixel window. Because there may be more pixels than processors, we allow a single processor to implement the action of several different processors over a period of time, that is, we adopt the Connection Machine's idea of *virtual processors* [12].

The Apply program works as follows:

1. Initialize: For $n \times n$ image processing, use a virtual processor network of $n \times n$ virtual processors.
2. Input: For each variable of type IN, send a pixel to the corresponding virtual processor.
3. Constant: *Broadcast* all variables of type CONST to all virtual processors.
4. Window: For each IN variable, with a window size of $m \times m$, shift it in a spiral, first one step to the right, then one step up, then two steps two the left, then two steps down, and so on, storing the pixel value in each virtual processor the pixel encounters, until a $m \times m$ square around each virtual processor is filled. This will take m^2 steps.
5. Compute: Each virtual processor now has all the inputs it needs to calculate the output pixels. Perform this computation in parallel on all processors.

Because memory on these machines is often limited, it may be best to combine the "window" and "compute" steps above, to avoid the memory cost of prestoring all window elements on each virtual processor.

6.2. Apply on Distributed-Memory General-Purpose Machines

Machines in this class consist of a moderate number of general-purpose processors, each with its own memory. Many general-purpose parallel architectures implement this model, such as the Intel iPSC [13] or the Cosmic Cube [14]. Other parallel architectures, such as the shared-memory BBN Butterfly [15, 16], can efficiently implement Apply in this way; treating them as distributed-memory machines avoids problems with contention for memory.

This implementation of Apply works as follows:

1. Input: If there are n processors in use, divide the image into n regions, and store one region in each of the n processors' memories. The actual shape of the regions can vary with the particular machine in use. Note that compact regions have smaller borders than long thin regions, so that the next step will be more efficient if the regions are compact.
2. Window: For each IN variable, processors exchange rows and columns of their image with processors holding an adjacent region from the image so that each processor has enough of the image to compute the corresponding output region.
3. Compute: Each processor now has enough data to compute the output region. It does so, iterating over all pixels in its output region.

7. SUMMARY

We have described our programming techniques for low-level vision on Warp. These techniques began with simple row-by-row image processing macros, which are still in use for certain kinds of algorithms, and led to the development of Apply, which is a specialized programming language for low-level vision on Warp.

We have defined the Apply language as it is currently implemented and described its use in low-level vision programming. Apply is in daily use at Carnegie-Mellon University for Warp and vision programming in general; it has proved to be a useful tool for programming under Unix, as well as an introductory tool for Warp programming.

The Apply language crystallizes our ideas on low-level vision programming on Warp. It allows the programmer to treat certain messy conditions, such as border conditions, uniformly. It also allows the programmer to get consistently good efficiency in low-level vision programming by incorporating expert knowledge about how to implement such operators.

One of the most exciting characteristics of Apply is that it may be possible to implement it on diverse parallel machines. We have outlined such implementations on bit-serial processor arrays and distributed memory machines.

Implementation of Apply on other machines will make porting of low-level vision programs easier, should extend the lifetime of programs for such supercomputers, and will make benchmarking easier.

8. ACKNOWLEDGMENTS

We would like to acknowledge the contributions made by Steve Shafer, who helped develop the Apply programming model. The Warp project is a large, and growing, project at Carnegie-Mellon University and General Electric Corporation. The authors are greatly indebted to this group, which has designed, built, and maintained the Warp machine, as well as implemented the W2 programming language, which is the basis for the Warp implementation of Apply. Apply itself grew out of work in the standard-vision programming environment at Carnegie-Mellon, which is based on C/Unix. Apply benefitted from the use and criticism of members of the Image Understanding Systems and Autonomous Land Vehicles group at Carnegie-Mellon.

The research was supported in part by Defense Advanced Research Projects Agency (U.S. Department of Defense) monitored by the Air Force Avionics Laboratory under Contract F33615-81-K-1539, and Naval Electronic Systems Command under Contract N00039-85-C-0134, in part by the U.S. Army Engineer Topographic Laboratories under Contract DACA76-85-C-0002, and in part by the Office of Naval Research under Contracts N00014-80-C-0236, NR 048-659, and N00014-85-K-0152, NR SDRJ-007.

REFERENCES

1. H. T. Kung, and J. A. Webb, "Mapping Image Processing Operations onto a Linear Systolic Machine," *Distributed Computing*, 1(1986): 246–257.
2. H. T. Kung, and O. Menzilcioglu, "Warp: A Programmable Systolic Array Processor," *Proc. SPIE Symp. Vol. 495, Real-Time Signal Processing VII*, Society of Photo-Optical Instrumentation Engineers, Aug. 1984, pp. 130–136.
3. E. Arnould, H. T. Kung, O. Menzilcioglu, and K. Sarocky, "A Systolic Array Computer," *Proc. 1985 IEEE Int'l, Conf. on Acoustics, Speech and Signal Processing*, March 1985, pp. 232–235.
4. M. Annaratone, E., Arnould, T. Gross, H. T. Kung, M. Lam, O. Menzilcioglu, K. Sarocky, and J. A. Webb, "Warp Architecture and Implementation," *Conf. Proc. 13th Annual Int'l Symp. on Computer Architecture*, June 1986, pp. 346–356.
5. M., Annaratone, E. Arnould, R. Cohn, T. Gross, H. T. Kung, M. Lam, O. Menzilcioglu, K., Sarocky, J. Senko, and J. A. Webb, "Warp Architecture: From Prototype to Production," *Proc. 1987 Nat'l Computer Conf.*, AFIPS, 1987.
6. T. S. Huang, G. J. Yang, and G. Y. Tang, "A Fast Two-Dimensional Median Filtering Algorithm," *Int'l Conf. on Pattern Recognition and Image Processing*, IEEE, 1978, pp. 128–130.
7. H. Tamura, S. Sakane, F. Tomita, N. Yokoya, K. Sakaue, and N. Kaneko, *SPIDER Users' Manual*, Joint System Development Corp., Tokyo, Japan 1983.
8. U.S. Department of Defense, AdaTEC, SIGPLAN Technical Committee on Ada, *Reference Manual for the Ada Programming Language*, MIL-STD 1815 ed., New York, N. Y. AdaTEC, 1982, Draft revised MIL-STD 1815. Draft proposed ANSI Standard document.
9. B. W. Kernighan and D. M. Ritchie, "The M4 Macro Processor." In *Unix Programmer's Manual*, Vol. 2, Bell Laboratories, Murray Hill, NJ, 1979.
10. T. Gross, and M. Lam, "Compilation for a High-Performance Systolic Array," *Proc. SIGPLAN 86 Symposium on Compiler Construction*, ACM SIGPLAN, June 1986, pp. 27–38.
11. K. E. Batcher, "Bit-Serial Parallel Processing Systems," *IEEE Trans. on Computers*, C-31(5): 377–384, 1982.

12. W. D. Hillis, *The Connection Machine*. Cambridge, MA: MIT Press, ACM Distinguished Dissertations, 1985.
13. Intel Corporation, *iPSC System Overview*, 1985.
14. C. Seitz, "The Cosmic Cube," *Comm. of the ACM*, 28(1): 22–33, 1985.
15. BBN Laboratories, *The Uniform System Approach to Programming the Butterfuly Parallel Processor*, First Edition, Cambridge, MA, 1985.
16. T. J. Olson, *An Image Processing Package for the BBN Butterfly Parallel Processor*, Butterfly Project Rep. 9, Department of Computer Science, University of Rochester, Rochester, NY, Aug. 1985.

11. AHR: A PARALLEL COMPUTER FOR PURE LISP

ADOLFO GUZMAN

1. INTRODUCTION

Parallel processing now constitutes a major direction for computer development, and the future of this field is very bright. At the same time, the field is very difficult due to the complexities inherent in parallel systems. In 1973, these complexities made parallelism seem to be impractical, yet results obtained from a project undertaken that year at the Institute for Research in Applied Mathematics and Systems (IIMAS) at the National University of Mexico demonstrated that parallel systems were more feasible than had previously been assumed.

In 1973, researchers at IIMAS outlined several organizational premises for parallel computers, specifically one for a reconfigurable Lisp machine [1, 2]. At that time, the proposal showed little promise of being fruitful. However, in spite of all the difficulties intrinsic to parallel systems, a computer designed along the lines proposed in 1973 was built and tested. Specific conditions existing in Mexico influenced the final form of AHR (an acronym for Arquitecturas Heterarquicas Reconfigurables), primarily in terms of staffing and the curtailment of second-generation work. Yet results obtained from the prototypes at IIMAS in 1980 and 1981 yielded information useful for future developments in parallel processing.

This work was carried out at the Institute for Research in Applied Mathematics and Systems (IIMAS), National University of Mexico, Mexico City. Other members of the AHR team were Luis Lyons, Luis Peñarrieta, Kemer Norkin, David Rosenblueth, Raul Gómez, Manuel Correa, Dora Gómez, and Norma A. de Rosenblueth.

The laboratory prototype of the AHR computer consisted of approximately 600 components, many of which were Large Scale Integration chips. Consequently, the AHR project represented, under classifications prevailing at that time, a complicated electronic design. This demand for such a huge amount of hardware devoted to a unique goal was new for IIMAS, and the project was a pioneering effort in computer research in Mexico. Although the main goal of AHR was educational, the projects aim was multipurpose: AHR was designed as a vehicle for future development, one that would, for instance, allow a programmer to write programs for a parallel machine without having to worry explicitly about parallelism. The first implementation of AHR supported pure parallel Lisp, but the ultimate goal for the machine was as a development tool for new languages and hardware for parallel systems. As part of its evolution as a development tool, the machine was available for students to use to learn and practice parallel concepts in hardware and software.

Four principal uses were envisioned for the machine:

To develop hardware and parallel processing languages
To explore new ways to perform parallel processing
To provide parallelism in a way that was transparent to the user
To provide a machine for students to use.

1.1. Characteristics of the AHR Machine

The design of AHR was predicated upon several architectural considerations, the chief of which are listed in Table 11–1. These design premises made the complexity of a parallel system more manageable. Because all the processors were at the same hierarchical level, no one of them was the "master"; hence, the AHR machine used a heterarchical organization, not a hierarchical one. Having pure Lisp as the main programming language eliminated side effects, setq's, and goto's. Up to a point, the computing power of the machine could be increased by simply adding more microprocessors. Communication between processors was minimized: since the design of the machine did not require processors to communicate directly with each other, they simply "left work" for some other processor to do, without knowing or talking to such a processor. Finally, all input/output (I/O)

Table 11–1. AHR Design Premises

A general purpose parallel processor.
The absence of hierarchical distinctions.
An asynchronous operation.
The use of pure Lisp as the main programming language.
The absence of processor-to-processor communications.
A gradually expandable hardware design.
An allocation of input/output to a host.
A small operating system.

was conducted by a host computer to which the AHR machine was attached as a slave or back-end processor.

Another factor in the management of the complexity dealt with the allocation of tasks normally associated with an operating system. The AHR machine, as such, had no software-written operating system. A normal operating system existed in the host processor, but it was not considered a part of the AHR machine. If the term *operating system* is taken to mean the "system's resources administrator," then the *grill*, or active memory—together with the *fifo* and the *distributor*—constituted an operating system. Even this small operating system, however, was embodied in the hardware. The majority of the Lisp operations, as well as the garbage collector, which was not parallel, were written in Z-80 machine language. Special hardware also helped with handling list structures, free-cell lists, and queues. The efficiency of the system was further increased by the use of "intelligent memories" that could be accessed in several modes, among them *read, write, free this cell,* and *give me a new cell.* All modes were implemented in the hardware.

Since the purpose of the AHR Project was mainly educational and scientific, not much attention was paid to the normal things that give good service to users, such as I/O facilities, utility programs, and service routines. Because such resources are very well known, the AHR team concentrated instead on the *new* aspects of the computer, its unique and novel parts. By doing so, the team ensured that the new ideas performed correctly, given the constraints of time and funds for the AHR project. The final report of the AHR project [3] contains further details of the IIMAS effort; the summary thus far in this chapter is based on that report.

1.2. Project Status

By the end of 1981, the AHR was operational to the extent of performing short test programs, which processed correctly. As a prototype, the AHR computer was not destined for normal use, but for verification of design ideas, a purpose for which it was completely sufficient. Consequently, the prototype became the "living proof" of the feasibility of the AHR premises. Because the machine had only a modest amount of memory, no large programs were run on it. As a prototype, it proved the correctness of its design assumptions and the validity of its way of operation. As a learning tool, it was invaluable because, in addition to confirming many design choices, it taught the AHR researchers many things to *avoid.*

The things to avoid primarily involved the issue of reliability for a sustained operation of several hours. The prototype failed frequently, due to the designers' insufficient experience in some technical aspects of its construction; some of the problems were due to the connections, weak contacts, a card size that was too large, short circuits, and reflections of pulses.

Because the prototype proved the success of the design, together with the fact that the machine was not able to support practical applications, Phase 1 of the AHR Project terminated; the first version of AHR ceased to exist at the end of

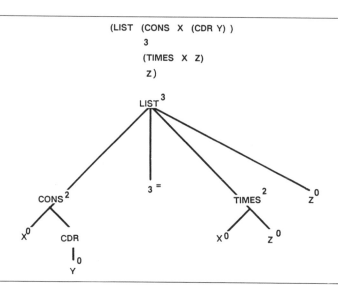

Figure 11–1. A Lisp program can be represented as a tree. The numbers near the nodes are the *nanes*, and nodes with a *nane* of "0" are ready for evaluation. Nodes with nane "=" are already evaluated (such as the constant 3).

1982. As detailed in the final report [3] of Phase 1 of the AHR project, a second version of the machine—improved, robust, and reliable—was proposed, but due to a lack of resources, work on this second version never began.

2. PARALLEL EVALUATION OF PURE LISP

Because the order of evaluation of the arguments of a function does not matter in a pure applicative language, such as pure Lisp, it is indeed possible to evaluate them in parallel. The only rule that a designer has to follow is *applicative order evaluation*, mean which that a program has to evaluate all of the arguments of a function before evaluating the function itself.

Thus, a pure Lisp program is analogous to a tree in which the leaves are ready for evaluation. This evaluation can proceed in parallel by several Lisp processors: as each leaf is converted into a value, the "parent" of that leaf must receive not only the value but also the notification that one more of its arguments has been evaluated. When a node has *all* of its arguments evaluated, that node becomes a leaf node, and is itself ready for evaluation. Figure 11–1 shows the tree corresponding to a particular Lisp expression. Notice that next to each node there is a number, called a *nane*, indicating the *number* of *arguments* *not* yet *evaluated*.

2.1. Idealized Evaluation Model

If the tree represented by Figure 11–1 is placed in a common memory, which is accessible to all Lisp processors, then the processors can be controlled with an

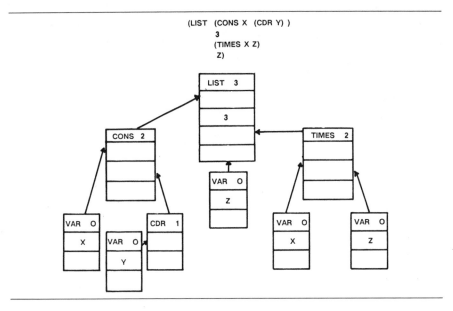

Figure 11-2. Representation inside the *Grill*. The nodes inside the grill represent the program to be evaluated in parallel.

instruction of the following generalized form:

Look for a node with *nane* = 0, and evaluate it.
After finding its value, give the value to its parent.
Then subtract one from the *nane* of the parent.

This rule permits the parallel evaluation of the tree from the leaves towards the root. As the internal nodes have their *nanes* diminished, the *nanes* eventually become 0 and, consequently, ready for evaluation. In other words, the nodes can then be captured by whatever Lisp processors are not busy evaluating a node; these processors search through the memory looking for "work to do," namely nodes with a *nane* of 0. Eventually, the whole tree is transformed into a Lisp result, namely, a list or an atom.

Figure 11-2 illustrates the foregoing principle: the tree has been drawn with nodes corresponding to each Lisp primitive, and each node points to its parent. Initially, only the nodes named *VAR*, or the variables, are ready to be evaluated, but soon the evaluation proceeds towards the root. As a node is evaluated, its value is inserted in the corresponding slot of its parent, and the *nane* of the parent subsequently decremented. VAR Z, for example, can be evaluated as having the value of 5; this value is then inserted in the slot for its parent process, and the value of the *nane* of the parent decreases by one.

The above design, as is, contains the possibility of having 64 Lisp processors fighting for access to the common memory where the program to be evaluated resides. In such a case, the memory port becomes a bottleneck. However, the problem can be avoided if another memory, called *fifo* or *blackboard*, contains only pointers to nodes with *nane* = 0. Additional details about the *fifo* can be found in the third section of this chapter entitled "The Parts of the AHR Machine." In the above model, the common memory where the program resides—called the *grill*—has the property to destroy the programs, since it converts them into Lisp results; therefore, a master copy of the definition of each user-defined function has to be kept outside the *grill*. As discussed later, these definitions are kept as list structures, together with the other Lisp data, in another common memory called the *passive memory*. The bindings of variables to values must also be kept outside the *grill*; consequently, there is another common memory, called the *variables memory*. In addition to having a separate logical use, these memories are actually separate memories in the AHR machine in order to allow simultaneous access by different Lisp processors.

2.2. The Handling of Conditionals

Evaluations of Lisp conditional expressions must be treated in a special manner for processing in a parallel system. For example, pure Lisp evaluates (*if p q r*) by first evaluating the predicate p. Then, exactly one of q or r is evaluated, depending on whether the value of p is "True" or "False." Consequently, the tree of (*if p q r*) cannot be placed into the *grill*, because this action calls for the parallel evaluation of p, q, and r. However, if the expression (*if1 p*) is placed into the grill, then whenever p is evaluated, *if1* decides to copy q or r on top of itself. Thus, *if1* becomes either q or r.

COND, AND and OR are handled in similar ways, because their "arguments" cannot be evaluated in parallel. Consequently, the program does not copy an entire list, as in *AND p q r s . . .* , into the *grill*; instead, p is copied with q r s . . . stay in the *passive memory*, waiting, perhaps, for a later evaluation.

In conclusion, a function can be *evaluated* merely by copying it into the *grill*; there the evaluation takes place "automatically" with the help of the Lisp processors that search for nodes with a *nane* = 0.

2.3. Handling Recursion in an Idealized Lisp Machine

When the call to a user-defined function, as in, for instance, *factorial z*, is placed on the *grill*, the node then has the name *factorial*, a procedure that allows the evaluation of z to occur. For example, suppose the value of z is 4; if so, the node (factorial 4) is replaced by the node

((lambda (n) (if (eq n 0) . . .))4)

In effect, this operation replaces "factorial" with its definition. The evaluation of a lambda expression, in which all of its arguments are already evaluated, produces

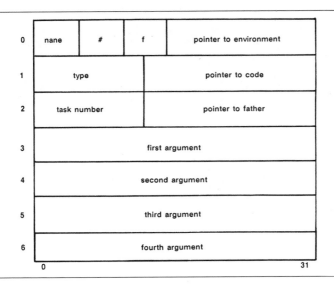

Figure 11–3. A node. This node contains seven words of 32 bits; the last four are for arguments to the Lisp primitive, as indicated in the field *type*. The fields "#" and "f" indicate number of arguments and flags, respectively. *Nane* contains the number of arguments not yet evaluated.

no special problem, except that new bindings have to be registered in the *variable memory* prior to the evaluation of the lambda body.

3. PARTS OF THE AHR MACHINE

Various parts of the AHR machine are discussed below: (a) the *mailbox* and injection mechanism for avoiding access bottlenecks, (b) the various forms of memory, (c) the Lisp processors, (d) the communication media, and (e) the host. Following the discussion of the parts is a section that describes how the machine works.

3.1. The Mailbox and Injection Mechanism

One of the most critical parts of the AHR design involves the management of the memory known as the *grill*. To make efficient use of the *grill*, a Lisp processor has to access it for as little time as possible. On the other hand, what is transmitted from the *grill* to the Lisp processor is a node—that is, a primitive function—with all its arguments already evaluated. Figure 11–3 depicts such a node.

A node contains seven words of 32 bits each; however, in the instance of the AHR, a Lisp processor (a Z-80A) can only access eight bits at a time. Thus, fetching a node from the *grill*, in this configuration, is quite slow. In addition, several Lisp processors may be trying to access the *grill*. To avoid this bottleneck, the situation is reversed: when a Lisp processor requests more work, the *grill* actually *injects* the node into the microprocessor. This "injecton" is done through

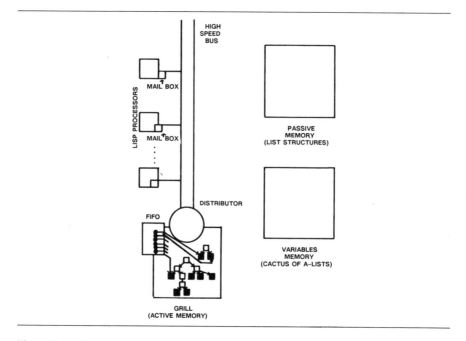

Figure 11–4. Diagram of the AHR Lisp machine. The *fifo* contains pointers to nodes with *nane* = 0. There are connections (not shown) from each Lisp processor to *passive memory* and also to *variables memory*. The *distributor* sends nodes with *nane* = 0 to each Lisp processor requesting for more work to do. These nodes are placed directly in the *mailbox* of the requester.

a *mailbox* in the private memory of each Lisp processor. The *mailbox* is a seven word (32-bits each) register that *shadows* some addresses in the Lisp processor memory. When a Lisp processor requests a new node, the processor goes into a wait state. The *grill* notices this request, extracts the previous result from the *mailbox*, and stores it in the corresponding slot of the parent node. The *grill* then subtracts one from the *nane* of the parent; this subtraction is an indivisible operation. The *grill* then checks to see if this new *nane* is zero; if so, the *grill* registers the parent in the *fifo*. At this point, the grill obtains a new node, with the help of the *fifo*, from the *grill* and injects this node into the *mailbox* of the (waiting) Lisp processor. Finally, the grill takes the Lisp processor out of its wait state.

Thus, the *grill* operates as a *smart memory*, and its capability as such is made possible by the construction of an additional piece of hardware, the *distributor*, which does all these things on behalf of the *grill*.

3.2. The Memories of AHR

There are five different types of memory: (1) *grill*, (2) *fifo*, (3) *passive memory*, (4) *variables memory*, and (5) *private memories*. Each of these is discussed below, and Figure 11–4 shows a diagram of the overall machine.

3.2.1. *The Grill*

The *grill*, also known as the "active memory," holds the programs that are being evaluated. With the help of the *fifo*, the *distributor* of the *grill* passes data to and from the Lisp processors requesting access to the *grill*. The *grill* has to be very fast, to distribute nodes quickly to the Lisp processors. The *grill* can consist of up to 512K words of 32 bits and is divided logically into nodes, each with seven words. Version 1 of AHR, which contained only 8K words, had an access time of 55 nanoseconds per word [4, 5].

3.2.2. *fifo*

Also called the "blackboard," the *fifo* holds pointers to the Lisp nodes that are ready for evaluation but have not yet been evaluated. When the *distributor* decides to send a new "ready for evaluation" node to some Lisp processor requesting it, it pops the top of the *fifo* to obtain its address.

3.2.3. *Passive Memory*

The *passive memory* contains "data," namely, lists and atoms; this memory also contains the Lisp programs in list form. In the beginning of a process, the programs to be executed reside in *passive memory*. From there, they are copied by the Lisp processors onto the *grill* for their execution. As new data structures, otherwise known as "partial results," are built, these structures also come to reside in the passive memory, which can have up to one million words of 22 bits, plus a parity bit. The tag bits are not implemented in hardware, but in software, as indicated in Figure 11–3.

In addition, the *passive memory* communicates with the memory of the *host computer* through a *window*. Version 1 of AHR had only a modest 64K words of passive memory with an access time of 150 nanoseconds per word. This memory is a single-port memory; an arbiter handles simultaneous requests from the Lisp processors, according to a fixed priority.

3.2.4. *Variables Memory*

The *variables memory* contains a tree of a-lists (association lists). Each element of an a-list is a variable name paired with its value. If AHR were a sequential machine, the *variables memory* would be a stack; instead, the variables memory looks more like a cactus, where branches and subbranches grow and shrink in parallel. A branch of this "cactus" grows after each lambda binding.

When the value of a variable is needed in a node, the Lisp processor in charge of the evaluation of that variable uses the appropriate part of the "cactus" to begin searching for its value. Accordingly, the node also has "pointer to the environment."

The *variables memory* consists of up to 512K words of 32 bits. Its lower half contains floating-point numbers, and its upper half has "environments" (the cactus of a-lists), which are lists of cells of five words each. Version 1 of AHR had a variables memory of 16K words with an access time of 150 nanoseconds. The variables memory is a single-port memory with a fixed-priority arbiter.

3.2.5. *The Private Memory of Each Lisp Processor*

Each Lisp processor has 16K bytes, with maximum of 64K, of private memory (RAM + ROM). This "private" memory is where the processor's own machine stack resides, as well as the code in Z-80 machine language that executes each Lisp primitive.

3.3. The Lisp Processors of AHR

Each Lisp processor is a Z-80A with 16K bytes of private memory, each one connecting to the AHR machine through a *coupler*. This coupler contains: (1) a *mailbox* for fast access to the *grill*, and (2) latches to indicate petition access either to the *grill*, the *passive memory*, or the *variables memory*. The Z-80 not only accesses these memories in the *write* or *read* modes, but the chip also addresses the *grill* in several other modes, namely, *give me new work* and *take my previous result* and others [6]. This plurality of modes to access memories proved to be valuable for simplifying the design of AHR.

All the Lisp processors are connected to the *distributor* of the *grill* through the high-speed bus, which transfers a word (32 bits) in 55 nanoseconds. Note that this transfer occurs directly between the *grill* and the *mailbox* of the Lisp processor, while the latter is in a **wait** state.

Each Lisp processor knows how to execute every Lisp primitive; each one works asynchronously, without communicating directly with other processors. The processors "communicate" by leaving their results in the corresponding slot of the parent process, as shown in Figure 11–3. Synchronization takes place whenever the *nanes* of nodes become 0. Nodes with a *nane* of zero signal a request, after their inscription in the *fifo*, for their evaluation.

Each Lisp processor is always either occupied in evaluating a node or ready to accept more work (another node). Only nodes with a *nane* = 0 come to the Lisp processor for evaluation; hence, the processor never has to wait, since all its arguments have already been computed. In the process of evaluation, the Lisp processor may have to access the *passive memory*, as in, for instance, taking CADR of a list. Likewise, the Lisp processor may also have to access the *variables memory* to obtain the value of a variable. If a processor wants to access the node that it is evaluating, that node is already in its *mailbox*; consequently, the node is available through the processor's own private memory.

Up to 64 Lisp processors are possible, but version 1 of AHR had only five. Figure 11–5 gives an overall view of version 1 of AHR.

3.4. Communication Media in AHR

The Lisp processors connect their mailboxes with the distributor of the grill through the high-speed bus. The AHR machine itself communicates with the host

Figure 11-5. Front view of the AHR machine. AHR is built as a circular structure. The top of this figure shows the Lisp processors, the different memories, the couplers, etc. The bottom left includes the *host computer*; to its right there is another Zilog Z-80, which is the *distributor* in its software version. The Lisp processors are not visible in this picture.

through a window. The *variable memory* and the *passive memory* each have a single port; thus, one of these memories can be accessed by a Lisp processor while the other memory is being accessed by another Lisp processor simultaneously.

3.4.1. *The High-Speed Bus*
The high-speed bus connects the *grill*, whenever the *distributor* decides to do so, to the *mailbox* of one of the Lisp processors requesting access to the *grill*. The bus transfers a node in 7 cycles of 55 nanoseconds each.

3.4.2. *Channels to Variables Memory and Passive Memory*
Each of these is a memory channel with an arbiter. The Lisp processors have a fixed priority in which the "closest" to the *distributor* has the highest priority. As soon as a Lisp processor requests access to a particular memory, it goes into a wait state; consequently, it can not request access to more than one memory at the same time.

3.4.3. *The Coupler and the Mailbox*

Each Lisp processor contains a *coupler*. As described in the preceding section and illustrated in Figure 11–7, this piece of hardware contains a *mailbox* and latches to indicate requests/grants from/to the Lisp processor.

3.4.4. *The Distributor*

The *distributor* monitors requests from the Lisp processors to access the *grill*. If requested, the *distributor* selects a processor and produces the desired access in accordance with the *mode* in which the request was made. Most frequently, the *distributor* is asked to do the following tasks:

Take, from the *mailbox*, the previous result
Store it in the parent
Substract one from the *nane* of the parent
Inscribe this parent into the *fifo* if its new *nane* becomes zero.

This entire process can be considered as a "take my previous result" request.
    After this procedure is done, the *distributor* is usually requested to "give me new work". The *distributor* responds by transferring a node through the *high-speed bus* to the *mailbox* of the requester. At this point, the *distributor* signals the requester to proceed.
    The first version of the AHR machine had a software *distributor* embodied inside another Z-80, as depicted in Figure 11–5. This software *distributor* was very useful for debugging purposes. Once the exact "code" for the *distributor* was known, a hardware *distributor* replaced it [7, 8].

3.4.5. *The Low-Speed Bus*

The *low-speed bus* is not really a part of the AHR machine. Its width is 16 bits, eight of which indicate which Lisp processor is addressed, and the others to carry data. This low-speed bus is used in the following situations:

To transmit to the Lisp processor, at initialization time, the code for the Lisp primitives
To gather statistics
To broadcast to all Lisp processors the number of a program that needs to be killed [6].

3.4.6. *The Window*

Part of the *passive memory* of AHR maps into the private memory of the host computer through the use of a movable *window* of 4K addresses. From the viewpoint of the user, the Lisp programs are loaded into the host-machine memory but they actually go into AHR's *passive memory*.

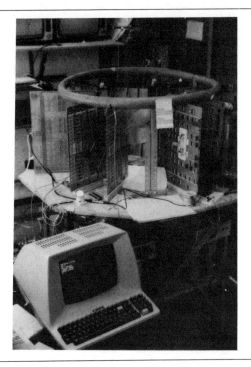

Figure 11–6. Host console with AHR. In the foreground sits the console attached to the host; the AHR machine appears in the middle ground. At the top of the picture are partially visible two *spies*; these are television screens that display in ASCII the contents of selected blocks of private memories of the Lisp processors. These were very useful for debugging, but they are not referenced in the text. Here, two Lisp processors are being debugged off-line.

3.5. The Host Computer

The host computer, as shown in Figure 11–6, is still another Z-80, although any other computer could be used. Though not actually part of the AHR design innovations, the host (1) transfers data to/from AHR through the *window*; (2) signals to AHR to start working; and (3) waits for the "work has finished" signal from AHR.

The host accesses the result to be printed through the *window*. The host, which is also called the "I/O machine" due to input/output taking place there, uses its normal operating system, disks, etc. The host uses the AHR machine as a back-end processor whenever the host desires to execute Lisp programs. While the AHR machine is executing, the host can be doing other jobs, including non-Lisp-related ones.

4. HOW THE AHR MACHINE WORKS
The section discusses the following topics: input, initialization, evaluation of programs, and output.

4.1. Input
Through the host, the user may develop a Lisp program, as, for example, in Figure 11–1. By loading the program from disk into the memory of the host, the user is really loading a Lisp list into the *passive memory* of AHR. After the program is loaded, the host signals AHR to begin execution and gives it the address in *passive memory* where the program to be evaluated resides. In a more realistic example, the user would have defined several functions, perhaps factorial, and then typed (**factorial 4**).

4.2. Starting
At this point each Lisp processor is assumed to have had its programs loaded into its private memory. This memory contains Z-80 machine code for Lisp primitives, together with routines that handle the special hardware, such as the *mailbox* and the memory's access modes. All Lisp processors are idle and, consequently, requesting *work to do*. When the AHR machine receives the "start" signal, the *distributor* makes available a node, called the RUN node, to some Lisp processor. This node points to the program, stored in *passive memory*, that is to begin to be evaluated.

The program in *passive memory* is then copied into the *grill*; in the course of being "copied," the program is transformed from list notation to node notation. The RUN node does the initial copy/transformation, but soon more and more Lisp processors aid in copying the program to the *grill*. The number of processors needed to copy a program is determined by the number of leaves or branches in that program. Copying is done in parallel: a processor that is copying (*foo x y z*), for example, can still copy *foo* while requesting some other processors to copy *x*, *y* and *z*, the latter of which, one can assume, are large S-expressions. This "request" on the part of the former processor takes the form of the creation of suitable nodes on the *grill*.

Nodes with *nane* = 0 are inserted, by the Lisp processors copying them, into the *fifo*, in order for other Lisp processors to execute them. At any given time, there are some Lisp processors copying the program while nodes with *nane* = 0 are being evaluated by other Lisp processors.

4.3. Evaluation
As explained in the section on the communication media and as shown in Figure 11–7, the *distributor* sends a node to each Lisp processor that requests more work. Before sending the node, the *distributor* extracts the previous result from the processor's *mailbox* and inserts the value into the parent. If no Lisp processor requests more work, the *distributor* sits idle, wasting *grill* cycles. If more than one Lisp processor request work, a fixed priority arbiter choses one of them.

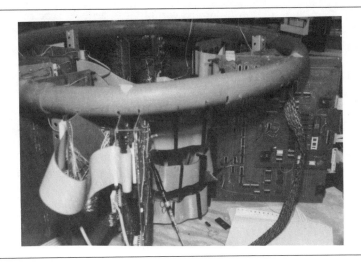

Figure 11–7. A Lisp processor. Here a Lisp processor, to which a fat cable of wires from a development system is connected, is evident, complete with its *coupler*. The empty connectors in the circular structure of AHR are where additional (up to 5) Lisp processors are attached.

Thus, nodes with *nane* = 0 are consumed by the Lisp processors and converted into results. At the same time, the substraction of 1 from the *nane* of the parent eventually creates more nodes with *nane* = 0. In addition, recursion—as indicated by the substitution of the word *factorial* by its definition (lambda (n) . . .)—creates more nodes in the *grill*, some with *nane* = 0 and some with *nane* > 0.

4.4. Output

When the complete program has been converted into a single result, for instance a list, residing in *passive memory*, the AHR machine signals the host, giving it also the address where the result is stored. The host proceeds to read the result through the *window* and to output the data to the user's terminal.

5. WHAT THE IIMAS TEAM LEARNED FROM THE AHR PROJECT

The following analysis of the results from the AHR project includes a consideration of the successful premises as well as a discussion of the technical weaknesses to be avoided in similar experiments. In addition, a list enumerates certain choices that could be varied in future experiments. Finally, the section concludes with an explanation of recommendations for further work.

5.1. Benefits of the AHR Project

Certain conclusions were far-reaching. The AHR project showed, by its very construction:

It is possible to build an entire parallel computer of a novel type in Mexico.
Simulation methods are reliable.
The AHR design is viable for other design projects.

The AHR design is very flexible: it offers concepts about interconnection and
parallel work that are applicable to many homogeneous and heterogeous
systems. The architecture was not only proven to be a well-designed concept, but
the prototype offered a myriad of practical checks during the course of
development. The research effort also proved the validity of simulation methods,
in this case the use of Simula on a Burroughs B6700. The simulation methods
developed by the team were checked in practice, and the simulation results had a
sufficient correspondence to actual measurements. Finally, the project yielded
practical data about the complexity of different parts of the computer [3] and
about time delays in different parts of the computer [6].

5.2. Key Decisions for the AHR Project

Several key architectural considerations, as listed in Table 11–2, contributed to
the success of AHR. The decision to use pure Lisp made the hardware design very
simple, because there were no worries about side effects. The use of pure Lisp also
freed the programmer from having to worry explicitly about parallelism, for
special commands such as DOALL, FORK, JOIN, etc., were unnecessary.

The design of a very fast grill also had repercussions for the success of the
experiment. One particularly valuable implementation was the procedure that
allowed the *grill* to inject and extract work from the *mailbox*. That design made it
possible to use a simple shared memory concept. In fact, if the time that it takes
the *grill* to receive a previous result and emit a new work is **k** times faster than the
average Lisp primitive, as executed in the Lisp processor, then up to **k** Lisp
processors can be supported by the *grill* without any bottlenecks. A bigger **k**
could be realized through several (not mutually exclusive) choices: (1) having a
hierarchy of memories, (2) having cache memories for data in each Lisp
processor, and (3) increasing the grain of parallelism. The latter option of
increasing the grain would be possible if larger Lisp primitives were constructed
that, in effect, would define a new Lisp-based language.

Table 11–2. Key Decisions for the AHR Project

To use pure Lisp.
To use a *grill* that was very fast relative to the slow Lisp processors.
To use simulation tools for the design of AHR.
Not to do garbage collection in the *grill*.
To use other modes besides *read* and *write* for memory access.
To use a host computer.

The small number of processors in Version 1 of AHR, as well as its memory constraints, prevented serious performance studies from being undertaken, yet the principles listed above could be the basis for new experiments.

As noted in Table 11–2, simulation was a key ingredient in the successful outcome of the project. The AHR project used simulation tools to detect the places and causes of noneffective work. By first simulating the operation of AHR, the design team found ways to simplify the design by migrating this noneffective work to the hardware. One can think of this type of work as "red tape," meaning noneffective, bureaucratic work. As a result, the *modes* of the *grill* were specially chosen to make the bureaucracy fast.

Another important factor was the elimination of the role of garbage collection from the *grill*. Because the *distributor* knows exactly when a node is no longer needed, it returns the node to the free-nodes list directly.

A key premise in the AHR design was the decision to use other modes in addition to *read* and *write* for memory access. This decision helped to blur the distinction between memory and processor. One example is the mode, *insert this node into the free-nodes list.*

The AHR experimental architecture would not have been possible, within the limits of the time and budget, without the use of a host machine. The use of a normal host allowed AHR to be designed as a back-end (memory-to-memory) processor for the host. In fact, the resources of the host, together with the use of the *window*, saved the team from having to write I/O routines, file management systems, editors, and so forth. The users had access to *unmodified* tools belonging to the host. Consequently, the team could concentrate on the novel parts of the AHR design.

5.3. Possible AHR Design Modifications

Some important decisions had definite alternatives, which were not, in all cases, thoroughly investigated at the time and machine was being constructed. In addition, there was a certain degree of arbitrariness in the chosen course of development. The AHR team does not know to what extent the following decisions would have improved the behavior of AHR:

List vs. node forms for Lisp program storage. A Lisp program is kept in list form in the *passive memory*. Each time a program is copied to the *grill*, it then has to be converted to the node form, as shown in Figure 11–2. Perhaps it would have been better to have also kept the Lisp programs in node form in the *passive memory*.

Fixed vs. variable size of nodes. As evident in Figure 11–3, the nodes are of a fixed size, and they can have as many as four arguments. Thus, Lisp on the AHR machine cannot directly handle functions with more than four arguments. Using nodes of variable size would maximize the use of space in the *grill*—at the expense of a more difficult memory management.

Serial vs. parallel garbage collection. The garbage collector on the AHR was a serial one. Since this factor caused all processors but one to wait, a parallel collector was clearly in order. However, the AHR team concentrated on other aspects of AHR machine and did not pursue this topic.

Immediate vs. delayed evaluation of *nanes* with a value of zero. When a Lisp processor, after subtracting 1 from the *nane* of a node, discovers it to be 0, it could go ahead and evaluate that node, instead of inscribing it in the *fifo*.

5.4. Weak Engineering Points

Some decisions had a negative impact either on the performance of AHR or on its design and construction. As such, these flaws need to be documented.

1. The AHR cards were too large, and they tended to bend causing printed-circuit connections to break or become loose. These flaws produced bugs and intermitent failures that were hard to diagnose.
2. Card interfaces initially were incompatible because the interfaces among the different cards were not precisely specified early in the construction phase. Consequently, slightly different—but incompatible—assumptions were made by the people building cards that were later interconnected. The decomposition of the computer into its constituent printed-circuit cards was not done in such a way as to make each card simple and easy to test.
3. The flat cables running among the different cards of AHR were just too long; there was no backplane. The length of the cables gave rise to pulse reflections and impedance mismatches, among other problems, as well as pulse distortions. There were too many lines going to each Lisp processor. The well-known techniques of multiplexing, time sharing, etc., were not used.
4. Debugging tools were insufficient because too little detail was devoted to debugging tools, mainly due to a scarcity of resources (people). Thus, debugging this parallel machine was difficult.

5.5. Recommendations for Further Work

Any additional work in parallel processing that considers the results gained from the AHR project will have a greater degree of success if the factors listed in Table 11–3 are observed.

5.5.1. *Introduce Impurities into Pure Lisp*

Most Lisp programs are written in impure Lisp, with setq's, rplacd's, goto's, etc. Learning pure Lisp in order to use a machine such as AHR may seem a very high price to pay. Moreover, there are some applications where there is not enough memory for continually replicating data when only a small part changes. A program that modifies an array of a million pixels, for example, may have changes affecting only a few pixels.

Consequently, there is a need to introduce the assignment concept (setq), and similar arguments can be made for other impurities. At the time of the AHR

Table 11–3. Recommendations for Further Work

Introduce impurities into pure Lisp.
Emphasize hardware improvements.
Increase the granularity of parallelism.
Provide natural parallel constructs.
Provide natural parallel data structures.

project, the AHR team proposed to define *suitable* impurities, perhaps by inventing a few *new* types, to add to pure Lisp. These "impurities" could have been introduced only if the overall design maintained the following features of the architecture: (1) the simplicity of the AHR schema, (2) the suitability of the program for parallel systems, and (3) the transparent user interface for a parallel system.

A programmer should, ideally, have little or no awareness of programming a machine that is a parallel system. The AHR design team did not want to load (not heavily, at least) the programmer with special parallel constructs, with worries about synchronization, assignment of tasks to processors, etc.

5.5.2. *Emphasize Hardware Improvements*
Once tasks that need to be done efficiently are identified, it is worth the effort to develop hardware that does them quickly. For instance, the different modes of AHR memories, in addition to *write* and *read*, greatly simplified the design and made the system run faster. Simulations using the B6700 allowed the AHR designers to discover what parts were worth improving and speeding up. Along the same lines, actual machines now contain tag bits and forward pointers in hardware.

Monoprocessors with a program counter work better with a memory buffer register bigger than one word. If, for instance, the memory buffer register can hold two words, then a fetch issued to the memory location **a** can bring both the contents of **a** and **a** + **1** to the central processing unit (CPU), thereby cutting the effective fetch time in half. This trick works because the next instruction is normally executed right after a prior one instruction is executed. Why not, then, when the Lisp processor asks for cell **a**, bring also the cell pointed to by the **car** of **a** as well as that pointed to by the **cdr** of **a**?

5.5.3. *Increase the Granularity of Parallelism*
The AHR machine sends nodes for evaluation to the Lisp processors that are too small, perhaps, compared with the overhead involved in using the *distributor*, the *high-speed bus*, etc. Thus, there could be a concept such as *send bigger nodes*. Implementing this concept would necessitate the invention of higher primitives in Lisp. Lisp could be enriched with functions that "compute more" once they have all their arguments. To some extent, Lisp already does that, for it provides

MEMBER as a primitive function, primarly for efficiency reasons, although MEMBER could easily be a user-defined function.

5.5.4. *Provide Natural Parallel Constructs*

A collection of Lisp function—such as Mapcar, Forall, For-the-first, Parallel-and, etc.—would entice the user to "think parallel." The use of *future* [9] is natural in this sense, since (future (foo x y)) means the same as (foo x y), but the "future" version is intended to be *computed in another processor*. Nevertheless, asynchronous evaluation creates indeterminism in the presence of side effects and assignments of global variables; therefore, it has to be used carefully with impure code. One example of a language that provides natural parallel constructs is L, a language developed for image processing [10].

A language that emphasizes natural parallel constructs can be described [11] as follows:

It would create primitives that operate on *all* processors;
It can be interpreted as an order to the *whole* parallel computer, as opposed to CAR, which is an order to *one* of the Lisp processor;
It captures, in a multiple instruction, stream, multiple data stream (MIMD) machine, the "spirit of programming" in a single instruction stream, multiple data stream (SIMD) architecture.

5.5.5. *Provide Natural Parallel Data Structures*

The **cdr** of a list is generally bigger than the **car**. This "unbalanced" data structure predisposes the programmer to a sequential mode of computation: there is a tendency to think, "First I will handle now the **car**, and then later I will take care of the rest." Perhaps something like the xapping construct [12] is needed.

6. CONCLUSION

The history of the AHR project was not only a precursor of later work with parallel systems, but it also posed some questions that are still of intrinsic interest to computer research.

ACKNOWLEDGMENTS

The AHR machine is the result of many hours of work by the AHR team. A special word of gratitude is due to the IIMAS director, Dr. Tomás Garza, and the IIMAS administration, all of whom made their best efforts to help the AHR project.

The financial support from CONACYT (grant #1632) is acknowledged, as well as CONACYT's help in the interchange of visiting scientists between IIMAS-UNAM and the Institute for Control Sciences, USSR Academy of Sciences.

Thanks are due to the parallel processing program at the Microelectronics and Computer Technology Corporation (MCC), Austin, TX, particularly

Dr. Stephen Lundstrom, its vice president and program director, for his continuous support. A special word of appreciation is also due to my colleagues of the MCC Lisp group for their fruitful comments and help.

REFERENCES

1. A. Guzman and R. Segovia, *A Configurable Lisp Machine.* IIMAS-UNAM Tech. Rep. Na 133 (AHR-76-1). National University of Mexico, Mexico City, 1976. (Hereinafter, all reports such as this one are signified by the note, "IIMAS Technical Report.")
2. A. Guzman and R. Segovia, "A Parallel Reconfigurable Lisp Machine," *Proc. Int'l Conf. on Information Science and Systems,* University of Patras, Greece, Aug. 1976, pp. 207–211.
3. A. Guzman and K. Norkin, *The Design and Construction of a Parallel Heterarchical Machine*: *Final Report of Phase 1* of the AHR Project. IIMAS Tech. Rep. Na 308 (AHR-82-21), 1982.
4. A. Guzman, "A Heterarchical Multi-Microprocessor Lisp Machine." *Proc. 1981 IEEE Workshop on Computer Architecture for Pattern Analysis and Image Database Management,* Hot Springs, VA., 1981. IEEE Catalog 81CH-1697-2.
5. A. Guzman, "A Parallel Heterarchical Machine for High Level Language Processing." In M. J. B. Duff and S. Levialdi (eds.) *Languages and and Architectures for Image Processing.* New York: Academic Press, 1981. (Also published in *Proc. 1981 Int'l. Conf. on Parallel Processing,* 64–71. IEEE Catalog 81CH-1634-5.)
6. A. Guzman, *et al. The AHR Computer*: *Construction of a Multiprocessor with Lisp as Its Main Language.* IIMAS Rep. Na 253 (AHR-80-10), 1980 (in Spanish).
7. N. Gayosso, *The Distributor for the AHR Machine*: *The Microprogrammable Hardware Version.* B.Sc. thesis, ESIME-National Polytechnic Institute, Mexico City, 1981 (in Spanish).
8. L. Peñarrieta and N. Gayosso, *Alternatives for the AHR Distributor.* IIMAS Tech. Rep. Na 302 (AHR-82-20), 1982.
9. P. McGehearty and E. Krall, "Potentials for Parallel Execution of Common Lisp Programs," *Proc. 1986 Int'l Conf. on Parallel Processing,* 696–702. IEEE Catalog 86CH2355-6.
10. R. Barrera and A. Guzman, *et al.,* "Design of a High-level Language (L) for Image Processing." In, M. J. B. Duff and S. Levialdi (eds.) *Languages and Architectures for Image Processing.* New York: Academic Press, 1981.
11. S. Lundstrom, Personal communication.
12. G. L. Steele and W. D. Hillis, "Connection Machine Lisp: Fine-Grained Symbolic Processing" *Proc. 1986 ACM Conference on Lisp and Functional Programming,* pp. 279–297. ACM Order No. 552860.

12. FAIM-1: AN ARCHITECTURE FOR SYMBOLIC MULTIPROCESSING

ALAN L. DAVIS

1. INTRODUCTION
1.1. Goals
The FAIM-1 system is an attempt to provide a significant performance gain over conventional machines in support of symbolic artificial intelligence (A1) processing. The primary performance-enhancement mechanism is to consistently exploit concurrency at all levels of the architecture. In designing FAIM-1, prime consideration was given to programmability, performance, extensibility, fault tolerance, and the cost-effective use of modern circuit and packaging technology.

1.1.1. *Programmability*
Although the FAIM-1 machine architecture is unconventional, the software environment provides a concurrent programming language and application development system based on models that are familiar to members of the AI community. This permits immediate evaluation of the FAIM-1 architecture using existing applications, as well as easing the burden on future application programmers.

1.1.2. *Performance*
Exploitation of concurrency is the primary mechanism employed by the FAIM-1 system to significantly increase performance over conventional sequential systems. Within the hardware, concurrency is exploited between processing

223

elements as well as within each processing element. Software concurrency is also exploited in a variety of ways permitting flexible parallel pipeline and task structures to be specified.

1.1.3. *Extensibility*

High priority was given to creating a design that permits arbitrary expansion of the hardware resources to permit the creation of machine instances containing virtually any number of processing elements. Such expansion requires minimal rewiring and no modification to either the user or the system software. The communication topology is planar and therefore will not become a liability as technology permits evolution from multiple-chip to single-chip processing elements (PE's). All hardware interfaces are self-timed [1] to permit individual components to evolve in performance, implementation technology, and functionality. The result is an architecture that is easy to modify and exhibits a favorable cost-performance ratio under scaling.

1.1.4. *Fault Tolerance*

Any solution to the fault-tolerance problem inherently contains redundancy. The FAIM-1 contains significant redundancy both in terms of processing elements and in the way they are interconnected. The resource allocation mechanism permits the reassignment of tasks to processors, the message-routing algorithm is capable of routing messages around failed paths and processors, and the system software supports self-diagnosis.

1.1.5. *Technology*

The architecture has been designed to take advantage of the cost and performance of both advanced very-large-scale-integration (VLSI) circuit technology and advanced packaging technology, such as immersion-cooled wafer hybridization [2], as they become available.

1.2. System Software Issues

The concurrent programming language for FAIM-1 is called OIL, for Our Initial Language [3]. OIL is intended to be a high-level, concurrent, symbolic programming language which when coupled with its programming environment supports the development of concurrent AI application programs. OIL is macro-expanded into our implementation language. KernOIL, which is a variant of SCHEME [4] and includes the *future* constructs of Multilisp [5]. KernOIL is then compiled to produce object code for the FAIM-1. We presently have little experience with OIL, but have coded the entire FAIM-1 run-time system in KernOIL and have found it to be a useful and powerful parallel programming language in its own right.

The OIL programming language is composed of components of object-oriented [6, 7], and logic [8], and procedural programming styles [9]. An OIL program is viewed as a cooperating ensemble of objects. OIL program execution, control, and synchronization are all a direct result of objects communicating via messages. Objects are uniquely generated, nameable entities capable of retaining local state and have associated operations or methods that may be written using either a declarative (an OR-parallel dialect of Prolog) or imperative (a subset of Common Lisp, which has been modified to incorporate concurrency) notation.

OIL programs are translated into loadable object code on a host Symbolics 3600 Lisp machine. User programs can be executed either by loading the object code onto the FAIM-1 hardware or by running it on a host-based FAIM-1 simulator. Critical decisions about where to load individual object-code tasks are made during a phase of compilation called *resource allocation*. The resource allocation process involves balancing the use of the parallel execution hardware with the cost of run-time communication overhead. Resource allocation is a configuration-dependent task that allows programmers to write parallel programs without a detailed understanding of the processing element, inter-connection structure, or communication costs.

The complexity of resource allocation for large programs makes it unlikely that explicitly programmer specified allocations will be a viable long-term solution. Dynamic (run-time) allocation inherently implies significant levels of run-time overhead. Hence, the primary focus for FAIM-1 is on static (compiled) methods. The OIL programmer can influence the static allocator by special annotations called *pragma's*, and some simple dynamic load balancing can be performed when run-time conditions indicate that it is necessary. The goal in FAIM-1 is to allocate a fair number of parallel tasks to each PE, e.g., ten to 20. This strategy improves PE utility by increasing the probability that at any given time, one task will be runnable in each PE. The hardware architecture of the PE has significant support for rapid task-switching as a result of this view.

1.3. Hardware

The remainder of this chapter focuses on the hardware of the FAIM-1 machine. The architecture permits an unbounded number of PE's called *Hectogons* to be interconnected by a *communication topology*. Hectogons communicate by passing messages. Although a Hectogon is directly connected to only six neighbors, nonlocal messages can be sent using intermediate Hectogons as forwarding agents. Each Hectogon is a medium-grain processing element containing a number of concurrent coprocessor subsystems including an evaluation processor (EP), a task-switching processor (SP), a communications subsystem (Post Office), and three special-purpose memories (ISM, PAM. and SRAM), which support respectively instruction storage and delivery, data storage, and structured pattern matching.

2. COMMUNICATION TOPOLOGY

The FAIM-1 communication topology comprises two levels. At the bottom level, a number of **PE's** are interconnected to form a *processing surface*. At the top level,

Hex Display with One Wrapped Axis

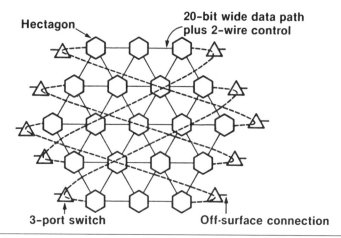

Figure 12–1. E-3 surface with three-way switches.

any number of surfaces can be interconnected to form a multisurface FAIM-1 configuration.

The topology used for a FAIM-1 surface is a regular hexagonal mesh. PE's communicate directly with six on-surface neighbors. The periphery of the surface is also hexagonal, and hence multiple surfaces may also be combined using a hexagonal mesh interconnection as well. In this case each surface connects to six neighbor surfaces. When wires leave a processing surface through the processing elements at the periphery, they are folded back onto the surface using a three-axis variant of a twisted torus [10]. In Figure 12–1 the basic surface topology is illustrated along with the wrap lines of a single axis (for clarity) and the off-surface switches that complete the interconnect structure.

This particular wrapping scheme results in a simple routing algorithm and provides a minimal (provable) switching diameter for a hexagonal mesh. The term *switching diameter* is defined as the worst-case communication distance between any two elements in an interconnection structure. The topology is homogeneous in that any PE can be viewed as if it is the center PE of the surface. In the worst case, a message requires at most two hops (for the 19-processor surface shown in Figure 12–1) to reach its destination. This topology permits routing decisions to be based on a two- or three-axis relative coordinate system, which specifies the axis offset between the sending and receiving PE's for each individual message. For fault tolerance reasons, FAIM-1 employs a three-axis coordinate system.

Each peripheral port of a surface communicates with an off-surface switch as well as being wrapped back to the opposite edge of the surface. These off-surface connections permit communications with I/O devices and other surfaces. The external and wrap connections are supported by the addition of a simple three-way switch shown in Figure 12–1. The switches have three ports: internal (local surface messages), external (adjacent surfaces, I/O devices, or the host), and wrap (local surface via the wrap line). Switching decisions are based on which of the three ports a message arrives on and the destination contained in the message header.

Notationally, the size of a surface is defined by the number of processors n on each *edge* of the hexagonal surface. The surface is then referred to as an E–n *surface*; the number of processors in a surface scales as $3n(n-1)+1$. For example, the E–3 surface shown in Figure 12–1 has three processors on each edge and contains a total of 19 processors. For surface sizes between E–1 and E–7 inclusive, the number of PE's is a prime number, which is advantageous from the standpoint of fault tolerance and initialization.

The internal connections of the hexagonal array and the external connections to the three-way switches are all planar; the wrap lines are the only nonplaner links. For each peripheral port, a three-way switch must be added along with two additional wires that allow connectivity among the external port, peripheral PE, and wrap line. The number of wrap wires therefore scales linearly while the number of processors scales as $O(n^2)$. This reduces wiring complexity when connecting the nonplanar wrap wires as larger surface sizes are used to increase processing power. However, the number of peripheral I/O devices on a surface can still grow as $O(n)$ to increase I/O bandwidth as the number of processors is increased.

A multisurface instance of FAIM-1 can therefore be simply constructed from a number of processor surfaces by simple abutment. Multisurface configurations have the advantage of increased on-surface locality and reduced communication diameter of the entire system when compared to a single-surface instance comprising approximately the same number of processors. These properties can be demonstrated by the following exmmple. An E–7 surface contains 127 processors and has a diameter of six, while seven E–3 surfaces can be tiled to form an S–2 E–3 machine as shown in Figure 12–2 that contains 133 processors with a diameter of five. The S–n notation is similar to the E–n notation, indicating the number of surfaces on each edge of the approximately hexagonal supersurface illustrated in Figure 12–2. The switching diameter improves dramatically as surface count and size scale up. A 58,381 processor E 140 has a diameter of 139 while a 58.807 processor S–9 E–10 FAIM instance results in a diameter of 89, a full 50 hops better (worst case) than the single E–140 surface.

Single surface configurations have the advantage of simplified routing, and inherently more flexible routing decisions due to the presence of the wrap lines. However for large PE counts, multiple-surface configurations are preferable due to improved communication within local surface boundaries, while global surface-to-surface communication does not degrade when compared with a single surface containing approximately the same number of PE's. The routing

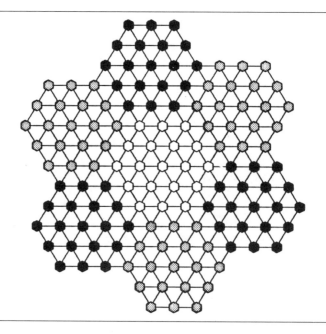

Figure 12–2. S-2 tessellation of E-3 surfaces.

algorithm for the single surface extends to multiple surfaces, providing uniform routing across the hierarchy.

The probability of component failure in a system statistically increases as more components are added to the system [11] making fault-tolerance an important aspect of highly replicated architectures. Fortuitously, distributed ensemble architectures intrinsically contain redundant elements that can be used to support fault-tolerant behavior. Koren has shown that hexagonal meshes are particularly attractive fault-tolerant topologies [12]. In addition, fault-tolerant message routing is possible due to the multiplicity of paths over which a message may be routed to its destination.

3. THE HECTOGON

The intent of the Hectogon's design is to provide highly efficient support for programs written in either OIL or KernOIL. The Hectogon can be viewed as the homogeneously replicated PE of the the FAIM-1 architecture on one hand and as a medium-grain, highly concurrent, heterogeneous, shared-memory multiprocessor on the other. This double view is the result of an attempt to consistently and aggressively exploit concurrency at all levels of the FAIM-1 system. Externally viewed, a large number of Hectogons can be tiled together to form a fully distributed (no shared memory or control) multiprocessing architecture. Internally, each Hectogon can be viewed as a shared-memory multiprocessor

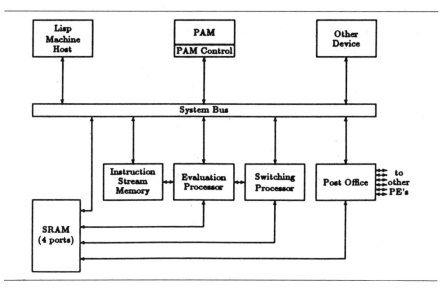

Figure 12–3. Hectogon block diagram.

containing multiple specialized coprocessor subsystems, which cooperatively evaluate the assigned tasks.

Intra-Hectogon subsystems communicate with each other using special-purpose self-timed interfaces for high frequency traffic. Infrequent subsystem communication is done via the System Bus or SBUS. All Hectogon subsystems contain an interface to the SBUS. The internal Hectogon SBUS's are interconnected to each other and to the host machine via a hierarchy of SBUS controllers. This organization permits the host machine to monitor individual subsystems and provides a convenient mechanism for initialization, monitoring, and testing. A Hectogon's subsystems and their interconnection are shown in Figure 12–3.

SBUS addresses are 24-bits wide, with the high-order four bits specifying a particular device, the host, or subsystem and the remaining 20 bits specifying an address within the device. The SBUS consists of parallel data and address lines, with additional signals for bus arbitration, interrupt handling, and miscellaneous control. A simple, speed-independent request/acknowledge protocol is used.

The six subsystems connected by the SBUS are:

Evaluation processor (EP). A streamlined, nonmicrocoded, stack-based processor responsible for evaluating machine instructions.

Switching processor (SP). A small-context switching processor that is responsible for interpreting the run-list in data memory (the SRAM) and moving blocked contexts out of processor registers and into SRAM-process control blocks, and then loading a new, runnable context into the processor registers.

Instruction stream memory (ISM). A specialized instruction memory that not only stores the instructions but is also responsible for finding the appropriate instruction, partially decoding it, and handing it to the EP.

Scratch random access memory (SRAM). The SRAM is the local data memory of the Hectogon. It is a four-ported subsystem that provides concurrent access to the EP. SP. SBUS. and Post office.

Pattern addressable memory (PAM). A parallel associative memory system capable of matching complex structures such as S-expressions, where *don't cares* may exist either in the query or in the data. In the present instantiation the match function is mock unification, i.e. the extent to which unification can be done without deferencing bound logical variable pointers.

Post Office. An autonomous communications subsystem responsible for all aspects of the physical delivery of inter-Hectogon messages.

4. THE PROCESSOR

4.1. A Two-Processor Partnership

To achieve the goal of rapid context switching, the processor is implemented as a partnership of two processors, the EP and the SP. The EP evaluates the currently active task, while the SP sets up the next runnable task. Tasks run in a context-specific register set, of which the processor contains two. Each set contains the stack buffers, processor status word, general purpose registers, etc. One set is marked *active* and is used by the EP, while the other is marked *idle* and is used by the SP to save the old context and load the next context from process-control blocks stored in the SRAM. This concurrent and cooperative partnership is also supported by the SRAM design in that both the EP and the SP have separate dedicated ports to the SRAM.

It will typically take a single instruction time to effect a context switch. This assumes that the SP has completed its next task prefetch activity. If this is not the case, then the EP will halt until the new context becomes valid. The EP is not explicitly aware that the SP is not ready. The self-timed hardware interface between the EP and SP will automatically and transparently inhibit the EP from evaluating an invalid context. Normally there are four ways that the currently running task can be suspended: interrupts, traps, task termination, and task block. A task block occurs when any long delay is incurred, such as a message send to a remote processor that requires a reply before the sending task can continue.

Both task termination and task block cause a context switch, and the next reasonable action is to run another task as nothing more can be done for a while on the evaluation of the current task. Since traps usually require the current context to be kept around, e.g., the arguments to the trapped instruction require modification by the service routine, trap service routines are run in the current context in a manner similar to that of a simple function call. Interrupt driven tasks inherently start and terminate cleanly and therefore can also be evaluated in the current context. The result is that context switches are explicitly forced by the currently running task, while exceptions (traps and interrupts) are dynamically spliced into the active context and therefore do not cause a context switch.

4.2. The EP

The EP executes instructions that it receives from the ISM using the active-context register set. To reduce the complexity of the EP, improve its performance, and utilize existing AI machine research [13, 14], a stack-based RISC [15] organization was chosen. The existence of a separate instruction delivery subsystem (the ISM) permits a simple two-stage pipeline to be employed for the EP. The first stage supports instruction decode, operand selection, and modification. The second stage performs the ALU operation, modifies the result if necessary, and stores the result. The ISM runs concurrently with the EP and effectively contains another two pipeline stages that perform effective-address translation, instruction fetch, and partial instruction decode.

The EP datapath is 28-bits wide. Four bits are reserved for garbage collection tag bits, and another four bits are used for type tags. The type-tags are processed in parallel by separate tag manipulation hardware. The type-tags are analyzed concurrently with the processing of the 20-bit data field and may generate a trap when the operand type-tags are inappropriate for a particular operation.

The EP contains the following context register set resources that the instruction set manipulates either explicitly or implicitly:

A processor status word (PSW) that encodes the status of the EP.

A 16-word expression stack buffer that contains most operand data. Associated with the stack buffer is an autonomous memory controller, which controls filling and unfilling the buffer as needed. The controller also generates the appropriate memory references for stack accesses that are deeper than the buffer size, and therefore reside in memory. Access to operands in the buffer is performed at register speed. Almost all of the dyadic data operations are performed by consuming the top two locations as input operands to the ALU and replacing them with the result value.

A four-word control-stack buffer that is used explicitly to store return addresses on a CALL. This buffer shares the memory controller. The existence of a separate control stack is motivated by the resulting simplification of the call and return sequence, the inherent datapath separation that exists for data and instruction storage (i.e., serviced by separate FAIM-1 subsystems), and the removal of the need for special-purpose registers such as a frame pointer.

Sixteen general-purpose pointer registers, which can be used for anything, but are typically used as index or offset registers. Instructions that manipulate them usually permit auto-increment and decrement modifications. These registers support systems that need to manipulate more than a single-expression stack, such as logic program interpreters [16].

The EP contains a full 20-bit-wide ALU that supports logical operators, integer arithmetic, and shifting instructions. The EP instructions combine the small instruction size of stack-organized processors and the streamlined style of the RISC methodology. This is achieved by trading register-based arithmetic and logical operations for stack-based operatons. In addition the instruction set supports a simple load-and-store model, which may also be indexed off any of the general-purpose index registers.

The 16 EP tag types are: uninterpreted bit field, two's complement integer, four-word floating-point number pointer, bignum pointer, immediate system constant, character, vector pointer, function pointer, invisible pointer, external pointer (data-pointer to an address on another Hectogon), string pointer, future pointer, symbol, code pointer, escape pointer. Immediate type discrimination is provided by evaluation of these tag types. If the word is an escape pointer then dereferencing that pointer leads to a word whose value is a user or system-defined type. The result is a type space of 15 immediate types and up to 2^{20} of system or user-defined types.

Traps are generated when instructions are evaluated and the tag values associated with their operand type tags are not of the expected type. The EP contains a trap and interrupt encoder that passes the proper trap-service routine address to the ISM when a trap occurs. When a trap occurs, the ISM takes this address over the SBUS and pushes the appropriate return address onto the control stack in the EP over the instruction bus.

The garbage collection tags do not have their own specialized data path as they are only used by the garbage collector in order to reduce the amount of free space required to perform garbage collection and to permit garbage collection to be more efficient by reducing the number of instructions in the inner loop of the garbage collection process.

The EP evaluates two basic types of instructions: short and long. A short instruction is a single eight-bit packet delivered by the ISM over the instruction bus. The format selector is the high-order bit of the instruction world. Short instructions either do not require operands or the operands are implicitly found on the expression stack. Long instructions either specify operand locations or contain a small immediate value.

Instructions exist to support functions in the following categories:

Stack manipulation. Duplicate top, exchange top two values, copy an indexed item to top, pop, push, etc.

Monadic arithmetic/logical. Operations on integer values and bit-field immediate types, which are found on the top of the data stack, e.g., increment, decrement, NOT. compare, negate, shift, and test for zero or negative.

Dyadic arithmetic/logical. Add, Subtract, Multiply, Divide, OR, XOR, AND, and bit-field extract, mask, or place. These instructions require that both operand tag types be either integer or bit-field. A trap will be generated if they are not.

Data movement instructions. Move data from register, stack top, or memory to some other register, stack top, or memory. Many of these instructions use the index registers and can optionally use an offset register and specify either auto-increment or auto-decrement of the selected index register.

Immediate instructions. Permit a small one-byte constant to be compared, pushed, or used as a mask against either the data or tag fields of the operand. They also permit some simple immediate arithmetic and logical functions.

State modification. Instructions that test, set, and manipulate condition codes and other PSW-specific fields.

Control. These instructions modify ISM addresses and save them in support of CALL, RETURN, and BRANCH constructs in the source program. Instructions in this area also exist to force explicit context switches and halt the EP. These instructions can be performed conditionally or unconditionally.

Interface. Instructions to read and write the SBUS and drive the interfaces of the ISM. Post Office, and SP.

The instruction set is tuned so that most instructions require only a single cycle. The only instructions that may consume additional cycles implicitly are instructions that generate memory references, and interface instructions to the other subsystems. The result is a simple, RISC-like processor that provides significant support for the efficient evaluation of OIL programs and that is physically small enough to permit the high levels of replication.

4.3. The SP

The context switcher is a small processor that loads and unloads the idle context register set with values found in a process control block (PCB) stored in the SRAM. This organization supports rapid context switching by not stealing EP cycles to set up the next task context. The main data structure manipulated by the SP is the *run-list.* The scheduler is an EP task that is run when necessary. The run-list is a linked list of PCB's where each PCB's first entry is a pointer to the next PCB in the list. The actual implementation is more complex than this, but additional detail is omitted here for clarity.

When the active EP task blocks, two interface bits to the SP are set. One bit indicates whether the now idle context set needs to be saved, and the other indicates that a context switch has occurred. In response to the switch bit being set, the SP examines the save bit. If save is set, then the SP unloads the idle context set into the appropriate PCB. The SP then examines the run list for the next runnable task and loads the context set with information contained in the next task's PCB and sets the valid bit to indicate completion of the *next-task-prepare* action. The SP will then halt until another context switch is signalled either by a blocking EP process or the scheduler.

Arriving message traffic from other Hectogons may cause idle processes to be rescheduled as runnable tasks. The message handler and scheduler support this by linking arriving messages with their target tasks and moving them to the run-list if the newly received message makes them runnable. The scheduler can therefore be invoked by a *message-delivered* interrupt from the Post Office or host machine. It can also be invoked by a *reschedule-timeout* interrupt from the real-time clock. The real-time clock provides periodic interrupts after a programmable interval.

Physically the SP is a medium-scale, finite-state machine that is capable of examining the run'list, nominating the next context, and generating a sequence of save-and-load instructions for moving the context register set contents to and from the corresponding PCB in the SRAM. The design fits on a single 64-pin LSI device.

5. THE ISM

The ISM [17] is designed to deliver instructions to the processor at high speed. To accomplish this task efficiently, the ISM performs several functions that are typically performed by the processor in a conventional system. These include calculation of instruction addresses, processing of branches and subroutine calls, and handling trap and interrupt vectors.

Implementing a separate instruction delivery module can have several advantages as demonstrated in the Dorado architecture [14]. Because only instructions are stored in the ISM, it can be optimized for its sole function of instruction delivery. Conventional solutions place a specialized intermediate piece of hardware between the processor and main memory such as an instruction cache [18] or translation look-aside buffer [19]. Performance can be enhanced by tightly coupling the instruction selection and delivery logic with the instruction storage. In addition to the advantage of higher performance instruction delivery, the design of the EP is simplified. The instruction-fetch stage of the traditional processor pipeline has effectively been transferred to the ISM, along with the program counter and all of the instructions address generation logic. The resulting shorter pipeline in the EP increases the throughput of the processor and simplifies exception handling duties.

The ISM capitalizes on the fact that instructions are not randomly accessed. In most programs, code is naturally partitioned into small sequences of linearly ordered instructions that terminate in branches or subroutine calls. Notationally these linear sequences of instructions will be called *tracks*. Logically, instruction tracks vary in length; however, the ISM's instruction storage maps these onto a set of fixed-length physical tracks. Linkage information corresponding to control instructions is associated with the physical tracks in a header field. Control point information is maintained in a *current track address register* or CTR, which is similar in function to the program counter of a conventional system. An individual instruction address consists of a track number and a track offset.

5.1. Branch and Exception Processing

Execution of branch-type instructions is quite complex in most large machines due to the large number of instructions that can cause a branch and the wide variety of addressing modes allowed. In keeping with the streamlined RISC theme, the FAIM-1 uses only a single jump format that is flexible enough to support conditional and unconditional branches, calls, and returns. Instruction decoding becomes simple both for the EP and ISM. The ISM examines each instruction as it is prepared for delivery to the EP. When a jump is detected, the ISM autonomously and concurrently processes that instruction, continuing delivery with the first instruction from the target stream.

Conditional branches are a canonical problem, which increase complexity and often limits the performance of pipelined processor architectures. They are usually the main bottleneck in lookahead and prefetch strategies [20]. In conventional pipelined systems, by the time the branch is executed and the correct path is resolved, some succeeding instructions have already entered the pipeline. If the branch is taken, the current contents of the pipeline must be discarded, incurring a delay while the pipe is filled again. The standard method of keeping the pipeline full is to use a delayed branch instruction as in the MIPs architecture [21].

In FAIM–1, the ISM decodes jump instructions before they even enter the pipeline, so a pipeline flush is not necessary and the delayed branch strategy is not applicable. This is because the required continuation of the instruction stream is always correctly delivered. There is, however, an analogous dependence problem in that the outcome of a conditional jump may depend on the result of a previous instruction that has not yet finished executing. To ensure that the branch condition has become valid by the time the ISM detects the jump, an *advance condition set* method is used.

If a sufficient number of filler instructions are inserted between the instruction that sets the condition and the instruction that checks it, it can be guaranteed that the condition code line (asserted by the EP) will be valid by the time the ISM decodes the jump instruction. Because the EP has a two-stage pipeline, only a single filler instruction is necessary. In the worst case. the filler instruction would be a NOP, but since many instructions do not modify the condition codes, they become candidates for placement between the condition-setting instruction and the conditional branch. Initial simulation statistics are similar to those produced under the delayed branch method [22], indicating approximately 75% success in NOP filler avoidance.

A subroutine or function call in the OIL language compiles to a simple jump instruction and is processed by the ISM in almost exactly the same manner as a normal jump. The only difference is that when a call is detected, the ISM pushes the return address contained in the CTR onto the EP's control stack over the instruction bus. On a return from subroutine, the ISM pops the return address off the control stack over the instruction bus. The self-timed nature of the ISM/EP interface permits the ISM to pop or push the control stack without disturbing the instruction evaluation duties of the EP datapath.

Traps and interrupts are additional factors that cause a break in the instruction stream. As such, they have an impact on the operation of the ISM. Traps cause an unexpected subroutine call in place of a scheduled instruction, whereas interrupts cause a call between two scheduled instructions. Exception calls are handled similarly to regular calls, with the exception that the ISM must calculate the proper return address and push it onto the control stack over the instruction bus and must receive the target service routine address from the EP's trap and interrupt encoder over the SBUS.

5.2. Implementation

The ISM design is simple enough to permit implementation using two custom LSI devices. One is the ISM-Controller, which provides all of the control signals and sequences the ISM's operation. The other custom device is the ISM-Buffer, which holds the current instruction buffers and also up to two prefetch buffers depending on the possible location of the next possible instruction targets. This buffering scheme permits full lookahead and prefetch for conditional jumps, calls, and returns. No prefetching is done for either trap or interrupt targets because they are too numerous to predict in a cost-effective manner. The rest of the implementation uses standard commercially available memory components. An ISM address is 20 bits. Due to the self-managing nature of the ISM, addresses seldom need to pass between the ISM and EP except for return addresses, which move between the ISM and the control stack, and trap or interrupt vectors, which are passed over the SBUS. However, in order to support functional arguments and multitasking, it is sometimes necessary for the EP to provide an initial instruction address to the ISM. These special ISM addresses are explicitly tagged as *code-pointer* in the EP.

6. THE SRAM

The SRAM is the local data memory system of the Hectogon and contains 28-bit-wide data words that are accessed by 20-bit addresses. The SRAM is a four-ported memory system that provides concurrent shared access to the EP, SP, Post Office, and SBUS. The word size internal to the SRAM may vary as needed to accommodate ECC. In the first prototype, no ECC is being implemented, and the internal word size is 29 bits to include only a simple parity bit. On a memory error, the SRAM interface sets an error flag in the PSW which may halt the machine if the SRAM-error-halt condition is set.

The physical structure of the SRAM is to partition memory into 16 concurrently accessible blocks. The high-order four bits of an address is the block selector, and the remaining 16 bits are the block offset. The memory in each block is implemented with standard memory chips. Each block is controlled by a SRAM block controller or (SBC). The role of the SBC is to take the request and block selection address bit from each port and determine whether the requested address lies within its local block. If the address is for the local block then this request is passed through four-input arbitration circuit which generates a GO signal for the port which will be serviced. The arbiter does not permit concurrent requests to any given block, but storage allocation is such that the SP, EP, and Post Office seldom conflict for access to any particular block.

The SBC is a custom 40-pin MSI circuit, which adds 12 nanoseconds onto the access times of whatever static RAM chips are used to implement the block storage. The SBC permits the use of external RC delay circuits to specify when the appropriate acknowledge signal should be sent back out the active port to indicate completion of the requisite memory operation. The low-order 16-address bits are multiplexed by control signals provided by the SBC. The SBC also passes the four GO lines to external logic, which must be used with the SBC device to do data and address steering.

The result is a four-ported data memory subsystem capable of servicing four concurrent access requests. In cases where concurrent requests are targeted at the same physical block in the SRAM, the self-timed interface provided by the SBC will sequence the accesses fairly on a first-come, first-served basis. This four-ported organization is essential to support the concurrent specialized coprocessor organization within the processing element.

7. THE POST OFFICE

7.1. Operational Responsibilities

The Post Office [23, 24] is an autonomous message delivery subsystem. It is responsible for all of the physical delivery aspects of inter-Hectogon message traffic. The Post Office is a seven-ported device: six external ports connect the Post Office to adjacent Hectogons as indicated by the communication topology, and an internal port connects to one of the local SRAM ports. The Post Office design allows all seven ports to be concurrently active.

The Post Office extracts a message from the SRAM and delivers it over the communication network to a receiving Post Office, which places the message in the destination PE's SRAM. The receiving Post Office will then notify its EP that a new message has arrived. Messages inherently vary in length. The Post Office physically delivers messages by breaking them up into a series of fixed-length packets. These packets are then delivered individually to their intended destination.

The Post Office contains a routing mechanism that can calculate the correct ports through which to transfer a packet. General communications efficiency can be significantly enhanced if the routing mechanism is capable of detecting congestion and routing packets around such congested areas in the communication network. The Post Office router is capable of detecting congestion dynamically and makes its routing decisions accordingly. This mechanism can also be extended to permit messages to be routed around nonfunctional nodes and ports.

The capability to dynamically route packets around congestion and failed components implies that the order of packet arrival may vary from the order in which the packets were sent. The capability to reorder packets at their final destination is essential to ensure both deterministic behavior and to permit proper reassembly of multiple-packet messages by the destination Post Office.

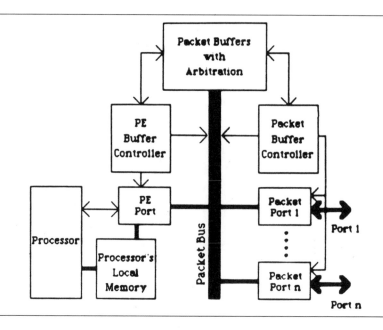

Figure 12–4. Post Office block diagram.

This also implies that each packet contains a unique message identifier, the packet number, and the number of total packets in the message. Although this increases the amount of work required at the receiving Post Office, it reduces congestion-related and failure-related message delays.

Messages are assumed to be delivered error-free. This assumption places the burden on the Post Offices to verify checksums for each packet, organize retransmission when an error is detected, and synchronize packet-copy destruction in a way that ensures that at least one correct copy of the packet exists in some Hectogon. To avoid deadlock, a mechanism must be employed that either guarantees deadlock will not occur, or ensures that the probability of deadlock is much less than the probability of an unrecoverable component failure. The Post Office guarantees that deadlock will not occur by preventing unrestricted incremental resource claiming, thereby ensuring that each Post Office will not be congested indefinitely.

7.2. Post Office Components

The Post Office is constructed from three types of basic components—*Port Controllers*, *Buffer Controllers*, and a *buffer pool* (as shown in Figure 12–4).

Most of the functions of the Post Office are performed by independent Post Controllers to enhance concurrency. There are two port types: packet ports and DMA ports. Each Post Office contains one DMA port and six packet ports. All seven of these ports use the same internal buffer pool. The Packet Port Controllers transmit packets between adjacent Post Office, while the DMA Port Controller transfers messages to and from the processor's local memory.

The function of the Buffer Controllers is to arbitrate and control access to the packet buffer pool. They are also responsible for emptying the buffers as fast as possible by matching free ports with the buffered packets that need to be routed through those ports. The Packet Buffer Controller also determines when messages are stagnating in the buffers. When this occurs, an alternate routing mechanism that dynamically reroutes packets via alternate links can be invoked. The Buffer Controllers also contain a deadlock-avoidance mechanism.

7.3. Message Control

Messages sent through the Post Office consist of a message header and a variable-length message body. The message header contains the routing information, a message identifier, the message size, and the destination of the message. The original message header loaded by the Post Office is augmented to include the number of packets that had to be formed to deliver the message, the packet sequence number, a checksum, and the most recent port through which the packet passed.

The normal mode of delivery is to have messages routed to their destination using a hardware-routing algorithm. This method only requires the address of the destination. The internal routing algorithm determines the shortest route to that location.

All routing in the Post Office is done dynamically. This is because it is possible for a packet to take multiple paths to a nonlocal destination in the richly connected hexagonal mesh network. Each of these paths will bring the message closer to the destination. The dynamic packet-delivery routing algorithm selects a prioritized list of port through which a given packet should be routed. The highest priority port is tried first. If efforts fail to gain access to the highest priority port then the packet's *stagnation count* is incremented. When the stagnation count reaches a pre-set level (that can be modified) then the next priority port is tried. Each failure to pass the packet through the desired port increments the stagnation count. When the count reaches a critical level, the first available port is chosen and the packet is sent out. Simulation studies show that this critical random routing effectively reduces congestion by selecting suboptimal paths when optimal paths are unavailable either because of malfunction or congestion.

7.4. Performance

Packets can flow concurrently on all seven ports of the Post Office. Using a pessimistic estimate of 20 MHz per port, this produces a burst communication bandwidth of about 3 Gigabits per second per processor. The speed-independent nature of the communication links automatically avoids problems if peak capacity is greater than the internal packet buffers permit due to conflict. While this performance level exceeds the need in an E-3 surface, it will be needed in multisurface implementations to support scalable performance in larger instances of the machine.

It is our belief that direct support for communications will be required in MIMD multiprocessors with many PE's. This requires a significant reallocation of the transistor budget in order to achieve the proper balance between processing and communication performance. The Post Office is an experiment that couples a scalable topology and architecture with a communication component that is completely responsible for the physical delivery of messages. By operating concurrently with program execution and allowing all ports to simultaneously transfer packets, the performance of the Post Office should be sufficient even for large-scale networks of processors. A single chip VLSI implementation of the Post Office is currently being designed.

8. THE PAM

One of the most common functions used in AI programming is pattern matching. It is also a fundamental part of unification [16], which in turn is the basis for logic program evaluation. The declarative component of OIL is an OR-parallel dialect of Prolog. We believe that special pattern-matching support is necessary to achieve high performance symbolic processing. The PAM provides that support.

The PAM is composed of a number of PAM memory chips and the PAM controller. In the FAIM-1 prototype, the PAM controller responds to commands from the EP and provides an interface to the rest of the Hectogon. In future implementations, the PAM controller may be extended to become an autonomous unification server. The PAM memory chips are highly parallel associative memory components capable of performing a *mock unification* matching function on structured entries.

Traditionally, content addressable memory (CAM) structures have had limited utility. The result has been that hashing techniques have been more applicable in broad system contexts. The reasons have typically been that CAM components have been expensive, small, inflexible memories that do not serve system needs in a cost-effective manner. CAM's usually only permit word-at-a-time matches, and usually structural matches are necessary in a system context. For example, the head of a Prolog clause is structure containing a primary functor and some arbitrary number of arguments, any of which may in turn be structures themselves. Hence, CAM's are not useful as a logic program clause indexing device.

Both the query and the entries in the PAM are Lisp-style S-expression structures. Structural nesting is permitted up to 255 levels deep. Individual words in the PAM memory are individually tagged and may be any of the following types:

1. Constants represented as a two's complement integers.
2. Variables represented as symbols.

3. Left structure markers represented as a positive integer indicating the associated nesting depth.
4. Right structure markers represented as a positive integer indicating the associated nesting depth.

An entry is a contiguous block of words corresponding to a linear encoding of the S-expression structure, including parentheses. Constants only match constants of the same value. Structure markers only match other structure markers of the same polarity and depth. Variables match any other constant, variable, or substructure.

The PAM controller responds to a *DoMatch* command from the EP, by taking a pointer from the EP that indicates the location in SRAM of the query structure. It then passes the query, one slot at a time, to the PAM chips until the query has been completely scanned. After a query has been processed, all PAM chips that have successfully matched the query on one or more of its entries will indicate by setting a *found* flag. If no matches were found to the query, the PAM controller will interrupt the EP with a *NoMatch* condition.

If a match was found, then the PAM builds a list in SRAM containing one entry for each matched structure in the PAM. Note that this list is semantically unordered, i.e., the order in which this result list is constructed can be considered random. Each entry in the result list contains the content field of the matched entries in SRAM. For logic program evaluation this content field would be a pointer to the right hand side of the rule. Once the result-list is built in SRAM, the PAM controller will interrupt the EP with a *MatchDone* indication and a pointer to the result-list.

The PAM can be thought of as being made up of a larger linear array, or stack, of symbol storage slots. Each slot stores one symbol, with name, tags, and index as appropriate. The storage elements used are capable of performing a full bit-wise compare of the stored data with an input query word in much the same way as does a CAM. The query is broadcast to all slots at once over a global data bus. CAM-style matches will not, however, handle the full complexity of the matching function. For this reason, each slot has additional logic attached to process tags. This tag logic is also responsible for keeping track of the matching process, which is done using "match tokens."

Matching involves starting tokens at the beginning of each expression and moving them on down as successive slots match the query, which is entered symbol by symbol. The match token is only passed on its the symbol it is marking matches the broadcast query symbol: if not, the token is consumed. Hence the token indicates the "readiness" of a symbol to continue a match through the expression. At the beginning of a query, all slots are initialized with such a token (to allow a match to start anywhere). At the end of the query, the only tokens remaining indicate the ends of entries that have successfully matched the query. Note that only one cycle is required per goal symbol entered. Hence, matching occurs on the fly as the query is passed from the PAM controller to the PAM memory chips.

The match token is implemented as part of the state enclosed in the finite state machine (FSM), which is the match logic. Other inputs to the matching FSM are the comparator result and the tags of both the stored and broadcast (query) symbols. The output from the match logic then sets or resets the match token in the next slot.

Due to the linear format there need be no one-to-one correspondence between symbols in the query and the entry being matched against. That is, a single variable in one can match a whole string of symbols representing a subexpression in the other. There are two cases to consider: one where the variable is in the query, the other when it is in the stored expression. In the first case, the match token must be *jumped* from the beginning of the subexpression to its end. In the second, the token must be held in position with the variable until the whole of the subexpression in the query has gone by or been *skipped*. Both these actions use the nesting level index to recognize the corresponding closing delimiter of a subexpression. The jumping is accomplished using a piece of circuitry included in the logic called the *jump wire*, which runs through the whole array. The jump only takes one cycle and so it can occur in parallel with a simple variable-variable match elsewhere in the PAM. The jump wire is an extremely powerful mechanism for parallel token transfers within the PAM.

The skip is effected by storing the match token away, so that it won't be passed on, as a second bit of state in the logic called the *skip bit*. This bit is released as a match token when the matching closing parenthesis is entered.

Reading and writing are performed using a global data bus. Thus every slot contains gating to connect its contents to this bus. Only one slot can be connected at a time, and this slot is selected by a single-bit pointer, rather than by an address and address decoders. There is one pointer each for reading and writing, the *read-slot* (RS) pointer and the *write-slot* (WS) pointer. For both registers; the pointer can be left where it is, incremented by one slot or reset to the beginning of the array. To enable the output of matched expressions, the read pointer can also be moved via the jump wire. While the read pointer is free to move about the array, the write pointer always points to the first free slot after the last entry. This implies that expressions can only be appended to the present contents of the PAM.

Removing expressions from the PAM is a two-stage process. In the first stage; the expression must be marked for deletion, i.e., for removal by the second stage, which is the garbage collection process. This requires an additional state bit called the *delete bit*. After an expression has been selected by matching, all the slots that contain elements of that expression can, by use of the jump wire, have their delete bits set.

Deletion and garbage collection are two independent processes, and it is not necessary to run one directly after the other. Garbage collection is a fairly lengthy process; hence it is only used when the number of deleted expressions grows large or when the amount of free space grows small. The garbage collection process

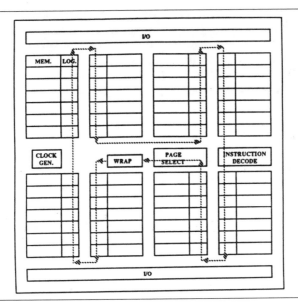

Figure 12-5. PAM memory chip floor plan.

uses the delete bits to control a read-write process that compacts out all deleted expressions.

The PAM memory chip is a single VLSI component. A floor plan of the chip is shown in Figure 12-5. The chip is composed of a number of blocks. Each block is comprised of the storage and logic parts. The storage part of the block contains the name and index fields, together with their tags, and the working bits. Storage for sixteen such words is provided. A standard three-transistor memory cell was used. This represents a fairly safe compromise between storage cell size and process parameter independence. The storage part also included the comparators, global connect, and refresh circuitry.

The logic contains three state machines. These are used to control the jump wire and to compute the new state of the working bits. The remainder of the logic implements the read and write pointers, the jump-wire circuitry, no-match sensors, local clock buffering, and a PLA which implements the finite-tate machine controller.

Die size constraints permitted 72 blocks to be placed on a single PAM chip. The blocks are arranged in four columns of 18: seven are placed on each side of the central spine. To make the transfer of tokens, pointers, and jump signals follow a reasonably continuous path, the blocks were oriented as shown within the array. The spine contains *wrap-around* circuitry to allow these signals to pass from one page to the next. This spine also contains the clock generator, instruction decode, and page-elect circuitry with busses and block buffers. The only other circuitry remaining is that to support data I/O. The buffers and sense amplifiers for writing, broadcasting, and reading to and from the PAM are distributed along the top and bottom edges, close to the pads they serve.

The resulting chip contains 1152 words of 20-bit symbols. If the average clause head size is seven PAM words, then one chip can store 164 such expressions. The chip is implemented in a two-micron-line-width, double-mental CMOS process and contains approximately 162,000 transistors.

If the desired storage capacity exceeds that of a single PAM chip, then the design permits a number of chips to be interconnected to provide any desired total capacity. Because the tokens, jump wire, and read/write pointers are not carried between chips, each is still managed as a separate store. Therefore, expressions cannot cross the chip boundary. Only when PAM's have to be accessed individually, i.e., for reading and writing, does the performance differ from that of a single PAM. The result is a highly parallel structure-matching storage subsystem whose performance is dependent only on the size of the query.

9. CONCLUSIONS

This chapter has presented a detailed overview of the physical architecture of a novel, high-performance, symbolic multiprocessing system known as FAIM-1. A small-scale prototype of FAIM-1, consisting of a single E-3 surface (19 Hectogons), is under construction. Operational hardware is expected late in 1987. The primary performance mechanism is the exploitation of concurrency at all levels of the system. From the top, the FAIM-1 appears as a medium-gain, homogeneous multiprocessor. The topology scales nicely to permit an arbitrary number of processing elements to be interconnected. Each processing element can be viewed from the bottom as a heterogeneous, shared-memory multiprocessor containing servers that are specialized to perform message delivery, mock-unification, data storage and delivery, instruction storage and delivery, instruction evaluation, and rapid context switching.

The architecture takes advantage of advanced circuit and packaging technology as a secondary performance enhancement mechanism. The present small-scale prototype is being implemented using custom CMOS VLSI circuits (the Post Office, and PAM sybsystems), two custom CMOS LSI components (the ISM) one custom CMOS MSI device (the SRAM's SBC), and commercially available components. The 19-Hectogon prototype will be attached to a host Symbolics 3600 Lisp Machine. The programming environment, OIL compiler, resource allocator, debugging tools, and a complete system simulator that can be used for initial application development all run on the Host machine. As such, the FAIM-1 prototype will serve as a symbolic accelerator to the host Lisp Machine.

We are not presently able to run large applications on FAIM-I due to the lack of operational hardware. We have written a few small programs and have run them on the simulator, and have done extensive simulations on the architecture and the custom VLSI designs. We expect the performance at each node to be 25

Mips. We expect that the machine's performance will scale approximately linearly for applications that consist of many communicating objects, and where the objects may vary in grain size from a few to several thousand machine instructions. The result should be a very high performance symbolic-processing accelerator for distributed AI applications.

Although the architecture represents a novel and significant reallocation of the conventional transistor budget to provide high performance and effecient evaluation of highly concurrent, symbolic programs, the programming environment departs from conventional AI program development systems only minimally to incorporate concurrency. This eliminates the need to reeducate programmers, while the architecture can be scaled to provide two to three orders of magnitude performance improvement over conventional AI machines.

ACKNOWLEDGMENTS

The work reported here is the joint work of the author and his colleagues in the AI Architectures group at Schlumberger Palo Alto Research. All of the group's members have played an important role in the invention and development of the FAIM-1 architecture. In addition to the author, the group's members are: Judy Anderson, Bill Coates, Bob Hon, Ian Robinson, Shane Robison, and Ken Stevens. I am also indebted to the following colleagues for their contributions to the ideas expressed in this document or for their help in refining them: John Conery, Gary Lindstrom, Barak Pearlmutter, Kevin Lang, Bill Athas, Kathy Weinhold, Vineet Singh, Dick Lyon, Tom Knight, Chuck Thacker, Erik Brunvand, Ken Olum, Alvin Despain, Dan Carnese, Allan Schiffman, Michael Deering, Shimon Cohen, and Rick Schediwy.

REFERENCES

1. C. L. Seitz, "System Timing." In *Introduction to VLSI Systems*, New York: McGraw-Hill, 1979.
2. H. Stopper, "A Wafer with Electrically Programmable Interconnections," In *Proc. 1985 IEEE International Solid State Circuits Conference*, 1985, pp. 268–269.
3. A. L. Davis and S. V. Robison, "An Overview of the FAIM-1 Multiprocessing System," *Proc. First Annual Artificial Intelligence and Advanced Computer Technology Conference*. Wheaton IL: Tower Conference Management Company, 1985, pp. 291–296.
4. W. D. Clinger, *The revised Revised Report on Scheme*. Tech. Rep. 174, Computer Science Department, Indiana University, 1985.
5. R. H. Halstead, Jr., "Parallel Symbolic Computing," *Computer*, 19(8):35–43.
6. A. Goldberg and D. Robson, *Smalltalk-80: The Language and its Implementation*. Menlo Park. CA: Addison Wesley, 1983.
7. W. C. Athas and C. L. Seitz, *Cantor User Report*. Tech. Rep. 5232:TR:86, Department of Computer Science, California Institute of Technology, Pasadena, CA, 1986.
8. W. F. Clocksin and C. S. Mellish, *Programming in Prolog*. New York: Springer-Verlag, 1981.
9. P. H. Winston and B. K. P. Horn, *Lisp*. Reading, MA: Addison-Wesley, 1980.
10. A. J. Martin, "The Torus: An Exercise in Constructing a Processing Surface," *Proc. of the 2nd Caltech Conference on VLSI*. 1981, pp. 527–538.
11. D. P. Siewiorek and R. S. Swarz, *The Theory and Practice of Reliable System Design*, Bedford, MA: Digital Press, 1982.
12. D. Gordon, I. Koren and G. M. Silberman, *Fault-Tolerance in VLSI Hexagonal Arrays*. Tech. Rep. Department of Electrical Engineering, Technion. Israel.

13. T. F. Knight, Jr., D. A. Moon, J. Holloway and G. L. Steele, Jr., *CADR*. Tech. Rep. 528, MIT Artificial Intelligence Laboratory, Cambridge, MA, 1981.
14. B. W. Lampson, K. A. Pier, G. A. McDaniel, S. M. Ornstein and D. W. Clark, *The Dorado: A High-Performance Perosnal Computer*. Tech. Rep. CSL-81-1. Xerox Palo Alto Research Center, Palo Alto, CA, 1981.
15. J. L. Hennessy, "VLSI Processor Architecture," *IEEE Trans. on Computers*, C-33 (12):1221–1246.
16. D. Warren, *Implementing Prolog*. Tech. Rep. 39. Edinburgh University, Edinburgh: Scotland, 1977.
17. W. S. Coates, *The Design of an Instruction Stream Memory Subsystem*. Master's thesis, Univeristy of Calgary, Calgary, Alberta, Canada, 1985.
18. M. D. Hill and A. J. Smith, "Experimental evaluation of on-chip microprocessor cache memories." *Proc. 11th Annual Symp. on Computer Architecture*, Ann Arbor. MI, 1984, pp. 158–166.
19. I. Flores, "Lookahead Control in the IBM System/370 Model 165P." *Computer*, 1974.
20. S. Weiss and J. E. Smith, "Instruction Issue Logic for Pipelined Supercomputers." *Proc. 11th Annual Sym. on Computer Architecture*. Ann Arbor, MI, 1984, pp. 110–118.
21. S. A. Przybylski, T. R. Gross, J. L. Hennessy, N. P. Jouppi and C. Rowen, "Organization and VLSI Implementation of MIPS." *Journal of VLSI and Computing Systems*, 1 (3): 170–208.
22. T. R. Gross, *Code Optimization of Pipeline Constraints*. PhD thesis, Stanford University, Stanford, CA, 1983.
23. K. S. Stevens, *The Communications Framework for a Distributed Ensemble Architecture*. AI 47. Schlumberger Palo Alto Research, Palo Alto, CA, 1986.
24. K. S. Stevens, S. V. Robison and A. L. Davis, "The Post Office—Communication Support for Distributed Ensemble Architectures," *Proc. 6th Int. Conf. on Distributed Computing Systems*, pp. 160–166.

13. OVERVIEW OF AI APPLICATION–ORIENTED PARALLEL PROCESSING RESEARCH IN JAPAN

RYUTAROU OHBUCHI

1. INTRODUCTION

The environment for parallel processing research has been changing in several aspects. For example, the availability of the very large scale integration (VLSI) technology has brought a precious tool to researchers to realize their ideas in hardware. Another change is in the application field of parallel processing. Previously, the word "supercomputer" used to mean "super fast number-cruncher." Now it is not uncommon for people to speak about "symbolic supercomputing." This trend is apparent in Japan. In some sense, the Japanese Fifth Generation Computer System (FGCS) project [1], which was started in 1982, was one of the key contributors to set this worldwide trend.

The purpose of this chapter is to give an overview of Japanese research projects in the field of parallel-processing architecture research oriented to artificial intelligence (AI) applications. The focus is on the architectural aspects of the parallel processing. In the following sections, machines are categorized into three groups based on the computational models primarily supported: (1) machines for logic-based languages, (2) machines for functional languages, and (3) machines for other applications, such as semantic networks or object-oriented languages.

For each category, a brief description of the machines and references to the published papers are given. Some of the machines are given more detailed descriptions.

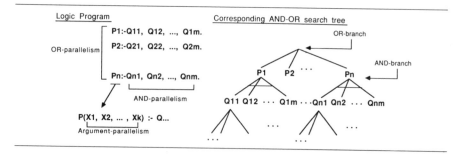

Figure 13-1. Parallelism in a logic program.

2. MACHINES FOR LOGIC LANGUAGES

The most visible trend in the Japanese parallel processing architecture research scene is the emergence of logic-language-oriented machines. Many projects based on logic languages are underway.

Before giving the overview of projects, a brief discussion on parallelism in logic languages would be beneficial. Logic program execution can be thought of as a search on an AND-OR search tree (Figure 13-1). Roughly speaking, there are three kinds of parallelism in a logic language. The OR-parallelism is to execute in parallel the OR-alternative clauses, which corresponds to the OR-branches in the search tree. The AND-parallelism is to execute in parallel the AND-terms in a clause, that is, the AND-branches in the search tree. Another source of parallelism, the argument-parallelism, is to unify several arguments in a clause header in parallel. The grain of parallelism increases from the argument-parallelism, to the AND-parallelism, to the OR-parallelism, roughly in that order. For various logic language models, see [2, 3].

2.1. Overview

The most publicized activity in Japan is the research conducted under the auspices of ICOT (Institute for New Generation Computer Technology), toward the realization of a Parallel Inference Machine (PIM).

ICOT's ten-year research period is divided into three stages: the initial stage (1982–1984), the intermediate stage (1985–1988), and the final stage (1989–1991). PIM-D (Dataflow PIM) [4], PIM-R (Reduction PIM) [5], and Kabu-wake method [6] were the first test-beds of ideas for the PIM line of machines during the initial stage.

PIM-D took a bottom-up approach and is based on the dataflow mechanism [4]. Programs written in Kernel Language version 1 (KL1), the language for PIM's based on the Guarded Horn Clause (GHC) [7], is compiled into dataflow graphs for execution. This machine is described in more detail below.

PIM-R took a top-down approach. The PIM-R execution model stems from the similarity among the reduction process and the logic program execution process [5, 8]. Basically, PIM-R reduces (sub) goals using the structure-copying strategy. It also incorporates distributed shared-memory modules (SMM's) to support interprocess communication among the AND-parallel processes via streams. The global machine structure consists of the IM's (inference modules) connected in a two-dimensional mesh by a packet switching network. SMM's are shared by several IM's. Two software simulators and a hardware simulator [9] have been constructed to evaluate the architecture.

The Kabu-wake method is also a part of the initial stage PIM research. It is a large grain OR-parallel model that can also be seen as a load-balancing mechanism [6]. This model will also be described in more detail later.

The research on intermediate stage PIM [10] has just started. The machine architecture is not clear yet, but it will be a collection of about 100 processing elements (PE's) connected in a hierarchical network, where each processing element is a sequential Prolog processor. The intermediate stage plan for PIM also stresses the importance of research on software, such as KL1 language, application programs, and PIMOS (parallel inference machine operating system). To this end, ICOT is developing two versions of the Multi-PSI (Personal sequential inference) system as a software research and development tool [10, 11]. Multi-PSI version 1 is basically a collection of six to eight PSI [12] processors interconnected by a packet switching network to form a two-dimensional mesh structure. Multi-PSI will accommodate a subset of GHC, the FlatGHC [13]. Multi-PSI version 2 will have 16 to 64 PSI-II processors. The processing element PSI-II is a successor to the PSI processor and is expected to perform at about 100 KLIPS (200 KLIPS [logical inference per second] for the append program) [14]; it will also be used as a stand-alone processor like the current PSI. Although Multi-PSI's are considered as software research tools, they can also be seen as fairly large (especially Multi-PSI version 2), relatively powerful, and realistic parallel logic machines.

Beside the work at ICOT, many other projects on parallel logic language machines are underway, both in industry and academia. Probably the parallel inference engine (PIE) is one of the most famous non-ICOT-related projects. PIE has been pursued by the researchers at the University of Tokyo for several years [15]. More details of PIE are given in the chapter.

Researchers at Kobe Univeristy have been actively working on language-oriented machines, including a sequential Prolog machine, PEK [16]. Their first parallel logic language implementation, K-Prolog [17], evolved to a parallel processor PARK, and a language called PARK-Prolog [18]. PARK (parallel processing system of Kobe University) is a bus-coupled multiprocessor system with four processing elements. Each processor consists of a MC68000 microprocessor with 128 Kbyte of local memory, and 512 Kbyte of memory that works as a logically shared memory among processors. PARK-Prolog incorporates both AND-parallelism and OR-parallelism.

Naganuma and colleagues at (NTT) Nippon Telephone and Telegraph are proposing a parallel logic language machine based on CAM (content addressable memory) technology [19]. It is derived from a sequential Prolog machine, ASCA [20], which employs CAM to associatively find the point to backtrack to, eliminating the trail stack. The ASCA prototype hardware, implemented in a bit-slice microprocessor and CAM chips, demonstrates performance of about 100 K LIPS in the append benchmark. A hardware algorithm for unification by Yasuura, and associates at Kyoto University [21] has been modified to accommodate CAM [22] and tested on ASCA [23].

There are several other models for parallel execution of logic language. Shibayama and co-workers at Kyoto University are proposing a reduction-based parallel logic language machine, KPR (Kyoto University Prolog machine based on parallel reduction model) [24]. It has a binary tree structure with up to 1000 ARP/ORP (AND reduction processor/OR reduction processor) pairs attached to the leaf nodes. A prototype system with two ORP's and two ARP's is under construction. A dataflow parallel processor, DFM (see 3.2) has a proposed execution model for logic language [25]. A parallel processor system coupled with a unique optical bus, Dialog H [26], has a model for logic language [27]. Shiohara and colleagues at Chiba University propose a dynamic dataflow-based execution model with an extended colored-token mechanism to cope with nondeterminism without a shared-stream data structure [28].

2.2. ICOT PIM-D

PIM-D is a parallel logic language machine based on the dataflow mechanism [4, 29, 30]. On PIM-D, a KL1 program is compiled into a dataflow graph for execution. It is executed by the instruction-level, colored-token, dynamic dataflow mechanism [31]. Several instructions are introduced to handle unification, stream, process synchronization, etc., which are inherent in the target language implementation. AND-parallelism and OR-parallelism, as well as argument-parallelism, are exploited in the execution model. Figure 13–2 shows the machine structure of the hardware prototype. It consists of PE's, structure memory modules (SM's) and a service processor (SVP, a VAX-11/730), interconnected by a hierarchical network. Four PE's and four SM's form a cluster connected by T-BUS. Several clusters, in turn, can be connected hierarchically. T-BUS is able to transfer a token (72 bits for a result packet) in one 500 ns cycle. To date, a system with 16 PE's, and one SVP has been implemented.

Each PE is a circular-pipeline dataflow processor. Instruction fetch and operand waiting/matching function are performed in the instruction control unit (ICU) that contains an instruction memory and an operand memory with a hardware hashing unit. Atomic processing units (APU's) execute atomic (non structure handling) instructions, while instructions to access structure data are sent out to the SM's for execution. The packet queue unit (PQU) is a FIFO queue to buffer result packets from two APU's. Local memory unit (LMU) stores various local data. Network node (NN) has FIFO buffers and a BA (bus arbitrator) to couple PE with T-BUS, or T-BUS with T-BUS. Shared data

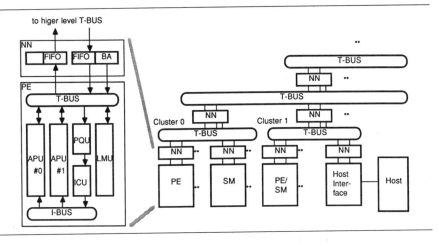

Figure 13–2. PIM-D prototype machine structure [4].

structures, such as streams, which are used to pass results among AND-parallel processes and to collect results from OR-parallel processes, are stored in the (SM). The SM allows multiple asynchronous accesses and implements the reference counting garbage collector.

The prototype machine constructed using TTL and bit-slice microprocessor technology attained 2.5 to 3.2 KRPS (reduction per second: number of successfully terminated goals per second) per PE [30]. According to Ito and colleagues [30], a slight modification to the architecture and faster technology will enable a PE to attain from 50 to 140 KRPS. Various evaluation results from both hardware prototype and a software simulator may be found in [32].

2.3. Fujitsu Kabu-wake

The Kabu-wake ("stock-subdivision") method [6, 33] is also a part of the PIM research at ICOT. Briefly, it is a load-balancing mechanism for the parallel Prolog execution. In the Kabu-wake method, every PE monitors its own load and the load of the other PE's. If a PE finds itself idle relative to the others, it requests a share of the load from another processor. The requested PE finds the oldest nonprocessed OR-alternative in the tree, subdivides the search tree at that point, and sends it to the requestor PE for execution. Because divided subtrees are in OR relation, the Kabu-wake method accomplishes a kind of large-grain OR-parallel execution model. An experimental system of the Kabu-wake method was constructed (Figure 13–3). Two networks, TASK-network and CONT-network, interconnect 15 PE's and a special PE called MA (manager). The TASK-network is an eight-bit-wide multistage packet switching network used to send subdivided tasks to the other PE's. The CONT-network is a 16-bit-wide ring network. A load-status packet for each PE constantly circulates the CONT-network to

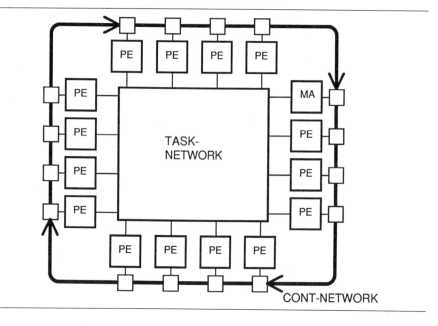

Figure 13–3. Kabu-wake experimental system structure [6].

notify its load to the other PE's. Each PE is an off-the shelf single-board computer based on the MC68000. The Kabu-wake language interpreter running on each processor has roughly a 0.5 KLIPS performance.

The number of interprocessor communications can be kept low in the Kabu-wake method mainly becuase the grain of parallelism increase with the size of the problem. Researchers plan to further reduce the task subdivision overhead, and speed up the language processor of each PE by compilation.

2.4. Tokyo University PIE

The PIE by Moto-oka and associates at Tokyo University [15, 34, 35] employs an OR-parallelism-based execution model called "Goal rewriting model."

Figure 13–4 shows the structure of PIE-II, the second version of PIE-II has many unification processors (UP's) to unify and reduce subgoal clauses. A UP is paired with a definition memory (DM), which holds the definition clause, i.e., the program. Each one of the DM's holds a complete copy of the entire program. There are working memories called memory modules (MM's) to store subgoals, and activity controllers (AC's) to monitor and control execution. The AC's hold the search tree as the computation proceeds and implement so-called meta-controls such as negation, cut, sequential execution, and gaurd, DM, UP, MM, and AC are packed together with the LFB (lazy fetch buffer) in a unit called IU (inference unit).

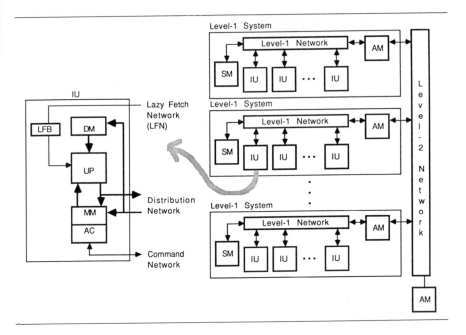

Figure 13–4. Parallel inference machine PIE 2 [15].

The PIE was started with a model in which each processor had a copy of the required data. Although this permited maximum parallelism, the overhead incurred by copying turned out to be large. The current PIE tries to merge complete copying and complete sharing strategies. To share a part of data structures, a component called the SM (structure memory) has been added to the level-1 network. While the MM in the IU stores a part of subgoal data structures with unbound variables, the SM stores subgoals without unbound variables (ground instances). These subgoals in the SM are shared among the IUs executing in an OR-parallel relation, to reduce subgoal copy overhead. The LFB in the IU works like a cache memory for the SM.

Several IU's and a SM are hooked to the level-1 network, which is actually a combination of DN (distribution network), CN (command network), and LFN (lazy fetch network). A level-1 system is attached to level-2 network via an AM (activity manager).

Various software simulations have been conducted, and several subsystems were prototyped. A hardware simulator for a single IU has been designed and implemented using a MC68000 and a bit-slice microprocessor [36]. Currently, the SM hardware simulator is under development.

3. FUNCTIONAL LANGUAGE–ORIENTED MACHINES

Despite the major shift of interest to the logic language machines, there are many persistent efforts on functional language-oriented machines, especially on dataflow architecture. We also will survey several projects on parallel Lisp machines.

3.1. Overview

Projects related to dataflow architecture have been active among the parallel architecture research community in Japan [37]. There is even a commercial dataflow machine for numerical application, whose peak performance reaches 160 MFLOPS [38]. For AI applications, several list-processing dataflow machine research projects have been active. Two of the most notable are EM-3 at ETL (Electro Technical Laboratory, under MITI) [39] and DFM (dataflow machine) at NTT [40]. Further description of these machines follows.

CORAL at Tokushima University is a general purpose, binary-tree structured parallel processor [41]. The first machine, CORAL prototype '83, consisted of 15 PE's based on the i8085 microprocessor. Experiments with logic languages and numerical problem as well as with functional language have been conducted. A new system called CORAL 68K, which consists of 63 processing elements based on the MC68000, is under development [42]. A CORAL 68K system with 15 PE's is already up and running.

In addition to these somewhat exotic architectures, there are several rather conventional parallel Lisp machines. EVLIS, pursued by the researchers at Osaka University [43,44], is an example. EVLIS is a shared-memory Lisp parallel processor with a few processors. The unit processor, called EVAL II, is a fairly powerful microprogrammed sequential Lisp processor. The speed of a Lisp interpreter running on single EVAL II is roughly comparable to the Zeta compiler on Symbolics-3600 [45]. Currently, an EVLIS machine with two EVAL II processors is running. A microprogrammed Prolog interpreter has also been reported [46].

Kurokawa and co-workers at Tohoku University are experimenting with a parallel Lisp on a machine in which multiple MC68000-based processor are connected by a crossbar switch [47]. The Synapse system at Keio University [48] is a shared-memory multiprocessor for multiuser environment. It also employs MC68000 and implements parallel garbage collection.

3.2. NTT DFM

The DFM is a instruction-level, colored-token, dynamic dataflow [31] machine, which is designed to execute a functional language Valid (*value identification*) [40, 49, 50]. DFM supports extensions to the basic data-driven computation mechanisms such as lenient (nonstrict eager) and lazy evaluation.

Figure 13–5 shows the structure of the NTT DFM prototype. Each PE is a dataflow processor with a circular pipeline structure. The IMU (instruction memory unit) stores the program, which corresponds to nodes in a dataflow graph. The OMU (operand memory unit) is the waiting/matching store, with various matching strategies. For example, "Color suppression match" is provided to realize loop invariant or global variable. The OMU is implemented

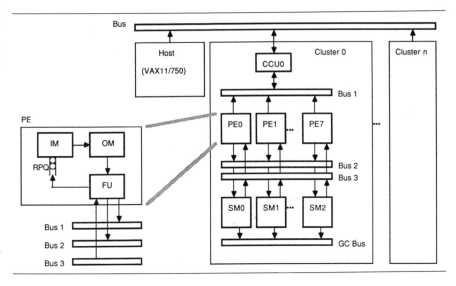

Figure 13–5. Machine structure of prototype DFM [40].

as a semi–content addressable memory. The OMU storage area is divided into many blocks, and each block is assigned to an active function instance. The function instance name is used to address a block, and, within a block, a cell is associatively accessed by a set-associative mechanism. The FUU (function unit) performs atomic operations, such as arithmetic operations, or conditional operations. All of the nonatomic operations like CAR, CDR, or CONS are sent to the SM and executed there. The GC (garbage collection) bus handles real-time garbage collection based on reference counting.

The network has a hierarchical structure. The first level is implemented in the bus and is called a cluster. A CCU (cluster control unit) is included in a cluster to handle intercluster communications and host communication, as well as intracluster dynamic load balancing. The higher level network structure has not yet been determined, but some load-balancing mechanism will be built into the network.

One of the implementation features in this system is the incorporation of intra-PE and intracluster dynamic-load-control schemes. In these schemes, each PE monitors the RPQ (result packet queue) length, the number of operands stored in the OMU, and the number of the active function identifiers. To implement intracluster load balancing, these values are encoded by a table and reported to the CCU. Upon function call, the PE that executes a function call instruction asks the CCU for the lowest load PE, and the called function is activated on that lowest load PE. For intra-PE load control, function activation in a PE is delayed if the RPQ length is longer than the predetermined threshold value.

A register-transfer-level software simulator has been written in Valid. A hardware prototype system with a cluster, which includes two PE's, two SM's, and a CCU, has been constructed and evaluated. It is implemented in TTL and bit-slice microprocessor technology, and runs Valid compiler-generated code at about five to seven times faster than the VAXLISP (CommonLisp) compiler running on a VAX-11/750.

Construction of the next version of the prototype with more PEs (DFM II), is underway. To date, four sorts of chips that implement the PE, SM, and network have been designed and fabricated in CMOS gate array [51], but the entire system has yet to be constructed.

3.3. ETL EM-3

The EM-3 is also a colored-token, dynamic dataflow machine designed to execute a Lisp-based parallel list-processing language, called EMLISP [39, 52, 53]. On EM-3, the grain of parallelism of both instruction level and function level is explored. A hardware prototype with eight PEs has been constructed. A PE of the prototype consists of a MC68000 microprocessor and a special hardware. The special hardware PMCU (packet memory control unit) has been added mainly to implement a matching store by hashing. Twenty 4 × 4 router LSI chips, fabricated in Bi-CMOS gate array, are used to realize a two-stage network.

A new hardware to experiment with various parallel-processing systems, including EM-3 architecture, is being developed. It has 16 MC68000 microprocessor-based PE's and a routing network similar to EM-3, but includes no special hardware like PMCU. Investigation of a large parallel processor up to 1000 PE's, where each PE is a single-chip dataflow processor, is underway [54].

4. OTHER MACHINES

Systems based on neither logic language nor functional language also exist. Systems for parallel object-oriented language or for direct processing of semantic networks, for example fall into this category. A knowledge-base machine is also included in this category.

4.1. Overview

A network of processors designed to accommodate semantic networks, called IXM [55], has been pursued by Higuchi and associates at ETL. This machine will be explained in somewhat more detail in Section 4.2.

ICOT has also started research on a knowledge-base machine called VLKBM [56]. It is based on the extended relational model with unification and is the successor to the relational data-base machine, Delta [57]. Architectural features include the incorporation of MPPM (multiport page memory) [58] and UEs (unification engines). MPPM is a large, multiple-ported staging memory, and UE performs extended-relational operations like unification-join or unification-restriction in a pipelined manner.

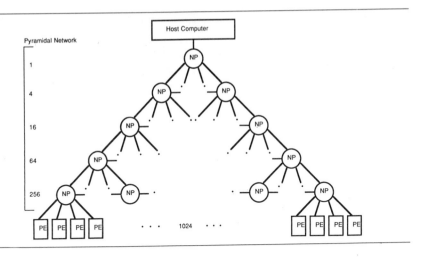

Figure 13–6. IXM machine organization [55].

Several groups are working on parallel object-oriented language machines, but none has made a substantial effort in concrete machine implemetation. One of these, the ORAGA (object-oriented architecture to govern abstraction) project at Tokyo University, covers a language called DinnerBell, a programming environment, and a machine called OragaItself [59, 60]. They are currently concentrating on the language and programming environment development. The concrete machine architecture is not clear yet.

4.2. ETL IXM

A network of processors, called IXM [55], designed to accommodate semantic networks (SN), has been pursued by Higuchi and colleagues, together with a language (IXL) [61] to express SN. IXM consists of 256 to 1000 PE's of medium size, in comparison with the Connection Machine [62], which is a collection of numerous very small processors. A characteristic of IXM is the heavy exploitation of associative memory.

Figure 13-6 shows the structure of IXM. PE's are at the leaf of 4-ary tree. Non-leaf nodes, NP's (network processors), mainly perform communication. Each PE contains two associative memory blocks, SNAM and IRAM. SNAM is to store several nodes of a SN. Each entry in SNAM represents a link in a SN and has fields for identifier of the link, destination pointer of the link, link name (IS-A, INSTANCE-OF, etc.), and marker bits. A bit in the marker bit field indicates membership in a specific set. Basic operations on a semantic network, such as association and set operations (union, intersection), are performed using the parallel, associative-access capability of SNAM. In this sense, although the PE's are fairly large, there exists a finer grain parallelism within a PE (within a SNAM).

The choice of larger PE's also makes it easier to realize a procedural part of knowledge, such as arithmetic operations.

Another associative memory element, IRAM, stores IXL programs. The propagation of markers in a SN, which mark elements that belongs to a certain set to establish set membership, occurs asynchronously from PE to PE. To exploit this parallelism, an instruction in a PE must be activated asynchronously by the presence of a bit in the marker-bits field of SNAM. The associative access capability of IRAM is used to realise this marker-driven activation of instruction. Some other ideas, such as "equivalence node" and its implementation by another associative memory element in the NP, helps to keep the degree of parallelism high. Currently, the design of the machine hardware is underway.

5. SUMMARY

An overview of various Japanese projects on AI application–oriented parallel processors has been given, along with the detailed description of a few machines.

The field of AI application–oriented parallel processing is relatively new, but it seems to be a fertile field. A number of systems with interesting ideas have been proposed and to some extent implemented. But it will take more research and development by researchers worldwide to prove that it is a truly fertile area for parallel processing. Further work through software simulation or construction of more realistic hardware prototypes or simulators is necessary.

ACKNOWLEDGMENTS

This survey was partilly carried out while the author was at Tokyo Research Laboratory (TRL), IBM Japan, Ltd., Tokyo, Japan. He would like to thank Dr. H. Kobayashi, who was the director of the laboratory at the time, for his strong encouragement to accomplish this work. Many of the colleagues at TRL contributed in many ways, but discussions with Dr. T. Fujisaki, Dr. N. Tamura, and Dr. S. Shimizu were particularly helpful. The author also would like to thank Dr. J. D. Brock, Dr. B. Jayaraman, and Mr. A. Omondi at University of North Carolina at Chapel Hill for their comments on the manuscript.

REFERENCES

1. *Proc. Int'l Conf. on Fifth Generation Computer Systems 1984 (FGCS'84)*, Tokyo, Japan, 6–9, 1984.
2. M. Bellia, et al., "The Relation Between Logic and Functional Language: A Survey," *Journal of Logic Programming*, 3, 1986.
3. E. Shapiro, "Concurrent Prolog: A Progress report," *Computer*, 19(8): 1986.
4. N. Ito, et al., "The architecture and Preliminary Evaluation Results of the Experimental Parallel Inference Machine PIM-D," *Proc. 13th ISCA Intl Sym. on Computer Architecture*, IEEE, 1986.
5. R. Onai, et al., *Architecture and Evaluation of a Reduction-Based Inference Machine: PIM-R*, ICOT Tech. Rep. TR-138, 1985.
6. K. Kumon, et al., "KABU-WAKE: A New Parallel Inference Method and its Evaluation," *Proc. COMPCON Spring*, 1986.
7. K. Ueda, "Guarded Horn Clauses," ICOT Tech. Rep. TR-103, 1985.
8. R. Onai, et al., "Architecture of a Reduction-Based Parallel Inference Machine: PIM-R," *New Generation Computing*, 3: 1985.

9. M. Sugie, et al., *Hardware Simulator of the Parallel Inference Machine PIM-R*, ICOT Tech. Rep. TR-119 (in Japanese).

10. A. Goto, et al., *Toward a High Performance Parallel Inference Machine—The Intermediate Stage Plan of PIM*, ICOT Tech. Rep. TR-201, in press.

11. K. Taki, "The Parallel Software Research and Development Tool: Multi-PSI System," *Proc. Japan-France Symp., 1986.*

12. K. Taki, et al., "Hardware Design and Implementation of the Personal Sequential Inference Machine (PSI)," *Proc. FGCS'84* 1984 (also in ICOT Tech. Rep. TR-075).

13. T. Miyazaki, et al., "Implementation Method of FlatGHC on Multi-PSI," *Proc. Logic Programming Conf. '86*, 1986 (in Japanese).

14. K. Nakajima, et al., "Architecture of Multi-PSI Element Processor (PSI-II)," *Proc. 33rd National Conf. of IPSJ*, 1986 (in Japanese).

15. T. Moto-oka, et al., "The Architecture of a Parallel Inference Engine—PIE," *Proc. FGCS'84*, 1984.

16. N. Tamura, et al., "Sequential Prolog Machine PEK." *Proc. FGCS'84*, 1984.

17. H. Matsuda, et al., "Implementing Parallel Prolog System 'K-Prolog,'" *Trans. IPSJ* 26(2): 1985 (in Japanese).

18. H. Matsuda, et al., "On Parallel Prolog Machine PARK," *Proc. Logic Programming Conf. '85*, 1985 (in Japanese).

19. J. Naganuma, et al., "Studies of a High-Speed CAM Based Parallel Inference Machine," *Proc. 33rd Natl Conf. of IPSJ*, 1986 (in Japanese).

20. J. Naganuma, et al., "Architecture of the CAM Based Prolog Machine (ASCA)," *Proc. Logic Programming Conf. '86*, 1986 (in Japanese).

21. H. Yasuura, et al., "A Hardware Algorithm for Unification Operation in Logic Languages," *IECE Japan WG* EC84-67, 1984 (in Japanese).

22. M. Ohkubo, et al., "A Hogh Speed Unification Algorithm Using Content Addressable Memory," *Proc. 33rd Natl. Conf. of IPSJ*, 1986 (in Japanese).

23. M. Ohkubo, et al., "Implementation and Evaluation of Unification Using CAM on ASCA," *Proc. 33rd Natl. Conf. of IPSJ*, 1986 (in Japanese).

24. K. Shibayama, et al., "The Architecture of a Logic Programming–Oriented Parallel Reduction Machine KPR," *IECE Japan WG* EC85-70, 1985 (in Japanese).

25. R. Hasegawa, et al., "Parallel Execution of Logic Program Based on Dataflow Concept," *Proc. FGCS'84*, 1984.

26. H. Tajima, et al., "A High Speed Optical Common Bus for a Multi-Processor System," *Trans. IECE Japan*, E66(1), 1983.

27. S. Umeyama, et al., "A Parallel Execution Model of Logic Programs," *Proc. 10th ISCA*, 1983.

28. R. Shiohara, et al., "Data-Flow Parallel Processing for Prolog," *IECE Japan WG* EC85-63, 1985 (in Japanese).

29. N. Ito, et al., "Data-flow Based Execution Mechanisms of Parallel and Concurrent Prolog," *New Generation Computing*, 3: 1985 (also in ICOT TR-099).

30. N. Ito, et al., "The Architecture and Preliminary Evaluation Results of the Experimental Parallel Inference Machine PIM-D," *Proc. 13th ISCA*, IEEE, 1986.

31. Arvind, et al., "An Asynchronous Programming Language and Computing Machine," TR-114e, *Dept. of ICS, University of California, Irvine*, CA, 1978.

32. M. Sato, et al., "Execution Mechanism of GHC on Parallel Inference Machine PIM-D, and its Evaluation on Experimental Machine," *Proc. Logic Programming Conference '86* 1986 (in Japanese).

33. Y. Sohma, et al., "A New Parallel Inference Mechanism Based on Sequential Processing," *Proc. IFIP TC-10 Working Confrence on Fifth General Computer Architecture*, 1985 (also in ICOT Tech. Memorandum TM-0131).

34. A. Goto, et al., "Highly Parallel Inference Engine PIE—Goal Rewriting Model and Machine Architecture," *New General Computing*, 2(1): 1984.

35. H. Tanaka, "A Parallel Inference Machine," *IEEE Computer*, 19(5): 1986.

36. M. Yuhara, et al., "A Unify Processor Pilot Machine for PIE," *Proc. Logic Programming Conference '84*, 1984.

37. T. Yuba, "Research and Development Efforts on Dataflow Computer Architecture in Japan," *Journal of Information Processing*, 9(2): 1986.

38. T. Kikuchi, et al., "The Architecture of a Data-Flow Computer NEDIPS," *Proc. Dataflow Workshop, IECE Japan*, 1986 (in Japanese).

39. Y. Yamaguchi, et al., "EM-3: A Lisp-Based Data-Driven Machine," *Proc. FGCS'84*, 1984.
40. M. Amamiya, et al., "Implementation of Evaluation of a List-Processing-Oriented Data Flow Machine," *Proce. 13th ICSA*, 1986.
41. Takahashi, Y., et al., "Efficiency of Parallel Computation on the Binary-Tree Machine CORAL'83," *Journal IPSJ*, 8(4): 1985.
42. K. Matsuo, et al., "Development of Processor Elements for Binary Tree Machine CORAL 68K," *Proc. 33rd Natl. Conf. of IPSJ*, 1986 (in Japanese).
43. H. Maegawa, et al., "Fast Lisp Machine and List-Evaluation Processor EVAL II—Processor Architecture and Hardware Configuration," *Trans. IPSJ*, 24(5): 1983.
44. T. Saito, et al., "Fast Lisp Machine and List-Evaluation Process EVAL II—Machine Evaluation on Interpreter," *Trans. IPSJ*, 24(5): 1983 (in Japanese).
45. H. Okuno, "The Report of the Third Lisp Contest and the First Prolog Contest," *IPSJ, WGSYM*, 33-4, 1985.
46. N. Odera, et al., "A Prolog Interpreter on the EVLIS Machine and its Dynamic Behavior," *IPSJ, WGSYM*, 27-4, 1984 (in Japanese).
47. H. Kurokawa, et al., "An Experimental Parallel Processing System Using MC68000," *IECE Japan WG EC85-44*, 1985 (in Japanese).
48. Y. Kato, et al., "Function and Operation in Synapse," *IPSJ WGSYM*, 30-3 1984 (in Japanese).
49. M. Amamiya, et al., "Data Flow Computing and Eager and Lazy Evaluation," *New Generation Computing*, 2(2): 1984.
50. R. Hasegawa, et al., "Performance Evaluation of List-Processing-Oriented Data Flow Machine Architecture," *IECE Japan WG EC-85-37*, 1985 (in Japanese).
51. M. Takesue, "Design and Implementation of LSI Chips for List-Processing Oriented Data Flow Machine," *Proc. Dataflow Workshop, IECE Japan*, 1986 (in Japanese).
52. Y. Yamaguchi, et al., "A Performance Evaluation of Lisp-Based Data-Driven Machine (EM-3)," *Proc. 10th ICSA*, IEEE, 1983.
53. K. Toda, et al., "Preliminary Measurement of the ETL LISP-Based Data-Driven Machine," *Proc. IFIP TC10 Working Conference on Fifth Generation Computer Architectures*, 1985.
54. Y. Yamaguchi, et al., "A Plan for a Parallel Computer Using Data-Driven Single Chip Processors," *Proc. Dataflow Workshop, IECE Japan*, 1986 (in Japanese).
55. T. Higuchi, et al., "The IX Supercomputer for Knowledge Based Systems," *Proc. FJCC '86*, 1986.
56. H. Yokota, et al., "A model and an Architecture for a Relational Knowledge Base," *Proc. 13th ISCA*, 1986.
57. S. Shibayama, et al., "Relational Database Machine with Large Semiconductor Disk and Hardware Relational Algebra Processor," *New General Computing*, 2(2): 1984.
58. Y. Tanaka, "MPDC: Massive Parallel Architecture for Very Large Databases," *Proc. FGCS'84*, 1984.
59. M. Abe, et al., "Visual Programming Tool ObjectPeeper," *IECE Japan WG EC85-71*, 1985 (in Japanese).
60. S. Kono, et al., "An Implementation of Concurrent Object Oriented Language DinnerBell," *IECE Japan WG EC85-72*, 1985 (in Japanese).
61. T. Higuchi, et al., "A Semantic Network Language Machine," *Proc. EUROMICRO '85*, 1985.
62. G. E. Hillis, *Connection Machine*, Cambridge, MA: MIT Press, 1985.

APPENDIX

A SURVEY ON SPECIAL–PURPOSE COMPUTER ARCHITECTURES FOR AI

BENJAMIN W. WAH and GUO-JIE LI

1. INTRODUCTION

Many of today's computers are single-processor von Neumann machines designed for sequential and deterministic numerical computations [23, 25, 358, 289], and are not equipped for artificial intelligence (AI) applications that are mainly parallel, nondeterministic, symbolic manipulations [16, 49, 127, 387]. Consequently, efficient computer architectures for AI applications would be sufficiently different from traditional computers [50, 104, 105, 134, 153, 187, 274, 281, 326, 407]. These architectures have the following requirements.

1. *Symbolic processing.* In the microlevel, AI applications require symbolic processing operations such as comparison, selection, sorting, matching, logic set operations (union, intersection, and negation), contexts and partition, transitive closure, pattern retrieval, and recognition. In a higher level, these applications may require the processing of nonnumerical data such as sentences, speech, graphics, and images. Efficient computers designed for these applications should possess hardware for symbolic processing functions [60, 191, 285]. The most important ones are tagged mechanisms [87, 191] and hardware stacks [117].

Research supported by National Science Foundation grant DCI 85-19649.

2. *Parallel and distributed processing.* Most AI problems are complex [84, 305] and must be evaluated by high-performance computers. Due to technological limitations of physical devices, parallelism is perhaps the only promising mechanism to further improve the performance of computers [182, 187, 198, 249, 315, 387]. To prevent the bottleneck of a centralized controller, intelligence in such a system should be decentralized. In applying multiprocessing and distributed processing to solve problems with exponential complexity, which is typical for problems in AI, one must realize that multiprocessing is useful in improving the computational efficiency, and *not in extending the solvable problem size* [404]. To extend the solvable problem space of such problems, the key is to find better models and more efficient heuristics.

3. *Nondeterministic processing.* Most AI algorithms are nondeterministic [78], that is, it is impossible to plan in advance the procedure to execute and to terminate with the available information. Therefore, dynamic allocation and load balancing of computational resources are essential in AI architectures [29, 187]. Further, an efficient interconnection network is needed to disseminate information for the scheduler. The tradeoff between the overhead of distributing the scheduling information and the overhead for the extra work needed wihout the scheduling information must be made. Morever, efficient garbage collection is important for AI architectures, owing to be dynamically allocated storage [29, 79, 248].

4. *Knowledge-base management.* Because a very large amount of information has to be stored and retrieved in AI applications, large knowledge bases are inevitable [20, 34, 319, 412]. An implementation using a common memory is inappropriate due to access conflicts. A decentralized memory system with distributed intelligence and capabilities for pattern matching and proximity search is required.

5. *Software-oriented computer architectures.* The efficiency of a computer system for an AI application depends strongly on its knowledge representation and the language used. An efficient AI architecture should be designed around the knowledge representations of the problems to be solved and the high-level AI languages to be supported. Further, the designed architectures should adapt to changes in granularity and data formats of various applications. Examples of these architectures are the dataflow machines [41, 205], object-oriented architectures [204, 381], Lisp machines [87, 105], and Prolog-like machines, such as the Fifth Generation Computer System [153].

Currently, extensive research is underway to design efficient AI architectures. Many existing concepts in computer architecture—such as dataflow processing [107, 388], stack machines [117], tagging [191], pipelining [198], direct execution of high-level languages [68, 144, 424], data base machines [237], multiprocessing, and distributed processing—can be incorporated into future AI architectures. New concepts in computer architectures are also expected.

2. AI LANGUAGES AND PROGRAMMING

One goal of computer scientists working in the field of AI is to produce programs that imitate the intelligent behavior of human beings [30, 44, 67, 313, 419]. Von Neumann-style programming that uses imperative languages, such as Fortran and Pascal, is inadequate due to its inability to specify parallel tasks and its unacceptable complexity [21, 224, 417]. To enhance programmers' productivity, a type of problem-oriented languages called declarative languages have been developed and widely applied in AI programming [121]. *Functional programming* [22, 183, 417] and *logic programming* [72, 226–228, 316] are the major programming paradigms of declarative languages.

Functional programming does not contain any notion of the present state, program counter, or storage. Rather, the "program" is a function in the true mathematical sense: it is applied to the input of the program, and the resulting value is the program's output. The terms *functional language, applicative language, dataflow language,* and *reduction language* have been used some-what interchangeably [57, 95, 199, 390]. Examples of functional languages are pure Lisp [26, 170, 260, 261, 321], Backus' FP [21], Hope [58], Val [264], and Id [15]. Interest in functional programming is steadily growing because it is one of the few approaches that offer a real hope of relieving the twin crises of AI-oriented computing today: the absolute necessity to reduce the cost of programming, and the need to find computer designs that make much better use of the power of very large scale integration (VLSI) and parallelism.

In its modest form, a logic program refers to the procedural interpretation of Horn clauses or predicate logic [226, 227]. The computer language Prolog [73, 75, 80, 81, 116, 406] is based on logic programming. Generally speaking, logic programming is reasoning-oriented or deductive programming. In fact, some ideas of logic programming, like automatic backtracking, have been used in early AI languages QA3 [30], PLANNER, MICROPLANNER, and CONNIVER [44, 363]. Logic programming has recently received considerable attention because of its choice by the Japanese as the core computer language for the Fifth Generation Computer System Project [284]. Although it seems on the surface that logic programming is an independent and somewhat separate notion from function programming, an ideal AI-programming style should combine the features of both languages and may be called "assertional programming" [316].

New languages and programming systems are being developed to simplify AI programming radically. It is expected that *object-oriented programming* [312] will be as important in the 1980s as structured programming was in the 1970s. The language Smalltalk [2, 160] is an example of object-oriented programming. Some ideas of object-oriented programming have been used in existing languages and systems, such as Simula, B5000, Lisp-AI notion of frame, ADA, and CLU. Other new object-oriented programming systems have also been developed [204, 272, 365, 381, 397].

AI programming languages have had a central role in the history of AI research. Frequently, new ideas in AI are accompanied by a new language in which it is natural for the ideas to be applied. Except for the widely used language Prolog, Lisp and its dialects, Maclisp [277], Interlisp [338, 376], Qlisp [318], Common Lisp [351], Franz Lisp [413], etc., many other AI language have been designed and implemented. Examples include IPL [296, 297] PLANNER [184], CONNIVER [363], KRL [46], NETL [126], SAIL [311], POP-2 [93], FUZZY [131], and first-order logic. In general, three capabilities, namely action, description, and reasoning, are needed for an AI language. Historically, languages strong in one of these capacities tended to be relatively weak in others. Prolog is a reasoning-oriented language that is limited by its inefficiency of description and action. Lisp, the second oldest programming language in present widespread use retains some features of von Neumann programming. Some new languages, such as Loglisp [316] and QUTE [325], which amalgamate Prolog and Lisp in natural ways, have been developed. On the other hand, to explore parallelism, parallel versions of Prolog and Lisp, such as Parlog [70], Concurrent Prolog [333, 335], and Concurrent Lisp [361, 367], have been proposed. Recent efforts have been aimed at automatic programming that will allow the program to be generated from a simple specification of the problem [31, 32, 242, 256, 343].

It has also been apparent to the AI community since the mid 1960s that inferences alone, even those augmented with heuristics, were often inadequate to solve real-life problems. To enhance the performance of AI programs, they must be augmented with knowledge of the problem domain rather than formal reasoning methods. This realization gave birth to *knowledge engineering* or the *knowledge-based system*, the field of applied AI [13, 240].

A *knowledge-based expert system*, or in short, expert system, is a knowledge-intensive program that solves problems in a specific domain normally requiring human expertise [56, 99, 157, 179–181, 294, 407]. An expert system consists of two parts: knowledge base and inference procedure. The knowledge base contains the facts and heuristics, while the inference procedure consists of the processes that search the knowledge base to infer solutions to problems, form hypotheses, and so on. What distinguishes an expert system from an ordinary computer application is that, in a conventional computer program, pertinent knowledge and the methods for utilizing it are all intermixed, whereas in an expert system, the knowledge base is separated from the inference procedure, and new knowledge can be added to the system without programming.

Contemporary expert-system development techniques are shifting towards the use of software development tools that resemble a programming language, but include internal user-accessible data bases and other high-level strategies for using knowledge to solve a class of problems [88, 157, 181, 220]. Each tool suggests some additional design properties, such as rule-base and backward reasoning, for the knowledge-system architecture. Three of the most popular families of expert-system tools are: (1) EMYCIN [267, 268], KS300, and S.1; (2) HEARSAY-III [125] and AGE [299]; and (3) OPS that incorporates the R1 (XCON) expert-system families [145]. Other expert-system tools include LOOPS [354], ROSIE [130], RLL [167] MRS, and KMS. Some of these tools aim to provide a mixture of representations and inference techniques. Knowledge-acquisition tools such as TEIRESIAS [97], EXPERT [411], KAS [120], and learning tools such as META-DENDRAL [55] and EURISKO [241] have also been developed.

3. MICRO-AND MACROLEVEL AI ARCHITECTURES

The VLSI technology has flourished in the past ten years [1, 54, 266, 329, 382], resulting in the development of advanced microprocessors [384], semiconductor memories [415], and systolic arrays [147, 148, 168, 231, 330].

The microlevel architectures consist of architectural designs that are fundamental to applications in AI. In the design of massively parallel AI machines [129], some of the basic computational problems recognized are set intersection, transitive closure, contexts and partitions, best-match recognition, Gestalt recognition, and recognition under transformation. These operations may not be unique in AI and may exist in many other applications as well. Due to the simplicity of some of these operations, they can usually be implemented directly in hardware, especially in systolic arrays using the VLSI technology. Many other basic operations can also be implemented in VLSI. Examples include sorting [35, 43, 51, 197, 229, 309, 378, 379, 395, 418] and selection [401, 425], computing transitive closure [171, 231], string and pattern matching [8, 13, 14, 162, 174, 192, 285, 374], selection from secondary memories [119, 161], dynamic programming evaluations [39, 64, 171], proximity searches [427], and unification [118, 146, 380, 399, 400].

Some AI languages such as Lisp differ from traditional machine languages in that the program/data storage is conceptually an unordered set of linked record structures of various sizes, rather than an ordered, indexable vector of numbers or bit fields of a fixed size. The instruction set must be designed according to the storage structure [353]. Additional concepts that are well suited for list processing are the tagged-memory [137, 191] and stack architectures [117].

The macrolevel is an intermediate level between the microlevel and the system level. In contrast to the microlevel architectures, the macrolevel architectures are (possibly) made up of a variety of microlevel architectures and perform more complex operations. However, they are not considered as a complete system that can solve problems in AI applications, but can be taken as more complex supporting mechanisms for the system level. The architectures can be classified into dictionary machines, data-base machines, architectures for searching, and architectures for managing data structures.

A dictionary machine is an architecture that supports the insertion, deletion, and searching for membership, extremum and proximity of keys in a data-base [18, 37, 61, 141, 238, 303, 348]. Most designs are based on binary-tree architectures; however, designs using radix trees and a small number of processors have been found to be preferable when keys are long and clustered [141].

A data-base machine is an architectural approach that distributes the search intelligence into the secondary and mass storage and relieves the workload of the central processor. Extensive research has been carried out in the past decade on optical and mass storage [270, 271], back-end storage systems [150], and data-base machines [19, 52, 156, 177, 196, 217, 236, 251, 336, 339]. Data-base machines developed earlier were mainly directed towards general-purpose relational data-base management systems. Examples include the DBC, DIRECT, RAP, CASSM, associative array processors, text retrieval systems [196, 236], and CAFS [19]. Nearly all current research on data-base machines to support knowledge data-bases assumes that the knowledge data-base is relational, hence research is directed towards solving the disk paradox [52] and enhancing previous relational data-base machines by extensive parallelism [287, 319, 340, 373]. Commercially available data-base and backend machines have also been applied in knowledge management [213, 214, 295].

Searching is an essential to many applications, although unnecessary combinatorial searches should be avoided. The suitability of parallel processing to searching depends on the problem complexity. the problem representation, and the corresponding search algorithms. Problem complexity should be low enough such that a serial computer can solve the problem in a reasonable amount of time. Problem representations are very important because they are related to the search algorithms. Parallel algorithms have been found to be able to dramatically reduce the average-time behavior of search problems, the so-called combinatorially implosive algorithms [222, 223, 408].

A search problem can be represented as searching an acyclic graph or a search tree. According to the functions of nodes in the graph, the problem is transformed into one of the following paradigms: (a) AND-tree (or graph) search: all nonterminal nodes are AND-nodes, (b) OR-tree (or graph) search: all nonterminal nodes are OR-nodes, and (c) AND/OR-tree (or graph) search: the nonterminal nodes are either AND- or OR-nodes. A divide-and-conquer algorithm is an example algorithm to search AND-trees; a branch-and-bound algorithm is used to search OR-trees; and an alpha-beta algorithm is used to search (AND/OR) game trees. Parallel algorithms for divide-and-conquer [195], branch-and-bound [10, 24, 106, 149, 234, 235, 245, 247], and AND/OR-graph search [140, 142, 258] have been developed. Various parallel architectures to support divide-and-conquer algorithms [307, 341] and branch-and-bound algorithms [108, 122, 139, 175, 201, 202, 359, 402–404] have been proposed.

Extensive research has been carried out in supporting dynamic data structures in a computer with a limited memory space. *Garbage collection* is an algorithm that periodically reclaims memory space no longer needed by the users [27–29, 33, 45, 79, 110, 114, 136, 188, 230, 248, 259, 298, 349, 352]. This is usually transparent to the users and could be implemented in hardware, software, or a combination of both. For efficiency reasons, additional hardware such as stacks and reference counters are usually provided.

4. FUNCTIONAL PROGRAMMING ORIENTED ARCHITECTURES

The origin of functional languages as a practical class of computer languages can perhaps be traced to the development of Lisp by McCarthy [261] in the early 1960s, but their ancestry went directly back to the Lambda Calculus developed by Church in the 1930s. The objective of writing a functional program is to define a set of (possibly recursive) equations for each function [91]. Data structures are handled by introducing a special class of functions called constructor functions. This view allows functional languages to deal directly with structures that would be termed "abstract" in more conventional languages. Moreover, functions themselves can be passed around as data objects. The design of the necessary computer architecture to support functional languages thus centers around the mechanisms of efficient manipulation of data structures (list-oriented architectures) and the parallel evaluation of functional programs (function-oriented architectures).

List-oriented architectures are architectures designed to efficiently support the manipulation of data structures and objects. Lisp, a mnemonic for list-processing language, is a well-known language to support symbolic processing. There are several reasons why Lisp and list-oriented computers are really needed. First, to relieve the burden on the programmers, Lisp was designed as an untyped language. The computer must be able to identify the types of data, which involves an enormous amount of data-type checking and the use of long strings of instructions at compile- and run-times. Conventional computers cannot do these efficiently in software. Second, the system must periodically perform garbage collection and reclaim unused memory at run-time. This amounts to around 10 to 30% of the total processing time in a conventional computer. Hardware implementation of garbage collection is thus essential. Third, due the nature of recursion, a stack-oriented architecture is more suitable for list processing. Lastly, list processing usually requires an enormous amount of space, and the data structures are so dynamic that the compiler cannot predict how much space to allocate at compile-time. Special hardware to manage the data structures and the large memory space would make the system more cost-effective and efficient [105, 132, 143, 290].

The earliest implementation of Lisp machines were the PDP-6 computer and its successors the PDP-10 and PDP-20 made by the Digital Equipment Corporation [261]. The half-word instructions and the stack instructions of these machines were developed with Lisp's requirements in mind. Extensive work has been done for the DEC-System 10's and 20's on garbage collection to manage and reclaim the memory space used.

The design of Lisp machines was started at MIT's AI Laboratory in 1974. CONS, designed in 1976 [36, 165, 219, 328], was superseded in 1978 by a second-generation Lisp machine, the CADR. This machine was a model for the first commercially available Lisp machines [22, 257, 291], including the Symbolics LM2, the Xerox 1100 Interlisp work station, and the Lisp Machine Inc. Series III

CADR, all of them delivered in 1981. The third-generation machines were based on additional hardware to support data tagging and garbage collection. They are characterized by the Lisp Machines Inc.'s Lambda, supporting Zetalisp and LMLisp [87, 257, 291]. The Symbolics 3600, supporting Zetalisp, Flavors, and Fortran 77 [19, 278, 405, 409], the Xerox 1108 and 1132, supporting Interlisp-D and Smalltalk [47, 280, 337], and the Fijitsu FACOM Alpha Machine, a back-end Lisp processor, supporting Maclisp [9, 178]. Most of the Lisp machines support networking using Ethernet. The LMI Lambda has a NuBus developed at MIT to produce a modular, expandable Lisp machine with multiprocessor architecture.

A single-chip computer to support Lisp has been implemented in the MIT SCHEME-79 chip [350, 353, 364]. Other experimental computers to support Lisp and list-oriented processing have been reported [111, 164, 166, 169, 292, 310, 322–324, 370]. These machines usually have additional hardware tables, hashing hardware, tag mechanisms, and list-processing hardware, or are microprogrammed to provide macroinstructions for list-processing. Experimental multiprocessoring systems have been proposed to execute Lisp programs concurrently [173, 186, 265, 273, 361, 362, 414]. Dataflow processing is suitable for Lisp because these programs are generally data driven [422, 423]. Other multiprocessing and dataflow architectures to support list-processing have been proposed and developed [11, 12, 77, 113, 159, 385].

Besides specialized hardware implementations, software implementations on general-purpose computers are also popular. The earliest Lisp compilers were developed on the IBM 704 and later extended to the IBM 7090, 360, and 370. Various strategies for implementing Lisp compilers have been proposed [60, 103, 170, 320, 321, 376], and conventional microcomputers have been used to implement Lisp compilers [216, 368]. Lisp is also available on various general- and special-purpose work stations, typically based on multiple 68000 processors [216, 368]. Lisp has been developed on Digital Equipment Corp.'s VAXstation 100, a MC68000-based personal graphics work station, and clusters of 11/782s running several dialects of Lisp and Common Lisp [360]. One dialect of Lisp, Franz Lisp, developed at the University of California, Berkeley, was written in C and runs under Unix and is available on many general-purpose work station.

Architectures have also been developed to support object-oriented programming languages which have been extended from functional languages to additionally implement operations such as creating an object, sending and receiving messages, modifying an object's state, and forming class-superclass hierarchies [185, 381, 421]. Smalltalk, first developed in 1972 by the Xerox Corp., is recognized as a simple but powerful way of communicating with computers. At MIT, the concept was extended to become the Flavors systems. Special hardware and multiprocessors have been proposed to directly support the processing of object-oriented languages [204, 308, 365, 397].

In *function-oriented architectures*, the design issues center on the physical interconnection of processors, the method used to "drive" the computation, the representation of programs and data, the method to invoke and control parallelism, and the optimization techniques [398]. Desirable features of such architectures should include a multiprocessor system with a rich interconnection structure, the representation of list structures by balanced trees, and hardware supports for demand-driven execution, low-overhead process creation, and storage management.

Architectures to support functional-programming languages can be classified as uniprocessor architectures, tree-structured machines, data-driven machines, and demand-driven machines. In a uniprocessor architecture, besides the mechanisms to handle lists, additional stacks to handle function cells and optimization for redundant calls and array operations may be implemented [6, 38, 63, 350, 390]. Tree-structured machines usually employ lazy evaluations, but suffer from the bottleneck at the root of the tree [94, 210, 251, 253, 300]. Dataflow machines are also natural candidates for executing functional programs and have tremendous potential for parallelism. However, the issue of controlling parallelism remains unresolved. A lot of the recent work is concentrated on demand-driven machines, which are based on reduction machines on a set of load-balanced (possibly virtual) processors [74, 90, 151, 194, 211, 212, 218, 221, 344, 383, 385].

Owing to the different motivations and objectives of various functional programming–oriented architectures, each machine has its own distinct features. For example, the Symbolics 3600 [278] was designed for an interactive program development environment where compilation is very frequent and ought to appear instantaneous to the user. This requirement simplified the design of the compiler and results in only a single-address instruction format, no indexed and indirect addressing modes, and other mechanisms to minimize the number of nontrivial choices to be made. On the other hand, the aim in developing SOAR [397] was to demonstrate that a Reduced Instruction Set Computer could provide high performance in an exploratory programming environment. Instead of microcode, SOAR relied on software to provide complicated operations. As a result, more sophisticated software techniques were used.

5. LOGIC- AND KNOWLEDGE-ORIENTED ARCHITECTURES

In logic- and knowledge-oriented architectures, the ideal goal is for the user to specify the problem in terms of the properties of the problem and the solution (logic or knowledge), and the architecture exercises the control on how the problem is to be solved. This goal is not fully achieved yet, and users still need to provide small but undue amounts of control information in logic programs, partly by ordering the clauses and goals in a program, and partly by the use of extra-logical "features" in the language.

Knowledge- and logic-oriented architectures can be classified according to the knowledge representation schemes. Besides incorporating knowledge into a program written in a functional programming language, some of the well-known schemes are logic programs and semantic networks. According to the search strategy, logic programs can further be classified into production systems and logical inference systems [48, 50, 118, 146, 326, 407].

Substantial research has been carried out on parallel computational models of utilizing AND-parallelism, OR-parallelism, and stream parallelism in logical inference systems [41, 62, 66, 69, 82, 83, 102, 215, 246, 250, 293, 302, 342, 396, 420, 426], production systems [301, 317, 377], and others [154]. The basic problem on the exponential complexity of logic programs remains open at this time.

Sequential Prolog machines using software interpretation [7, 200], emulation [76, 429], and additional hardware support such as hardware unification and backtracking [207, 372, 380] have been proposed. Single-processor systems for production systems using additional data memories [239] and a RISC architecture [146] have been studied.

New logic programming languages suitable for parallel processing have been investigated [193]. In particular, the use of predicate logic [123], extensions of Prolog to become Concurrent Prolog [53, 233, 331, 334, 366, 375, 393], Parlog [71], and Delta-Prolog [306], and parallel production systems [394] have been developed. Concurrent Prolog has also been extended to include object-oriented programming [331] and has been applied as a VLSI design language [366]. One interesting parallel language is that of systolic programming, which is useful as an algorithm design and programming methodology for high-level-language parallel computers [332].

Several prototype multiprocessor systems for processing inference programs and Prolog have been proposed, some of which are currently under construction. These systems include multiprocessors with a shared memory [53], ZMOB, a multiprocessor of Z80's connected by a ring network [65, 208, 314, 389, 410], AQUARIUS, a heterogeneous multiprocessor with a crossbar switch [109], and MAGO, a cellular machine implementing a Prolog compiler that translates a Prolog program into a formal functional program [225]. Techniques for analyzing Prolog programs such that they can be processed on a dataflow architecture have been derived [40, 176, 203, 205]. DADO is a multiprocessor system with a binary-tree interconnection network that implements parallel production systems [172, 355–357]. An associative processor has been proposed to carry out propositional and first-order predicate calculus [115].

It has been recognized that a combination of Lisp, Prolog, and an object-oriented language such as Smalltalk may be a better language for AI applications [369]. A computer of this type that implements a combination of the AI languages may use microprogramming to emulate the various functions. Prolog is also available as a secondary language on some Lisp machines. A version of Prolog interpretor with a speed of 4.5 KLIPS has been developed for Lisp Machine's Lambda [257]. Some of the prototype multiprocessors, such as ZMOB [65, 208, 314, 389, 410] and MAGO [225] were developed with a flexible architecture that can implement object-oriented, functional, and logic languages. FAIM-1, a multiprocessor connected in the form of a twisted hex-plane topology, implements the features of object-oriented, functional, and logic programming in the OIL programming language [96].

Besides being represented in logic, knowledge can also be represented in terms of semantic nets. Proposed and experimental architectures have been developed. NETL [126, 128, 138], and its generalization to THISTLE [129], consists of an array of simple cells with marker-passing capability to perform searches, set-intersections, inheritance of properties and descriptions, and multiple-context operations on semantic nets. Thinking Machine's Connection Machine is a cellular machine with 65,536 processing elements. It implements marker passing and virtually reconfigures the processing elements to match the topology of the application semantic nets [86, 186]. Associative processors for processing semantic nets have also been proposed [275, 276].

Some AI architectures are based on frame representations and may be called object-oriented architectures. For example, the *Apiary* developed at MIT is a multiprocessor actor system [186]. *Actor* is an object that contains a small amount of state and can perform a few primitive operations: sending a message, creating another actor, making a decision, and changing its local state. An efficient AI architecture also depends on the problem-solving strategy. The basic idea of the *Boltzmann machine* developed at the Carnegie-Mellon University is the application of statistical methods to constraint-satisfaction searches in a parallel network [190]. The most interesting aspect of this machine lies in its domain-independent learning algorithm [17].

With the inclusion of control into stored knowledge, the resulting system becomes a distributed problem-solving system. These systems are characterized by the relative autonomy of the problem-solving nodes, a direct consequence of the limited communication capability [98, 100, 133]. With the proposed formalism of the Contract Net, contracts are used to express the control of problem solving in a distributed processor architecture [345–347]. Related work in this area include Petri-net modeling [304], distributed vehicle-monitoring testbed [84, 243], distributed air-traffic control system [59], and modeling the brain as a distributed system [152, 158].

6. FIFTH GENERATION COMPUTER SYSTEM

The Fifth Generation Computer System (FGCS) project was a project that started in Japan in 1982 to further the research and development of the next generation of computers. It was conjectured that computers of the next decade will be used increasingly for nonnumeric data-processing such as symbolic manipulation and applied AI. The goals of the FGCS project are

1. To implement basic mechanisms for inference, association, and learning in hardware
2. To prepare basic AI software in order to utilize the full power of the basic mechanisms implemented

3. To implement the basic mechanisms for retrieving and managing a knowledge base in hardware and software
4. To use pattern recognition and AI research achievements in developing user-oriented man-machine interfaces
5. To realize supporting environments for resolving the "software crisis" and enhancing software production

The FGCS project is a marriage between the implementation of a computer system and the requirements specified by applications in AI, such as natural-language understanding and speech recognition. Specific issues studied include the choice of logic programming over functional programming, the design of the basic software systems to support knowledge acquisition, management, learning, and the intelligent interface to users, the design of highly parallel architectures to support inferencing operations, and the design of distributed-function architectures that integrates VLSI technology to support knowledge data-bases [42, 153, 209, 282, 284, 386].

A first effort in the FGCS project is to implement a sequential inference machine, or SIM [392, 428]. Its first implementation is a medium-performance machine known as a personal sequential inference, or PSI, machine [371, 430]. The current implementation is on the parallel inference machine, or PIM [163, 205, 206, 283, 287, 288, 391]. Another architectural development is on the knowledge-base machine, Delta [286–319, 340]. Lastly, the development of the basic software system acts as a bridge to fill the gap between a highly parallel computer architecture and knowledge information processing [155, 263, 269]. Currently, all the projects are progressing well; however, the struggle is still far from over [255].

The Japanese FGCS project has stirred intensive responses from other countries [3–5, 89, 90, 92, 101, 124, 279, 344, 416]. The British project is a five-year $550 million cooperative program between government and industry that concentrates on software engineering, intelligent knowledge-based systems, VLSI circuitry, and human-machine interfaces. Hardware development has focused on ALICE, a Parlog machine using dataflow architectures and implementing both Hope, Prolog, and Lisp [89, 90, 92, 101, 279, 344]. The European Comission has started the $1.5 billion five-year European Strategic Program for Research in Information Technologies (Esprit) in 1984 [4]. The program focuses on microelectronics, software technology, advanced information processing, computer-integrated manufacturing, and office automation. In the United States, the most direct response to the Japanese FCGS project was the establishment of the Microelectronics and Computer Technology Corp. in 1983 [3]. The project has an annual budget of $50 million to $80 million per year. It has a more evolutionary approach than the revolutionary approach of the Japanese and should yield technology that the corporate sponsors can build into advanced products in the next 10 to 12 years. Meanwhile, other research organizations have formed to develop future computer technologies of the United States in a broader sense. These include DARPA's Strategic Computing and Survivability, the semiconductor industry's Semiconductor Research Corporation, and the Microelectronics Center of North Carolina [3].

7. CONCLUSIONS

This survey briefly summarizes the state of the art in AI architectures. Conventional von Neumann computers are unsuitable for AI applications because they are designed mainly for deterministic numerical processing. To cope with the increasing inefficiency and difficulty in coding algorithms in AI, *declarative languages* have been developed. *Lambda-based* and *logic-based* languages are two popular classes of declarative languages.

One of the architect's starting point in supporting applications in AI is the language. This approach has been termed the *language-first approach*. A possible disadvantage of this approach is that each language may lead to a quite distinct architecture which is unsuited to other languages, a dilemma in high-level language computer architectures. In AI applications, the lambda-based and logic-based languages have been considered seriously by novel architects. Recent research lies in integrating the logic and lambda languages, and the work on lambda and logic oriented architectures provides useful guidelines for parallel architectures that support more advanced languages. On the other hand, AI architectures are also related to knowledge representations. This approach has been called the *knowledge-first approach*. Several architectures have been designed to support multiple knowledge representations.

An appropriate methodology to design an AI architecture should combine the top-down and bottom-up design approaches. That is, we need to develop functional requirements based on the AI problem requirements and map these requirements into architectures based on technological requirements. Parallel processing is a great hope to increase the power of AI machines. However, parallel processing is not a way to overcome the difficulty of combinatorial explosion. It cannot significantly extend the solvable problem space on problems that we can solve today. Hence the problem complexity is an important consideration in designing AI machines. Problems of lower complexity may be solved by sequential computation; problems of moderate complexity may be solved by parallel processing; while problem of high complexity should be solved by heuristic and parallel processing. Since the complexities of most AI problems are high, an appropriate approach should start by first designing good heuristics to reduce the serial-computational time, and using parallel processing to pursue a near-linear speed-up.

Although many AI architectures have been built or proposed, the Lisp machines are the only architectures that have had widespread use for solving real AI problems. Most underlying concepts in AI architectures are not new and have been used in conventional computer systems. For example, hardware stack and tagged memory were proposed before they were used in Lisp machines. On the other hand, some popular architectural concepts in currnet supercomputers will have restricted use in some AI applications. For example, the large amount of branch and symbolic processing operations in AI programs reduces stream parallelism in pipelining.

The question of how AI programs can be executed directly in hardware efficiently is still largely unanswered. The following are some key issues in designing AI architectures:

1. Identification of parallelism in AI programs
2. Tradeoff between the benefit and the overhead on the use of heuristic information
3. Efficient interconnection structure to distribute heuristic-guiding and pruning information
4. Granularity of parallelism
5. Dynamic scheduling and load balancing
6. Architecture to support the acquisition and learning of heuristic information
7. Prediction of performance and linear scaling
8. Management of the large memory space.

REFERENCES

1. *Proc. 2nd Caltech Conf. on Very Large Scale Integration.* Rockville, MD: Computer Science Press, 1981.
2. "Special Issue on Smalltalk," *Byte*, Aug. 1981.
3. "Special Issue on Tomorrow's Computers," *Spectrum*, 20(11):51–58, Nov. 1983.
4. "ESPRIT: Europe Challenges U.S. and Japanese Competitors," *Future Generation Computer Systems*, 1(1):61–69, 1984.
5. *Proc. ACM '84 Annual Conference: The Fifth Generation Challenge*, ACM, 1984.
6. P. S. Abrahms, *An APL Machine.* Ph.D. thesis, Stanford University, Menlo Park, CA, Feb. 1970.
7. J. P. Adam, et al., *The IBM Paris Scientific Center Programming in Logic Interpreter: Overview.* IBM France Scientific Center, Oct. 1984.
8. S. R. Ahuja and C. S. Roberts, "An Associative/Parallel Processor for Partial Match Retrieval Using Superimposed Codes," *Proc. 7th Annual Symp. on Computer Architecture.* IEEE/ACM, May 1980, pp. 218–227.
9. H. Akimoto, S. Shimizu, A. Shinagawa, A. Hattori, and H. Hayashi, "Evaluation of the Dedicated Hardware in FACOM Alpha," *Proc. COMPCON Spring*, IEEE, 1985, pp. 366–369.
10. S. G. Akl, D. T. Barnard, and R. J. Doran, "Design, Analysis and Implementation of a Parallel Tree Search Algorithm," *IEEE Trans. on Pattern Analysis and Machine Intelligence*, PAMI-4(2):192–203, 1982.
11. M. Amamiya, R. Hasegawa, O. Nakamura, and H. Mikami, "A List-Processing-Oriented Data Flow Machine Architecture," *Proc. Natl Computer Conf.* AFIPS Press, 1982, pp. 144–151.
12. M. Amamiya and R. Hasegawa, "Dataflow Computing and Eager and Lazy Evaluations," *New Generation Computing*, 2(2):105–129, 1984.
13. J. Aoe, Y. Yamamoto, and R. Shimada, "A Method for Improving String Pattern Matching Machines," *IEEE Trans. on Software Engineering*, SE-10(1):116–120, 1984.
14. A. Apostolico and A. Negro, "Systolic Algorithms for String Manipulations," *IEEE Trans. on Computers*, C-33(4):361–364, 1984.
15. Arvind, K. Gostelow, and W. Plouffe, *An Asynchronous Programming Language and Computing Machine.* Technical Report. 114a, University of California, Irvine, CA, Dec. 1978.

16. Arvind and R. A. Iannucci, "A Critique of Multiprocessing von Neumann Style," *Proc. 10th Annual Int'l Symp. on Computer Architecture*, pp. 426–436, IEEE/ACM, June 1983.
17. D. H. Askley, G. E. Hinton, and T. J. Sejnowski, "A Learning Algorithm for Boltzmann Machines," *Cognitive Science*, 9(1):147–169, 1985.
18. M. J. Atallah and S. R. Kosaraju, "A Generalized Dictionary Machine for VLSI," *Trans. on Computers*, C-34 (2):151–155, 1985.
19. E. Babb, "Joined Normal Form: A Storage Encoding for Relational Databases," *Trans. on Database Systems*, 7(4):588–614, 1982.
20. E. Babb, "Functional Requirements for Very Large Knowledge Bases," *Proc. ACM'84 Annual Conf.*, pp. 55–56, ACM, Oct. 1984.
21. J. Backus, "Can Programming be Liberated from the von Neumann Style? A Functional Style and Algebra of Programs," *Comm. of the ACM*, 21(8):613–641, 1978.
22. J. Backus, "Function-Level Computing," *Spectrum*, 19(8):22–27, 1982.
23. J.-L. Baer, *Computer Systems Architecture*. Rockville, MD: Computer Science Press, 1980.
24. J. L. Baer, H. C. Du, and R. E. Ladner, "Binary Search in a Multiprocessing Environment," *IEEE Trans. on Computers*, C-32(7):667–677, 1983.
25. J. L. Baer, "Computer Architecture," *Computer*, 17(10):77–87, 1984.
26. H. G. Baker, Jr., "Shallow Binding in Lisp 1.5," *Comm. of the ACM*, 21(7):565–569, 1978.
27. H. C. Baker, Jr., and C. Hewitt, "The Incremental Garbage Collection of Processes," *Proc. Symp. on Artificial Intelligence and Programming Languages* (*also SIGART Newsletter*, pp. 55–59), ACM, Aug. 1977.
28. H. G. Baker, Jr., "List Processing in Real Time on a Serial Computer," *Comm. of the ACM*, 21(4):280–294, 1978.
29. H. G. Baker, Jr, "Optimizing Allocation and Garbage Collection of Spaces." In P. H. Winston and R. H. Brown (eds.), *Artificial Intelligence: An MIT Perspective*, vol. 1. Cambridge, MA: MIT Press, 1979, pp. 391–396.
30. A. Barr and E. A. Feigenbaum, *The Handbook on Artificial Intelligence*, 2. Los Altos, CA: William Kaufman, 1982.
31. D. Barstow, "A Perspective on Automatic Programming," *Proc. 8th Int'l Joint Conf. on Artificial Intelligence*. Los Altos, CA: Aug. 1983, William Kaufman, pp. 1170–1179.
32. D. R. Barstow, "An Experiment in Knowledge–Based Automatic Programming." In B. L. Webber and N. J. Nilsson (eds.), *Readings in Artificial Intelligence*. Palo Alto, CA: Tioga, 1981. pp. 289–312.
33. J. M. Barth, "Shifting Garbage Collection Overhead to Compile Time," *Comm. of the ACM*, 20(7):513–518, 1977.
34. M. Bartschi, "An Overview of Information Retrieval Subjects," *Computer*, 18(5):67–84, 1985.
35. G. Baudet and D. Stevenson, "Optimal Sorting Algorithms for Parallel Computers," *Trans. on Computers*, C-27(1):84–87, 1978.
36. A. Bawden, R. Greenblatt, J. Holloway, T. Knight, D. Moon, and D. Weinreb, "The Lisp Machine." In P. H. Winston and R. H. Brown (eds.), *Artificial Intelligence: An MIT Perspective*, vol. 1, Cambridge, MA: MIT Press, 1979, pp. 343–373.
37. J. L. Bentley and H. T. Kung, "A Tree Machine for Searching Problems," *Proc. Int'l Conf. on Parallel Processing*, IEEE, 1979, pp. 257–266.
38. K. J. Berkling, "Reduction Languages for Reduction Machines," *Proc. Int'l Symp. on Computer Architecture*, IEEE/ACM, 1975, pp. 133–140.
39. D. P. Bertsekas, "Distributed Dynamic Programming," *IEEE Trans. on Automatic Control*, AC-27 (3):610–616, 1982.
40. L. Bic, "Execution of Logic Programs on a Dataflow Architecture," *Proc. 11th Annual Int'l Symp. on Computer Architecture*, IEEE/ACM, June 1984, pp. 290–296.
41. L. Bic, "A Data-Driven Model for Parallel Interpretation of Logic Programs," *Proc. Int'l Conf. on Fifth Generation Computer Systems*, ICOT and North-Holland, 1984, pp. 517–523.
42. L. Bic, "The Fifth Generation Grail: A Survey of Related Research," *Proc. ACM '84 Annual Conf.*, ACM, Oct. 1984, pp. 293–297.
43. D. Bitton, D. J. DeWitt, D. K. Hsiao, and J. Menon, "A Taxonomy of Paralle Sorting," *Computing Surveys*, 16(3): 1984.
44. D. Bobrow and B. Paphael, "New Programming Languages for AI research," *Computing Surveys*, 6(3):153–174, 1974.

45. D. Bobrow and D. Clark, "Compact Encoding of List Structure," *ACM Trans. on Prog. Language and Systems*, 1(2): 266–286, 1979.
46. D. G. Bobrow and T. Winograd, "An Overview of KRL—A Knowledge Representation Language," *Cognitive Science* 1(1):3–46, 1976.
47. D. G. Bobrow, *The LOOPS Manual*, Technical Report KB-VLSI-81-13, Xerox PARC, Palo Alto, CA, 1982.
48. D. G. Bobrow, "If Prolog Is the Answer. What is the Question?," *Proc. Int'l Conf. on Fifth Generation Computer Systems*, ICOT and North-Holland, 1984, pp. 138–145.
49. H. Boley, "A Preliminary Survey of Artificial Intelligence Machines," *SIGART Newsletter*, 72: 21–28, 1980.
50. H. Boley, "AI Languages and AI Machines: An Overview," *Proc. German Workshop on Artificial Intelligence*, Springer-Fachberichte, 1981.
51. M. A. Bonuccelli, E. Lodi, and L. Pagli, "External Sorting in VLSI," *IEEE Trans. on Computers*, C-33(10):931–934, 1984.
52. H. Boral and D. DeWitt, "Database Machine: An Idea Whose Time has Passed?," *Database Machines*. New York: Springer-Verlag, 1983, pp. 166–167.
53. P. Borgwardt, "Parallel Prolog using Stack Segments on Shared-Memory Multiprocessors," *Proc. Int'l Symp. on Logic Programming*, IEEE, Feb. 1984, pp. 2–11.
54. R. Bryant (ed.), *Proc. 3rd Caltech Conf. on Very Large Scale Integration*. Rockviller, MD: Computer Science Press, 1983.
55. B. G. Buchanan and E. A. Feigenbaum, "Dendral and Meta-Dendral: Their Applications Dimension," *Artificial Intelligence*, 11(1–2):5–24, 1978.
56. B. G. Buchanan, "New Research on Expert Systems." In Hayes, D. Michie, and Y.-H. Pao, (eds.), *Machine Intelligence 10*. Chichester, Eng.: Ellis Horwood Ltd., 1982, pp. 269–299.
57. R. Burstall, "Programming with Modules as Typed Functional Programming," *Proc. Int'l Conf. on Fifth Generation Computer Systems*, ICOT and North-Holland, 1984, pp. 103–112.
58. R. M. Burstall, D. B. MacQueen, and D. T. Sannella, "HOPE: An Experimental Applicative Language," *Conf. Record of Lisp Conf.*, Stanford University, Menlo Park, CA, 1980, pp. 136–143.
59. S. Cammarata, D. McArthur, and R. Steeb, "Strategies of Cooperation in Distributed Problem Solving," *Proc. 8th Int'l Joint Conf. on Artificial Intelligence*. Los Altos, CA: William Kaufman Aug. 1983, pp. 767–770.
60. J. Campbell and J. Fitch, "Symbolic Computing With and Without Lisp," *Conf. Record of Lisp Conf.*, Stanford University, Menlo Park, CA, 1980.
61. M. J. Carey and C. D. Thompson, *An Efficient Implementation of Search trees on O(log N) Processors*. Tech. Rep. UCB/CSD 82/101, Computer Science Division, University of California, Berkeley, CA, April 1982.
62. D. A. Carlson, "Parallel Processing of Tree-Like Computations," *Proc. 4th Int'l Conf. on Distributed Computing Systems*, IEEE, May 1984, pp. 192–198.
63. M. Castan and E. I. Organick, "M3L: An HLL-RISC Processor for Parallel Execution of FP-Language Programs," *Proc. 9th Annual Symp. on Computer Architecture*, pp. 239–247, IEEE/ACM, 1982, 239–247.
64. J. Casti, M. Richardson, and R. Larson, "Dynamic Programming and Parallel Computers," *J. of Optimization Theory and Applications*, 12(4):423–438, 1973.
65. U. S. Chakravarthy, S. Kasif, M. Kohli, J. Minker, and D. Cao, "Logic Programming on ZMOB: A Highly Parallel Machine," *Proc. Int'l Conf. on Parallel Processing*, IEEE, Aug. 1982, pp. 347–349.
66. J. H. Chang, A. M. Despain, and D. DeGroot, "AND-Parallelism of Logic Programs Based on A Static Data Dependency Analysis," *Proc. COMPCON Spring*, IEEE, 1985, pp. 218–225.
67. E. Charniak, C. Riesbeck, and D. McDermott, *Artificial Intelligence Programming*. New York: Lawrence Erlbaum Press, 1980.
68. Y. Chu, "Direct-Execution Computer Architecture." In B. Gilchrist (ed.), *Information Processing 77*. North-Holland, 1977, pp. 18–23.
69. A. Ciepielewski and S. Haridi, "Execution of Bagof on the OR-Parallel Token Machine," *Proc. Int'l Conf. Fifth Generation Computer Systems*. ICOT and North-Holland, 1984, pp. 551–560.
70. K. Clark and S. Gregory, "Note on System Programming in PARLOG," *Proc. Int'l Conf. Fifth Generation Computer Systems*, ICOT and North-Holland, 1984, pp. 299–306.
71. K. Clark and S. Gregory, *PARLOG: Parallel Programming in Logic*. Research Rep. DOC 84/4, Imperial College, London, England, 1984.
72. K. L. Clark and S.-A. Turnlund (eds), *Logic Programming*, New York: Academic Press, 1982.

73. K. L. Clark and F. G. McCabe, "Prolog: A Language for Implementing Expert Systems." In J. Hayes, D. Michie, and Y. H. Pao, *Machine Intelligence 10.* Chichester, England: Ellis Horwood Ltd., 1982, pp. 455–471.

74. T. Clarke, P. Gladstone, C. Maclean, and A. Norman, "SKIM—The S, K, I Reduction Machine," *Conf. Record of Lisp Conf.*, Stanford University, Menlo Park, CA, 1980.

75. W. F. Clocksin and C. S. Mellish, *Programming in Prolog.* New York: Springer-Verlag, 1981.

76. W. F. Clocksin, "Design and Simulation of a Sequential Prolog Machine," *New Generation Computing*, 3(2): 101–120, 1985.

77. G. Coghill and K. Hanna, "PLEIADES: A Multimicroprocessor Interactive Knowledge Base," *Microprocessors and Microsystems*, 3(2):77–82, 1979.

78. J. Cohen, "Non-Deterministic Algorithms," *Computing Surveys*, 11(2):79–94, 1979.

79. J. Cohen, "Garbage Collection of Linked Data Structures," *Computing Surveys*, 13(3):341–367, 1981.

80. A. Colmerauer, H. Kanoui, and M. Van Caneghem, "Last Steps Towards an Ultimate Prolog," *Proc. 7th Int'l Joint Conf. on Artificial Intelligence.* Los Altos, CA: William Kaufman, Aug. 1981, pp. 947–948.

81. A. Colmerauer, "Prolog in 10 Figures," *Proc. 8th Int'l Joint Conf. on Artificial Intelligence.* Los Altos, CA: William Kaufman, 1983, pp. 488–499.

82. J. S. Conery and D. F. Kibler, "Parallel Interpretation of Logic Programs," *Proc. Conf. on Functional Programming Languages and Computer Architecture*, ACM, 1981, pp. 163–170.

83. J. S. Conery and D. F. Kibler, "AND Parallelism and Nondeterminism in Logic Programs," *New Generation Computing*, 3(1):43–70, 1985.

84. S. A. Cook, "An Overview of Computational Complexity," *Comm. of the ACM*, 26(6):401–408, 1983.

85. D. D. Corkill and V. R. Lesser, "The Use of Meta-Level Control for Coordination in a Distributed Problem Solving Network," *Proc. 8th Int'l Joint Conf. on Artificial Intelligence.* Los Altos, CA: William Kaufman, Aug. 1983, pp. 748–756.

86. Thinking Machines Corporation, *The Connection Machine Supercomputer: A Natural Fit to Application Needs.* Tech. Rep., Thinking Machines Corporation, Waltham, MA, 1985.

87. M. Creeger, "Lisp Machines Come Out of the Lab.," *Computer Design*, Penn Well, Nov. 1983, pp. 132–137.

88. A. S. Cromarty, "What Are Current Expert System Tools Missing?" *Proc. COMPCON Spring*, IEEE, 1985. pp. 411–418.

89. J. Darlington and M. Reeve, "ALICE: A Multi-processor Reduction Machine for the Parallel Evaluation of Applicative Languages," *Proc. Conf. on Functional Programming Languages and Computer Architecture*, ACM, 1981, pp. 65–74.

90. J. Darlington and M. Reeve, "ALICE and the Parallel Evaluation of Logic Programs." Preliminary Draft, Dept. of Computing, Imperial College of Science and Technology, London, England, June 1983.

91. J. Darlington, "Functional Programming". In F. B. Chambers, D. A. Duce, and G. P. Jones (eds.), *Distributed Computing.* London: Academic Press, 1984, Chap. 5.

92. J. Darlington, A. J. Field, and H. Pull, *The Unification of Functional and Logic Languages*, Tech. Rep., Imperial College, London, England, Feb. 1985.

93. D. Davies, et al., *POPLER 1.5 Reference Manual.* University of Edinburgh, Edinburgh, Scotland, 1973.

94. A. L. Davis, "A Data Flow Evaluation System Based on the Concept of Recursive Locality," *Proc. National Computer Conf.*, AFIPS Press, 1979, pp. 1079–1086.

95. A. L. Davis and R. M. Keller, "Data Flow Program Graphs," *Computer*, 15(2):26–41, 1982.

96. A. L. Davis and S. V. Robinson, "The FAIM-1 Symbolic Multiprocessing System," *Proc. COMPCON Spring*, IEEE, 1985, pp. 370–375.

97. R. Davis and B. Buchanan, "Meta-level Knowledge: Overview and Applications," *Proc. 5th Int'l Joint Conf. on Artificial Intelligence.* Los Altos, CA: William Kaufman, 1977, pp. 920–928.

98. R. Davis, "Report on the Workshop on Distributed Artificial Intelligence," *SIGART Newsletter*, 73: 43–52. 1980.

99. R. Davis, "Expert Systems: Where Are We? And Where Do We Go From Here?' *AI Magazine*, AAAI, Spring 1982, pp. 3–22.

100. R. Davis, "Report on the Second Workshop on Distributed Artifical Intelligence," *SIGART Newsletter.* 80: 13–83, 1982.

101. M. Dawson, *A LISP Compiler for ALICE*, Tech. Rep. Imperial College, London, Eng., 1985.

102. D. DeGroot, "Restricted AND-Parallelism," *Proc. Int'l Conf. on Fifth Generation Computers,* ICOT and North-Holland, Nov. 1984, pp. 471–478.
103. M. Deering, J. Faletti, and R. Wilensky, "PEARL—A Package for Efficient Access to Representations in Lisp," *Proc. 7th Int'l Joint Conf. on Artifical Intelligence.* Los Altos, CA:William Kaufman, Aug. 1981, pp. 930–932.
104. M. F. Deering, "Hardware and Software Architectures for Efficient AI," *Proc. National Conf. on Artifical Intelligence,* AAAI, Aug. 1984, pp. 73–78.
105. M. F. Deering, "Architectures for AI," *Byte,* April 1985, pp. 193–206.
106. E. Dekel and S. Sahni, "Binary Trees and Parallel Scheduling Algorithms," *IEEE Trans. on Computers,* C-32(3):307–315, 1983.
107. J. B. Dennis, "Data Flow Supercomputers," *Computer,* 13(11):48–56, 1980.
108. B. C. Desai, "A Parallel Microprocessing System," *Proc. Int'l Conf. on Parallel Processing,* IEEE, Aug. 1979, p. 136.
109. A. M. Despain and Y. N. Patt, "Aquarius—A High Performance Computing System for Symbolic/Numeric Applications," *Proc. COMPCON Spring,* IEEE, Feb. 1985, pp. 376–382.
110. L. Deutsch and D. Bobrow, "An Efficient Incremental, Automatic Garbage Collector," *Comm. of the ACM,* 19(9):522–526, 1976.
111. P. Deutsch, "Experience with a Microprogrammed Interlisp Systems," *Proc. MICRO,* vol. 11, ACM/IEEE, Nov. 1978.
112. P. Deutsch, "ByteLisp and its Alto Implementation," *Conf. Record of Lisp Conf.,* Stanford University, Menlo Park, CA, 1980.
113. H. Diel, "Concurrent Data Access Architecture," *Proc. Int'l Conf. on Fifth Generation Computer Systems,* ICOT and North-Holland, 1984. pp. 373–388.
114. E. W. Dijkstra, L. Lamport, A. J. Martin, C. S. Scholten, and E. F. M. Steffens, "On-the-Fly Garbage Collection: An Exercise in Cooperation," *Comm. of the ACM,* 21(11):967–975, 1978.
115. W. Dilger and J. Muller, "An Associative Processor for Theorem Proving," *Proc. Symp. on Artifical Intelligence,* IFAC, 1983, pp. 489–497.
116. B. Domolki and P. Szeredi, "Prolog in Practice," In R. E. A. Mason (ed.), *IFIP Information Processing.* New York: Elsevier, 1983, pp. 627–636.
117. R. Doran, "Architecture of Stack Machine." In Y. Chu (ed.), *High-Level Language Computer Architecture,* New York: Academic Press, 1975.
118. R. J. Douglass, "A Qualitative Assessment of Parallelism in Expert Systems," *Software* 2(2): 70–81, 1985.
119. H. C. Du, "Concurrent Disk Accessing for Partial Match Retrieval," *Proc. Int'l Conf. on Parallel Processing,* IEEE, 1982, pp. 211–218.
120. R. O. Duda, J. G. Gaschnig, and P. E. Hart, "Model Design in the PROSPECTOR Consultant System for Mineral Exploration." In *Expert System in the Micro-Electronics Age,* Edinburgh, Scotland: Edinburgh University Press, 1979.
121. S. Eisenbach and C. Sadler, "Declarative Languages: an Overview," *Byte,* Aug. 1985, pp. 181–197.
122. O. I. El-Dessouki and W. H. Huen, "Distributed Enumeration on Between Computers," *IEEE Trans. on Computers,* C-29(9):818–825, 1980.
123. M. H. van Emden and G. J. de Lucena-Filho, "Predicate Logic as a Language for Parallel Programming." In S.-A. Tarnlund and K. Clark (eds.), *Logic Programming,* New York: Academic Press, 1982.
124. M. van Emden, "Towards a Western Fifth-Generation Computer System Project." *Proc. ACM'84 Annual Conf.* ACM, Oct. 1984, pp. 298–302.
125. L. Erman, P. London, and S. Fickas, "The Design and Example, Use of HEARSAY-III." *Proc. 7th Int'l Joint Conf. on Artifical Intelligence.* Los Altos, CA: William Kaufman, 1981, pp. 409–415.
126. S. Fahlman, *NETL: A System for Representing and Using Real-World Knowledge.* Series on Artifical Intelligence. Cambridge, MA: MIT Press, 1979.
127. S. Fahlman, "Computing Facilities for AI: A Survey of Present and Near-Future Options," *AI Magazine,* AAAI, Winter 1980–1981, pp. 16–23.
128. S. E. Fahlman, "Design sketch for a Million-Element NETL Machine," *Proc. 1st Annual Nat'l. Conf. on Artifical Intelligence,* AAAI, Aug. 1980, pp. 249–252.
129. S. E. Fahlman and G. E. Hinton, "Massively Parallel Architectures for AI: NETL, THISTLE, and BOLTZMANN Machines," *Proc. Nat'l. Conf. on Artifical Intellgence,* AAAI, 1983, pp. 109–113.

130. J. Fain and F. Hayes-Roth, et al., *Programming in ROSIE: An Introduction by Means of Examples.* Tech. Note N-1646-ARPA, Rand Corp., Santa Monica, CA, 1982.
131. R. A. Le Faivre, *FUZZY Reference Manual.* Computer Science Dept., Rutgers University, New Brunswick, NJ, 1977.
132. R. Fateman, "Is a Lisp Machine Different from Fortran Machine?," *SIGSAM Bulletin*, 12(4): ACM, 1978.
133. M. Fehling and L. Erman, "Report on the Third Annual Workshop on Distributed Artificial Intelligence," *SIGART Newsletter*, (84):3–12, 1983.
134. E. A. Feigenbaum, F. Hayes-Roth, D. Waltz, R. Reddy, and V. Zue, "The Building Blocks," *Spectrum*, IEEE, Nov. 1983, pp. 77–87.
135. E. A. Feigenbaum, "Knowledge Engineering: The Applied Side." In J. E. Hayes and D. Michie (eds.), *Intelligent Systems: The Unprecedented Opportunity.* Chichester, England: Ellis Horwood Ltd., 1983, pp. 37–55.
136. R. Fenichel and J. Yochelson, "A Lisp Garbage-Collector for Virtual Memory Computer Systems," *Comm. of the ACM* 12(11):611–612, 1979.
137. E. A. Feustel, "On the Advantages of Tagged Architecture," *IEEE Trans. on Computers*, C-22(7): 644–656, 1973.
138. N. V. Findler, *Associated Network.* New York: Academic Press, 1979.
139. R. Finkel and U. Manber, "DIB—A Distributed Implementation of Backtracking," *Proc. 5th Int'l Conf. on Distributed Computing Systems*, IEEE, May 1985, pp. 446–452.
140. R. A. Finkel and J. P. Fishburn, "Parallelism in Alpha-Beta Search," *Artifical Intelligence*, 19(1): 89–106, 1982.
141. A. L. Fisher, "Dictionary Machines with a Small Number of Processors," *Proc. 11th Annual Int'l Symp. on Computer Architecture*, IEEE/ACM, June 1984, pp. 151–156.
142. D. H. Fishman and J. Minker, "π-Representation: A Clause Representation for Parallel Search," *Artificial Intelligence* 6(2):193–127, 1975.
143. J. Fitch, "Do We Really Want a Lisp Machine?" *SEAS/SMC Annual Meeting*, ACM, Jan. 1980.
144. M. J. Flynn, "Directions and Issues in Architecture and Language," *Computer* 13(10):5–22, 1980.
145. C. Forgy and J. McDermott, "OPS—A Domain-Independent Production Systems Language," *Proc. 5th Int'l Joint Conf. on Artifical Intelligence.* Los Altos, CA: William Kaufman, 1977, pp. 933–939.
146. C. Forgy, A. Gupta, A. Newell, and R. Wedig, "Initial Assessment of Architectures for Production Systems," *Proc. National Conf. on Artifical Intelligence*, AAAI, Aug. 1984, pp. 116–120.
147. J. A. B. Fortes, K. S. Fu, and B. W. Wah, "Systematic Approaches to the Design of Algorithmically Specified Systolic Arrays," *Proc. Int'l Conf. on Accoustics, Speech, and Signal Proc.*, IEEE, 1985, pp. 8.9.1–8.9.4.
148. M. J. Foster and H. T. Kung, "The Design of Special-Purpose VLSI Chips," *Computer*, 13(1): 26–40, 1980.
149. M. A. Franklin and N. L. Soong, "One-Dimensional Optimization on Multiprocessor Systems," *IEEE Trans. on Computers*, C-30(1):61–66, 1981.
150. H. A. Freeman (ed.) "Special Issue on Backend Storage Networks," *Computer*, 13(2): Feb. 1980.
151. D. P. Friedman and D. S. Wise, "Aspects of Applicative Programming for Parallel Processing," *IEEE Trans. on Computers*, C-27(4):289–296, 1978.
152. W. Fritz and The Intelligent System, *SIGART Newsletter*, 90:34–38, 1984.
153. K. Fuchi, "The Direction the FGCS Project Will Take," *New Generation Computing*, 1(1):3–9, 1983.
154. B. V. Funt, "Whisper: A Problem-Solving System Utilizing Diagrams," *Proc. 5th Int'l Joint Conf. on Artifical Intelligence.* Los Atlos, CA: William Kaufman, 1977, pp. 459–464.
155. K. Furukawa and T. Yokoi, "Basic Software System," *Proc. Int'l Conf. on Fifth Generation Computer Systems*, ICOT and North-Holland, 1984, pp. 37–57.
156. D. Gajski, W. Kim, and S. Fushimi, "A Parallel Pipelined Relational Query Processor: An Architectural Overview," *Proc. 11th Annual Int'l Symp. on Computer Architecture*, IEEE/ACM, June 1984, pp. 134–141.
157. W. B. Gevarter, *An Overview of Expert Systems.* Tech. Rep. NBSIR 82-2505, National Bureau of Standards, Washington, DC, 1982.
158. A. S. Gevins, "Overview of the Human Brain as a Distributed Computing Network," *Proc. Int'l Conf. on Computer Design: VLSI in Computers*, IEEE, 1983, pp. 13–16.
159. W. K. Giloi and R. Gueth, "Concepts and Realization of a High-Performance Data Type

Architecture," *Int'l J. of Computer and Information Sciences*, 11(1):25–54, New York: Plenum Press, 1982.

160. A. J. Goldberg and D. Robson, *Smalltalk-80: The Language and Its implementation.* Reading, MA: Addision-Wesley, 1983.
161. R. Gonzalez-Rubio, J. Rohmer, and D. Terral, "The Schuss Filter: A Process for Non-Numerical Data Processing," *Proc. 11th Annual Int'l Symp. on Computer Architecture.* IEEE/ACM, June 1984, pp. 64–73.
162. K. Goser, C. Foelster, and U. Rueckert, "Intelligent Memories in VLSI," *Information Sciences*, 34(1):61–82, 1984.
163. A. Goto, H. Tanaka, and T. Moto-oka, "Highly Parallel Inference Engine PIE—Goal Rewriting Model and Machine Architecture," *New Generation Computing* 2(1):37–58, 1984.
164. E. Goto, T. Ida, K. Hiraki, M. Suzuki, and N. Inada, "FLATS, A. Machine for Numerical, Symbolic and Associative Computing," *Proc. 6th Int'l Joint Conf. on Artificial Intelligence.* Los Altos, CA: William Kaufman, 1979, pp. 1058–1066.
165. R. G. Greenblatt, T. F. Knight, J. T. Holloway, and D. A. Moon, "A Lisp Machine," *Proc. 5th Workshop on Computer Architecture for Non-Numeric Processing*, ACM, March 1980, pp. 137–138.
166. N. Greenfeld and A. Jericho, "A Professional's Personal Computer System," *Proc. 8th Int'l Symp. on Comp. Architecture*, IEEE/ACM, 1981, pp. 217–227.
167. R. Greiner and D. Lenat, "A Representation Language," *Proc. First National Conference on Artificial Intelligence.* Los Altos, CA: William Kaufman, 1980, pp. 165–169.
168. J. Grinberg, G. R. Nudd, and R. D. Etchells, "A Cellular VLSI Architecture," *Computer* 17(1): 68–81, 1984.
169. M. Griss and M. Swanson, "MBALM/1700: A Microprogrammed Lisp Machine for the Burroughs B1726," *Proc. MICRO-10*, ACM/IEEE, 1977.
170. M. L. Griss and E. Benson, "Current Status of a Portable Lisp Compiler," *Proc. SIGPLAN Symp. on Compiler Construction*, ACM, June 1982, pp. 276–283.
171. L. J. Guibas, H. T. Kung, and C. D. Thompson, "Direct VLSI Implementation of Combinatorial Algorithms," *Proc. Caltech Conf. on VLSI*, Caltech, Pasadena, CA, 1979, pp. 509–525.
172. A. Gupta, "Implementing OPS5 Production Systems on DADO," *Proc. Int'l Conf. on Parallel Processing.* IEEE, 1984, pp. 83–91.
173. A. Guzman, "A Heterarchical Multi-Microprocessor Lisp Machine," *Proc. Workshop on Computer Architecture for Pattern Analysis and Image Database Management.* IEEE, Nov. 1981, pp. 309–317.
174. P. A. V. Hall and G. R. Dowling, "Approximate String Matching," *Computing Surveys*, 12(4): 381–402, 1980.
175. J. A. Harris and D. R. Smith, "Simulation Experiments of a Tree Organized Multicomputer," *Proc. 6th Annual Symp. on Computer Architecture*, IEEE/ACM, April 1979, pp. 83–89.
176. R. Hasegawa and M. Amamiya, "Parallel Execution of Logic Programs based on Dataflow Concept," *Proc. Int'l Conf. on Fifth Generation Computer Systems*, ICOT and North-Holland, 1984, pp. 507–516.
177. P. B. Hawthorn and D. J. DeWitt, "Performance Analysis of Alternative Database Machine Architectures," *IEEE Trans. on Software Engineering*, SE-8(1):61–75, 1982.
178. H. Hayashi, A. Hattori, and H. Akimoto, "ALPHA: A High-Performance Lisp Machine Equipped with a New Stack Structure and Garbage Collection System," *Proc. 10th Annual Int'l Symp. on Computer Architecture*, IEEE/ACM, June 1983, pp. 342–348.
179. F. Hayes-Roth, D. A. Waterman, and D. B. Lenat, *Building Expert Systems*, Reading, MA: Addison-Wesley, 1983.
180. F. Hayes-Roth, "The Knowledge-Based Expert System: Z Tutorial," *Computer*, 17(9):11–28, 1984.
181. F. Hayes-Roth, "Knowledge-Based Expert Systems," *Computer*, 17(10):263–273, 1984.
182. L. S. Haynes, R. L. Lau, D. P. Siewiorek, and D. W. Mizell, "A Survey of Highly Parallel Computing," *Computer*, 15(1):9–24, 1982.
183. P. Henderson, *Function Programming, Application and Inplementation*, New York: Prentice-Hall, 1980.
184. C. Hewitt, *Description and Theoretical Analysis (Using Schemas) of PLANNER: A Language for Proving Theorems and Manipulating Models in Robots*, PhD. thesis, Artificial Intelligence Laboratory, MIT, Cambridge, MA, 1971.

185. C. Hewitt, "Viewing Control Structure as Patterns of Passing Messages," *Artificial Intelligence*, 8(3):323–364, 1977.
186. C. Hewitt, "The Apiary Network Architecture for Knowledgeable Systems," *Conf. Record of Lisp Conf.*, Stanford University, Menlo Park, CA, 1980, pp. 107–117.
187. C. Hewitt and H. Lieberman, "Design Issues in Parallel Architectures for Artificial Intelligence," *Proc. COMPCON Spring*, IEEE, Feb. 1984, pp. 418–423.
188. Y. Hibino, "A Practical Parallel Garbage Collection Algorithm and Its Implementations," *Proc. 7th Annual Symp. on Computer Architecture*, IEEE/ACM, May 1980, pp. 113–120.
189. W. D. Hills, "The Connection Machine: A Computer Architecture Based on Cellular Automata," *Physica*, North-Holland, 1984, pp. 213–228.
190. G. E. Hinton, T. J. Sejnowski, and D. H. Askley, *Boltzmann Machine: Constraint Satisfaction Network that Learns*. Tech. Rep. Carnegie-Mellon University, Pittsburgh, PA, 1984.
191. A. Hirsch, "Tagged Architecture Supports Symbolic Processing", *Computer Design*, PennWell, June 1984.
192. C. Hoffmann and M. O'Donnell, "Pattern Matching in Trees," *J. of the ACM*, 21(1):68–95, 1982.
193. C. J. Hogger, "Concurrent Logic Programming." In *Logic Programming*, S.-A. Tarnlund and K. Clark (eds.), New York: Academic Press, 1982, pp. 199–211.
194. F. Hommes, "The Heap/Substitution Concept—An Implementation of Functional Operations on Data Structures for a Reduction Machine," *Proc. 9th Annual Symp. on Computer Architecture*, IEEE/ACM, April 1982, pp. 248–256.
195. E. Horowitz and A. Zorat, "Divide-and-Conquer for Parallel Processing," *Trans. on Computers*, C-32(6):582–585, 1983.
196. D. K. Hsiaso (ed.), "Special Issue on Database Machines," *Computer*, 12(3):1979.
197. C. C. Hsiao and L. Snyder, "Omni-Sort: A Versatile Data Processing Operation for VLSI," *Proc. Int'l Conf. on Parallel Processing*, IEEE, 1983, pp. 222–225.
198. K. Hwang and F. A. Briggs, *Computer Architecture and Parallel Processing*, New York: McGraw-Hill, 1984.
199. T. Ida and J. Tanaka, "Functional Programming with Streams—Part II," *New Generation Computing*, 2(3):261–275, 1984.
200. Y. Igawa, K. Shima, T. Sugawara, and S. Takagi, "Knowledge Representation and Inference Environment: KRINE—An Approach to Integration of Frame, Prolog and Graphics," *Proc. Int'l Conf. on Fifth Generation Computer Systems*, ICOT and North-Holland, 1984, pp. 643–651.
201. M. Imai and T. Fukumura, "A Parallelized Branch-and-Bound Algorithm Implementation and Efficiency," *Systems, Computers, Controls*, 10(3):62–70, 1979.
202. M. Imai, Y. Tateizumi, Y. Yoshida, and T. Fukumura, "A Multicomputer System Based on the Binary-Tree Structure: DON(2)," *TGEC*, EC83-23(1):19–30, IECE of Japan, 1983.
203. K. B. Irani and Y. F. Shih, "Implementation of Very Large Prolog-Based Knowledge Bases on Data Flow Architectures," *Proc. 1st Conf. on Artifical Intelligence Applications*, IEEE, Dec. 1984, pp. 454–459.
204. Y. Ishikawa and M. Tokoro, "The Design of an Object-Oriented Architecture," *Proc. 11th Int'l Symp. on Computer Architecture*, IEEE/ACM, 1984, pp. 178–187.
205. N. Ito, H. Shimizu, M. Kishi, E. Kuno, and K. Rokusawa, "Data-Flow Based Execution Mechanisms of Parallel and Concurrent Prolog," *New Generation Computing*, 3:15–41, 1985.
206. N. Ito and H. Shimizu, "Dataflow Based Execution Mechanisms of Parallel and Concurrent Prolog," *New Generation Computing* 3(1):15-41, 1985.
207. M. S. Johnson, "Some Requirements for Architectural Support of Software Debugging," *Proc. SIGPLAIN Symp. on Compiler Construction*, ACM, June 1982, pp. 140–148.
208. S. Kasif, M. Kohli, and J. Minker, "PRISM: A Parallel Inference System for Problem Solving," *Proc. 8th Int'l Joint Conf. on Artificial Intelligence*, Los Altos, CA: William Kaufman, 1983, pp. 544–546.
209. K. Kawanobe, "Current Status and Future Plans of the Fifth Generation Computer System Project," *Proc. Int'l Conf. on Fifth Generation Computer Systems*, ICOT and North-Holland, 1984, pp. 3–36.
210. R. M. Keller, G. Lindstrom, and S. Patil, "A Loosely Coupled Applicative Multiprocessing System," *Proc. National Computer Conf.*, AFIPS Press, 1979, pp. 613–622.
211. R. M. Keller and F. C. H. Lin, "Simulated Performance of a Reduction-Based Multiprocessor," *Computer*, 17(7). 70–82, 1984.

212. R. M. Keller, F. C. H. Lin, and J. Tanaka, "Rediflow Multiprocessing," *Proc. COMPCON Spring*, IEEE, 1984, pp. 410–417.

213. C. Kellogg, "Knowledge Management: A Practical Amalgam of Knowledge and Data Base Technology," *Proc. National Conf. on Artificial Intelligence*. AAAI, 1982, pp. 306–309.

214. C. Kellogg, "Intelligent Assistants for Knowledge and Information Resources Management," *Proc. 8th Int'l Joint Conf. on Artificial Intelligence*. Los Altos, CA: William Kaufman, 1983, pp. 170–172.

215. T. Khabaza, "Negation as Failure and Parallelism," *Proc. Int'l Symp. on Logic Programming*, IEEE, Feb. 1984, pp. 70–75.

216. T. King, "Expert Systems with 68000 and Lisp," *Microprocessors and Microsystems*, Vol. 8, no. 7, IPC Business Press, England, Sept. 1984, pp. 374–376.

217. M. Kitsuregawa, H. Tanaka, and T. Moto-oka, "Application of Hash to Data Base Machine and its Architecture," *New Generation Computing*, 1(1):63–74, 1983.

218. W. E. Kluge, "Cooperating Reduction Machines," *Trans. on Computers*, C-32(11):1002–1012, 1983.

219. T. Knight, "The CONS Microprocessor." AI Working Paper 80, MIT, Cambridge, MA, Nov. 1974.

220. V. P. Kobler, "Overview of Tool for Knowledge Base Construction," *Proc. Data Engineering Conf.*, IEEE, 1984, pp. 282–285.

221. W. A. Kornfeld, "ETHER—A Parallel Problem Solving System," *Proc. 6th Int'l Joint Conf. on Artificial Intelligence*. Los Altos, CA: William Kaufman, 1979, pp. 490–492.

222. W. A. Kornfeld, "The Use of Parallelism to Implement a Heuristic Search," *Proc. 7th Int'l Joint Conf. on Artificial Intelligence*. Los Altos, CA: William Kaufman, Aug. 1981, pp. 575–580.

223. W. A. Kornfeld, "Combinatorially Implosive Algorithms," *Comm. of the ACM*, 25(10):734–738, 1982.

224. B. D. Kornman. "Pattern Matching and Pattern-Directed Invocation in Systems Programming Languages," *J. of Systems and Software*, 3:95-102, 1983.

225. A. Koster, "Compiling Prolog Programs for Parallel Execution on a Cellular Machine," *Proc. ACM'84 Annual Conf.*, ACM, Oct. 1984, pp. 167–178.

226. R. Kowalski, "Predicate Logic as a Programming Language," *IFIP Information Processing*, North-Holland, 1974, pp. 569–574.

227. R. Kowalski, *Logic for Problem Solving*, North-Holland, 1979.

228. R. Kowalski, "Logic Programming." In R. E. A. Mason (ed.), *IEIP Information Processing*. New York: Elsevier, 1983, pp. 133–145.

229. C. P. Kruskal, "Searching, Merging, and Sorting in Paralle Computation," *Trans. on Computers*, C-32(10) 942–946, 1983.

230. H. Kung and S. Song. *An Efficient Parallel Garbage Collection Systems and Its Correctness Proof*. Tech. Rep. Department of Computer Science, Carnegie-Mellon University, Pittsburgh, PA, Sept. 1977.

231. H. T. Kung, "Let's Design Algorithms for VLSI Systems," *Proc. Caltech Conf. on VLSI*, Caltech, Pasadena, CA, Jan. 1979, pp. 65–90.

232. T. Kurokawa, "Lisp Activities in Japan," *Proc. 6th Int'l Joint Conf. on Artificial Intelligence*. Los Altos, CA: William Kaufman, 1979, pp. 502–504.

233. A. J. Kusalik, "Serialization of Process Reduction in Concurrnet Prolog," *New Generation Computing*, 2(3):289–298. 1984.

234. T. H. Lai and S. Sahni, "Anomalies in Parallel Branch-and-Bound Algorithms," *Comm. of the ACM*, 27(6):594–602, 1984.

235. T. H. Lai and A. Sprague, "Performance of Parallel Branch-and-Bound Algorithms," *Trans. on Computers*, C-34(10):962–964, 1985.

236. G. G. Langdon, Jr. (ed), "Special Issue on Database Machines," *Trans. on Computers*, C-28(6):1979.

237. G. G. Langdon, Jr., "Database Machines: An Introduction," *Trans. on Computers*, C-28(6):381–384, 1979.

238. C. E. Leiserson, "Systolic Priority Queues," *Proc. Caltech Conf. on VLSI*, Caltech, Jan. 1979.

239. D. B. Lenat and J. McDermott, "Less Than General Production System Architectures," *Proc. 5th Int'l Joint Conf. on Artificial Intelligence*. Los Altos, CA: William Kaufman, 1977, pp. 923–932.

240. D. B. Lenat, "Computer Software for Intelligent Systems," *Scientific American*. 251(3):204–213, 1984.

241. D. B. Lenat and J. S. Brown, "Why AM and EURISKO Appear to Work?" *Artificial Intelligence*, 23(3) 269–294, 1984.
242. E. J. Lerner, "Automating Programming," *Spectrum*, 19(8):28–33, 1982.
243. V. R. Lesser and D. D. Corkill, "The Distributed Vehicle Monitoring Testbed: A Tool for Investigating Distributed Problem Solving Networks," *AI Magazine*, Fall 1983, pp. 15–33.
244. S. P. Levitan and J. G. Bonar, "Three Microcomputer Lisps," *Byte*, Sept. 1981, pp. 388–412.
245. G.-J. Li and B. W. Wah, "Computational Efficiency of Parallel Approximate Branch-and-Bound Algorithms," *Proc. Int'l Conf. on Parallel Processing*, IEEE, 1984, pp. 473–480.
246. G.-J. Li and B. W. Wah, "MANIP-2: A Multicomputer Architecture for Evaluating Logic Programs," *Proc. Int'l Conf. on Parallel Processing*. IEEE, June 1985, pp. 123–130.
247. G.-J. Li and B. W. Wah, "Coping with Anomalies in Parallel Branch-and-Bound Algorithms," *IEEE Trans. on Computers*, C-35(6):568–573, 1986.
248. H. Lieberman and C. Hewitt, "A Real-Time Garbage Collector Based on the Lifetimes of Objects," *Comm. of the ACM*, 26(6):419–429, 1983.
249. N. R. Lincoln, "Technology and Design Tradeoffs in the Creation of a Modern Supercomputer," *Trans. on Computers*, C-31(5):349–362, 1982.
250. G. Lindstrom and P. Panangaden, "Stream-Based Execution of Logic Programs." *Proc. Int'l Symp. on Logic Programming*, IEEE, Feb. 1984, pp. 168–176.
251. G. Mago, "A Network of Microprocessors to Execute Reduction Languages, Part I," *Int'l J. of Computer and Information Sciences*, 8(5):349–385, 1979.
252. G. Mago, "A Network of Microprocessors to Execute Reduction Languages, Part II," *Int'l J. of Computer and Information Sciences*, 8(6):435–471, 1979.
253. G. Mago, "Making Parallel Computation Simple: The FFP Machine," *Proc. COMPCON Spring*, IEEE, 1985, pp. 424–428.
254. F. J. Malabarba, "Review of Available Database Machine Technology," *Proc. Trends and Applications*, IEEE, 1984, pp. 14–17.
255. T. Maneul, "Cautiously Optimistic Tone Set For 5th Generation," *Electronics*, Dec. 3, 1984, pp. 57–63.
256. Z. Manna and R. Waldinger, "A Deductive Approach to Program Synthesis," *Proc. 6th Int'l Joint Conf. on Artificial Intelligence*. Los Altos, CA: William Kaufman, 1979, pp. 542–551.
257. T. Manuel, "Lisp and Prolog Machines are Proliferating," *Electronics*, Nov. 1983, pp. 132–137.
258. T. A. Marsland and M. Campbell, "Parallel Search of Strongly Ordered Game Trees," *Computing Surveys*, 14(4):533–551, 1982.
259. J. J. Martin, "An Efficient Garbage Compaction Algorithm," *Comm. of the ACM*, 25(8):571–581, 1982.
260. J. McCarthy, P. Abrahams, D. Edwards, T. Hart, and M. Levin, *Lisp 1.5 Programmer's Manual*. Cambridge, MA: MIT Press, 1962.
261. J. McCarthy, "History of Lisp," *SIGPLAN Notices*, 13(8):217–223, 1978.
262. W. M. McCormack, F. G. Gray, J. G. Tront, R. M. Haralick, and G. S. Fowler, "Multi-Computer Parallel Architectures for Solving Combinatorial Problems." In K. Preston, Jr., and L. Uhr (eds.), *Multicomputers and Image Processing Algorithms and Programs*. New York: Academic Press, 1982, pp. 431–451.
263. C. D. McCrosky, J. J. Glasgow, and M. A. Jenkins, "Nial: A Canadidate Language for Fifth Generation Computer Systems," *Proc. ACM'84 Annual Conf.*, ACM. Oct. 1984, pp. 157–166.
264. J. R. McGraw, "Data Flow Computing: Software Development," *Trans. on Computers*, C-29(12):1095–1103, 1980.
265. D. McKay and S. Shapiro, "MULTI—A Lisp Based Multiprocessing System," *Conf. Record of Lisp Conf.*, Stanford University, Menlo Park, CA, 1980.
266. C. Mead and L. Conway, *Introduction to VLSI Systems*. Reading, MA: Addison-Wesley, 1980.
267. Van Melle, E. H. Shortliffe, and B. G. Buchanan, "EMYCIN: A Domain-Independent System that Aids in Constricting Knowledge-Based Consultation Programs," *Machine Intelligence: Infotech State of the Art Report 9*. Infotech International, London, England, 1981.
268. Van Melle, A. C. Scott, J. S. Bennett, and M. Peairs, The EMYCIN Manual, Tech. Rep. HPP-81-16, Computer Science Dept., Stanford University. Menlo Park, CA, 1981.
269. D. Michie, "Inductive Rule Generation in the Context of the Fifth Generation," *Proc. Int'l Machine Learning Workshop*, University of Illinois, Urbana, IL, June 1983, pp. 65–70.
270. S. W. Miller (ed.), "Special Issue on Mass Storage Systems Evolution of Data Center Architectures," *Computer*, 15(7): July 1982.
271. S. W. Miller (ed), "Special Issue on Mass Storage Systems," *Computer*, 18(7): July 1985.

272. F. Mizoguchi, H. Ohwada, and Y. Katayama, "LOOKS: Knowledge Representation System for Designing Expert Systems in a Logic Programming Framework," *Proc. Int'l Conf. on Fifth Generation Computer Systems,* ICOT and North-Holland, 1982, pp. 606–612.

273. M. Model, "Multiprocessing via Intercommunicating Lisp Systems," *Conf. Recrod of Lisp Conf.,* Stanford University, Menlo Park, CA, 1980.

274. D. I. Moldovan, *Survey of Computer Architectures for Artificial Intelligence.* Tech. Rep. PPP-84-6, University of Southern California, Los Angeles, CA, July 1984.

275. D. I. Moldovan and Y. W. Tung, *SNAP: A VLSI Architecture for Artificial Intelligence Processing.* Tech. Rep. PPP 84-3, University of Southern California, Los Angeles, CA, 1984.

276. D. I. Moldovan, "An Associative Array Architecture Intended for Semantic Network Processing," *Proc. ACM'84 Annual Conf.,* Oct. 1984, pp. 212–221.

277. D. Moon, *Maclisp Reference Manual.* Cambridge, MA: MIT Press, 1974.

278. D. A. Moon, "Architecture of the Symbolics 3600," *Proc. 12th Annual Int'l Symp. on Computer Architecture,* IEEE/ACM, June 1985, pp. 76–83.

279. I. W. Moor, *An Applicative Compiler for a Parallel Machine.* Research Rep. DoC83/6, Imperial College, London, Eng., March 1983.

280. J. Moore, *The Interlisp Virtual Machine Specification.* Tech. Rep. CSL 76-5, Xerox PARC, Palo Alto, CA, Sept. 1976.

281. T. Moto-oka, et al. "Challenge for Knowledge Information Processing Systems," *Proc. Int'l. Conf. on Fifth Generation Systems.* ICOT, and North-Holland, 1981, pp. 3–89.

282. T. Moto-oka, "Overview to the Fifth Generation Computer System Project," *Proc. 10th Annual Int'l Symp. on Computer Architecture.* IEEE/ACM, June 1983, pp. 417–422.

283. T. Moto-oka, H. Tanaka, H. Aida, K. Hirata, and T. Maruyama, "The Architecture of a Parallel Inference Engine (PIE)," *Proc. Int'l Conf. on Fifth Generation Computer Systems.* ICOT and North-Holland, 1984, pp. 479–488.

284. T. Moto-oka and H. S. Stone, "Fifth-Generation Computer Systems: A Japanese Project," *Computer,* 17(3):6–13, 1984.

285. A. Mukhopadhyay, "Hardware Algorithms for Nonnumeric Computation," *Trans. on Computers,* C-28(6):384–394., 1979.

286. K. Murakami, T. Kakuta, N. Miyazaki, S. Shibayama, and H. Yokota, "A Relational Data Base Machine: First Step to Knowledge Base Machine," *Proc. 10th Annual Int'l Symp. on Computer Architecture.* IEEE/ACM, June 1983, pp. 423–425.

287. K. Murakami, T. Kakuta, and R. Onai, "Architectures and Hardware Systems: Parallel Inference Machine and Knowledge Base Machine," *Proc. Int'l Conf. on Fifth Generation Computer Systems.* ICOT and North-Holland, 1984, pp. 18–36.

288. K. Murakami, T. Kakuta, R. Onai, and N. Ito, "Research on Parallel Machine Architecture for Fifth-Generation Computer Systems," *Computer,* 18(6):76–92, 1985.

289. G. Myer, *Advances in Computer Architecture.* New York: Wiley, 1978.

290. E. Myers, "Machine that Lisp," *Datamation,* 27(9):105–108, 1981.

291. W. Myers, "Lisp Machine Displayed at AI Conf.," *Computer,* 15(11):79–82, 1982.

292. M. Nagao, J. I. Tsujii, K. Nakajima, K. Mitamura, and H. Ito, "Lisp Machine NK3 and Measurement of Its Performance," *Proc. 6th Int'l Joint Conf. on Artificial Intelligence.* Los Altos, CA: William Kaufman, 1979, pp. 625–627.

293. S. I. Nakagawa and T. Sakai, "A Parallel Tree Search Method," *Proc. 6th Int'l Joint Conf. on Artificial Intelligence.* Los Altos, CA: William Kaufman, 1979, pp. 628–632.

294. D. S. Nau, "Expert Computer System," *Computer,* 16(2):63–85, 1983.

295. P. M. Neches, "Hardware Support for Advanced Data Management Systems," *Computer* 17(11):29–40, 1984.

296. A. Newell, J. C. Shaw, and H. A. Simon, "Programming the Logic Theory Machine," *Prof. 1957 Western Joint Computer Conference.* IRE, 1957, pp. 230–240.

297. A. Newell, J. C. Shaw, and H. A. Simon, "Empirical Explorations with the Logic Theory Machine." In E. A. Feigenbaum and J. Feldman (eds.), *Computers and Thought.* 1963, pp. 109–133.

298. I. A. Newman and M. C. Woodward, "Alternative Approaches to Multiprocessor Garbage Collection," *Proc. Int'l Conf. on Parallel Processing.* IEEE, 1982, pp. 205–210.

299. H. P. Nii and N. Aiello, "AGE (Attempt to Generalize):A Knowledge-Based Program for Building Knowledge-Based Programs," *Proc. 6th Int'l Joint Conf. on Artificial Intelligence.* Los Altos, CA: William Kaufman, 1979, pp. 645–655.

300. J. T. O'Donnel, *A Systolic Associative Lisp Computer Architecture with Incremental Parallel Storage Management.* Ph.D. dissertation, University of Iowa, Iowa City, IA, 1981.
301. K. Oflazer, "Partitioning in Parallel Processing of Production Systems," *Proc. Int'l Conf. on Parallel Processing.* IEEE, 1984, pp. 92–100.
302. H. Ogawa, T. Kitahashi, and K. Tanaka, "The Theorem Prover Using a Parallel Processing System," *Proc. 6th Int'l Joint Conf. on Artificial Intelligence.* Los Altos, CA: William Kaufman, 1979, pp. 665–667.
303. T. A. Ottmann, A. L. Rosenberg, and L. J. Stockmeyer, "A Dictionary Machine (for VLSI)," *IEEE Trans. on Computers.* C-31(9):892–897, 1982.
304. J. Pavlin, "Predicting the Performance of Distributed Knowledge-Based Systems: A Modeling Approach," *Proc. National Conf. on Artificial Intelligence.* AAAI, 1983, pp. 314–319.
305. J. Pearl, *Heuristics: Intelligent Search Strategies for Computer Problem Solving.* Reading, MA: Addison-Wesley, 1984.
306. L. M. Pereira and R. Nasr, "Delta-Prolog, A Distributed Logic Programming Language," *Proc. Int'l Conf. on Fifth Generation Computer Systems.* ICOT and North-Holland, 1984, pp. 283–291.
307. F. J. Peters, "Tree Machine and Divide-and-Conquer Algorithms," *Lecture Notes CS 111 (CONPAR81).* New York Springer-Verlag, 1981, pp. 25–35.
308. A. Plotkin and D. Tabak, "A Tree Structured Architecture for Semantic Gap Reduction," *Computer Architecture News,* 11(4):30–44, 1983.
309. F. P. Preparata, "New Parallel-Sorting Schemes," *Trans. on Computers.* C-27(7):669–673, July 1978.
310. E. von Puttkamer, "A Microprogrammed Lisp Machine," *Microprocessing and Microprogramming.* 11(1):9–14, 1983.
311. J. F. Reiser, ed., SAIL, Tech. Rep. STAN-CS-76-574, Computer Science Dept. Stanford University, Menlo Park, CA, 1976.
312. T. Rentsch, "Object Oriented Programming," *SIGPLAN Notices,* 17(9):51–57, 1982.
313. E. Rich, "The Gradual Expansion of Artificial Intelligence," *Computer.* 17(5):4–12; 1984.
314. C. Rieger, R. Trigg, and B. Bane, "ZMOB: A New Computing Engine for AI," *Proc. 7th Int'l Joint Conf. on Artificial Intelligence.* Los Altos, CA: William Kaufman, 1981, pp. 955–960.
315. J. P. Riganati and P. B. Schneck, "Supercomputing," *Computer,* 17(10):97–113, 1984.
316. J. A. Robinson, "Logic Programming—Past, Present and Future," *New Generation Computing,* 1(2):107–124, 1983.
317. M. D. Rychener, "Control Requirements for the Design of Production System Architectures," *Proc. Symp. on Artificial Intelligence and Programming Languages (also SIGART Newsletter),* ACM, Aug. 1977, pp. 37–44.
318. E. D. Sacerdoti, R. E. Fikes, R. Reboh, D. Sagalowicz, R. J. Waldinger, and B. M. Wilber, "Qlisp—A Language for the Interactive Development of Complex Systems," *Proc. National Computer Conf.,* AFIPS Press, 1976, pp. 139–146.
319. H. Sakai, K. Iwata, S. Kamiya, M. Abe, A. Tanaka, S. Shibayama, and K. Murakami, "Design and Implementation of Relational Database Engine," *Proc. Fifth Generation Computer Systems,* ICOT and North-Holland, 1984, pp. 419–426.
320. H. Samet, "Code Optimization Considerations in List Processing Systems," *Trans. on Software Engineering,* SE-8(2):107–113, 1982.
321. E. Sandewall, "Programming in an Interactive Environment: the Lisp Experience," *Computing Surveys.* 10(1):35–71, 1978.
322. J. Sansonnet, D. Botella, and J. Perez, "Function Distribution in a List-Directed Architecture," *Microprocessing and Microprogramming,* 9(3):143–153, 1982.
323. J. P. Sansonnet, M. Castan, and C. Percebois, "M3L: A List-Directed Architecture," *Proc. 7th Annual Symp. on Computer Architecture.* IEEE/ACM, May 1980, pp. 105–112.
324. J. P. Sansonnet, M. Castan, C. Percebois, D. Botella, and J. Perez, "Direct Execution of Lisp on a List-Directed Architecture," *Proc. Symp. on Architectural Support for Programming Languages and Operating Systems.* ACM, March 1982, pp. 132–139.
325. M. Sato and T. Sakurai, "QUTE: A Prolog/Lisp Type Language for Logic Programming," *Proc. 8th Int'l Joint Conf. on Artifical Intelligence.* Los Altos, CA: William Kaufman, 1983, pp. 507–513.
326. D. Schaefer and J. Fischer, "Beyond the Supercomputer," *Spectrum,* 19(3):32–37, 1982.
327. H. Schmeck and H. Schroder, "Dictionary Machines for Different Models of VLSI," *Trans. on Computers,* C-34(5):472–475, 1985.

328. S. R. Schoichet, "The Lisp Machine," *Mini-Micro Systems*, June 1978, pp. 68–74.

329. C. L. Seitz (ed.), *Proc. Caltech Conf. on Very Large Scale Integration*, Caltech, Pasadena, CA, Jan. 1979.

330. C. L. Seitz, "Concurrent VLSI Architectures," *Trans. on Computers*, C-33(12):1247–1265, 1984.

331. E. Shapiro and A. Takeuchi, "Object Oriented Programming in Concurrent Prolog," *New Generation Computing*, 1(1):25–48, 1983.

332. E. Shapiro, "Systolic Programming: A Paradigm of Parallel Processing," *Proc. Int'l Conf. on Fifth Generation Computer Systems*, ICOT and North-Holland, 1984, pp. 458–470.

333. E. Y. Shapiro, "Object Oriented Programming in Concurrent Prolog," *New Generation Computing*, 1(1):25–48, 1983.

334. E. Y. Shapiro, *Subset of Concurrent Prolog and its Interpreter*. Tech. Rep. TR-003, ICOT, Tokyo, Japan, 1983.

335. E. Y. Shapiro, *A Subset of Concurrent Prolog and its Interpreter*. Tech. Rep. TR-003, ICOT, Tokyo, Japan, 1984.

336. D. E. Shaw, *Knowledge-Based Retrieval on a Relational Database Machine*, Ph.D. dissertation, Stanford University, Menlo Park, CA; also Tech. Rep., Columbia University, New York, NY, Aug. 1980.

337. B. Sheil, "Family of Personal Lisp Machines Speeds AI Program Development," *Electronics*, Nov. 1983, pp. 153–156.

338. B. Sheil, "Power Tools for Programmers," *Datamation*, Technical Publishing, Feb. 1983, pp. 131–144.

339. J. Shemer and P. Neches, "The Genesis of a Database Computer," *Computer*, 17(11):42–56, 1984.

340. S. Shibayama, T. Kakuta, N. Miyazaki, H. Yokota, and K. Murakami, "A Relational Database Machine with Large Semiconductor Disk and Hardware Relational Algebra Processor," *New Generation Computing*, 2(2):131–155, 1984.

341. M. R. Sleep and F. W. Burton, "Towards a Zero Assignment Parallel Processor," *Proc. 2nd Int'l Conf. on Distributed Computing Systems*, IEEE, April 1981, pp. 80–85.

342. C. Smith, "The Power of Parallelism for Automatic Programming Synthesis," *Proc. 22nd Annual Symp. on Found. of Computer Science*, ACM, 1981.

343. D. R. Smith, "A Design for an Automatic Programming System," *Proc. 7th Int'l Joint Conf. on Artificial Intelligence*, Los Altos, CA: William Kaufman, Aug. 1981, pp. 1027–1029.

344. K. Smith, "New Computer Breed Uses Transputers for Parallel Processing," *Electronics*, Feb. 24, 1983, pp. 67–68.

345. R. G. Smith, "The Contract Net: A Formalism for the Control of Distributed Problem Solving," *Proc. 5th Int'l Joint Conf. on Artificial Intelligence*. Los Altos, CA: William Kaufman, Aug. 1977, p. 472.

346. R. G. Smith, "A Framework for Distributed Problem Solving," *Proc. 6th Int'l Joint Conf. on Artificial Intelligence*. Los Altos, CA: William Kaufman, Aug. 1979, pp. 836–841.

347. R. G. Smith and R. Davis, "Frameworks for Cooperation in Distributed Problem Solving," *Trans. on Systems, Man and Cybernetics*, SMC-11(1):61–70, 1981.

348. A. K. Somani and V. K. Agarwal, "An Efficient VLSI Dictionary Machine," *Proc. 11th Annual Int'l Symp. on Computer Architecture*, IEEE/ACM, June 1984, pp. 142–150.

349. D. Spector, "Minimal Overhead Garbage Collection of Complex List Structure," *SIGPLAN Notices*, 17(3):80–82, 1982.

350. G. Steel and G. Sussman, Design of Lisp-Based Processor, or SCHEME: A Dielectric Lisp or Finite Memories Considered harmful, or LAMBDA: The Ultimate Opcode. AI Memo 514, MIT, Cambridge, MA, March 1979.

351. G. L. Steele, Jr, "An Overview of Common Lisp," *Conf. Record of the 1982 Symp. on Lisp and Function Programming*, ACM, 1982. pp. 98–107.

352. G. Steele, "Multiprocessing Compactifying Garbage Collection," *Comm. of the ACM*, 18,(9):495–508, 1975.

353. G. L. Steele Jr. and G. J. Sussman, "Design of a Lisp-Based Microprocessor," *Comm. of the ACM*, 23(11):628–645, 1980.

354. M. Stefik, D. Bobrow, S. Mittal, and L. Conway, "Knowledge Programming in LOOPS: Report on an Experimental Course," *AI Magazine*, Fall 1983, pp. 20–30.

355. S. J. Stolfo and D. E. Shaw, *DADO: A Tree-Structured Machine Architecture for Production Systems*. Tech. Rept, Columbia University, New York, NY, March 1982.

A survey on special-purpose computer architectures for AI **289**

356. S. J. Stolfo and D. P. Miranker, "DADO: A Parallel Processor for Expert Systems," *Proc. Int'l Conf. on Parallel Processing*, IEEE, Aug. 1984, pp. 74–82.
357. S. J. Stolfo, "Five Parallel Algorithms for Production System Execution on the DADO Machine," *Proc. National Conf. on Artificial Intelligence*, AAAI, Aug. 1984, pp. 300–307.
358. H. S. Stone, *Introduction to Computer Architecture*, Second Ed. Science Research Associates, 1980.
359. Q. F. Stout, "Sorting, Merging, Selecting and Filtering on Tree and Pyramid Machines," *Proc. Int'l Conf. on Parallel Processing*, IEEE, Aug. 1983, pp. 214–221.
360. W. D. Strecker, "Clustering VAX Superminicomputers into Large Multiprocessor Systems," *Electronics*, Oct. 20, 1983, pp. 143–146.
361. S. Sugimoto, K. Tabata, K. Agusa, and Y. Ohno, "Concurrent Lisp on a Multi-Micro-Processor System," *Proc. 7th Int'l Conf. on Artificial Intelligence*, Los Altos, CA: William Kaufman, 1981, pp. 949–954.
362. S. Sugimoto, K. Agusa, K. Tabata, and Y. Ohno, "A Multi-Microprocessor Systems for Concurrent Lisp," *Proc. Int'l Conf. on Parallel Processing*, IEEE, 1983, pp. 135–143.
363. G. J. Sussman and D. V. McDermott, "From PLANNER to CONNIVER—A Genetic Approach," *Fall Joint Computer Conf.*, vol. 41, AFIPS Press, 1972, pp. 129–137.
364. G. J. Sussman, J. Holloway, G. L. Steel, Jr., and A. Bell, "Scheme-79—Lisp on a Chip," *Computer*, 14(7):10–21, 1981.
365. N. Suzuki, K. Kubota, and T. Aoki, "SWORD32: A Bytecode Emulating Microprocessor for Object-Oriented Languages," *Proc. Int'l Conf. on Fifth Generation Computer Systems*, pp. ICOT and North-Holland, 1984, pp. 389–397.
366. N. Suzuki, "Concurrent Prolog as an Efficient VLSI Design Language," *Computer*, 18(2):33–40, 1985.
367. K. Tabata, S. Sugimoto, and Y. Ohno, "Concurrent Lisp and its Interpreter," *J. of Information Processing*, vol. 4, no. 4, Information Processing Society of Japan, Feb. 1982.
368. S. Taff, "The Design of an M6800 Lisp Interpreter," *Byte*, Aug. 1979, pp. 132–152.
369. I. Takeuchi, H. Okuno, and N. Ohsato, "TAO—A Harmonic Mean of Lisp, Prolog, and Smalltalk," *SIGPLAN Notices*, 18(7): 65–74, 1983.
370. K. Taki, Y. Kaneda, and S. Maekawa, "The Experimental Lisp Machine," *Proc. 6th Int'l Joint Conf. on Artificial Intelligence*, Los Altos, CA: William Kaufman, 1979, pp. 865–867.
371. K. Taki, M. Yokota, A. Yamamoto, H. Nishikawa, H. Uchida, H. Nakashima, and A. Mitsuishi, "Hardware Design and Implementation of the Personal Sequential Inference Machine (PSI)," *Proc. Int'l Conf. on Fifth Generation Computer Systems*, ICOT and North-Holland, 1984, pp. 398–409.
372. N. Tamura, K. Wada, H. Matsuda, Y. Kaneda, and S. Maekawa, "Sequential Prolog Machine PEK," *Proc. Int'l Conf. on Fifth Generation Computer Systems*, ICOT and North-Holland, 1984, pp. 542–550.
373. Y. Tanaka, "MPDC-Massive Parallel Architecture for Very Large Databases," *Proc. Int'l Conf. on Fifth Generation Computer Systems*, ICOT and North-Holland, 1984, pp. 113–137.
374. S. L. Tanimoto, "A Boolean Matching Operator for Hierarchical Cellular Logic," *Proc. Computer Society Workshop on Computer Architecture for Pattern Analysis and Image Database Management*, IEEE, Oct. 1983, pp. 253–256.
375. A. Taueuchi and K. Furukawa, "Bounded Buffer Communication in Concurrent Prolog," *New Generation Computing*, 3(2):145–155, 1985.
376. W. Teitelman and L. Masinter, "The Interlisp Programming Environment," *Computer*, 14(4):25–33, 1981.
377. M. F. M. Tenorio and D. I. Moldovan, "Mapping Production Systems into Multiprocessors," *Proc. Int'l Conf. on Parallel Processing*, IEEE, 1985. pp. 56–62.
378. C. D. Thompson and H. T. Kung, "Sorting on a Mesh-Connected Parallel Computer," *Comm. of the ACM*, 20(4):263–271, 1977.
379. C. D. Thompson, "The VLSI Complexity of Sorting," *Trans. on Computers*, C-32(12):1171–1184, 1983.
380. E. Tick and D. H. D. Warren, "Towards a Pipelined Prolog Processor," *New Generation Computing*, 2(4):323–345, 1984.
381. M. Tokoro and Y. Ishikawa, "An Object-Oriented Approach to Knowledge Systems," *Proc. Int'l Conf. on Fifth Generation Computer Systems*, ICOT and North-Holland, 1984, pp. 623–632.

382. B. P. Treleaven and C. Philip (eds.), *VLSI Architectures*. Englewood Cliffs, NJ: Prentice-Hall, 1983.

383. P. Treleaven and G. Mole, "A Multi-Processor Reduction Machine for User-Defined Reduction Languages," *Proc. 7th Int'l Symp. Computer Architecture*, IEEE/ACM, 1980, pp. 121–130.

384. P. C. Treleaven, "VLSI Processor Architectures," *Computer*, 15(6):33–45, 1982.

385. P. C. Treleaven and R. P. Hopkins, "A Recursive Computer Architecture for VLSI," *Proc. 9th Annual Symp. on Computer Architecture*, IEEE/ACM, April 1982, pp. 229–238.

386. P. C. Treleaven and I. G. Lima, "Japan's Fifth-Generation Computer Systems," *Computer*, 15(8):79–88, 1982.

387. P. C. Treleaven, "The New Generation of Computer Architecture," *Proc. 10th Annual Int'l Symp. on Computer Architecture*, IEEE/ACM, June 1983, pp. 402–409.

388. P. C. Treleaven and I. G. Lima, "Future Computers: Logic, Data Flow, . . . , Control Flow?" *Computer*, 17(3):47–55, 1984.

389. R. Trigg, "Software on ZMOB: An Object-Oriented Approach," *Proc. Workshop on Computer Architecture for Pattern Analysis and Image Database Management*, IEEE, Nov., 1981, pp. 133–140.

390. D. A. Turner, "A New Implementation Technique for Applicative Languages," *Software—Practice and Experience*, 9(1):31–49, 1979.

391. S. Uchida, "Inference Machine: From Sequential to Parallel," *Proc. 10th Annual Int'l Symp. on Computer Architecture*, IEEE/ACM, June 1983, pp. 410–416.

392. S. Uchida and T. Yokoi, "Sequential Inference Machine- SIM Progress Report," *Proc. Int'l Conf. on Fifth Generation Computer Systems*, ICOT and North-Holland, 1984, pp. 58–81.

393. K. Ueda and T. Chikayama, "Efficient Stream/Array Processing in Logic Programming Languages," *Proc. Int'l Conf. on Fifth Generation Computer Systems*, ICOT and North-Holland, 1984, pp. 317–326.

394. L. M. Uhr, "Parallel-Serial Production Systems," *Proc. 6th Int'l Joint Conf. on Artificial Intelligence*. Los Altos, CA: William Kaufman, 1979, pp. 911–916.

395. J. D. Ullman, "Some Thoughts About Supercomputer Organization," *Proc. COMPCON Spring*, IEEE, Feb. 1984, pp. 424–432.

396. S. Umeyama and K. Tamura, "A Parallel Execution Model of Logic Programs," *Proc. 10th Annual Symp. on Computer Architecture*, IEEE/ACM, June 1983, pp. 349–355.

397. D. Ungar, R. Blau, P. Foley, D. Samples, and D. Patterson, "Architecture of SOAR: Smalltalk on RISC," *Proc. 11th Annual Int'l Symp. on Computer Architecture*, IEEE/ACM, 1984, pp. 188–197.

398. S. R. Vegdahl, "A Survey of Proposed Architectures for the Execution of Functional Languages," *Trans. on Computers*, C-33(12):1050–1071, 1984.

399. J. S. Vitter and R. A. Simons, "Parallel Algorithms for Unification and Other Complete Problems," *Proc. ACM'84 Annual Conf.*, ACM, Oct. 1984, pp. 75–84.

400. J. S. Vitter and R. A. Simons, "Parallel Algorithms for Unification and Other Complete Problems," *Trans. on Computers*, to appear 1986.

401. B. W. Wah and K. L. Chen, "A Partitioning Approach to the Design of Selection Networks," *IEEE Trans. on Computers*, C-33(3):261–268, 1984.

402. B. W. Wah, G.-J. Li, and C. F. Yu, "The Status of MANIP—A Multicomputer Architecture for Solving Combinatorial Extremum-Search Problems," *Proc. 11th Annual Int'l Symp. on Computer Architecture*, IEEE/ACM, June 1984. pp. 56–63.

403. B. W. Wah and Y. W. E. Ma, "MANIP—A Multicomputer Architecture for Solving Combinatorial Extremum-Search Problems," *Trans. on Computers*, C-33(5):377–390, 1984.

404. B. W. Wah, G.-J. Li, and C. F. Yu, "Multiprocessing of Combinatorial Search Problems," *Computer*, 18(6):93–108, 1985.

405. L. Walker, "Lisp Language Gets Special Machine," *Electronics*, Aug. 25, 1981, pp. 40–41.

406. D. H. Warren, L. M. Pereira, and F. Pereira, "Prolog—The Language and Its Implementation Compared with Lisp," *Proc. Symp. on Artificial Intelligence and Programming Languages*, ACM, Aug. 1977 (also in *SIGART Newsletter*, 64: 109–115).

407. D. A. Waterman and F. Hayes-Roth, *Pattern-Directed Inference Systems*. New York: Academic Press, 1978.

408. B. W. Weide, "Modeling Unusual Behavior of Parallel Algorithms," *Trans. on Computers*, C-31(11):1126–1130, 1982.

409. D. Weinreb and D. Moon, Flavors, Message Passing in the Lisp Machine. AI Memo 602, MIT Laboratories Cambridge, MA, Nov. 1980.

410. M. Weiser, S. Kogge, M. McElvany, R. Pierson, R. Post, and A. Thareja, "Status and Performance of the ZMOB Parallel Processing System," *Proc. COMPCON Spring*, IEEE, Feb. 1985, pp. 71–73.

411. S. M. Weiss and C. A. Kulikowski, "EXPERT: A System for Developing Consulting Models," *Proc. 6th Int'l Conf., Artificial Intelligence*. Los Altos, CA: William Kaufman, 1979, pp. 942–947.

412. G. Wiederhold, "Knowledge and Database Management," *Software* 1(1):63–73, 1984.

413. R. Wilensky, *Lispcraft*. New York: W. W. Norton, 1984.

414. R. Williams, "A Multiprocessing System for the Direct Execution of Lisp," *Proc. 4th Workshop on Computer Architecture for Non-Numeric Processing*, ACM, Aug. 1978.

415. T. Williams, "Semiconductor Memories: Density and Diversity," *Computer Design*, Penn Well, Aug. 1984, pp. 105–116.

416. K. G. Wilson, "Science, Industry, and the New Japanese Challenge," *Proc. IEEE*, 72(1):6–18, 1984.

417. T. Winograd, "Beyond Programming Languages," *Comm. of the ACM*, 22(7):391–401, 1979.

418. L. E. Winslow and Y. C. Chow, "The Analysis and Design of Some New Sorting Machines," *Trans. on Computers*, C-32(7):677–683, 1983.

419. P. H. Winston and B. Horn, *Lisp*, Second Edition. Reading, MA: Addison-Wesley, 1984.

420. M. J. Wise, "EPILOG = Prolog + Data Flow: Arguments for Combining Prolog with a Data Driven Mechanism," *SIGPLAN Notices*, 17(12):80–86, 1982.

421. The Xerox Learning Research Group, "The Smalltalk-80 System," *Byte*, Aug. 1981, pp. 36–48.

422. Y. Yamaguchi, K. Toda, and T. Yuba, "A Performance Evaluation of a Lisp-Based Data-Driven Machine (EM-3)," *Proc. 10th Annual Int'l Symp. on Computer Architecture*, IEEE/ACM, June 1983, pp. 363–369.

423. Y. Yamaguchi, K. Toda, J. Herath, and T. Yuba, "EM-3: A Lisp-Based Data-Driven Machine," *Proc. Int'l Conf. on Fifth Generation Computer Systems*, ICOT and North-Holland, 1984, pp. 524–532.

424. M. Yamamoto, "A Survey of High-Level Language Machines in Japan," *Computer*, 14(7):68–78, 1981.

425. A. C. C. Yao, "Bounds on Selection Networks," *SIAM J. on Computing*, 9(3):566–582, 1980.

426. H. Yasuhara and K. Nitadori, "ORBIT: A Parallel Computing Model of Prolog," *New Generation Computing*, 2(3):277–288, 1984.

427. P. N. Yianilos, "Dedicated Comparator Matches Symbol Strings Fast and Intelligently," *Electronics*, 1983, pp. 113–117,

428. T. Yokoi, S. Uchida, and ICOT Third Laboratory, "Sequential Inference Machine: SIM—Its Programming and Operating System," *Proc. Int'l Conf. on Fifth Generation Computer Systems*, ICOT and North-Holland, 1984, pp. 70–81.

429. M. Yokota, et al., "A Microprogrammed Interpreter for Personal Sequential Inference Machine," *Proc. Int'l Conf. on Fifth Generation Computer Systems*, ICOT and North-Holland, 1984, pp. 410–418.

430. M. Yokota, A. Yamamoto, K. Taki, H. Nishikawa, and S. Uchida, "The Design and Implementation of a Personal Sequential Inference Machine: PSI," *New Generation Computing*, 1(2):125–144, 1983.